Rebekah

RELENTLESS PERSISTENCE

Nonviolent Action in Latin America

Edited by
Philip McManus & Gerald Schlabach

Published in cooperation with the
Resource Center for Nonviolence

New Society Publishers

Philadelphia, PA   Santa Cruz, CA

Gabriola Island, BC

Editors' royalties from this book will go to support nonviolent struggles for justice and peace in Latin America.

Inquiries regarding requests to reprint all or part of *Relentless Persistence: Nonviolent Action in Latin America* should be addressed to:
New Society Publishers
4527 Springfield Avenue
Philadelphia, PA 19143

ISBN USA 0-86571-181-X Hardcover
ISBN USA 0-86571-182-8 Paperback
ISBN Canada 1-55092-012-X Hardcover
ISBN Canada 1-55092-013-8 Paperback

Printed in the United States of America on partially recycled paper by BookCrafters

Cover art by Rini Templeton, from *The Art of Rini Templeton: Where There Is Life and Struggle/El arte de Rini Templeton: Donde hay vida y lucha*, Real Comet Press, is used with permission of the Capp Street Foundation/Rini Templeton Memorial Fund. Cover design by Anita Heckman.

Book design by Tina Birky

To order directly from the publisher, add $1.75 to the price for the first copy, 50¢ each additional. Send check or money order to:
New Society Publishers
PO Box 582
Santa Cruz, CA 95061

New Society Publishers is a project of the New Society Educational Foundation, a nonprofit, tax-exempt, public foundation. Opinions expressed in this book do not necessarily represent positions of the New Society Educational Foundation.

Grateful acknowledgment is made for permission to reprint previously published and copyrighted articles and material from the following sources:
— "Like You," from *Clandestine Poems*, translated by Jack Hirschman, first published in 1984 by Solidarity Publications, is reprinted by permission of Curbstone Press and is now distributed by the Talman Company, 150 Fifth Ave., New York, NY 10011.
— "Miracle in Bolivia: Four Women Confront a Nation" by Wilson T. Boots is reprinted with permission. Copyright 1978, *Christianity and Crisis*, 537 West 121st Street, New York, NY 10027.
— "Peru: Furrows of Peace in a Blood-stained Land" by Edmundo León y León & Oscar Aliaga-Abanto is reprinted by permission of Centro de Estudios y Acción para la Paz (CeaPaz), Apdo. 11-0764, Lima 11, Peru (63-1112).
— "Preparing for Nonviolence" by Secretariado Justiça e Não-Violência and "Firmeza Permanente: Labor Holds the Line in Brazil" by Mário Carvalho de Jesus are adapted from *A Firmeza Permanente—A Força da Não-Violência* [*Relentless Persistence: The Power of Nonviolence*] by permission of Edições Loyola, Caixa Postal 42.335, 04216 São Paulo, SP Brasil (274-6068).
— *The Spritual Basis of Nonviolence* by Domingos Barbé is reprinted by permission of Edições Paulinas, Av. Indianópolis 2752, 04062 São Paulo, SP Brasil (276-5566).

Velazquez

ACKNOWLEDGMENTS

Many people contributed generously of their time, energy and ideas for this book. In particular we would like to thank Betsy Fairbanks and Joetta Handrich for their patience, good humor and unending— even if not always tireless—support.

The Mennonite Central Committee and the Resource Center for Nonviolence supported us throughout this project. We are deeply grateful for that assistance and trust.

Others who deserve special thanks include Elizabeth Seton Stone, Theron F. Schlabach, Marie Bloom, Mev Puleo, Melinda Melone, Anita Heckman, Doug Rand, Ofelia Gómez, Julie Knop, Arthur Powers, David Sweet, Tom Quigley, Earl Hostetler Martin, Margaret Wilde, Judy Brown, Fernando Aliaga, Naomi Parker, Keith Elliot, Creuza Maciel, Francisco Undurraga, Mário Carvalho de Jesus, Paul Dix, Maria Dolores Cordeiro de Melo, Mark Snyder, Jose Alamiro Andrade Silva, Marilyn Lorenz-Weinkauff, José Westercamp, Alicia Sanguinetti, Bill Deutsch, César Chelala, Catherine Dacre, Marion Casey, William McManus, Marion McManus, John Sinclair, Scott Kennedy, George Vickers, Richard Taylor, Louis Vitale, Alain Richard, Barbara Graves, Richard Chartier, Phillip Berryman, Betsy Crites, Don Irish, John R. Burkholder, Gene Stolzfus, Joe Eldridge, Virginia Bouvier, Linda Shelly, Arnold Snyder, John Paul Lederach, Rod King, Ron Flickinger, Colleen Kliewer, John Doyle, Gerald Mumaw, Monica Larenas, Beverly Keene, Yolanda Provoste, Andrés Thomas Conteris, Renato Frota, Robert Fairbanks.

—Philip McManus and Gerald Schlabach

iii

CONTENTS

iv

II: Testimonies

To those who inspired this book: the base-level community workers in Latin America whose faith does move mountains, whose eyes always hold the prize, whose hope is contagious, whose love is home.

Like You

Like you I
love love, life, the sweet smell
of things, the sky-blue
landscape of January days.

And my blood boils up
and I laugh through eyes
that have known the buds of tears.

I believe the world is beautiful
and that poetry, like bread, is for everyone.

And that my veins don't end in me
but in the unanimous blood
of those who struggle for life,
love,
little things,
landscape and bread,
the poetry of everyone.

—Roque Dalton

FOREWORD

Active Nonviolence
The Political and Moral Power of the Poor
Leonardo Boff

Frei Leonardo Boff, O.F.M., 1989
Photo by Philip McManus

Besides everyday violence, three great forms of violence confront us today: originating violence, consequential violence, and revolutionary violence.

Originating violence has its roots in the elite institutions of power, in a social structure that protects the interests of the dominant groups, and in the extreme right, which will not tolerate any social change out of fear of losing its privileged status. As a result, many countries of the Third World are in the grips of state terrorism. Those who oppose the interests of capital or of the totalitarian state find themselves monitored, imprisoned, tortured, "disappeared" or assassinated.

vii

2)   Out of this first violence comes a second: consequential violence. To counter the first violence, or to show that they can and will fight back, resistance groups or terrorists use violent means. Undeniably, consequential violence has a component of legitimate indignation at injustice. At the same time it reflects a less admirable sentiment: revenge. Revenge is an attempt to pay back in kind. But returning violence to the violent does not change the social structure that produces the violence. To the contrary, as the Brazilian religious leader Dom Hélder Câmara says, it creates an endless spiral of violence.

3)   Finally, there is revolutionary violence. Behind revolutionary movements there is an immense thirst for justice in the face of a fundamentally unjust social system. A revolutionary desires an alternative society that offers a greater possibility of life, the full participation of all citizens, and greater equity among them. Revolution is complex, perhaps the most complex process of history. After all, it involves nothing less than remaking an entire social edifice and cultivating new values and new ways of relating. A revolution has many fronts: the popular, the legal, the diplomatic, the political, the pedagogical, the religious, the class, and, historically, also the military front. It is with the military front that the question of violence as a means to overthrow the old, oppressive regime surfaces most obviously. For revolutionary violence may have a different purpose than originating violence, but it also produces victims.

      History is full of examples of these three responses to a situation of social inequity. Can we break this vicious cycle of violence? Is it at least possible to limit violence in such a way that we neither become accomplices of injustice nor lose our human dignity?

      Throughout the world an alternative movement called *active nonviolence* answers with an emphatic "Yes!" This answer is inspired in part by the extraordinary example of persons who have successfully demonstrated another way of confronting highly conflictive situations. Some of the best known are Mahatma Gandhi, Martin Luther King, Jr., Dom Hélder Câmara, and Adolfo Pérez Esquivel.

      This book brings together a collection of beautiful examples of nonviolence, sometimes from a Nobel Laureate like Pérez Esquivel, but often from people with no dreams of winning a Nobel Prize. They demonstrate that the path of active nonviolence is viable and, in a world threatened by nuclear holocaust and the destruction of its ecosystems, is perhaps the only way to safeguard creation and life in all of its forms.

      These stories reveal that behind every concerted nonviolent struggle there is a powerful *mística*[1]: the conviction that truth, justice, and love are ontological. That is to say, these are objective forces tied to the very structure of reality, of human society, of being human. No matter how much they are violated, they always persist, and they find an echo in both the consciousness of people and in historical processes. These are the banners that never fall. Under them people accept death with honor.

The *mística* of active nonviolence implies changing ourselves as well as working to change the world. We must live the truth. We must be just, our integrity transparent. We must be peacemakers. It is not enough simply to confront external violence. We must also dig out the roots of violence in our own hearts, in our personal agendas, and in our life projects. In both a personal and a political sense we must seek to live today in miniature what we are seeking for tomorrow. Otherwise the glorious tomorrow of the revolution will never come.

Nothing is more subversive and transforming than love. The examples in this collection show the real power of love and solidarity. They show the power of completely renouncing the spirit of vengeance. Not being violent—in and of itself—is not the key to the praxis of Christ. The key is the capacity to love, which in turn means to be in solidarity with the socially and religiously marginalized.[2] Such solidarity is faithful to the promise of the coming of the Kingdom, even at risk of death. These are the ideas which committed Christ to nonviolence and made him a preacher and peacemaker.

Human history is not ruled by our desires, nor by the high-mindedness of our ethical and political ideals. It is dramatic and at times tragic. For Christians, the brokenness of our world reflects the presence of sin and evil. And that brokenness results in violence, whether through weakness, malice, or the selfish interests of individuals or groups. In this world the struggle is for life, for justice, and for solidarity in social relations. It is not against the bosses or the powerful. Struggle *with* passion but never *for* passion. And always struggle with compassion. With good reason Gandhi used to say, "Nonviolence has as an essential condition the ability to both move others and to be moved to compassion by others."

The theology of liberation is not an alternative to active nonviolence, nor vice versa. On the contrary, they are born of the same inspiration, which is the commitment to transform a violent social reality to one based on justice and fraternity through peaceful means. Theologians of liberation always speak with confidence of the historic power of the poor. The process of liberation comes from the oppressed themselves.

It begins with a pedagogy of liberation. Paulo Freire, the great pedagogue of the poor of the Third World, has outlined this. The first task of the process consists of ejecting the oppressor who lives within the oppressed. The goal is not to become another oppressor, but to be free and to establish ties of solidarity, which are the building blocks of collective freedom. When popular movements turn to action, their vision may be initially more tactical than strategic. They may struggle to fill a very particular need or to claim a specific right. But their small victories serve both to redeem hope and gradually to destabilize the oppressive system.

In this struggle, theologians of liberation give clear preference to peaceful means because these are the means that generate life. We find in the gospel the renunciation of all vengeance, of all domination of one over another. We learn solidarity and love of enemy. But traditionally this gospel has only been preached at the personal level. We must reclaim it for our politics as well.

Like liberation theology, active nonviolence—also called *firmeza permanente* or relentless persistence—is centered on the conviction that liberation is only possible when the oppressed are the subjects of their own history. Active nonviolence has contributed to the theology of liberation through its pedagogy, through its gospel-based *mística* of peace based on justice, and through its creative means of confronting conflict by applying gospel teachings in political action.

Thus active nonviolence and liberation theology are two facets of a single reality. The two facets are not opposed. On the contrary, they inform and complete each other. As the Chilean bishop Jorge Hourton observed at an international meeting on active nonviolence in 1977, nonviolence is "a vibrant, rich, and valid vein of liberation theology."[3]

To a great degree the future of active nonviolence depends on nurturing a culture of solidarity, dialogue, and participation. It is in the absence of these practices that a society turns violent. When such values are real social practices, they constitute the necessary preconditions for a network of cooperative relationships and for controlling the violence that continues to plague humanity.

Finally, we must not limit the renunciation of violence to human relations. It must also include relations with nature. The stones, the plants, the animals, the air, and the water are our sisters and brothers. We need to cultivate tenderness for all beings. Democracy should be not only political, but cosmic. When there are open relationships based on solidarity with all of creation and especially between people, then we can hope that the era of violence will belong to the dark past of humanity and that a new era of universal love will be inaugurated.

The testimonies in this book indicate that history is pointing in this direction. They anticipate the future and they provide a foundation for the hope that a more tender and fraternal humanity is still possible, even amid our tired historical trajectory.

Leonardo Boff, O.F.M.
Petrópolis, Brazil, September 1989

Translated from Portuguese by Philip McManus

Notes

1. *"Mística"* is a much richer word than its literal English translation "mystique." It refers to a shared vision or inspiration capable of motivating, guiding, and giving cohesion to a group, institution or movement. By implication, participation is a privilege that is its own reward.—Trans.

2. Latin American thinkers often characterize their societies in terms of the center, and the periphery or margin. The concept has a geographic basis. The major cities are the centers of industrial power and wealth. Often the largest rural landowners make their homes there and may visit their vast holdings only rarely. Shantytowns of the poor surround almost all Latin American cities.·Beyond them lie rural areas populated largely by impoverished peasants. Underlying this geographic configuration is a more fundamental social and political one. The poor are excluded—"marginalized"—from real participation in the political process, from anything approaching a fair share of the economic wealth of their societies, and even from access to basic human necessities.—Eds.

3. Quoted in Eds. Goss, Jean and Goss-Mayr, Hildegard, *La No Violencia Evangélica: Fuerza de Liberación*; Barcelona: Editorial Fontanella, 1978, p. 9.

LATIN AMERICA

(see inset)

VENEZUELA

COLOMBIA
ECUADOR
Guayaquil

Caracas
Bogotá
Quito
Amazon River

GUYANA
SURINAME
FRENCH GUIANA

João Pessoa

PERU
Puno
BOLIVIA
Antofagasta
CHILE
Santiago

Lima
Andes Mtns.
La Paz
Andes Mtns.
Asunción
Buenos Aires

Brasilia

BRAZIL

Rio De Janeiro
São Paulo
PARAGUAY
Porto Alegre
Rio Grande
Montevideo
URUGUAY

Andes Mtns.

ARGENTINA

● = cities mentioned
    in the book
o = capital cities

SCALE:
⊢――――⊣
= 520 Miles

MEXICO

BELIZE
HONDURAS

GUATEMALA
EL SALVADOR
NICARAGUA
COSTA RICA

PANAMA

INTRODUCTION

In Search of the Shalom Society
Philip McManus

At the point that we committed ourselves to this struggle, we began
to understand that victory was ours. Each day we took another step
forward. In the end, the outcome was no surprise.[1]

—Zé Galego

All of his life, peasant leader Zé Galego has worked the hot, dry fields
of Camucim, a rural community in Brazil's impoverished Northeast.
The story of Camucim is the story of many areas of Latin America
today. In 1978 the community united to face the attempts of wealthy
absentee landowners to drive them off their land. Hired goons and
corrupt local police beat some of the peasants, imprisoned others,
poisoned wells, and plowed their crops down. Community houses were
burned; the school was destroyed four times.

During eight years of relentless nonviolent struggle the people of
Camucim organized, resisted, suffered. They marched, gathered
signatures, and even camped for a month at the governor's office.
Because of their nonviolent attitude, their unity, and their compelling
demand for simple justice, the public began to sympathize. Meanwhile
they continued to plant. At last in 1986 they won: the government
recognized their claim to the land.

There are many Camucims in Latin America. This book is about
people like the Camucim peasants and about courage like theirs. It is

1

about the kind of determination and faith that empowered Zé Galego to detect the fruit of struggle even as he and his community planted the first seeds.

The collection of stories here certainly is not exhaustive. But it does show that through the great diversity that is Latin America, many people have found that active nonviolence (by whatever name) is indeed an effective means of struggle for social change, often against great odds and great repression. Here are contemporary accounts of factory workers, miners' wives, peasants, Indians, and middle-class mothers of the "disappeared." They tell of dramatic actions, of lengthy campaigns, of mass actions, and of the day-to-day work of building change through popular education. But above all they tell how many Latin Americans—especially the poor—experience, love, nurture, and defend the precious gift of life today.

A struggle for life

Latin America is in upheaval—caught between the vestiges of feudalism and the dislocations of modern life, rocked by the disequilibrium of powerful, wealthy elites facing impoverished masses. Modernization is putting tremendous pressure on Latin American economic and social structures. Attempts to industrialize have raised expectations yet have not invigorated Latin American economies in any sustained way. Modern life has driven millions from the countryside to sprawling urban shantytowns. It has brought new forms of communication and tantalized the poor as well as the rich with images of conspicuous consumption. Yet in the cities the majority of people are unemployed or underemployed, and in the countryside the people suffer the heavy weight of semi-feudal land tenure systems.

The eruption of the poor. Amid all the upheaval, one fact stands out: The region's poor will no longer be passive victims of changes that do not address the fundamental injustices of the status quo. Latin America has never been without social strife; yet there is no precedent for the breadth and depth of the participation of the poor in movements for change during the last thirty years. This increased participation is so significant that there has emerged a new word—*concientización* in Spanish, *conscientização* in Portuguese—to describe its underpinning.[2] The emergence of the poor as a self-conscious political force has created a fundamentally new reality. In the words of the Peruvian priest Gustavo Gutiérrez, a key theologian of liberation, "What is most central and irreversible in these last few years in Latin America is this eruption of the poor. The social and political life of our countries as well as the life of the church and theological reflection revolve around this fact."[3]

At least in name Latin America is almost universally Christian and eighty-eight percent Roman Catholic. Religious faith is strong, especially among the poor. Historically, with some notable exceptions, the church has been a conservative force. But over the last thirty years that pattern has begun to change. In the Catholic Church, especially since the Second Vatican Council,[4] the role of the laity has increased and the church has acknowledged a historical dimension in the gospel's liberating message. Increasingly Christians see injustice not as the inevitable result of "the will of God" but rather as the product of human failing. As such, it is a challenge the church must address.

Of course there are many cases in which church groups continue to play a conservative or even reactionary role in society. In both Catholic and Protestant churches there are powerful efforts to attack and undermine faith-based movements for structural change. Yet in most of Latin America's popular movements today, faith nurtures and some kind of church support bolsters the people's commitment to their struggle. It is simply impossible to understand social change in Latin America without understanding the role of the people's Christian faith, especially in its expression as a cry for liberation.

The process of change is step-by-step. During the independence movement in India, Gandhi used to say that his goal, *swaraj,* the authentic self-rule of the Indian people, was a spiritual goal with economic and political trappings. He saw independence from the British as merely a significant milestone that the Indian people needed to pass along the way. The most important work, the work to which he devoted the great majority of his efforts, was not the famous resistance campaigns but rather the slow and methodical work of rebuilding India's village life.

In a parallel way some of the most significant work for social change in Latin America today is that of the thousands and thousands of community organizing projects that empower the poor and marginalized. Typically these projects are not built on charismatic leaders and faceless masses. Rather, as this book illustrates, they are the fruit of communities of solidarity and accountability. Through such projects people become economically productive, develop self-reliance, rescue their human dignity and their cultural identity, and construct the framework of a new social order.

The increased activism of the church and the rebuilding of community come together in the formation of thousands of *"comunidades eclesiales de base,"* or "Christian base communities." These small groups of neighbors, of which there are 100,000 in Brazil alone, gather to study the scriptures in the light of their own experiences. Their revolutionary potential lies in the fact that the poor themselves interpret and then apply the gospel message.[5]

The growth of the Christian base communities closely parallels the development of liberation theology. Liberation theology owes much to the reflections of the base communities. For it is not so much a body of thought as it is a way of doing theology from the perspective of the poor. When read from the viewpoint of the poor, the gospel message that Jesus came "to proclaim good news to the poor, release to the captives and recovering of sight to the blind, and to liberate those who are oppressed" (Luke 4:18) is a rich source of inspiration. In it they find not only consolation but also a new boldness: "In the *favelas* [shantytowns] in São Paulo, when the police come to throw the people out, the people have met them with the Bible in their hands. They quote Genesis and say, 'The contract that we signed with God is that the earth is for all of us. You can read it here. And this contract is higher than any human contract.' "[6]

The explosion of base-level organizing and popular movements,[7] *conscientización*, liberation theology, and Christian base communities are all expressions of the creative force of life in contemporary Latin America. But to understand the significance of these expressions, one must also recognize the faces of death.

Structural violence—the human face. In a modern, industrialized country like the United States, it is not uncommon to find infants born mid-term in a pregnancy surviving to lead healthy lives. But in parts of Latin America, as many as half of the children born after normal full-term pregnancies die before the age of five for lack of adequate nutrition and health care. The overt political violence in Latin America that makes the evening news is the product of another, more insidious violence—that of economic and political structures.

The measure of this violence is not the amount of death squad activity, shootings or disappearances. It is a child mortality rate of 176 per 1,000 in Bolivia, a life expectancy of forty-eight years in parts of the Peruvian highlands, the tragedy of the seven million homeless children in Brazil, or a forty-one percent rate of unemployment in Honduras.[8] When either dictatorships or nominally democratic' governments place their own interests above the priority of changing the economic and political structures, they share responsibility for this slow but steady strangling of their citizens.

Yet the greed of rich national elites would be less of a match for the poor's demands for justice if it were not for an international dimension. International attitudes and economics only reinforce Latin America's structural violence. In the industrialized countries of the North we may know little of the displacement of Latin American peasants. Yet many things connect us to their Camucims. First of all, large landholders in Latin America include many transnational corporations. Even where that is not the case, there have been numerous instances in which U.S. tax dollars, channeled through institutions like the World Bank, have financed the displacement of poor peasant farmers in favor of large agricultural or industrial projects. And while peasants typically produce for their own consumption or for domestic markets, most large landholdings produce export crops such as coffee, beef, or sugar, which eventually find their way to our tables.

The enormous foreign debt in most of Latin America—$400 billion in 1989—has created economic depression and added considerably to the structural violence. A third of Latin America's population, one hundred and thirty million people, lives in extreme poverty, denied access to adequate food, housing, health care, and education. Yet a 1989 UNICEF report noted that, "taking everything into account—loans, aid, repayments of interest, and capital—the southern world (including Latin America) is now transferring at least $20 billion a year to the northern hemisphere." The transfers continue even as the poor starve. UNICEF noted that child mortality rates, which had steadily declined during the 1970s, are no longer improving. The organization estimates that *in 1988 alone* this stagnation cost the lives of 250,000 children in just six Latin American countries.[9]

Peaceful popular movements, armed insurgencies, and occasional spontaneous rioting have been among the predictable results. And all have been repressed. Much of this repression has sought legitimacy in what has become known as the National Security Doctrine.[10] Through its counterinsurgency programs, the United States has taught military officers from throughout the hemisphere that "communism" in the form of internal subversion threatens not just the security of a particular nation but Western, Christian civilization itself. In this life and death struggle, the poor are suspect simply for organizing to seek desperately needed change.

Yet physical repression does not eliminate legitimate grievances and desperate needs. Hence all such governments remain unstable. At the close of the 1980s the military with its National Security Doctrine remained the dominant force in most of Latin America, including in countries with elected governments like El Salvador and Guatemala.

The path of liberation

This then is the context in much of Latin America today: grinding poverty, limited options, continual repression. These are the challenges facing movements for social change. In the 1980s elected civilian governments succeeded a number of military dictatorships. In most cases, this reduced the level of official violence somewhat and increased the space for political debate. However, it has not led to significant improvement in the lives of the poor majorities in those countries.

The eruption of the poor and their cry for liberation continues. But what does "liberation" mean? In recent years the 1948 Universal Declaration of Human Rights by the United Nations has increasingly served to define its parameters. The declaration insists firmly on guarantees of the life, physical integrity, and liberties of the individual person. It also charts the fundamental rights people have to such basic necessities as food, shelter, and work, without which individual rights have little meaning. It has helped make human rights the universal language of the poor and a concrete sign of the commitment of the world community to a truly human future.

In order to liberate, then, any political project must provide political and religious freedoms for the individual. But it must also seek a society that meets all the needs of the poor majority. It must build a society that offers access to basic necessities, that promotes equality of opportunity, that ensures the right of full participation for all to the point that democracy truly is government by the people.

What about the *means* of the struggle for liberation? How will such change be possible? It seems that most of the news about Latin America that reaches the countries of the North involves political violence. But in Latin America, many are discovering the path of liberation daily through thousands of concerted nonviolent struggles. Such struggles are bringing the poor both immediate relief and long-term hope.

Capturing the essence of these struggles is the term *"firmeza permanente."* In some places it serves as a substitute for the term "nonviolence." For movements whose first challenge is to overcome the traditional passivity of the dispossessed, the passive connotation of "nonviolence" is a handicap. Clearly "nonviolence" does not adequately describe the dynamism, courage, and commitment that have characterized its classic struggles, such as India's campaign for independence from the British or the U.S. civil rights movement.

"Firmeza permanente" might best translate into English as "relentless persistence." It puts emphasis on what to do rather than what not to do. It echoes *"satyagraha,"* the term that Mahatma Gandhi coined to describe his struggle. In its etymological roots *satyagraha* means "firm grasping after the truth." The same sense of keeping faith and courageously holding on to what is right gave rise to the term *"firmeza permanente."* While not used widely, especially outside of Brazil where it originated, *"firmeza permanente"* aptly characterizes nonviolent action throughout Latin America.

Adolfo Pérez Esquivel, the Argentine winner of the 1980 Nobel Peace Prize, captured its essence when he said:

> Nonviolence is not passivity or conformism. It is a spirit and a method. It is a spirit of prophecy, for it denounces all sundering of a community of brothers and sisters and proclaims that this community can only

be rebuilt through love. And it is a method—an organized set of ruptures in the civil order so as to disturb the system responsible for the injustices we see around us. . . . The means are manifold, depending on the creative capabilities of the people. Here we see the power of the dispossessed, the weapon of the poor. The struggle, then, will be the people's struggle. . . . Our strength will wax great, for it will be the accumulated strength of many forces.[11]

In the midst of the structural and political violence in Latin America and the rising demands for change there are many signs that interest in active nonviolence as a social change strategy is on the increase. When fraud was apparent in the presidential election in Mexico in 1988, and people began to mobilize en masse, "civil resistance" became a rallying cry. Before a national plebiscite in Chile in the same year, opponents of the military dictatorship held dozens of nonviolence training sessions throughout the country. In El Salvador there was more than one occasion in which massive civil disobedience of thousands of refugees intent on returning home from camps in Honduras brought results. The Salvadoran government changed its regulations and accommodated the returnees. In Brazil, rubber tappers in the Amazon rain forest have placed their bodies in front of bulldozers and also joined with environmental groups worldwide in an effective campaign to defend their traditional livelihood in the face of expanding rain forest destruction.

When Latin America's Catholic bishops met in Puebla, Mexico in 1979, and sought an "evangelical means . . . of special effectiveness . . . to re-establish justice,"[12] they explicitly called for developing the strategies of nonviolence. In her landmark work, Cry of the People, Penny Lernoux cited a widespread sense at the Puebla meeting that "the future struggle in Latin America will depend upon . . . the techniques used by Martin Luther King and Mahatma Gandhi, the two leaders in contemporary history most respected by Latin American churchmen. . . . The principal base for this new thrust toward active nonviolence, the bishops said, will be the Christian [base] communities, which are growing by the thousands every year. So while the techniques will be those employed by Gandhi and King, they will capitalize on specific Latin American traits, such as popular religiosity."[13]

National programs by the Catholic church in Brazil, Peru, and elsewhere have focused on education in active nonviolence. Historic peace churches such as the Mennonites are grappling with active nonviolence as a means of integrating the gospel call to seek justice with their traditional pacifism. An international network committed to promoting active nonviolence as a means of liberation struggle, called Servicio Paz y Justicia (SERPAJ) (Service for Peace and Justice), has chapters in eleven countries from Mexico to Chile and Argentina which offer workshops, educational materials, and assistance in organizing.[14]

This is not to suggest that nonviolence is an everyday topic of discussion in the strategy sessions of popular organizations such as unions, peasant associations, or women's groups. There the urgency of each situation results in an unambiguous focus on the needed change. When discussion turns to strategy and tactics, it tends to be concrete and pragmatic rather than theoretical. Nonetheless in the means that popular organizations choose, there is most often a practical nonviolence that is faithful to the cultural and religious values of the people.

Active nonviolence offers pragmatic advantages. A refusal to use violence keeps the moral authority of the poor unclouded. Moreover, relentless persistence builds on the fundamental strengths of the poor majority: their numbers, their unity and capacity for organization, their essential role in the production process, and their ability—in fact their need—to persist and come back again and again. Finally, nonviolence is a strategy that is accessible, one in which all may participate fully: old and young, weak and strong, poor and not-so-poor.

In some areas, another element influencing the choice of nonviolent means is the cultural tradition of nonviolent resistance by indigenous peoples. Over the centuries they have foiled completion of the Conquest, not for the most part with armed struggle but through determined noncooperation—a refusal to assimilate into the Ladino culture. With varying degrees of success they have sought to maintain their way of life, including their language, dress, customs, and communal social structure.

Pacifism—the consistent, principled refusal to use violence as a means of resolving disputes—is rare. However, many are drawn to active nonviolence as a strategy that is both morally adequate and politically efficacious. In a reflection born of long involvement with Christian base communities, a Mexican priest named Oscar Salinas has referred to "the people's intuitive rejection of violence." There is a sense, he says, that "right from the start, the means must clearly correspond with the end. . . . Simply put, we are people who have a hard time seeing that the society of Shalom, of peace based on justice, can be forged by recourse to arms. War to combat war? . . . Death to combat death? When and where does the spiral end?"[15]

In order to understand the practice of nonviolence in Latin America, then, one must keep in mind both of these dimensions: the calculated *pragmatism* of people faced with great needs and limited choices, and the religious and cultural *principles* that give meaning and order to life. This combination is what gives Latin American nonviolence its distinctive character.

Of course the contemporary crisis in Latin America can and does lead individuals to different conclusions about whether armed struggle is necessary or whether nonviolent struggle will be adequate. But the result is often a dynamic rather than fractious tension. The Brazilian archbishop Dom Hélder Câmara, one of Latin America's best known proponents of active nonviolence, reflected the sentiments of many when he said, "I respect those who have felt obliged in conscience to opt for violence, not the facile violence of armchair guerrillas, but that of those who have proved their sincerity by the sacrifice of their lives. It seems to me the memory of Camilo Torres and Che Guevara deserves as much respect as that of Dr. Martin Luther King, Jr."[16]

It is not that the strategy for change is of no consequence. Clearly it matters, and people of different views feel passionately about it. But the choice is not an abstract one. Rather it is rooted in the concrete experience of struggle. And in the end it is the commitment to *struggle actively* for change that determines more than anything who is or is not an ally.

Embracing the nonviolent option

Although the eruption of the poor and their *concientización* is proving to be irreversible and cumulative, there are no magic formulas. Neither are there any guarantees that nonviolent strategies can muster the strength to carry out the structural change that Latin America desperately needs. Of course the same is surely true of armed struggle. Moreover active nonviolence is in its infancy. As a consciously organized strategy for social change it dates back only to 1906 when Gandhi began to struggle in South Africa. Even today nonviolent action in Latin America draws on the Bible more than on the modern experience of Gandhi, Martin Luther King, Jr., or other determined and serious practitioners. Relatively few popular struggles in Latin America have benefited from formal training in the theory, history, or practice of nonviolence. Generally they seek to avoid violence as much as to embrace what we call active nonviolence. But for that very reason the successes of spontaneous nonviolent movements are all the more tantalizing. Still, their limitations underscore the need for greater self-consciousness, strategic thinking, and preparation.

At another level, the efficacy of nonviolence in Latin America depends in part on cooperation from the developed North. Given the many forms of foreign intervention in those countries, concrete international collaboration must complement national popular movements. The simple writing of a letter to a government official in support of a community threatened with violence may save lives. Public education and support for sound development projects are also crucial areas of action. Sometimes more direct action is appropriate.

Yet the question is not only what to do. It is also when to do it. All too often, international solidarity movements develop only when popular movements have turned to armed struggle. In El Salvador during the 1970s and up until 1980, popular organizations held marches of hundreds of thousands of people. Yet a broad international solidarity movement did not emerge until the early 1980s when official violence had choked these organizations off.

The first step toward reducing our distance and working together is to recognize the humanity we share in common with Latin America's suffering poor. In 1987, Vietnam War veteran Brian Willson was run down while nonviolently blockading a munitions train carrying U.S. arms bound for Central America. Miraculously he survived, but he lost both of his legs. His action was a powerful symbol of the meaning of solidarity. Shortly before his peaceful protest he summed up his determination by saying, "One truth seems clear: If the munitions train moves past our blockade other human beings will be killed and maimed. We are not worth more. They are not worth less."

The stories in this book call for the kind of active love that Brian Willson expressed at risk to life and limb. To be sure these stories inform and analyze. But with no apology, and with much passion, they also call out an invitation to help build a new hemispheric community.

Like Zé Galego and the peasants of Camucim whose story began this chapter, the first fruits of that new community are found in the very act of sowing its seeds. Even in small acts of caring and solidarity, when people stand together in witness to deeply cherished values, a new reality is created. Hope arises.

Notes

1. Quoted in Creuza Maciel, *Não-Violência: Uma Estratégia Revolucionária* (São Paulo: Editora FTD, 1988), p. 46.

2. *Concientización* refers to the process whereby the poor acquire critical consciousness of their role as actors in the world, the creators of their own history. The translation that sometimes appears in English—"consciousness-raising"—is inadequate because it may suggest that the person with latent consciousness is a passive recipient in a process where becoming actors in history is everything. Because the English term "conscientization" is clumsy and not widely used, the Spanish *"concientización"* appears throughout this book, except in a chapter directly related to Brazil.

3. From a talk delivered at the IV Congresso Internacional Ecumênico de Teología, São Paulo, February 21 to March 2, 1981.

4. The Second Vatican Council (1962-65) was a watershed experience that redefined the role of the Roman Catholic Church in the modern world. The 1968 meeting of the Conference of Latin American Bishops (CELAM) in Medellín, Colombia applied

the spirit of Vatican II to the harsh reality of Latin America and produced a sweeping mandate for change.

5. Three of the best sources in English on the nature and practice of Christian base communities are: Dominique Barbé, *Grace and Power: Base Communities and Nonviolence in Brazil* (Maryknoll, N.Y.: Orbis Books, 1987), especially Chapter 6; Phillip Berryman, *The Religious Roots of Rebellion: Christians in Central American Revolutions* (Maryknoll, N.Y.: Orbis Books, 1984); and Guillermo Cook, *The Expectation of the Poor: Latin American Base Ecclesial Communities in Protestant Perspective* (Maryknoll, N.Y.: Orbis Books, 1985).

6. Domingos Barbé, "To Eat and to Love," *IFOR Report* February 1985, p. 6.

7. "Base-level" is to be distinguished from "grassroots" by the social strata of the constituency. "Grassroots" is used primarily in developed countries to connote a local focus. Most often it refers to a middle-class constituency if for no other reason than that the middle sectors include the majority of the population in such countries. "Base-level" comes from societies whose structure is characterized by a social pyramid: a small elite, a somewhat larger middle class, and a vast majority of poor. In this case the constituency is the poor. Likewise, in most cases the Christian base communities are made up of the poor. The term "popular" is similarly used to refer to the poor majority. Popular movements would not exclude members of the middle class, but their core constituency is generally the poor.

8. *New York Times,* July 20, 1982; cited in Barry, Wood, and Preusch, *Dollars and Dictators* (Albuquerque: The Resource Center, 1982), p. 124; UNICEF, *The State of the World's Children, 1989* (New York: UNICEF, 1989), p. 94. Child mortality refers to the annual number of deaths of children under five per 1000 live births. The corresponding rate in the United States is 13 per 1000. Consejo Nacional de Población, *Perú: Guía demográfica y socio-económica* (Lima: 1985); Conferência Nacional dos Bispos do Brasil, "Quem Acolhe o Menor, A Mim Acolhe," (São Paulo: Campanha da Fraternidade-1987, Texto Base), p. 14; Centro de Documentación de Honduras (CEDOH), *Boletín Informativo* 62, June 1986: p. 2, cited in Medea Benjamin, "Honduras: The Real Loser in U.S. War Games," *Food First Action Alert* (San Francisco: Institute for Food and Development Policy, 1987), p. 3. To these statistics may also be added the fact that in some countries, the fallout from crumbling economies has included a burgeoning drug trade which has only added another dimension of violence and distortion.

9. UNICEF, *The State of the World's Children—1989* (New York: Oxford University Press, 1989), pp. 1, 15, 16. The UNICEF report also notes that "in the last ten years, real prices for the developing world's principal commodities . . . have fallen by approximately 30%." Elaborating on the $20 billion transfer of wealth from South to North worldwide, it continues: "And if we were also to take into account the effective transfer of resources implied in the reduced prices paid by the industrialized nations for the developing world's raw materials, then the annual flow from the poor to the rich might be as much as $60 billion each year."

According to UNICEF, this reversal of declining infant mortality rates is primarily "a result of unprecedented borrowing, rising interest rates, falling commodity prices, inadequate investment of borrowed funds, and the domestic and international management of the resulting debt crisis" (p. 8). (It is widely acknowledged that (1) the "unprecedented borrowing" was heavily promoted by international banks flush with surplus funds as a result of spiraling oil prices in the 1970s; (2) decisions regarding borrowing and investment were often made by dictatorships or governments with only limited popular participation; and (3) the resultant debt crisis, i.e., the absolute impossibility of debt repayment according to previously established terms, has generally been managed through the collusion of international banks and wealthy elites in the individual countries. Despite the progressive impoverishment of Latin America, within the region the rich have continued to get richer while the backs of the poor are being broken.)

For an analysis of the debt crisis, see George Ann Potter, *Dialogue on Debt* (Washington, D.C.: Center of Concern, 1988).

10. In chapter one, Pablo Stanfield describes how in Guatemala in 1954 the U.S. Central Intelligence Agency conducted the first full-fledged experiment with the National Security Doctrine.

11. Adolfo Pérez Esquivel, *Christ in a Poncho* (Maryknoll, N.Y.: Orbis Books, 1983), pp. 52-53.

12. *Puebla, Final Document*, nos. 486, 533.

13. Penny Lernoux, *Cry of the People*, (New York: Penguin Books, 1982), p. 447-448.

14. While it is only in recent years that active nonviolence has become the subject of much discussion in Latin America, there are historical roots not addressed here. From the first century of Spanish conquest, priests like Bartolomé de las Casas and Bishop Antonio Valdivieso charted a regrettably small but nonetheless important tradition of witness in the Catholic church. De las Casas suffered expulsion and isolation, and Valdivieso lost his life for defending the rights of the indigenous peoples.

In the early part of this century, groups affiliated with the International Fellowship of Reconciliation (IFOR) emerged among Protestants in several Latin American countries. While these groups were staunchly pacifist, they did not always complement their pacifism with an equal commitment to active struggle for basic social change.

In the 1960s, IFOR International Secretaries Hildegard and Jean Goss-Mayr traveled throughout Latin America cultivating a network of contacts interested in active nonviolence as a means of liberation struggle. Their work had a far-reaching impact and contributed to the creation of the SERPAJ network. Their work and the origins of SERPAJ are chronicled in *Reseña Histórica del SERPAJ-AL*, vol. I, 1986. (Rio de Janeiro: Servicio Paz y Justicia). Some of the earlier history of the Fellowship of Reconciliation groups is found in John Nevin Sayre, "The FOR and Latin America: Outline of Work Carried on, 1919-1960," *Solidarity* (Newsletter of the Committee in Solidarity with Latin American Nonviolent Movements and the FOR Task Force on Latin America and the Caribbean): vol. II, no. 3; vol. III, nos. 2, 4; vol. IV, no. 2.

15. Salinas, Oscar, "La No-Violencia y las Comunidades Eclesiales de Base," p. 8 (unpublished mimeograph).

16. Quoted in Hall, Mary, "I have a dream . . . ", *Reconciliation Quarterly*, June 1980, p. 22.

For further reading

Barbé, Dominique. *Grace and Power Base Communities and Nonviolence in Brazil.* Maryknoll, NY: Orbis Books, 1987.

Boff, Clovodis. *Feet-on-the-Ground Theology.* Maryknoll, NY: Orbis Books, 1987.

Boff, Leonardo and Boff, Clovodis. *Introducing Liberation Theology.* Maryknoll, NY: Orbis Books, 1987.

Câmara, Dom Hélder. *The Spiral of Violence.* Denville, NJ: Dimension Books, 1971.

Fragoso, Antônio et al. A Firmeza-Permanente—A Força da Não-Violência. São Paulo: Loyola-Vega, 1977.

Fragoso, Dom Antônio B. *Face of a Church.* Maryknoll, NY: Orbis Books, 1987.

Galeano, Eduardo. *Open Veins of Latin America.* New York: Monthly Review Press, 1973.

Gutiérrez, Gustavo. *We Drink From Our Own Wells: The Spiritual Journey of a People.* Maryknoll, NY: Orbis Books, 1984; Melbourne, Australia: Dove Books, 1984.

Lernoux, Penny. *Cry of the People.* New York: Penguin Books, 1982.

Maciel, Creuza. *Não-Violência: Uma Estratégia Revolucionária.* São Paulo: Editora FTD, 1988.

Pérez Esquivel, Adolfo. *Christ in a Poncho.* Maryknoll, NY: Orbis Books, 1983.

Schlabach, Gerald. *Bibliographia en Español sobre la No Violencia.* Akron, PA: Mennonite Central Committee, 1989.

I
CASE HISTORIES

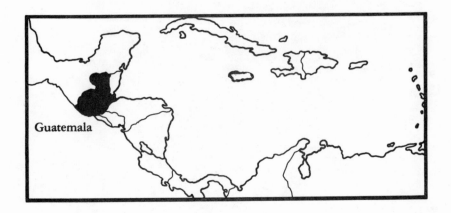

Guatemala

ONE

Introduction

In 1979 revolutionary change in Central America led many North Americans to take new notice of Latin America. For the first time in years, the region's events caught and held the attention of U.S. news media and (for better or worse) of U.S. presidents.

For twenty-five years, since 1954, it might have seemed that nothing newsworthy was happening in the isthmus. In the 1960s the United States had promoted reform through an Alliance for Progress, but the Alliance had come and gone. A common market had developed in the five key Central American states, but had fallen victim to a border dispute and U.S. manipulation. Where there had been elections they had often been rigged and had usually been inconclusive. In Honduras one military regime had indeed pushed social and land reform, but only for three years.

Of course for millions of Central Americans *everything* happened during those years. They grew up, went to school, sought work, and started families, struggling against hunger, poverty, and violence.

Yet in a way nothing did happen in Central America in those twenty-five years that events in 1954 did not foreshadow. In 1954 Central American history was aborted. Since then, whenever change has been conceived within the Central American womb, it has almost always miscarried. In 1954 the United States government, acting through its Central Intelligence Agency at the urging of the United Fruit Company, overthrew a decade of peaceful, democratic reform in Guatemala.

The previous Guatemalan decade, which had begun with the largely nonviolent overthrow of a dictator in 1944, had captured imaginations throughout the continent. Guatemala's new leaders had taken eight years to get down to the really serious business of restructuring Guatemalan society through land reform. Yet what was happening in the country so intrigued Latin Americans that they called it "The Guatemalan Revolution."

The demise of this peaceful revolution was a watershed for all Latin America. It told Latin Americans in no uncertain terms that if they expected the United States to help them vanquish fascism in the Americas, as it had done for Europeans, they were wrong. It quashed Latin hopes that Franklin Roosevelt's "Four Freedoms"—freedom of speech, freedom of religion, freedom from want, freedom from fear— might become their freedoms, too. It belied the 1933 Montevideo Declaration in which the United States had finally agreed to interpret its century-old Monroe Doctrine in a way that ruled out unilateral U.S. intervention and called for truly mutual security. The 1954 U.S. intervention in Guatemala promised an unfriendly response—at best impatient, at worst violent—to authentically Latin American democracy. Guatemala had created the most inspiring fusion of electoral and economic democracy the region had seen to date. Now its experiment was dead, a victim not of natural causes but of U.S. intervention and the growing chill of the Cold War.

For electoral democracy to function with meaning anywhere in Latin America, there must first be a base of economic democracy. Nowhere is that more clear than in Central America. Except in Costa Rica, the Spanish colonizers who settled there came not to work the land but to amass it and exploit it through the labor of the indigenous people who had traditionally cared for the land as their holy mother. Though the isthmus disappointed the first gold-hungry conquistadors, others soon discovered what Pablo Stanfield calls its "alchemy." In the twentieth century its fertile fields and hardworking people still make magic for a tiny group of large landholders—daily they convert sweat and sunshine into gold, or at least into dollars. If the key ingredient in this alchemic wizardry is ownership of the land, the key to change is land redistribution.

From 1944 to 1954, change began in Guatemala. The Great Depression, World War II, and Franklin Roosevelt had helped set the stage. But the Guatemalans had drawn as well on their own resources. Historian Jim Handy has written that through 450 years of peasant uprisings, "with amazing consistency, protest has always first taken a nonviolent, 'legal' form. Only with repeated demonstration of the inability or unwillingness of government to respond effectively to these protests have peasants turned violent."[1]

In June 1944, spontaneously and creatively, without benefit of any theory or training in nonviolence, the Guatemalan people drew on these roots. They demonstrated. They called a general strike. They turned cultural symbols like the national anthem and religious mourning into expressions of protest. They maintained a disciplined, dignified, and peaceful front that welded public opinion and won over the dictator's former supporters. Thus, his repression rebounded against him.

When a small nation begins to create a new model of democracy it can capture the imagination of a continent or even the world. In 1979 the Nicaraguan Sandinistas did that through a more violent revolution in their nation of three million people. But it is important for both sympathizers and detractors of that experiment to recall that Central Americans had earlier worked peacefully for reform when they had a chance to do so without outside interference.

At mid-century Guatemala also had about three million people. Their captivating experiment demonstrated that they were more and more recognizing the need for structural change. It showed more trust in FDR-style democratic reform than the United States was showing by that time. And it drew on an instinctive heritage of nonviolent action.

Is it too late to hope for other nonviolent revolutions in Latin America? Throughout this book the reader will keep facing that question. But for the moment there may be a prior question: To what lengths will the United States go to try to prevent nonviolent revolution in Latin America?

Guatemala: When Spring Turned to Winter
Pablo Stanfield

This is a story of the Guatemalan people and democracy, a story of mythic proportions. Like an epic tragedy it has defined one way a people name both a passion for life and the mortal perils that, time and time again, snuff out their best hopes. Like a classic romance it imposes meddling relatives on a short-lived love affair, yet evokes lingering memories of what could have been, or—against many odds— what still could be.

Alas, the story of Guatemala's courtship, honeymoon, and estrangement from democracy is no mere legend. In 1944 Guatemala did embrace democracy in a strikingly gentle way. During the next ten years that union gave birth to one social reform after another and inspired hopes throughout Central and South America. Then in 1954 the United States Central Intelligence Agency (CIA) sponsored a coup that dashed Guatemalan reform and much of the hope for peaceful democratic change in the rest of Latin America. This bitter story is all too real and, like the best of myths, it has provided rich, varied, and sometimes contradictory lessons to both Latin Americans and sympathetic observers.

A dictator falls

In 1944 Guatemala had an opportunity that at first it barely recognized. As in other Central American countries an astute and powerful dictator ruled. General Jorge Ubico, an admirer of Hitler, tolerated no dissent. A massacre he directed in 1934 shortly after he became president brutally drove the point home. "Scores of students, workers, [and] prominent citizens suspected of plotting a rebellion were seized in their homes, killed without formality. Hundreds were thrown into prison, tortured, executed. Cried Ubico . . ., 'I am like Hitler, I execute first and give trial afterwards. . . . ' "2

Nevertheless a commercial and professional middle class was growing in Guatemala and was increasingly unhappy with the general's iron rule. During World War II Guatemala officially joined the fight against fascism. The middle class sensed the irony of fighting for freedoms they could not enjoy themselves. They saw the Ubico government, under U.S. pressure, take away lands from German coffee growers and call it an act of war. But they knew that Ubico together with his close friends in the U.S.-based United Fruit Company could take their properties and futures from them as well.

In May 1944 the people of neighboring El Salvador successfully rose up against their dictator, General Maximiliano Hernández Martínez. Hernández was a brutal—some say psychotic—tyrant who in 1932 had massacred between ten and thirty thousand people during a single month. Yet through a massive general strike, despite bloody retaliation, the Salvadoran people managed to depose him. El Salvador's events quickly became Guatemala's events. Notes one historian: "The success of the Salvadoran uprising emboldened the

Guatemalan opposition and provided exiles with a base of operations on the border."[3]

Among the few groups of politically organized Guatemalans were students; indeed students "constituted almost the only group capable of initiating a challenge to the administration."[4] When a new University Students Association petitioned for a change in deans, Ubico surprised them with unexpected flexibility. Yet after he had negotiated on their first demands his patience quickly evaporated. On June 22 the students asked for more, including autonomy for the University of San Carlos. In authoritarian Guatemala, Ubico viewed their demands not as a minor nuisance but as a direct personal challenge. For only the second time in his presidency the general called his cabinet together. Immediately the government rejected the students' demands and suspended constitutional rights. Ubico claimed that the people of the country expected him to keep "peace and order."

But the country was not so quiescent. For a month or more dissatisfaction had been surfacing. Forty-five lawyers had petitioned Ubico for the removal of a biased judge. Two hundred school teachers had asked for higher pay. Plans for an opposition party were in the works.

So when on June 23 the university students swiftly matched Ubico's crackdown with a call for a general strike, many people were ready. Teachers joined them immediately. At noon the next day the first large demonstration occurred with the students marching through town, holding a mass gathering, and publicly reading the Atlantic Charter. The Charter, of course, was the 1941 Roosevelt-Churchill document that set out "Four Freedoms" as the official goals of the war against fascism (freedom of speech and expression, of worship, from want, and from fear). The same day, 311 prominent professionals signed a petition asking the dictator to lift the state of emergency and resign. Their action was something of a surprise, for many of those professionals were long-time supporters of Ubico. But they were also members of professional societies which included striking students. So they published their petition and joined the growing demonstrations in the National Palace plaza.

General Ubico had regularly feigned a desire to retire to private life. Even so he continued in office beyond constitutional limitations, saying that his fellow citizens insisted he do so. And now he reacted in a way that obliterated all remaining memory of his "selfless" public service. On the evening of June 24, 1944, he ordered police to attack groups violating a curfew in neighborhoods of the capital. The police did so ferociously, further outraging the nation.

The next morning, a Sunday, Guatemalans woke up to find the capital militarized. Armed cavalry charged a group of women dressed in mourning as they marched from a downtown church to the National Palace. A school teacher named María Chinchilla was killed, and many were wounded.

On Monday the country responded with a general strike. Stores, theaters, banks, schools, clinics, and offices were closed. Even market vendors left their stalls to join the protests, and brought their housewife clients with them. Ubico organized reprisals. The government harassed opposition leaders and put striking transportation and communications workers under military control. Police threatened shopkeepers if they joined the strike.

Amid the quickening pace of events the students attempted to provide some leadership. They distributed leaflets urging the public to continue its "dignified and peaceful attitude and to avoid any incivil or hostile act that might prejudice the happy accomplishments of our objects and those of the people."[5]

No longer did Ubico have even the passive consent of the people. Towns around the country joined the strike. Pressure mounted steadily on the increasingly isolated dictator. Faced with such dissent, his troops could not make the country governable. He yielded slightly by firing his strongest supporter, General David Ordóñez, head of his secret police. But this had no effect.

Early on July 1, the president called in his secretary, signed a resignation he had ordered drawn up, and named the first three generals who showed up for the morning's military staff meeting as Guatemala's new ruling junta. Retiring to his home he was bitter that the nation he thought loved him had forgotten all his years of striving to maintain law and order and all the economic advantages he had showered on supporters. He thought he deserved credit for saving his country from a protracted civil war, and he bragged that he had not left like Hernández Martínez in El Salvador, "with his hands dripping blood." Both United States and British envoys sent messages lauding the years of stability he had provided for business, even though he had never done much to hide his pro-Franco and fascist outlook.

When word reached the people that Ubico had stepped down, the streets exploded with celebration. The junta, with General Federico Ponce Vaides at its head, pledged to hold elections as soon as possible. Exiles began streaming home. Political parties formed. Ponce, who announced he would run for president, restored constitutional controls. Yet he also plotted to secure his position. Guatemalans, flush with the new taste of freedom, reacted at once. Demonstrators, yelling in the hall, ended a special session of the National Assembly that was to name him provisional president.

Ponce responded by clamping down. He had reason for concern. More than the head of state had changed. For fourteen years the old dictator had cowed Congress; suddenly intimidation no longer worked. Stories abounded of citizens standing up to the authorities with demands for freedom. The people were now demanding a liberality the new regime was not prepared to give. Ponce did not understand how the nation was changing. When one exile, philosopher Dr. Juan José Arévalo, returned to Guatemala to run for president as the main opposition candidate, crowds applauded him as if he were a conquering hero. Ponce tried unsuccessfully to have Arévalo assassinated. Elections took place on October 13, but the ruling junta sought ineptly and transparently to use the ballot box as an opportunity for political elimination. As the U.S. Embassy's chargé d'affaires reported: The government slate "won by a handsome, not to say fantastic, margin, garnering 48,503 votes out of a total 44,576 ballots cast."[6]

Others in the government understood the people far better. The fantastic election results did not amuse. Among the disgusted were several disaffected junior officers of the Army and some businessmen and functionaries who encouraged the officers to act. In the early morning hours of October 20 the officers took over the Honor Guard of the Presidential Palace. They shot the commanding officer when he resisted, and commandeered the nation's only tanks plus most of the arms in the capital. Ponce ordered loyal troops to attack the mutiny, but crowds of people rushed to protect the rebellious soldiers. Students took up rifles from the garrison or stones from the pavement and defied the loyalist troops. Loyalist officers could not keep their men from deserting. By evening, Ponce, Ubico, and all the old guard were seeking asylum in foreign embassies. A new triumvirate called for a democratic constitution and open elections, and this time kept the promises.

Given the contrast between the events of June and October, the question arises: Why a violent military coup to depose a regime less than four months old when nonviolence had shown its success against the far more deeply entrenched, thirteen-year rule of Jorge Ubico?

Ubico had worn out his welcome with too many years and too much brutality, but even his opponents admitted he had earlier been an astute politician. Ponce was a shallow opportunist. Once he took over the reins he also took to getting drunk every afternoon. His intent to pilfer while in office was so crass that fellow junta members soon denounced him.[7] His days, it would have seemed, were numbered. Yet Guatemalan democrats—so recently flush with the power of popular mobilization in the face of Ubico's repression—quickly grew discouraged when Ponce used all the tired tactics of dictatorship against them. When a second general strike sputtered in October, the most creative tactic Ponce's opponents could muster was an alliance with disgruntled military men. Why?

Guatemala's nonviolence of June 1944 was like much of the nonviolence in Latin American history—culturally authentic and tantalizing yet fragmentary and spontaneous. The Guatemalan militants of 1944 may scarcely have known their own strength. Or perhaps, since many were part of the emerging middle-class, they were ambivalent about extending that strength to Guatemala's vast underclass and above all to the native Mayas. If any did consider toppling Ponce by expanding the opposition movement, it undoubtedly seemed safer to turn to an alliance with a more traditional kind of power. After all, such allies were readily available and World War II had imbued a few of them with the ideals of representative democracy. Yet the role that opposition leaders asked military men to play in the birth of the Guatemalan revolution would come back to haunt all who loved democracy.

The springtime of democracy

Guatemalans still refer to the decade from 1944 to 1954 as their springtime. They were in a honeymoon with democracy. A new constitution contained a lengthy bill of rights. Their new leader was Arévalo, an idealist who took his inspiration from Franklin Roosevelt and Plato. No longer did Mayan chain-gangs march through the streets to work on coastal plantations. Goon squads no longer beat up anyone who formed a trade union. Newspaper editors would never again be shot for printing an opinion, or so they thought. The soldiers in the army no longer looked down when confronting their own people; they looked them in the eye and felt themselves to be part of the same nation that had taken on its own freedom, its own democracy. Arévalo and his successors would often repeat that this October Revolution had been for everyone, and that all sectors of the "Guatemalan family" would benefit.

For its part, the U.S. government played a low-key role during the transition. Earlier and later the United States reacted in the region with active intervention. To be sure, just after the coup the U.S. ambassador did call on the three interim leaders to insist that the former head of Ubico's secret police be named the new President. The triumvirate ignored him. After the elections the new government named the ambassador *persona non grata*. Still the United States stood by. Plotting was to come later.

For the most part the focus of the U.S. press, government, and people was on the war in Europe and the Pacific. The fall of a banana dictator did not count as much of a loss. Ubico had only attacked German interests in his country when the U.S. government pressured him. But if North Americans had paid attention, they might have been encouraged to discover that the Guatemalan Revolution was idealizing and imitating the U.S. system.

The leaders of the revolution were young and fascinated with what they saw as the egalitarian society and the expanding material benefits of the United States. They took to heart slogans of the Allies' fight on the fronts. "Democracy is in danger not only in Europe," said President Arévalo, "and it is defended in places besides just the battlefield."[8] To defend it in Central America all people had to be accorded dignity and opportunity. The new government took the United States as a model for building justice. Arévalo thanked Roosevelt for showing the world that democracy, private initiative, and government could work together to improve the lives of the poor. Although there were some communists in the coalition supporting Arévalo he himself rejected communism out of hand. He believed it ignored real men and women and reduced them to economic animals rather than a mix of good and bad, of social and selfish interests. Arévalo also rejected individualistic capitalism because it failed to account for the collective interests of society as a whole.[9] Arévalo termed his alternative "spiritual socialism."

Unknown to the people of Guatemala, who were amid an explosion of culture and material benefits, the government to the North was leaving behind the ideals with which it had combatted the Great Depression. So it was becoming less of a "Good Neighbor" and more of a "Big Brother." Having broken its anti-Nazi alliance with the Soviet Union it was concentrating on a new enemy. Cold War polarity was creating new priorities, a new world system, and blunt impatience for ill-fitting experiments at anything like "spiritual socialism." When the United States finally took notice, its new biases were against the sorts of changes taking place in Guatemala.

An early act of the Guatemalan Congress was to establish a labor code that fostered union organizing, collective bargaining, and the right to strike—all of which the Ubico government had totally restricted as being "red." Already during the Ponce regime after the nonviolent uprising of June 1944, trade unions had begun springing up. That July, six thousand workers on a United Fruit Company plantation near Tiquisate had gone on strike, and had maintained their discipline despite efforts by three trainloads of Ponce's troops to provoke them. With the fall of Ponce union rivalry broke out and hampered labor's effectiveness more than did the government. Nevertheless by 1952 labor leaders managed to form a single bloc that could claim some 400 affiliated unions with more than 200,000 members.[10]

The Constitution of 1945 forbade racial discrimination and guaranteed equal opportunity and universal access to legal redress. Once in place, the Arévalo government began providing health clinics and potable water even in neglected rural areas, and sewers in urban neighborhoods. Historian Jim Handy has written that "these measures, coupled with higher income levels, insured that the [infant] mortality rate fell an average of 2.5 percent per year over the ten years of spring."[11] Since the 1870s primary education had been compulsory in Guatemala, though the majority Mayan population would never have known it. Now the Arévalo government began literacy campaigns and boosted education expenditures by 155 percent over four years.[12] In 1946 the country enacted its first social security law, a law that still survives.

Slowly the revolution that had begun among Guatemala City's middle classes began spreading to the rural Mayan majority. The new government promptly canceled vagrancy laws with which the Ubico government had forced Mayan males to work on road projects and private plantations.[13] Increasingly the Mayas began participating in national life. Political parties began organizing to win their support.[14]

But there was one primordial part of the nation's structure that did not change so quickly—the pattern of land ownership. Ever since the Spanish had taken their lands in wars of conquest, the Mayan people had paid tribute just to stay alive. Liberal reforms of the 19th century had favored large coffee growers and ravaged the ancient Mayan system of collective land ownership. The Mayas no longer had a sufficient area of their sacred Mother Earth on which to grow food for their own families.

Yet sixty percent of the land on Guatemala's large plantations lay fallow. The Boston-based United Fruit Company, known as "la frutera," was the country's largest single landowner. It had over 400,000 acres "in reserve" and for tax purposes valued them at less than three dollars per acre.

Land tenure is the crux of many of the problems all over Latin America. For centuries the way to keep access to cheap labor of the peasants, and to exploit it, has been to limit their access to the most basic resource, land. In 1952 a mere two percent of the population owned seventy-two percent of Guatemalan farm land, while about half of the agricultural population owned less than four percent.[15] Sadly, those statistics have only gotten worse since then. Nor are they much different from land tenure patterns throughout Latin America. Hence, land reform programs are the basis of any valid proposal for improving the economies and lives of the people of the Americas.

Not until 1962 would a U.S. administration acknowledge as much. But by then the land reform that the Guatemalan Revolution eventually enacted, and which might have served as a model for the hemisphere, had disappeared along with Guatemalan democracy.

In 1949 the Arévalo administration took the first steps toward land reform. It did so by sponsoring a law to require landholders to rent uncultivated plots to the landless. The law was weak and had little effect; peasants had to request land in person, but most landowners were absentee, living in the capital. In 1951, the second administration of Guatemala's springtime, under President Jacobo Arbenz, tinkered with this "Law of Forced Rental." But again, results were hardly impressive.

Finally, on June 17, 1952, Congress passed Decree 900, the agrarian reform law. In cases of farms over a certain acreage Decree 900 allowed the state to exercise its right of eminent domain to expropriate land that had not been cultivated for at least three years. The government would pay for the land with twenty-five-year bonds at three percent interest, with the amount of principal based on the owners' tax declarations of land value. The president himself saw a large part of his family farm distributed to peasants under this law. One hundred thousand families soon found themselves tilling their own fields.[16] Crop yields rose, and for once there was enough corn and beans to meet the demand. Export production grew as well, and by 1954 Guatemala enjoyed a favorable balance of trade. A few years later a U.S. agronomist working for the United Nations Food and Agriculture Organization concluded: "For all the furor it produced, Law 900, which had its root in the constitution of 1945, is a remarkably mild and fairly sound piece of legislation."[17]

For ten years Guatemalan society had changed and grown faster than during all the years since the fall of the Mayas. The Guatemalan experiment was the curiosity of all Latin America, whose only previous experience with a real social revolution had been the bloody Mexican one. Here was a chance for Latin Americans to develop their resources and take their place among Western democracies, while inventing their own path to that goal. Here was the revival of independence leader Simón Bolívar's dream that all America would one day be the vanguard of freedom and hope for the world. Of course, the experiment was imperfect. As usual, the majority indigenous population was still the last to benefit. Social divisions were still deep and the economy imposed constraints. But no one knows how the dream might have developed had Guatemalans been permitted to resolve these questions among themselves.

Ever since 1954, Latin Americans have wondered if Guatemala's springtime was the way development would look if the Latin American nations were left to themselves.

Winter returns on the wind of Cold War

Then came June 1954, exactly ten years after the people had gone into the streets to achieve liberty and democracy. Now, instead, the people hid in the shelter of their homes amid a blackout. Planes from an invading army bombarded the capital. Suddenly President Jacobo Arbenz resigned. His hope was that the Army would now act to defend the nation, but he hoped in vain. Two days later the U.S. Ambassador flew to San Salvador and brought in an unknown colonel, Carlos Castillo Armas, to "lead" the country. Democracy was out; decades of military dictatorship, oppression, violence, and grief were beginning. Guatemala was in the grips of an untimely winter.

It was apparent to everyone that the United States of America was responsible for the overthrow of the constitutionally elected government. Before the invasion Guatemala had asked both the Organization of American States and the United Nations to investigate the tightening noose of threats against it, but U.S. political strength had thwarted even an investigation of the charges. Journalists Stephen Kinzer and Stephen Schlesinger have since used the U.S. Freedom of Information Act to document what was an open secret for twenty-five years. Their book, *Bitter Fruit: the Untold Story of the American Coup in Guatemala*, tells the story of "Operation Success."[18] It was a plan that United Fruit promoted, the CIA carried out, and President Eisenhower approved. Although the plan required a few bombs and bullets, it relied much more on disinformation.

John Foster Dulles, U.S. Secretary of State, had once been legal counsel to the United Fruit Company of Boston, Massachusetts, his home town. His brother, Allen Dulles, director of the CIA, had served on the board of trustees. Both owned stock in the corporation. For a base of operations against the Guatemala of Arévalo and Arbenz, they turned to Anastasio Somoza García, Nicaragua's dictator, who had his own reasons for stifling the Guatemalan example. Somoza furnished a site for training a few hundred mercenaries, who then feigned an invasion of Guatemala as a liberating army. He also provided a landing strip for CIA-owned planes, which strafed and dropped a few real bombs on Guatemala's capital to make the ragtag mercenary band at the border seem part of a real threat.

However, the air attacks would hardly have been credible without a barrage of fabricated reports from a clandestine radio station dubiously dubbed "The Voice of Liberation." Despite obligatory flourishes about broadcasting "from somewhere deep inside Guatemala," CIA operatives recorded the broadcasts in Florida and beamed them from Nicaragua and a U.S. base on the Caribbean's Swan Island. In their propaganda they announced fictitious air drops and military victories for the "Liberation Army" of Colonel Castillo Armas all over Guatemala. In fact, the sorry troops barely made it into Esquipulas, ten miles inside the border, and had one small battle at Zacapa, twenty-five miles away.

Clearly the three pillars of Guatemala's status quo—oligarchy,

Roman Catholic Church, and Army—had never really accepted the reforms that threatened their ability to profit from the alchemy that had long exploited sweat and turned it into gold. But until outside powers intervened, the three forces had not proven strong enough to undo the era of democratic reform.

The fact was that popular forces, organized in a broad range of unions, syndicates, peasant leagues, and cooperatives, were becoming a new pillar at the center of a new order. The Guatemalan revolution might have survived even CIA intervention if Arbenz had placed more trust in the power of a people united, the power that had resisted the repressive dictatorship of General Ubico in June 1944. When Arbenz went on the radio with a final speech, even a CIA operative working in the disinformation campaign thought the president had marshalled the populace to defeat the mock invasion. "We expected him to tell his people he had won," David Atlee Phillips told Kinzer and Schlesinger years later. "We thought we'd lost. . . . We were so surprised by his departure."[19]

So were many of Arbenz's most ardent supporters, who were waiting for his leadership when the unexpected news came. Participants in Guatemala's springtime of progressive democracy have agonized ever since about why the president deserted the cause so abruptly. Obviously the disinformation campaign had taken its toll. By all accounts Arbenz was despondent. Whether the threat to Guatemalan sovereignty was real or fabricated, it became increasingly clear that the Army would not support him, and his resolve ebbed. The only alternative he considered was distributing arms to student and worker militias, and that only hastened the Army's desertion.

But then, Arbenz was first of all a military man himself. He had been one of the main plotters of October 1944's violent palace coup. He had served in the transitional three-man junta that turned over the presidency to Arévalo, and had then been Arévalo's minister of defense. From October 1944 onward the Guatemalan revolution had actually consolidated the military's role in national politics. The transitional junta that included Arbenz created a virtually autonomous military council. It was the seed of a military elite that dominates Guatemala to this day.

When in October 1944 Guatemalan democrats turned to military men to do what the people had done themselves only months before, they gave the revolution an Achilles heel, one the CIA could later exploit. To avoid coups the Arévalo and Arbenz governments had to look continuously over their shoulders and placate the military with perquisites and privileges. It seems quite likely that there was a link between the military shortcut of October 1944 and the untimely demise of Guatemala's spring-like revolution in June 1954.

For all that, in the early 1950s the U.S.-based United Fruit Company was still Arbenz's most strident critic, inside or outside Guatemala. For *la frutera* the Arbenz reforms were insufferable. The Arbenz government was asking it to obey the laws of a country it seemed to believe it owned. And of course it did own more Guatemalan soil than any other landowner—over 500,000 acres. It also owned the railroad, monopolized the country's transportation, and operated the communications network. When the government bought nearly 210,000 unused acres at their declared value, and later another 171,000 acres, United Fruit screamed. The government simply pointed out that for years the company's own tax declarations had listed the value of the land at a mere $627,000. The company belatedly demanded nearly $16 million in compensation. But like other large landowners, it saw other losses looming as well. A hundred thousand peasants working their own lands might not find it necessary to migrate seasonally to coastal plantations to make ends meet. The law of supply and demand would drive up labor costs.[20]

"*¡Comunistas!*" the monopolies had cried as reform laws removed their manipulative leverage. The barb had clung to every step Guatemala took on behalf of its common people. The United Fruit Company was able to take its cries to the U.S. Congress at the height of Senator Joseph McCarthy's era of redbaiting; so the simplistic label fell on receptive ears. A few members of the communist Guatemalan Workers Party were prominent leaders in labor unions, and clearly, as other sectors turned against him, Arbenz relied more and more on the labor movement for political support. But as historian Walter LaFeber puts it, when the United Fruit Company, the U.S. government, and right-wing Guatemalans cried "*¡Comunista!*" upon seeing reform, they actually "allowed the Communists to take undeserved credit for correcting centuries of injustice."[21]

If the Guatemalan revolution of 1944-54 tended toward any one element in the synthesis that Arévalo termed "spiritual socialism," that element was capitalist modernization. And nowhere was this truer than with the agrarian reform. The basis of Decree 900, the agrarian reform law, was a 1950 study that the eminently capitalist World Bank had sponsored. Prepared by a Canadian economist and based on a 1950 agricultural census, it concluded that the poverty of the highland Mayas was a brake on the entire nation's economic growth. Giving the Mayas access to land and livelihood would turn them into small capitalists and consumers. The agrarian reform took aim not at capitalism but at entrenched vestiges of feudalism.[22]

In his inaugural speech Arbenz proposed to "convert our country from a dependent nation with a semi-colonial economy to an economically independent country; to convert Guatemala from a backward country with a predominantly feudal economy into a modern capitalist state. . . . " To do this he promised to strengthen "private initiative and develop . . . Guatemalan capital, in whose hands rests the fundamental economic activity of the country."[23] His vision was one of development, but it was also profoundly nationalistic. And that was the real source of United Fruit Company irritation.

After the coup, Castillo Armas's firing squads executed hundreds. The new regime canceled 533 labor union registrations and repealed labor protections. By 1957 less than 0.5 percent of those who had received plots under the agrarian reform still held their lands.

The decimation of the social gains of 1944-54 has required a continuing quotient of repression. In the mid-1960s, the ultraconservative Movement for National Liberation invented death squads—shadowy right-wing groups operating at night and killing with impunity. The Guatemalan military has used both its visible might and a clandestine death-squad network to maintain an iron grip, brutally squashing armed rebellions and peaceful organizing alike.

The toll is staggering. Two hundred thousand Guatemalans are now in exile. Over 500,000 have been displaced, usually into slums but sometimes into concentration-camp-like "development poles." Since 1978 the Army by its own account has destroyed over four hundred Indian villages. Since 1966, 100,000 people have been killed, the large majority being unarmed civilians. There are at least that many identified orphans, and Guatemala has the highest per capita ratio of widows in the world. Most chilling of all, since 1966 more than 38,000 more people have been "disappeared" in a peculiarly Latin American tactic of terror that leaves relatives and colleagues floundering in an uncertainty even more debilitating than news of assassination. This is more than in any other country in the world! Although the Guatemalan military allowed an official return to civilian rule in 1986, the nation's real ruler is still fear. Meanwhile, seventy-six percent of Guatemalan children still suffer from malnutrition. The sad litany could include statistics of infant mortality, illiteracy, poverty, and disease.[24]

Without U.S. interference more Latin American countries would probably have developed along lines similar to those Guatemala was discovering when the Revolution of 1944 was aborted. U.S. administrations now regularly bemoan Latin extremism of right and left, but the Guatemala of mid-century was beginning to rein them in and forge a national consensus. It was balancing traditional powers with trade unions and community groups. An explosive development of a new professional class offered some promise of innovation, local economic development, and cultural growth. Guatemala's Congress was becoming a forum in which all social strata could express their will and learn the dynamics of compromise. Newspapers were centers of ideological debate and exchange. This was an experiment in what democracy could bring to a formerly closed society, showing that it is possible for Latin American nations to develop policies that respect both their traditions and the adjustments necessary in the modern world.

Yet if Latin America was the loser in 1954, the judgment of history suggests that the United States was not really the winner. Even in some Washington circles the decades since 1954 have brought a certain forlorn longing for the Guatemalan spring. As one U.S. official put it in 1980, "What we'd give to have an Arbenz now."[25]

A lingering chill

Had the CIA coup been an aberration of the McCarthy era—a nasty episode to regret and learn from as Guatemalan politics spun further out of control, even U.S. control—that would be one matter. But Guatemala 1954 proved to be the pilot project for the United States' role in the Western Hemisphere in the Cold War. In Guatemala the United States tested tactics that became a pattern throughout the continent—massive disinformation, state terror under the guise of counterinsurgency, and the polarization of society to squeeze out the most articulate and compelling proponents of moderate social change. While most U.S. citizens take for granted their human rights to live, have a voice in public policies, and be equal before the law and equal in opportunity, the U.S. government has actively countered its neighbors' aspirations for this kind of social change.

When Latin American activists mobilized in 1944 against classic military strongmen like Jorge Ubico of Guatemala and Maximiliano Hernández of El Salvador, their spontaneous, authentically Latin nonviolence toppled the dictators with relative ease. But since 1954 movements for social change in Latin America have confronted something else again. Behind each dictator, and behind many civilian frontmen besides, stands the apparatus of a national security state, which justifies its brutality and authoritarian control in the name of preserving "Western, Christian civilization." And behind each national security state lie years of active, hemisphere-wide U.S. promotion, officer training, funding, and sponsorship—all in the name of combatting communism.[26]

Even if the Cold War and fears of Soviet expansionism meant the world had to divide into competing spheres of influence, more far-sighted Washington policymakers could have seized on the Guatemala of Arévalo and Arbenz as one of its strongest allies. In a more high-minded competition between East and West, Guatemala's revolution and the democratic reforms that followed would have been an attractive model. As Roosevelt's New Deal had inspired Guatemala, its springtime would have inspired other developing nations.

Instead, a brash and overbearing anti-communism kept the Cold Warriors from comprehending, much less learning from, a Guatemalan leader like Arévalo when he pointed to North-South realities, proposed a "spiritual socialism," and in fine Hispanic tradition valued cultural, philosophical, and social relations and not only commercial profits. On the occasion of his farewell speech to the Guatemalan Congress in 1951, Arévalo summed up the effects of emerging U.S. policies on the world:

> According to certain international norms, . . . little countries do not have a right to sovereignty. . . . The war that began in 1939 ended, but in the ideological dialogue between the two worlds and two leaders, Roosevelt lost the war. The real winner was Hitler. Little caricatures of Hitler sprang up and multiplied . . . here in the Americas. It is my personal opinion that today's world is ruled by the same ideas that served as the basis for raising Hitler to power.[27]

If U.S. citizens of today are to have any chance of helping undo the damage their government did to all of Latin America in 1954, they will need a more responsible and accurate understanding of national security. The true cost of believing that one nation can take upon itself the right to dominate others and intervene in their internal affairs may long go hidden but still remains high.

In 1961 John F. Kennedy said: "Those who make peaceful revolution impossible, will make violent revolution inevitable." He ignored his own advice by creating the Green Berets to one-up armed insurgents who had given up on peaceful change. The Green Berets soon found themselves in the jungles not only of Vietnam but also of Guatemala, where their students took the training they offered, went back to the capital, and perfected the tactics of death squad terror against civilians.

Still, Kennedy's counsel stands. If Guatemalans or any other Latin Americans choose armed struggle rather than the way Guatemalans stood in nonviolent unity in 1944, the choices North Americans make will be part of the reason.

Notes

1. Jim Handy, *Gift of the Devil: a History of Guatemala* (Boston: South End Press, 1984), p. 280.
2. *Time*, June 26, 1944, p. 45, quoted in John Swomley, Jr., *Liberation Ethics* (New York: Macmillan, 1972), p. 69.
3. Kenneth J. Grieb, *Guatemalan Caudillo: The Regime of Jorge Ubico, Guatemala 1931-44* (Athens, OH: University Press, 1979), pp. 270ff.
4. Ibid.
5. New York Times, July 3, 1944; quoted by George Lakey and Patricia Parkman,

Guatemala 31

"They Didn't Call it Nonviolence, But . . . : Three Cases of Civilian Insurrection in Latin America," unpublished.
6. Grieb, p. 277.
7. William Krehm, *Democracies and Tyrannies of the Caribbean*, with introduction and notes by Gregorio Sélser (Westport, CT: Lawrence Hill, 1984), p. 50.
8. Quoted in Gregorio Sélser, *El Guatemalazo: La Primera Guerra Sucia* (Buenos Aires: Ediciones Iguazú, 1961), p. 8.
9. Walter LaFeber, *Inevitable Revolutions: The United States in Central America* (New York: W.W. Norton, 1983) p. 112.
10. Krehm, p. 51; Mario Rosenthal, *Guatemala: The Story of an Emergent Latin-American Democracy* (New York: Twayne Publishers, 1962), p. 222; Handy, p. 118.
11. Mario Monteforte Toledo, *Guatemala: Monografía Sociológica* (Mexico City, 1959), pp. 47-50; cited in Handy, p. 107.
12. Handy, p. 107.
13. Peter Calvert, *Guatemala, a Nation in Turmoil* (Boulder: Westview Press, 1985), p. 70.
14. Handy, p. 126.
15. LaFeber, p. 115.
16. LaFeber, p. 116; Handy, p. 128; Morris J. Blachman, William M. LeoGrande, Kenneth Evan Sharpe, *Confronting Revolution: Security through Diplomacy in Central America* (New York: Pantheon Books, 1986), p. 28.
17. Thomas F. Carroll, "The Land Reform Issue in Latin America" in *Latin American Issues: Essays and Comments*, ed. Albert O. Hirschman (New York: The Twentieth Century Fund, 1961), pp. 178-79.
18. Stephen Schlesinger and Stephen Kinzer, *Bitter Fruit: the Untold Story of the American Coup in Guatemala* (Garden City, New York: Doubleday & Company, 1982).
19. Ibid., p. 204.
20. Marjorie and Thomas Melville, *Guatemala: the Politics of Land Ownership* (New York: Free Press, 1971), p. 61; Schlesinger and Kinzer, pp. 75-76.
21. LaFeber, p. 113. See also: Ronald Schneider, *Communism in Guatemala*, p. 49; Richard N. Adams, *Crucifixion by Power: Essays on Guatemalan National Social Structure, 1944-1966* (Austin: University of Texas Press, 1970), pp. 186-87; Stokes Newbold, "A Study of Receptivity to Communism in Rural Guatemala," quoted in John Gerassi, *The Great Fear in Latin America*, revised edition (New York, Collier Books, 1965), p. 181.
22. Handy, pp. 103-04,116.
23. *El Imparcial*, March 16, 1951, quoted in Handy, p. 116.
24. Sources for statistics in this paragraph are: Washington Office on Latin America (WOLA), "Uncertain Return: Refugees and Reconciliation in Guatemala" (May 1988), p. 8; Chris Krueger and Kjell Enge, *Security and Development Conditions in the Guatemalan Highlands*, (published by WOLA, August 1985), p. 2; Robert M. Carmack, ed., *Harvest of Violence: The Maya Indians and the Guatemalan Crisis*, (Norman and London: University of Oklahoma Press, 1988), p. x; Asociación Centroamericana de Familiares de Detenidos-Desaparecidos (ACAFADE), "La Práctica de la Desaparición Forzada de Personas en Guatemala," (1988); and UNICEF E/ICEF/1987/P/L.16, 1987.
25. Alan Riding, "Guatemala: State of Siege," *New York Times Magazine*, August 20, 1980, pp. 66-67.
26. National Security Council directive no. 52.
27. Excerpts of Arévalo's speech are from quotes by Cole Blasier, *The Hovering Giant: United States Responses to Revolutionary Change in Latin America* (Pittsburgh: University of Pittsburgh Press, 1976, [revised edition, 1985]), p. 63; and Schlesinger and Kinzer, p. 47.

For further reading

Adams, Richard N. *Crucifixion by Power: Essays on Guatemalan National Social Structure,*
1944-1966. Austin, TX: University of Texas Press, 1970.

Blasier, Cole. *The Hovering Giant: United States Responses to Revolutionary Change in Latin*
America. Pittsburgh: University of Pittsburgh Press, 1976. (Revised edition, 1985.)

Fried, Jonathan, et al., eds. *Guatemala in Rebellion: Unfinished History.* New York:
Grove Publishers, 1983.

Handy, Jim. *Gift of the Devil: A History of Guatemala.* Boston: South End Press, 1984.

Krehm, William. *Democracies and Tyrannies of the Caribbean.* Introduction and notes
by Gregorio Sélser. Westport, CT: Lawrence Hill, 1984.

Melville, Marjorie and Thomas. *Guatemala: the Politics of Land Ownership.* New York:
Free Press, 1971.

Parkman, Patricia. *Nonviolent Insurrection in El Salvador: The Fall of Maximiliano*
Hernández Martínez. Tucson: University of Arizona Press, 1988.

Schlesinger, Stephen and Stephen Kinzer. *Bitter Fruit: the Untold Story of the American*
Coup in Guatemala. Garden City, NY: Doubleday & Co., 1982.

Brazil

TWO

Introduction

In the history of Latin America, nowhere is the use of nonviolent action better established than in the efforts of organized labor. Strikes, marches, and other forms of public protest have been integral to social gains for workers throughout the region. Organizing efforts have had to confront both the institutionalized violence of subhuman working conditions and wages, and the reactionary violence of often brutal repression of efforts for change.

There are many examples of heroic struggle against such violence. The most successful of these include extraordinary determination and creative use of nonviolent strategies. A good example is the protracted struggle of workers at the PERUS cement factory on the outskirts of São Paulo, Brazil. In the early 1960s the growing awareness and organization of the workers prompted the owner, J.J. Abdalla, to draw the battle lines and declare war. Previous struggles had prepared the workers. In 1962, when the owner reneged on signed agreements and challenged them to strike, they dug in and held on to a deeply felt sense of justice.

Abdalla's status as a wealthy Brazilian businessman gave him substantial political influence. He had the police, some corrupt judges, and prominent politicians at his bidding. He tried strike-breaking, police repression, setting up another union under his control, "influencing" the judges. After a military coup in 1964, he took advantage of the national security state dictatorship to bring charges against his opponents. Yet through it all the large majority of workers stood firm.

There were many dramatic moments. One came when the owner succeeded in cajoling ten percent of the workers to return and hired a large number of new employees. The police had virtually militarized the area in a strong show of force. When the first trucks were ready to ship cement from the plant, some of the strikers threw themselves in front, saying, "Kill us, for what you are doing only helps exploit and ruin the Brazilian worker. What you are doing, do directly: Crush us." The drivers, themselves victims of the system, moved ahead. Suddenly several policemen, deeply impressed by the steadfast and uncompromising witness of the strikers, broke ranks, jumped onto the trucks, and stopped them. As word spread about this incident, people began more and more to notice an extraordinary struggle.

Most of the time, however, the long and difficult struggle was quite ordinary—leaflet distribution, public speaking, raising strike support funds. It took the strikers seven years to win back their jobs and five years more, until 1974, to receive full compensation. Brazilian courts heard the case eleven different times. In the meantime, the strikers suffered deprivation, imprisonment, takeover of their union, and other persecution. Through it all, it was the *firmeza permanente* or "relentless persistence" of the workers that eventually brought victory.

Firmeza permanente almost met its match in J.J. Abdalla, who fanatically refused to compromise. Abdalla never did pay. Instead, the government paid after confiscating his property. Years later he managed to get his plant back. But he also antagonized the cartel of cement producers who, by 1987, had ganged up to nearly run his business into the ground.

Today the PERUS workers, in many cases the sons of those who walked out in 1962, still have the same reputation for tough resistance. They are once again agitating for a government confiscation. This time, they want the plant turned over to them. In this campaign they have united with shantytown dwellers under the slogan, "Cheap cement to get out of the shack."

The author of this chapter, Mário Carvalho de Jesus, has served the workers' movement in Brazil for almost forty years. He is a tireless example of *firmeza permanente,* which he considers the only way to achieve workers' rights and still fully respect the human person.

For all his work with organized labor, the influence of Carvalho de Jesus on the Roman Catholic bishops of Brazil has perhaps been an even more important contribution. Through unflagging witness as a lay activist and insistent calls to conscience, he has done much to raise the social awareness of quite a few Brazilian bishops in what is today the most progressive Catholic church in the world.

Firmeza Permanente
Labor Holds the Line in Brazil
Mário Carvalho de Jesus

In the 1950s the one thousand workers of the Portland Cement Company of Brazil (PERUS) were divided between two sites: a factory in the town of Perus, near São Paulo, and, twelve miles away, quarries in Cajamar that provided the raw material for cement production. At that time PERUS was the only cement factory in São Paulo, and was one of thirty subsidiaries owned by the Abdalla Group.

Around the end of 1954, the Union of Cement, Lime and Plaster Workers of São Paulo invited me to be its lawyer. I found the workers isolated and fearful. With time we filed a series of successful complaints. In each case, by participating in these actions and evaluating their results the workers gained confidence and the union became stronger.

In October of 1958 the union struck successfully against Abdalla for better wages. Owners and the police tried to provoke the workers, but a spirit of peaceful protest blunted such attempts. Peaceful protest also enabled the workers' wives and families to participate in a round-the-clock picket and to help build public support through twice-weekly demonstrations in São Paulo. Meanwhile, strike committees visited other factories, schools, and universities.

The workers sought to tie their wage hike to a planned increase in the price of cement. By offering to take the smaller raise that the owners proposed if the owners in turn would reduce their disproportionate rise in cement prices, they strengthened public support. Seeing the workers hold firm in the face of great pressure, one of the lawyers helping them said that they reminded him of *queixadas.* He explained that *queixadas,* or wild boars, "are the only animals who, when in danger, will pull together in a group, snarling and grinding their teeth, and directly confront the hunter. He [the hunter] has to hide himself in a tree or else they will run him down. You are like the *queixadas, queixadas* who confront the predator."

This chapter first appeared in a different form in Fragoso, Antônio, et al., *A Firmeza Permanente—A Força da Não-Violência,* São Paulo: Loyola-Vega, 1977, pp. 39-90.

Finally, after forty-six days, the workers won the wage hike they had demanded. Winning future struggles would prove much more difficult.

By 1962, Abdalla Group president J.J. Abdalla had reneged on several agreements. Despite a number of good-faith efforts on the part of the union to accommodate him, he appeared intent on doing away with the *queixadas* altogether. Union leaders at three other Abdalla Group factories invited the PERUS union to join them in pressuring the owners to honor their contracts. By that time, the PERUS workers had had enough. Even their salaries were late. They gladly signed a joint letter listing their complaints. Abdalla did not even reply.

The unions continued to insist that their complaints be heard, saying otherwise they would have no choice but to strike. Abdalla, who was rich, powerful and at that time a member of the National Assembly, responded with cold calculated indifference: "Go ahead and strike, if you have the courage. . . . "

The provocation was obvious. And when people are committed to seeking justice, certain words are like a hard shove. On May 14, 1962, the day we had agreed to act, two hundred police occupied PERUS. Nonetheless, 3,500 workers peacefully paralyzed work in all four factories. Later, an assembly of the strike leaders agreed that no group would settle separately and that the strike would end only when the Abdalla group addressed the complaints of all the groups.

As union lawyer I filed four lawsuits in the government's Regional Office of Labor. The Minister of Labor tried without success to mediate the strike.

Abdalla is "hiding milk," or pretending to be poor, said the workers, who refused to resign themselves to the silence and indifference of the *mau patrão* (bad boss). Meanwhile, the united stand of the workers garnered increasing public support.

But thirty-two days after the start of the strike we received disconcerting news. The president of the Federation of Food Industry Workers of São Paulo sought me out at home on a Saturday afternoon. Downcast, he told me that the workers of the three other factories had reached an agreement with Abdalla. On Monday more than two thousand would return to their jobs. I was disappointed. Why did the agreement not include the PERUS *companheiros?*,[1] I asked. His reply: "Abdalla wants to put an end to the *queixadas*."

Later we learned that Abdalla had declared: "I am the lamp and the employees the butterflies; one by one they will come to me and I will destroy them."

After the agreement with the other groups Abdalla broke his silence. Using his great financial resources and political prestige, he publicly denounced the continuation of the strike of the *queixadas*. Our participation in the common strike, he argued, had been merely for solidarity, not to press our own complaints; there was no further reason for workers to stay out.

The Regional Labor Court, by a four to three vote, refused to hear our complaints and instead ordered a return to work. Apparently the sand Abdalla had thrown into the eyes of the public had worked its damage. But even as he obstinately sought to liquidate us, we began efforts to expropriate PERUS.

At that time, the union took a secret vote on whether to continue the strike. The results were: 1,257 in favor of continuing, nineteen opposed, and seven abstaining.

The workers' demands were straightforward. Besides the call for paying salaries on time, demands centered around the fulfillment of previous agreements. For example, for several years the company had deducted five percent of salaries to finance workers' purchase of company-owned lots for home sites. But the company never released the lots, and the workers demanded reimbursement. The company had also agreed to production incentives that it had never honored. Further issues included other legally obligated payments plus union recognition for a group of affiliated wood workers.

João Breno Pinto, then president of the union, later recalled some of the lessons union members learned:

> In a position of weakness, active nonviolence is more effective than violence. PERUS is a cement factory where the work is rough. So the typical worker there is an aggressive person. The small organized group was aware that to encourage violence was very easy but also that violence would achieve nothing, since the forces of repression would answer with better-organized violence. Our members were disgusted when we restrained them from letting the police and the traitors have it. However today, after it is all over, they acknowledge that while they did not deeply understand nonviolence, the path they were invited to walk was the best one.
>
> We saw that the violent person tries to provoke the nonviolent opponent to get him to abandon his main weapon: the use of active nonviolence. Even our oppressors understood that we were not joining in the game as they had expected. For example, one day during an attempt to break the strike, a worker in our group threw a stone at the windshield of a police car that was accompanying a truckload of strikebreakers. Of course the police started beating people. But there was no reaction by the strikers. A day or so earlier, this man had been seen in the factory, working harmoniously with the police and the management chief. This proved that the oppressors had set up a trap to use this worker as a provocateur to spark an act of violence, to create an ugly scene in which they would be sure to win.

Execution of the diabolic plan

With cool calculation, the Abdalla Group waited to wear down the workers. After May 14, 1962, in its efforts to crush the *queixadas*, the company suspended production of almost 600,000 bags of cement per month. In the beginning of August, their diabolical plan began to take shape.

The company lured two dozen tired workers, directing them to seek the help of Conceição da Costa Neves, a "labor leader" in the State Assembly. As a result she began to accuse us of being "communists" who impeded "honest workers" from returning to work. She went more than once to Perus and Cajamar to meet with the workers to induce them to break the strike.

About 100 workers among the 1,300 on strike presented a request for intervention in the union to the Labor Minister. Ten of the one hundred, who were portrayed as the "most enlightened," signed a power of attorney so that a lawyer in the pay of Abdalla would present two complaints against the leaders of the union and its lawyer. We were accused of embezzlement and of impeding "free workers" from returning to work. Paid ads in the principal newspapers of São Paulo and Rio de Janeiro publicized the complaints, as did thousands of leaflets. Then Abdalla promised an early wage payment of thirty percent to any workers who would return to work.

On August 21, the hundredth day of the strike, the Assemblywoman Conceição da Costa Neves herself led the breaking of the strike by 100 PERUS workers with the assistance of the police. Newspapers, radio, and television looked on. At the same time the company brought in a large number of new workers.

Strike leader João Breno recalls:

> The company mobilized the entire police force there and also brought in others from outside. They arrived with water cannons, which were a novelty then. They had the most modern equipment for dispersing crowds. At 5:00 A.M. our neighborhood awoke to a parade of all sorts of vehicles. Flyers explaining management's viewpoint were distributed. The flyers called the striking workers vagabonds, said that the union was made up of communists and thieves who wanted to ruin everything, including our neighborhood, and asked the housewives to force their sons, neighbors, and husbands to go back to work.[2]
> With all this effort the company was able to put the factory back into operation. Repression and the hunting down of all strikers started at this time. They were subject to being seized, beaten, arrested—all types of persecution were used.

In Cajamar, where the strike was broken a week earlier, the police took over the workers' club and began using it as a dormitory. The new pastor in Cajamar, Father Bianchi, was entirely on the side of the workers. So Abdalla ordered that the street which led to the workers' cooperative and the pastor's house be closed and that Father Bianchi vacate the company-owned house.

Closing in so as to crush the *queixadas*, Abdalla advised the merchants of Perus and Cajamar to quit providing foodstuffs to the workers. (Many of the merchants were campaign organizers in Abdalla's electoral bids.)

At the end of September 1962, PERUS began an inquest in the Labor Court to sanction the firing of 501 tenured employees. The company alleged that they had practiced a serious misdeed: participation in an "illegal strike" and "abandonment of the job." All those except the 100 who had requested intervention in the union were blacklisted. However the firing of the 501 tenured workers required a special court order. Afterwards, we took three claims on behalf of the tenured workers to court.

The resistance of the *queixadas*

To be truthful, I must confess that we were almost crushed. We suffered many hardships, shed many tears. Two workers committed suicide.

One day a *queixada*, a sixty-year-old northerner, called on me. "Get me twenty contos [approximately sixteen dollars] and I'll put an end to this strike," he said.

"How?" I asked.

"I'll kill Abdalla and disappear."

"Okay, Rodolfo, you know that we decide everything at meetings. I will not quote your name, but I'll present your proposal."

He agreed. My first intention was to try to dissuade him. Our work always respects the human being, distinguishing the person from the acts that the person practices. Everyone is capable of erring and everyone is capable of changing his or her position. But, knowing that other *companheiros* had also expressed the same intention as Rodolfo, I felt it would be a good opportunity to put the principles of *firmeza permanente* to the test.

Among the workers at the meeting that night I saw traces of satisfied smiles as they learned that someone was seriously disposed to liquidate the "bad boss."

I added, "The *companheiro* who wants to get Abdalla said that he will end the strike. But what's more important, to end the strike or to win the strike?"

I believed that any physical violence, even if it did not come to homicide, would give the police a motive to fall all over us. They would arrest the union leaders and me immediately. And the strike could really end. We could end up losing.

Everyone's anticipation increased when another *queixada* interrupted me: "Do you guarantee we'll win this strike?"

"No. No one can give this guarantee. The outcome of the lawsuit depends on many things: it depends on what we say in the presence of the judge; it depends on witnesses, on documents. Finally, it depends on the judge; not only one judge, but many judges. What I can guarantee is that we have a very strong case and that I will go to the end of the road with you, whatever happens."

Sergio interrupted: "This strike is a test of the existence of God. God can't possibly protect what Abdalla is doing to us."

I concluded more or less with the following words: "Abdalla with all his dirty tricks is a human being. We can't kill him. The laws are very weak in reaching the powerful, but if we believe in God, there will be a way for us to end this strike. Our visible aggressor is Abdalla, but behind him exists economic and political power. It's capitalism. We can't confront the aggressors with their weapons. That's what they want, because they can easily destroy us. Our weapon is our lives. Stay cool, *companheiros.*"

In fact, the workers assimilated well the method of struggle inspired in the Sermon on the Mount and the witness of the apostles, a method that Gandhi and Martin Luther King, Jr. took up again in the political sphere. In modern times it's called nonviolence. In Brazil, we call it *firmeza permanente* (relentless persistence) in search of justice.

There were many examples of resistance and solidarity in the strike, which began to seem like a war. The number of donations we received from all corners of the state of São Paulo easily thwarted the siege of hunger Abdalla wanted to impose. The governors of two other states lent their support. Leonel Brizola, Governor of Rio Grande Do Sul, sent us a hundred sacks of rice. From Parana, Ney Braga sent us a truckload of potatoes and beans. The owner of a bakery in Perus lent us an oven for use by two *queixadas* who were bakers. The Catholic Church furnished us flour.

At a hearing in which inspectors from the Labor Ministry and the Assemblywoman Conceicão da Costa Neves participated, we successfully warded off a petition for government intervention in the union. The inspectors verified that the accusations against the union leaders, who had the solid support of the workers, were unfounded. Even so, the Labor Ministry postponed union elections. To hold elections we had to obtain a court injunction.

Once more we resorted to the courts, hoping to oust the police who had transformed the workers' club into a dormitory in order to better protect the Abdalla Group. The court ordered the "bad boss" to demolish a wall he had raised in the street. Its purpose was to obstruct passage to Father Bianchi's house and to the striking workers' cooperative.

Knowing that the struggle in the Labor Court would be a long one, we argued that Brazil's president could intervene and expropriate PERUS. We developed a big campaign in this respect, with popular support and support from the students and teachers at the university. We circulated petitions, gave talks, and arranged meetings with political authorities.

However, with the factory returning to normal production levels without them, the workers were dejected, some desperate. The strikers called a meeting. Some workers wanted to invade the factory during the night and beat up the "*pelegos*," or sell-outs.[3] Others even wanted to set fire to the factory. The idea took shape. They even marked the date.

Then someone raised a question: "We know that physical violence can be practiced after all other possibilities have been exhausted. Have we already done everything we can?"

The question posed, the participants eyed each other. "Do you remember the passage of the gospel in which the apostles came to complain to Christ because they couldn't perform certain cures? Christ responded: 'Certain kinds of devils are expelled only with fasting and prayer.' "

In an instant, a worker suggested: "A hunger strike?" Others welcomed the idea. In early December we began. We spent Christmas and New Year's Eve of 1962 fasting in the Plaza of São Francisco. While one group was fasting, others would carry placards and distribute flyers to passersby. We stayed there for four weeks.

João Breno later reflected on the significance of that experience:

> Our assembly decided that we should, like Gandhi, have a hunger strike in public, in the open area in some plaza in São Paulo. The objective would be to mobilize public opinion. Things were dragging out and everyone was forgetting about the PERUS strike.
>
> The hunger strike seemed to us an act of humility rather than of protest. To attain our objective—mobilizing public opinion on our side—we had to halt all activity and just stay there in the square, standing or sitting, without eating. In spite of the noise of passersby, this forced us to meditate among ourselves. We talked about the conversations we had with the people who came by. After the hunger strike, I was totally convinced that this was the way, that nonviolence was not just a tactic but that it was the core of our work. From that time onwards we had to develop it.

With the inauguration of Governor Adhemar de Barros in the

beginning of 1963, Cardinal Motta, who always showed us complete solidarity, addressed a pastoral appeal to the Governor, asking him to mediate.

We—J.J. Abdalla and the leaders of the union—were summoned to the Government Palace. The employer never wanted to have a face-to-face meeting with the workers. At the time Abdalla made no proposal. Then a few days later, the company offered us twenty percent of lost wages. But it had underestimated the strength of the *queixadas*.

Personally I did not understand the obstinacy of the Abdalla Group very well. "Why do they want to destroy us?" I asked myself many times. Father Bianchi calmed us with a comparison: "Abdalla is the new Pharaoh. Apparently he is strong. But the small, led by God, dethrone the powerful. The struggle will take time. We too must purify ourselves."

Rafael, an ever-confident union leader, said, "We have to go through various sieves. At the end there will be a small group in the fine sieve. This group can't become discouraged. It will be responsible for the journey."

We had taken out various loans, already renewed. Finally, we had to begin paying on them. We began by selling the small bus of the National Labor Front, my car, and the union's small bus. The debts were many. Soon after that I sold a plot of land and a garage.

But no solution was in sight. In all honesty we had to tell the workers: "It's necessary to look for another job. The return to work of the tenured workers depends on the Labor Court. While we cannot get the untenured workers rehired, they should be indemnified. However, this also depends on the Labor Court."

Continuation of the exodus (1964-1969)

The military coup of March 31, 1964 reverberated immediately in the life of our union, which was the first in São Paulo to suffer official intervention. The new dictator-president named the head of PERUS' Personnel Department as intervener, a temporary governor serving as the chief executive's direct agent. We were arrested—various union leaders and I.

The courts had suspended the August 1962 police inquests initiated against us for embezzlement and interfering with the workers, but now the government reactivated them. We were pointed at like criminals. Abdalla hired two criminal lawyers onto the case as assistants to the government.

After an exhaustive inquiry, the courts again dropped the inquests against us. Meanwhile our other cases wound their way through the court system. We lost the case of the untenured workers. We lost the

São Paulo case of the 501 tenured workers, then won an appeal before the Superior Labor Court. This forced a retrial in São Paulo, which took place in early 1967.

As the hearing began, the atmosphere was one of expectation and apprehension. After all, we had lost the suit on behalf of the untenured workers. But now our diligence in using all available means to publish the reasons for the strike and make clear the Abdalla Group's brazen intent to crush the *queixadas* brought liberal compensation. One of the judges, in reexamining the six volumes of proceedings, changed his his position and swung the vote in our favor. The tenured workers won the right to return to work at PERUS. PERUS was obligated to pay their salaries—with readjustments, interest, and correction for inflation—from August 1962 until the date they actually began work again.

The workers questioned why we had won one lawsuit and lost another. Why did the tenured workers get to go back to work while the untenured could not? After all, the cause of dismissal was the same. There was another, deeper doubt: Would Abdalla be able to overturn this decision in Brasilia (the capital)?

Abdalla did try. In fact, the courts evaluated the issue eleven times. Throughout, the wear and tear on the Abdalla Group was great. The epithet of "bad boss" appeared frequently in the papers.

Finally, in the Superior Labor Court in Brasilia, we were successful. In January 1969, 309 tenured employees (all but the deceased, the retired, and those who had made agreements) returned to work in the presence of court officials. The impossible was happening.

We looked for a way to have PERUS pay salaries from the time of the lawsuit's duration—January 1962 to 1969—through an increase in productivity. Production at the factory was well below normal. The old employees, who knew the factory well, pledged to strive diligently to increase the production of cement. We drew up a petition of agreement. The talks with management were progressing when the dictatorship's General Committee of Investigations summoned several workers, union leaders, and me for a few days. We were all arrested as a result of Abdalla's accusations. The authorities subjected us to long interrogations. As for myself, I was held at the air force base in Cumbica for twenty-nine days.

When I finally returned to the union, we talked about the continuing repression and our prospects. I warned union members about possible future pressures and arrests; I felt they were standing firm. Rafael—the same Rafael who, after the breaking of the strike in 1962 had alerted us to the need for the *queixadas* to pass through various sieves—said in a loud voice, "I'm not afraid of going to jail. My suitcase is already packed."

At this time we also sought to reestablish contact with the employer in order to receive the strike wages (estimated at five million *cruzeiros*, or $815,000, plus interest and correction for inflation.) We planned to receive the delayed payment based on the increase in production, and we wanted to find a way to share it with the untenured workers who had not been rehired.

The Abdalla Group, however, changed the subject. Knowing they would be able to take advantage of the inertia of the public powers, they had in mind a new and dangerous ploy against the *queixadas*.

The new ruse (1970 to 1973)

Although the Abdalla Group had more than thirty enterprises (besides numerous estates and buildings), much of their property did not officially appear in the Group's name. In order to disguise the blow they were preparing, they took advantage of one of their enterprises— SOCAL S.A.

First the Abdalla Group installed the SOCAL office in a workers' house in Cajamar and began to hire new employees to work in PERUS' quarries. Because it was a different company, they claimed the workers could not belong to the PERUS workers' union. However, there was no other union in Cajamar, and some of those new employees worked together with the PERUS workers at the same job. Slowly, under Abdalla's direction, PERUS transferred the employees it had admitted after the 1962 strike to SOCAL. If they did not accept the transfer they were fired. Later PERUS managed to have the tenured employees themselves—the strikebreakers of August 1962—become part of SOCAL. They also coerced the workers of Railroad PERUS-PIRAPORA (a railroad that links Perus to Cajamar for the transport of limestone) to be transferred to SOCAL. PERUS even put SOCAL employees to work in the factory at Perus. The only thing they did not achieve was the transfer to SOCAL of about a hundred employees—the *queixadas* who had been reintegrated in January 1969.

We went back to court and revealed the facts: compulsory transfers, blocking of unionization, and the fraudulent PERUS document written for SOCAL authorizing it to work the quarries.

Since Abdalla did not want to have any friendly contact, much less pay the strike wages he still owed, I pushed forward the labor lawsuit. But when the court moved to force Abdalla to pay what he owed within forty-eight hours, we discovered that PERUS was insolvent—all its assets had liens on them from other claimants. Abdalla offered up another property, Sitio Santa Fe, as compensation. We refused, proving that the Federal Court had already filed twenty-eight liens on that property for fines owed to the government.

The Abdalla Group had planned to deflate PERUS and then have it bought at auction by another of the Abdalla Group's enterprises or by a trusted person. The Abdalla Group had done this before with another of its organizations. Thus SOCAL would come to replace PERUS.

We suspended the collection of wages in the Labor Court and called for PERUS' bankruptcy. But the Civil Court thought the Abdalla Group still had other properties for which it could file liens. The Court proposed we claim the production of cement. So we returned to the lawsuit in the Labor Court. Before claiming the cement production, we filed a lien on PERUS' eucalyptus grove (twenty million trees standing) only to discover that Abdalla had already sold it. We also asked President Medici to confiscate PERUS' property.

After much delay, President Medici did confiscate PERUS' property in July 1973. The confiscation aimed at collecting payment of Abdalla's debts to the Public Treasury (about one billion *cruzeiros*, or $63,000,000), payment of the strike wages (almost twenty million *cruzeiros*, or $3,260,000), and the end of pollution in Perus.

The confiscation proved weak; the union felt it had to intervene once more. Federal officials confiscated the factory in Perus, but they did not get as far as Cajamar. Given the incomplete confiscation, the union found itself in a humiliating situation. The factory, in order to function, needed to buy limestone from the Abdalla Group, from SOCAL, which continued to direct PERUS' quarries in Cajamar.

Through the union, following the workers' decision, we resubmitted our petition to President Medici; but with this government we achieved nothing. In fact, the Abdalla Group had gotten Minister Alfredo Buzaid to order another police inquest against me. I was indicted again under the National Security Law. (After an investigation, the charge was finally dropped.)

The truth wins out

With the inauguration of a new military president we renewed our efforts. On the first of May, 1974, we sent President Geisel a petition. Three thousand five hundred workers, their families, and community organizations from Perus and Cajamar signed. All were committed to *firmeza permanente* in search of justice. Among the demands were the following:

1) complete confiscation of PERUS;
2) payment of the overdue salaries, valued at nearly 20 million *cruzeiros*, for more than 400 workers and their heirs;
3) the end of government intervention in the union;

4) the withdrawal of SOCAL from Cajamar so that PERUS would once again operate the quarries, with the approval of all SOCAL workers who would then become part of PERUS.

We waited patiently, without ceasing our accusations against Abdalla's tricks with SOCAL. Press coverage was always very valuable.

In October 1974, President Geisel corrected the first failed confiscation by allowing the union to take possession of the quarries. SOCAL was turned out of Cajamar and all the workers went back to rendering service to PERUS.

In November of the same year the union received more than eighteen million *cruzeiros* ($2,934,000) to pay the workers' salaries for the time of the lawsuit's duration—from 1962 to January 1969. By candlelight, in front of the union headquarters in Perus, the workers finally received their payment. A share went to those who had not been rehired. Two years later, the government finally lifted its intervention in the union.

After twelve years on strike, PERUS workers and families celebrate victory and finally receiving their back pay with a candlelight vigil in front of union headquarters on November 11, 1974.

The human wear and tear had been great. But *firmeza permanente* knows that the truth appears with time, if we do not grow discouraged. What is authentic prevails. The masquerader fails.

I believe it is useless to try to get rid of the group that fights for justice, when it knows how to resist and discovers ways to denounce fraud, using courage, loyalty, skill, wisdom, acumen, and, if possible, faith. All of these are attributes of *firmeza permanente*. The important thing is not that we be brave or violent once in a while, but resolute all the time, all our lives, in all of our attitudes, whether in the family, in the factory, or in society. To be resolute does not mean to be the owner of the truth. Rather, it means to always be willing to discover the truth, in the search for justice for the whole person and for all people.

Translated from Portuguese
by Naomi Parker, Keith Elliot, and Philip McManus

Notes

1. "Companions"—frequently used to denote those involved in a shared struggle. [Eds.]
2. At least some did just the opposite. One worker who broke the strike came home one day to find that his wife had moved to her parents' house. When he caught up with her, she told him, "I will come back to live with you only if you go back out on strike." He did, and they returned home together.
3. "*Pelego*" is the blanket worn under the saddle of a horse. The term is used for labor leaders who stick with the bosses, not their fellow workers, thus making the owners more comfortable. [Eds.]

For further reading

Carvalho de Jesus, Mário. *PERUS—Os 'Queixadas' Resistem As Artimanhas Do Grupo Chofi-Abdalla Em Cajamar*. Frente Nacional do Trabalho.
Carvalho de Jesus, Mário, & Equipe dos Queixadas. *A 'Máfia' Do Cimento*. São Paulo: Edições Loyola, 1985.
Erickson, Kenneth P. *The Brazilian Corporative State and Working-Class Politics*. Berkeley: University of California Press, 1977.
Moreira Alves, Maria Helena. *State and Opposition in Military Brazil*. Austin: University of Texas Press, 1985.
Permanent Commission of PERUS Workers. "The 150 Months of Resistance: The 'Snarlers' of the PERUS Cement Company." In *Christ in a Poncho*, Adolfo Pérez Esquivel. Maryknoll, New York: Orbis Books, 1983.

Bolivia

THREE

Introduction

In early 1978 four Bolivian women, wives of imprisoned miners, did more than confront their nation's leaders. They also inspired their people, using a hunger strike as their tactic, if one may call it a tactic. Begun in the offices of the Archbishop of La Paz, in the waning days of 1977 when even their sympathizers doubted that a nation on holiday would notice, the strike was first of all a cry from the heart. Others joined the cry, and eventually twelve hundred people around the country joined in the fast. Newspapers backed it and a wide spectrum of political organizations found reason to express support. After twenty-three days, more from shock than repentance, a seven-year dictatorship took a step it surely found humiliating: it agreed, in writing, to virtually all the four women's demands.

The event, which the Reverend Wilson Boots witnessed and tells here in some detail, brought a sudden if somewhat chaotic new beginning of popular and political mobilization to Bolivia. General Hugo Bánzer and his military regime had wanted to lift the lid on

48

democracy only enough to win international legitimacy—and only slowly, to insure the outcome it desired. On December 21, 1977 the regime had announced an amnesty against which the fasting women protested. That announcement made clear that the government would be blatant in its manipulation, for it offered freedom to only a fraction of the nation's political exiles and prisoners, then turned around and prosecuted more than half of those few on other counts. Yet political groups hesitated to do more than unite in calling the amnesty a "*burla*," or farce. It required four women, desperately frustrated that the amnesty had passed over their husbands, to wake up the country.

"Although it was to be some time before it was fully evident," writes James Dunkerley, "the hunger strike was the single most important factor in bringing the [Hugo Bánzer regime] to an end and laying the basis for mass mobilization over the coming period." Other observers have called it "the event that completely changed the Bolivian political picture," and "a truly extraordinary development." Within weeks, not only were prisoners released but political parties were formed and began realigning. Labor unions replaced government-imposed officials, exiles started returning, peasants organized, progressive sectors of the church spoke out more boldly, and popular sectors found new hope. [1]

The hunger strike alone could hardly usher in democracy. It had unmistakably demonstrated the weakness of the military dictatorship, but when Bolivia's Permanent Assembly for Human Rights compiled a book on the strike only a few months later, it had reason to warn: "Twenty-three days of struggle has not annihilated an institutional apparatus constructed over seven years. The loss inflicted has been important, but has not managed to transform the structure of power. No one should underestimate the adversary's capacity to react." [2]

Sure enough, it took three years and three general elections, five presidents, and four coups d'etat before Bolivia inaugurated an elected civilian president, Hernán Siles Zuazo. Along the way, Bolivia's people suffered a level of repression new even in a country known for its long string of coups. During a two-year rule, General Luis García Meza introduced paramilitary death squads to eliminate opposition and impose what James M. Malloy and Eduardo Gamarra have called "a terrified apathy on Bolivian society." [3] For help he turned to a systematically brutal source—the military regime in Argentina. Eventually, the García Meza government's deep involvement in narcotics smuggling forced the Reagan administration in Washington to disown Meza and his rule.

Democracy is a long process and the legacy of military rule only makes it longer. When Siles Zuazo finally led a center-left coalition government to power in 1982 he faced an economic crisis that had been building for years. Successive military regimes had managed to postpone all tough social and economic decisions; that way civilians would take the blame for mistakes military regimes had been stacking up for years.

This is where the message of the four women who confronted their nation is so eloquent in its blunt simplicity. Democracy is a long process, but it can only begin at one point—the participation of the people. What ought to be a truism rarely is. Nevertheless, when Bolivia's military men crassly disregarded democracy's core meaning they soon tangled with the fact that four impoverished citizens (and women at that!) might represent the nation better than they. They might even lead it. The women's eloquent message was simply that anything called a democratic opening must actually open the door to the voice of the people. An amnesty is not an amnesty if only 14 of 348 alleged "political dissidents" go free. Democracy is not democracy until the government's most credible opponents can return from prison or exile, or until fired union organizers can return to work free from army control. Those were their demands.

In their demands, the Bolivian people discovered that it had a voice. As the Permanent Assembly for Human Rights concluded: "Bolivia, the Bolivian people, has learned to recognize itself, to once again search within itself, recovering the distinct image that a regime wanted to steal from it. . . . This may turn out to be the first and greatest consequence of the hunger strike, and a huge step toward liberation. When a people discovers its own force and its own truth, it is able to forge its own history."[4]

Miracle in Bolivia
Four Women Confront a Nation
Wilson T. Boots

From late December 1977 to mid-January 1978 a kind of miracle took place in Bolivia. It was not an otherworldly apparition or a series of physical cures; that kind of phenomenon would be better known by now. What happened was that a group of four women and fourteen children set out to change the course of their country's history. And succeeded.

They were a tiny band with practically no resources. The women were politically aware and religiously devout, but they had little education and no experience on the national stage. The only group behind them—other than their own children, ages eight through fourteen—were fifty others who like them were wives of tin miners banned from their jobs for union activity.

Nellie Paniagua, a tin miner's wife, with her children at the end of her successful hunger strike during which she lost 22 pounds. January 1978. Photo courtesy of Asamblea Permanente de Derechos Humanos de Bolivia.

In the Bolivian context what the women demanded went beyond reason. They asked an immediate, unrestricted amnesty for political exiles and refugees, restoration of jobs for workers fired for organizing, reinstatement of labor unions, and removal of the army from the mines. A remarkable set of aspirations for such a group. But less than a month after they announced these goals, the movement they launched had forced the military dictatorship of General Hugo Bánzer to grant the substance of all their demands. Three months later an informed observer just back from La Paz reported that the government was still honoring the commitments it made to the women and their allies. Not only were the unions functioning again; so were political parties. A political campaign was being conducted for an election in July 1978 that was to restore civilian government and constitutional processes in Bolivia.

In a fallen world all victories for truth and justice are fragile. There

This chapter first appeared in *Christianity and Crisis,* May 1, 1978, pp. 101-107. Reprinted with permission. Copyright 1978, Christianity and Crisis, 537 West 121st Street, New York, New York 10027.

are hard-line, anti-democratic, anti-worker forces still very much in place in Bolivia. And the United States government, even though its representatives played a helpful role in the negotiations of January 1978, promptly created grave new risks by a March announcement of a plan to sell 45,000 tons of tin from its strategic reserve. The mere announcement immediately depressed the world price of tin, seriously threatening the Bolivian economy and endangering the budding hope of political stability under an elected regime.

Yet there was a victory, and one that deserves to be celebrated throughout the world. It has especially great significance to those whose commitment to social justice rises from the gospel, who believe in the power of nonviolence to effect social change and who understand the immense potential of Third World women to move their societies.

At a Mass of thanksgiving offered in the courtyard of San Calixto school the day after the government had given way, a woman who took part in the strike rose and said, "I want all of you to realize that it was the women who did this, and that we are good for something more than cooking, cleaning, and looking after children."

For a brief period during the climactic hours of the struggle I was privileged, as one of three on the scene representing U.S. and world churches, to watch the drama unfold and even to have some part in nurturing the tense negotiations. I was there to represent the National and World Councils of Churches. The other observers were Sister Jo Marie Griesgraber, C.PP.S., deputy director of the Washington Office on Latin America (WOLA), and the Reverend Alan McCoy, O.F.M., representing the (U.S.) National Conference of Catholic Bishops.

As observers we were not neutrals and as participants we were not privy to all that took place. Acknowledging these limitations, I offer this account of a series of events that still astonish me as I record them.

Weapon of the weak

First, the women: four persons at once very ordinary and most extraordinary. They were Nellie Paniagua, forty-five, and Angélica Flores, thirty-one, whose husbands' arrests and firings precipitated the women's decision; Aurora Lora, twenty-five, who was expecting a child and whose husband was in hiding; and Luzmila Pimentel, twenty-four, whose husband was in jail. Serving as spokesperson for the four, but not herself joining in the strike, was Domitila Chungara, about forty, whose autobiography (transcribed from tape recordings) has been published in Spanish and in English translation: *Si Me Permiten Hablar* [Let Me Speak!].

The weapon the women wielded against the entrenched Bolivian establishment was, of course, a weapon of the weak—a hunger strike.

It is a weapon used only at great risk. On Sunday, January 15, 1978, when we observers first encountered them, they lay stretched on cots in the residence of the Archbishop of La Paz. By that time they had been fasting from all but liquids and glucose for a period of nineteen days. Their faces were remarkable: bronze with their Aymara Indian background, filled with strength and determination, but marked also with suffering. Two of them were too weak even to raise their hands, and yet as we touched the women we gained some sense of power flowing to us. The day, we noted, was the anniversary of the birthday of Martin Luther King, Jr.

The developments leading to that moment had begun on October 11, 1977, when a member of the local human rights assembly at Siglo XX (Twentieth Century) tin mine, eight hours driving time from La Paz, was arrested, beaten, and tortured. Eleven days later another member of the same assembly underwent the same experience. Eventually the two miners were released but forbidden to return to their jobs or even to their homes. Their wives waited for the traditional Christmas amnesty to be announced by the government, but when it came their hopes were dashed: the amnesty did not reinstate workers dismissed for political or union activity. Nor did it permit political and union leaders living in exile to re-enter Bolivia.

The episode struck the women—both those directly involved and others with similar experiences—as a final provocation. The life of Bolivian tin miners and their families is a desperate affair. Though tin prices were then at their highest level in years, miners received wages of thirty-five pesos (about $1.50) a day. They lived in one-room houses, four meters by five. Their children could attend school, and they had access to the company stores. The stores sold limited amounts of rice, meat, bread, and sugar at lower-than-market prices, but when a miner lost his job the family had to move out of its home, the children had to leave school and the company store would not serve them. One woman showed Sister Jo Marie her husband's pay statement: after the company store had been paid off, he received ninety-two pesos ($4.60) to feed eight children for a month. A miner's life expectancy is thirty-five years; statistically he can expect to die of silicosis.

The military government had ruled Bolivia with a firm and oppressive hand since 1971, when it gained power in a coup. That takeover meant wealth for some military leaders and for a small business and financial elite, while poverty worsened for a full seventy percent of the people. Though the Bánzer regime did not resort to the extremes found in Chile, Argentina, and Uruguay, there were many summary arrests, exiles, disappearances, and instances of torture. In 1974, in response to unrest, the government suspended all political parties and all unions. It also instituted universal obligatory civil service, under which the government could assign any worker to any job. The price of protest was exile or prison, always with the possibility of torture.

The government appeared secure and determined, and there was always the possibility that new protests would bring even harsher measures. But to the women at Siglo XX mine the latest beatings and arrests served as a spark; like Rosa Parks boarding a segregated bus in Montgomery, they were tired of merely enduring, and were ready to involve themselves directly. The fifty wives of miners not permitted to work met, decided on a hunger strike, and chose four from their number—including the wives of the two men tortured—to go to La Paz.

In the capital city they met with the Roman Catholic archbishop, the Most Reverend Jorge Manrique, and announced their plans. The choice was shrewd; the archbishop himself was a man of the people, with Aymara blood in his veins—strong, simple, devoted to the poor, and fully aware of their plight and its causes. (In the course of the struggle that followed the government was to request a formal apology from Rome in response to a prophetic sermon he preached in the presence of President Bánzer and his Cabinet.) The archbishop not only gave his blessing to the hunger strike but granted the women and children sanctuary in his own residence, a scant 200 yards from the presidential palace.

And so the stage was prepared for a long, tense, wavering confrontation between the people and their government. At first the clash went badly for the women. When their far-reaching program and the drastic strategy they had chosen was explained to their most natural allies, the Permanent Assembly for Human Rights, the response was negative. Formed the previous year by a group of individuals with the strong support of the Catholic, Evangelical Methodist, and Lutheran churches, the Assembly was dedicated to nonviolent action for human rights. But its members thought that the women had not acted correctly; they should not have begun their protest without first presenting their complaints and their demands to the Ministry of Labor and the Ministry of the Interior. And they had chosen a time when it would be hard to get public attention: during the post-Christmas and New Year's season. Above all, how could they involve their own children in a fast that might be prolonged, arduous, and dangerous?

The season for justice

But the women had come to inform the Assembly of their decision, not to ask advice. For them the Christmas season was exactly right; it celebrates the coming of the Lord of justice. They began their protest with a public reading of the Beatitudes from the Gospel of Matthew—

recalling Martin Luther King, Jr.'s comment more than a decade before that it was the Sermon on the Mount that moved the black people of Montgomery to begin organized, dignified, unyielding action for justice.

As for the children, the hunger strike began on December 28, celebrated throughout the Catholic world as the Feast of the Holy Innocents. The feast commemorates the infants martyred, as Matthew tells it, by the soldiers of King Herod in his vain effort to destroy Jesus. Yes, it was dangerous for the children, but so was a life without meaning or dignity. Reflecting later on this episode, I thought of the harsh obedience of Abraham as he led his son Isaac to the altar of sacrifice.

And the women were not only wise as doves but as cunning as serpents. Responding on the third day of their fast to more protests about the children's fasting, they announced that the children would be allowed to eat as soon as adults came forward to take their places. Several members of the assembly then joined the strike, taking up residence together in the offices of the Catholic daily newspaper, *Presencia*. Meantime the public was being informed; there was a degree of press freedom in Bolivia and the Permanent Assembly for Human Rights included a number of writers and others adroit in the use of the media.

The strike began to grow. First dozens, then scores, then hundreds of women and men joined the hunger strike. At last more than 1,380 people were fasting, among them Dr. Luis Adolfo Siles Salinas, a former president of Bolivia. Churches and university buildings became centers of peaceful demonstrations, not only in La Paz but in Cochabamba, Santa Cruz, Sucre, Potosí, and other cities. Even in countries as distant as Mexico, groups joined the strike on behalf of the Bolivian people.

Not that the response was universally favorable. *Presencia* itself reported the strike with sympathy; so also did the country's two leading radio stations, one Baptist, the other Jesuit. But the general press downplayed the strike and dismissed it as a political maneuver. Ads began to appear signed by paramilitary organizations deploring the government's lack of action against the strikers, and threatening to take matters into their own hands. These groups were known to be creatures of the government, but their threats gave some color of legitimacy to warnings by the Minister of the Interior that he would soon have to imprison the strikers "for their own protection."

In Bolivia a hunger strike is not a novel stratagem; it has been used even by a president while in office. Yet it retains dramatic force, especially when on so large a scale and so strongly religious in character as this one. The government could not ignore the strike, but instead of dealing directly with the strikers it went over their heads. The regime appealed to José Cardinal Maurer, Archbishop of Sucre and Roman Catholic Primate of Bolivia, presenting him with a "working document" containing a promise of "general amnesty."

Ill-advised and unwary, the Cardinal gave his approval to the document, failing to observe the presence of a technically worded clause that had the effect of excluding union or political organizers from the amnesty. Despite the Cardinal's response the strikers rejected the proposal, but did soften their own demands. They agreed to drop their requests for reinstatement of unions and for removal of the army from the mines. They still insisted, however, on an unrestricted amnesty and restoration of dismissed miners to their jobs. When the government would not agree, the strikers went back to their original position.

Call for observers

With the strike continuing and both sides hardening their positions, the situation was becoming extremely tense. By January 13, 1978 there were widespread rumors that government troops would soon storm the strikers' sanctuaries and carry out mass arrests. The possibility of violence on a large scale was very real. Human rights and church leaders became so alarmed that they issued formal requests to major Christian groups in the United States and Europe to send official representatives to Bolivia as quickly as possible. Their mission would be to observe the situation, try to promote negotiations, and inform the world community.

It was in response to these requests that Father McCoy, Sister Jo Marie, and I arrived in La Paz on Sunday, January 15. The next four days were as tense and tumultuous as any I have experienced, each promising development followed by a new menace, so that our emotions roller-coastered almost continuously from hope to fear to hope again. Then on Tuesday, January 17, dawn broke at midnight.

Immediately on our arrival we plunged into a series of meetings that had been arranged for us and that continued into the week. We talked with the women strikers; with leaders of the assembly and the strike spokesperson; with church leaders, including Archbishop Manrique and Archbishop Guiseppe Laigueglia, Papal Nuncio; with U.S. Ambassador Paul H. Boeker and members of his staff; with Jiménez Gallo, Minister of the Interior and, perhaps most importantly, with General Bánzer's closest civilian advisers, Javier Arce and Edwin Tapia. Their opposite numbers, the negotiators for the strikers, were Dr. Siles Salinas, Father Julio Tumiri, and Hugo Fernández.

At the time of our arrival the negotiating situation was clearly frozen. Some of those who had been fasting longest were becoming dangerously weak—a fact that led some government spokespersons to accuse the other side of hoping for a "victim," a martyr. The threat of paramilitary violence or government action was strong. Our objectives were to advocate continued talking, to convey to each side the views of the other, to keep emphasizing humanitarian and human rights concerns—and most of all to underscore, if only by our presence and the organizational titles we bore, the concern of the world community. That time did not allow the formation of an international rather than totally U.S. delegation may have been a happy circumstance. It soon became clear that the Carter administration's emphasis on human rights had made a strong impression in Bolivia. It was clear also that the Bánzer regime cared deeply about its international image as a nation moving toward democratization and economic growth.

Still, after our round of meetings on Sunday the first developments on Monday were disappointing: the government arranged for a one-day work stoppage to demonstrate the "spontaneous" support of workers for its policy. But then in the evening a government representative met with leaders of three political parties and the three strike representatives to consider the forging of a pact, similar to those made in Spain and Portugal, that all parties would observe in the process of democratization. The hunger strike was only one point on the agenda, but it quickly became the primary focus of the discussion. At 8:00 P.M. the group recessed so that its members could consult their respective groups; it appeared that a breakthrough was near, and the negotiators were to reassemble at 11:00.

But the government line immediately hardened; instead of resuming the discussion it issued an ultimatum to the strikers. They were given until midnight to disassemble. It was no empty threat, as we observers learned when we were roused from our beds at 3:30 in the morning so that we could make our presence felt as government soldiers entered the sanctuaries of the strikers. A Jesuit priest drove Sister Jo Marie, along with Sister Amparo Carvajal, a leader of the Permanent Assembly for Human Rights, to the university. Father McCoy and I were taken to the offices of *Presencia*.

Entering the newspaper offices we saw the arrests being made. The strikers went limp, so that they had to be carried out. There were literally hordes of soldiers, perhaps fifty in one small room. From another part of the building we heard a shout and hurried along a corridor to find soldiers and police already at work rifling files and confiscating film. Our escort called attention to us, and we presented ourselves as human rights observers from the United States who would make a full report of all we saw and heard. There was a hurried conference, and the order was given to cease the attack on the files. But the strikers were gone.

Meantime Sisters Jo Marie and Amparo and their escort were able to drive within a block of the university, then walked toward it past three armed guards. Then more soldiers and police blocked their way and forbade them to enter the university's plaza. Worse, when they turned back toward their jeep the commander called out Sister Amparo's name. Twice he ordered her to return; twice she refused. Two soldiers seized her and dragged her to an unmarked police car, refusing to allow Sister Jo Marie to go along. Nor was the jeep allowed to follow. Two other sisters and three priests also were arrested that night.

Message to the world

At this point we assembled at San Calixto, the Jesuit school. The phone lines had been cut but we were able to use the school's radio equipment to send messages to New York, Washington, and Geneva, reporting the situation and asking for protests by the groups we represented. Our signals got through and the protest messages began arriving. Whether because of them or for other reasons, it seemed the situation was easing when, later that Tuesday morning, Father McCoy and I met with the president's advisers, Javier Arce and Edwin Tapia. They guaranteed humane treatment of the prisoners and security for those still striking; we were assured we could visit the priests and nuns arrested the previous night.

But there were conflicting signs as well. Another priest was put under arrest: Father Gregorio Iriarte, the Permanent Assembly of Human Rights' international secretary, who had initially invited us to La Paz and was our host. We could not learn where he and Sister Amparo were being held; meantime we received word that one university student had been killed by shots apparently fired from an unmarked police car, and that five other students had been severely beaten.

It was then (Tuesday afternoon) that the power and prestige of the Catholic Church in Bolivia began coming fully into play. First, a letter from Cardinal Maurer, the Primate, co-signed by twenty other religious leaders, arrived from Sucre, clearly and strongly affirming the justice of the workers' demands. It added:

> We must underline the importance of this nonviolent movement that supports fundamental values for all humanity. For the first time in the history of Bolivia and perhaps of humanity we have seen the phenomenon of so many persons who sacrifice themselves in such a way in defense of their fellow humans who are in such need of justice, liberty, and employment.

The letter completely undercut the government's contention that the Cardinal's earlier statements had ranged the Church on the government's side.

Then came the blockbuster. Archbishop Manrique issued an ultimatum: either the strike would be settled within twenty-four hours, beginning at midnight Tuesday, or he would place the Archdiocese of La Paz under interdict. Except for the necessary care of the seriously ill and dying, there would be no religious services of any kind on Friday, Saturday, and Sunday. Further, those responsible for planning and carrying out the invasion of church sanctuaries to arrest strikers were threatened with excommunication. Any solution offered by the government must include the immediate release of arrested strikers.

For an outsider there was a kind of culture shock in the announcement, a translation in time back to the Middle Ages. But in La Paz it was a serious matter—and not only for Bolivians. A U.S. diplomat confided that it had shaken his wife, a Catholic. To the government as well, the threat was most serious. To ignore or defy it would unite the people behind the church and endanger the regime's international standing.

Meanwhile the four women who had launched the whole train of events took a hand once more. Responding to the breakdown of discussions Monday and to the massive arrests of strikers, they announced that henceforth they would abstain even from water until agreement was reached. They were already extremely weak; two days without liquids might well be fatal.

At midnight Tuesday, with the social fabric of Bolivia nearly at the tearing point, the government began to give way. General Bánzer appeared on television to announce an immediate and general amnesty. But still the strikers were not satisfied, for the president's promise of amnesty to "enemies of the nation" was ambiguous—it could be used to exclude any number of political or union exiles. Moreover the announcement was not clear about provisions for dismissed workers or about future guarantees for those who had taken part in the strike.

On Wednesday, however, negotiations continued. Dr. Jorge Rojas Tardio, a former government minister and close friend of key leaders on both sides (including Archbishop Manrique and Dr. Siles Salinas), offered his services as mediator. Three times during the course of the day proposals shuttled back and forth between the strikers and the Ministry of the Interior. By eight o'clock, agreement had been reached. On behalf of the government and the armed forces, the Minister signed an accord that provided a general amnesty for all political prisoners, exiles, and refugees (an estimated 19,000 people); reinstatement in their jobs of all miners dismissed for union or political activities, with full seniority rights; and freedom for all arrested in connection with the strike or detained because of peaceful protest. (Freedom for union activity was announced the following Saturday.)

Prisoners released

Hours later, prisoners were being released from police centers and clinics. Among them were Sister Amparo and Father Gregorio, who had been held at the Ministry. Medical doctors were circulating advice to the strikers on how to break their fast safely. There was ample reason for the rites of thanksgiving celebrated that evening and the next day.

Tin miners' wives receive medical attention at the end of their successful 23-day hunger strike. January 1978. Photo courtesy of Asamblea Permanente de Derechos Humanos de Bolivia.

Why did it happen as it did? Not even a well-informed and reflective Bolivian national with access to all parties could give a complete answer; my own must be even less adequate. But there are things worth saying.

The courage and determination of the women must be kept central. Needless to say, however, such qualities do not emerge from an historical vacuum. Political and social awareness among Bolivia's tin miners and their families goes back a long way, and we observers felt its effects in the disciplined cohesion of the movement that responded to the initiative of the women.

So also with the strong role of the churches and the unity among them. At one point in the strike some 400 delegates of the Evangelical

Methodist Church meeting in national assembly voted their support of the strike, and joined with the Lutherans in backing the evangelical churches in La Paz that offered sanctuary, along with Catholic churches, for hunger strikers. It was clear to us that Bolivia's social protest movement draws much of its vitality from a solid faith that has been nurtured by biblical and liturgical themes out of the Old Testament prophets, the Magnificat, the Beatitudes, and the whole life and witness of Jesus. It seems apparent to me—and it came as joyful news—that the past decade and more of evangelization and *conscientización* had had effects more profound than we knew.

Because similar occasions may arise in the future it is necessary to include a word about the effect of our own presence as observers. As outsiders we were not equipped to handle the subtleties of final arbitration. As church persons invited by a church-supported human rights group, we could not credibly claim impartiality. Yet we felt our presence was appropriate—in that we came by invitation of local human rights groups—and that we were able to become catalytic agents in the process of negotiation. What this told us was that "world opinion" is not a phantom reality, and that the influence of the world church community on opinion is taken seriously. This basic attitude was evident in the reception we had throughout our stay, from key government figures and U.S. and U.N. representatives as well as from our hosts. In view of recent critiques of national and international church bodies, that is a reality that deserves recognition.

As I have already said, there are no final victories. The workers of Bolivia and their allies need to maintain their discipline, take new risks, nurture their spirits. The rest of us must continue our support in all ways open to us. But though there is a long journey yet to be made, this one stride covered many leagues. It offers a model that can have significance in many places on earth.

Notes

1. James Dunkerley, *Rebellion in the Veins: Political Struggle in Bolivia, 1952-82* (London: Verso Editions, 1984), p. 241; Robert J. Alexander, *Bolivia: Past, Present, and Future of its Politics* (New York: Praeger, 1982), p. 112; Herbert S. Klein, *Bolivia, the Evolution of a Multi-ethnic Society* (New York: Oxford University Press, 1982), p. 262; Asamblea Permanente de los Derechos Humanos (APDH), *La Huelga de Hambre* [The Hunger Strike] (La Paz: APDH, 1978), pp. 239-42.
2. APDH, p. 246.
3. James M. Malloy and Eduardo Gamarra, *Revolution and Reaction: Bolivia, 1964-1985* (New Brunswick, N.J. and Oxford: Transaction Books, 1988) p. 145.
4. APDH, p. 245.

For further reading

Alexander, Robert J. *Bolivia: Past, Present, and Future of its Politics.* New York: Praeger, 1982.

Asamblea Permanente de los Derechos Humanos. *La Huelga de Hambre* [The Hunger Strike]. La Paz: APDH, 1978.

Barrios de Chungara, Domitila. *Let me speak!: Testimony of Domitila, a Woman of the Bolivian mines.* New York: Monthly Review Press, 1978.

Dunkerley, James. *Rebellion in the Veins: Political Struggle in Bolivia, 1952-82.* London: Verso Editions, 1984.

Malloy, James M. and Eduardo Gamarra. *Revolution and Reaction: Bolivia, 1964-1985.* New Brunswick, N.J. and Oxford: Transaction Books, 1988.

Honduras

FOUR

Introduction

How to recognize Latin American nonviolent action when one sees it? In the question, more than idle speculation is at stake. Hope is never idle, for it fuels action and gives solidarity its sinew. Social activists in Europe and North America must recognize nonviolence at work in Latin America before they can hope in it, and mobilize to offer support.

The shape of authentic Latin American nonviolence may be unfamiliar. People at the grassroots draw on their own cultural heritage, religious traditions, and communal resources, not on Gandhi, Tolstoy or Martin Luther King, Jr. Progressive intellectuals, liberation theologians, and leaders of popular movements may be more familiar with such figures but they are likely to consider nonviolent action to be merely one tactic in the arsenal of popular struggle. Even such a prominent apostle of nonviolence as Brazil's Dom Hélder Câmara has made a point of calling Camilo Torres, the martyred Colombian guerrilla-priest, "my brother," even though he chose to use violence. After all, the primary bond of those struggling for liberation in Latin

America is the yearning for justice, not a particular approach to achieving it.

To recognize nonviolence in Latin America, then, one must first recognize a kind of nonviolence that grows neither from ethical pacifism nor from political science. It is the nonviolence of those who scarcely know its name. It is the spontaneous and instinctive nonviolence of those who would not have the resources to mount an armed insurrection if they wanted to, yet are highly resourceful. It is the nonviolence of desperation.

The story of the struggle of Honduran *campesinos* (peasants), for land is a good illustration of such nonviolence. Like others throughout Latin America, the rural poor in Honduras have developed a largely unconscious style of nonviolence. Christian faith and peasant culture have molded their actions. Openings and obstacles in Honduran political life have guided their course. But above all, hunger has prodded them to act. As a result, organizing farming cooperatives and "recovering" the land has evolved into a veritable Honduran folk tradition.

To Honduran peasants, what observers would call nonviolence is neither an ethic nor a tactic but pursuit of common sense born of necessity. Their power is their numbers, stubborn persistence, courage, and organization. The incessant efforts of Honduras's ruling elites to divide peasant unions into factions, buy off their leaders, and intimidate or repress the unwavering is a tribute to that power.

The Nonviolence of Desperation
Peasant Land Action in Honduras
Gerald Schlabach

"Our children are dying of hunger anyway . . ."

It is Holy Week, 1973. In northwest Honduras, at a place called Quebrada Seca, the time is near for the year's first planting.

For the rural poor throughout Central America, it is the season of desperation. Two or three months ago last year's crop, or the money from its sale, began running out. Of those fortunate enough to own or rent land only a few have enough to feed their families modestly well for a full twelve months. For those without land altogether—day laborers, gatherers and vendors of firewood, maids, and laundresses in the houses of the wealthy—the price of basic grains is at its annual peak.

Yet this year in Honduras, like a new machete flashing in the sunlight, word of the chance for land has hacked a hopeful notch in the gnarly stump of fatalism and despair. A few months earlier, in late 1972, an

The determination of the peasants of the Ivan Bettancourt Cooperative in Honduras was key to their successful nonviolent "recovery" of idle land in Honduras. February 1984. Photo courtesy of Fellowship of Reconciliation Task Force on Latin America and the Caribbean.

ironic version of the Latin American coup d'état had taken place. Reform-minded sectors of the military—fed up with the corruption of civilians more interested in dividing the spoils of government among old entrenched political parties than in developing the nation—had seized power. Backing them was organized labor. Abetting them were peasants with plans for a massive hunger march on the capital. Among the reformers' first acts: a new, provisional agrarian reform law.

Agrarian reform, born in the era of Kennedy's Alliance for Progress, had actually been on the books for a decade. But the National Agrarian Institute (INA), the agency the government had set up to carry it out, was at best a fitful operation. A sickly child, it was subject to every change in the national political climate. On its own the INA lacked the force to push through such a basic but potentially volatile structural change as land redistribution.

But word was out: INA was finally working overtime! Its technical personnel had spread out through the countryside to respond to legal claims, research deeds, assess land values, and identify idle arable land that the law said should pass to those who would use it. Still, the task was so great and the clamor for arable land so acute that most peasant groups had to do more than fill out proper forms and ask for an interview if they were to get INA's attention. The only sure way to get an interview with INA representatives was simply to go ahead and occupy idle land en masse.

So it was that, in nationally coordinated actions on the same day in Holy Week, two hundred peasant groups occupied idle land. Throughout the country groups quickly set up makeshift houses of scrap lumber, rusty old roof sheeting, and plastic, and began to clear land for planting. In Quebrada Seca sixty families occupied more than one thousand acres of mostly idle land that one of the area's richest families controlled. The influential landowner, in addition to cultivating tobacco on what land he used, was a major bank shareholder and would later run for president.

But sixty families were too few and the military's supposed conversion to the people's cause was far from thorough. On their first attempt, the only response the Quebrada Seca peasants won was beatings and eviction at the hands of soldiers. The following week, their numbers growing to one hundred families with the help of neighboring communities, they re-occupied the land. But again the authorities evicted them.

Only on the third week's attempt did the peasants capture INA's interest in the case. By then the number of families had swelled to a more formidable two hundred; food provisions from the National Union of Campesinos (UNC) were allowing them to stay put; and makeshift stone walls and hastily dug trenches gave protection. Among INA representatives accompanying the contingent of soldiers called to the peasant site was a young agricultural technician and cooperative organizer who sympathized with the peasants. He recalls that the oldest men, the women, and the children met the soldiers when they arrived. The military, as usual, first asked to speak with the group's leaders.

Ragtag and sweating under the hot sun, the people were nonetheless proud. They replied that everyone was a leader, and whoever would speak would be speaking for all. The military men said they were there to negotiate, but that they wanted to see the leaders so they could go together to a meeting with INA. The people insisted that this was the place to negotiate, with everyone together, and that they were waiting to hear what the authorities had to say. The military men replied that they had orders to evict the group, and that the trucks along the road were waiting to carry out those orders.

One of the old men stood up on a mound of stones. "I want these military men to hear what the people think," the agricultural technician remembers him saying. "Are you ready to abandon the land?"

Everyone yelled, "NO, NO! It would be better to die!"

Another peasant leader stood up to address the officer in charge. "Listen, my Colonel," said the peasant, "rather than die little by little, we'd rather die at once. Either way, our children are already dying of hunger, and if you decide to shoot, well, you'll kill us all. But we are definitely not going to leave. What are you going to do with us? Your bullets will run out, but our machetes will live on!" At that everyone lifted his machete in the air with a shout. The authorities—with the "colonel" almost trembling in rage—backed down.

INA soon began negotiating with the landowner. He insisted that the government agency follow through on orders to evict the people, but INA refused. By now a month had passed since the first takeover, and the peasants had cleared the land and settled in. Of course the military could easily have evicted them. But INA did not want a massacre. Its representatives told the landowner and his lawyers: "Look, you have two alternatives. There is pressure from peasants all over the country and a massacre will only make things worse. Either you negotiate a price for the land, or we take it from you outright."[1]

Land actions: a Honduran folk tradition

"Recoveries." "*Las recuperaciones.*" That is what peasants throughout Honduras call such land actions. They emphasize that they are only recovering what the rich have taken either from them or from their forebears, and what the law, if enforced, would return to them. In the end the Quebrada Seca recovery inspired many others in that region of the country.

In fact it is just such a magnetic effect, rather than conscious training by peasant unions, that has turned *las recuperaciones* into something of a national folk tradition. The peasants may have no more explicit commitment to active nonviolence than did the Quebrada Seca group with its raised machetes. Yet their most powerful weapons are numbers, organization, and the same desperate willingness to risk suffering again and again. With these "weapons" Honduran peasants have developed a strategy of "relentless persistence" that is authentically their own. Often improvising, like people throughout history, they have turned to nonviolent action out of necessity rather than out of ethical, pacifist conviction.

Almost by definition, such a spontaneous phenomenon has at times lacked national cohesion and consistency. The peasants have rarely proposed a full program for political and social transformation. Yet for that very reason, what peasant organizations have achieved is all the more remarkable. At almost every critical juncture in Honduran history it is the peasants and the fruit company workers who have played the pivotal roles.

When they have hung back, the peasants have lent their inertia to the status quo. As late as the early twentieth century, in quasifeudalistic fashion, the oligarchy settled its disputes and contended for political power (with corresponding access to huge tracts of land as prize!) by using favors and promises to marshal the peasants to fight its civil wars.[2]

When mobilized on behalf of their own interests, however, the peasants have repeatedly shifted the balance of power toward progressive social change. Doing so, they have provided a classic case of what nonviolence theorist Gene Sharp insists is the true basis of political power: not brute force, nor the threat of its use, but the granting or withdrawal of consent.[3] Repeatedly, ruling Honduran regimes or foot-dragging INA directors have fallen when peasants from all over the country have converged on the capital for a hunger march—or even when they have merely threatened to do so.

To be sure, such palace turnovers have seldom produced enduring structural change. INA has rarely maintained the pace of agrarian reform on its own without relentless peasant pressure from below, often through coordinated and nationwide campaigns of land recovery. One reason for these limitations is that the nation's ruling elites almost seem more aware of the latent power of the peasant masses than are the peasants themselves. Accordingly, the elites have devised astute tactics to preempt, co-opt and divide the peasant movement. Their tactics add up to ruling-class tradition matching the folk tradition of land actions. And that fact, though tragic, is a kind of tribute.

Reckoning with desperation: revolution or reform?

In 1952 when Honduras conducted its first agrarian census, the richest landowners—4.2 percent of the total—owned 56.8 percent of the nation's arable land, and usually the best. The poor majority, 65.1 percent of landowners, owned only 15.7 percent.[4] If the large landowners had been using their resources productively, perhaps their wealth would have provided some service to society by fueling national development with export earnings while providing greater employment for rural workers. But such was seldom the case. Foreign fruit companies kept nearly three-quarters of their holdings in idle reserve, claiming they needed insurance against plant epidemics. Meanwhile, large Honduran landowners often dedicated fertile land to inefficient cattle ranching or were more concerned with preserving a genteel way of life dating from colonial feudalism than with employment or national development.

By the early sixties, then, even persons who conceived of such development in purely capitalist terms were seeking land reform. For markets to expand the rural poor would need to join the national economy. To invigorate commerce, manufacturing, and agro-industry, the large traditional landowners would need to become vigorous entrepreneurs and transfer their capital investment from stagnant land use into the modern economy. Honduras's first agrarian reform law, passed in 1962, explicitly sought to force both moves.

But for those at all inclined to conceive of development in its human as well as economic dimensions, the need for agrarian reform was even more poignant. After all, Latin America's archetypical "banana republic" was and still is among its poorest, vying with Haiti for last place. Moreover, brute statistics on land distribution, discouraging as they are, and poor as some of the land may be, often leave out the most appalling fact of all: more than forty percent of the rural poor, according to the United States Agency for International Development (USAID), own no land at all.[5] The economic and social consequences were and are predictable: in 1983, even after more than twenty years of agrarian reform, more than ten of every hundred newborn infants were dying before their first birthday. Of those lucky enough to reach age five, ninety percent were suffering from malnutrition.[6]

Admittedly, redistribution of land in Honduras became a permissible political topic only when, in the early 1960s, reformed-minded governments held office in both Washington and Tegucigalpa. Yet to credit these governments with initiating land reform in Honduras is to put the politician's bandwagon before the peasant's horse. In each capital a prime motive of the policymakers was the simmering threat that the desperate ones would somehow erupt. President John F. Kennedy, in promoting his Alliance for Progress proposals in 1961, implied as much when he coined the adage forever attached to that initiative: "Those who make peaceful revolution impossible, make violent revolution inevitable." In Honduras, the liberal government that held power from 1957 to 1963 owed much to the ferment that surfaced irreversibly in 1954 when a spontaneous strike against the United Fruit Company quickly spread into a general strike.

Now known simply as the Great Strike, it became *the* watershed in Honduran labor relations. The strike had begun in April 1954 when dock workers, first in one port, then another, protested that according to law they should be receiving double holiday pay. Within a month, and with only a hastily assembled central strike committee, workers had shut down the entire banana industry. During the second month, tobacco, beer, textile, and mine workers—then students, teachers, and artisans—joined in with solidarity strikes. The wildcat-turned-general strike virtually shut down the country.

The Great Strike helped spawn the organized peasant movement in both direct and indirect ways. In some respects the strike was a failure, since the fruit company left loopholes in the ensuing contract and was able to retaliate with massive layoffs. Forced to return to traditional subsistence agriculture, however, thousands of recently unemployed fruit company workers took their newly gained organizing skills and consciousness directly into the countryside. By the end of the decade, the first enduring peasant unions were forming.

Less directly but just as importantly, the Great Strike succeeded in making decisively clear to all who would govern Honduras that, one way or another, they would have to take the working classes into account.[7] If with only minimal organization the discontent of a few dock workers could spark a general strike, what could a well-organized movement do? Some pre-emptive attention to the demands and conditions of workers was clearly necessary.

By the early 1960s it was obvious that the peasants—not only industrial and fruit company workers—would have to be part of the national reckoning as well. In 1961 and 1962, a series of actions demanding land reform and the elimination of large landholdings were carried out by some 15,000 peasants affiliated with the newly organized Central Committee for Campesino Unification (soon renamed FENACH, the National Federation of Honduran Campesinos).

The agrarian reform law of 1962 was the climax to nearly a decade of social ferment. Despite its limitations, the law established a legal framework for the Honduran peasant movement by affirming the "social function" of the land: Because the entire nation depends on agriculture, the state has a responsibility to ensure that whoever controls land uses it to benefit the nation as well as the individual. From 1962 on the peasants would have every right to speak not merely of "invading" but of "recovering" idle land that failed to serve Honduran society in some way.

A military-peasant alliance?

By the late 1960s, the phenomenon of land recovery was beginning to mushroom. Three different peasant blocs were working nationally: the UNC, FENACH, and the National Association of Campesinos (ANACH). Increasingly these peasant unions were demanding not just land but credit, technical resources, and a voice in INA policy. While ANACH was the most politically acceptable (and stridently anti-communist) of the three, it had shown that no regime could take its support for granted. When in 1966 ANACH and other labor leaders began announcing plans for a "hunger march," the increasingly vulnerable and unpopular military regime of General Oswaldo López Arellano quickly negotiated. One result: a restructuring of INA.

By the 1970s, government had again changed from military to civilian hands. But civilian elites soon began squandering resources with infighting, party sectarianism, nepotism, and general corruption.

A potentially more fundamental realignment was taking place within the military itself. A rising sector of officers was wondering whether its interests lay in an alliance with workers and peasants. The armed forces, so claimed its top general in an unprecedented Labor Day speech on May 1, 1972, "are made up of workers and peasants, which is why the armed forces are not the enemy of the workers and peasants."

The last half of 1972 saw worker and peasant organizations leading a groundswell of opposition to the civilian government. Then on December 4, two days before thousands of peasants were to converge on Tegucigalpa in a massive "hunger march," the military carried out a coup d'état. It was a coup different from any previous one. Instead of citing the threat of international communism as its cause, it cited the people's unhappiness and the great national problems that endangered national development. The high priority the military reformers intended to assign the agrarian problem was evident in a prompt decree with a new, provisional agrarian reform law. That commitment was also explicit in the National Development Plan that the government released in early 1973. The plan called agrarian reform a "fundamental task of the Armed Forces," and it sought to deal a decisive blow to the power base of the landowning oligarchy while consolidating the new regime's alliance with reform-minded elements within the business community.

INA distributed more land during the next four years than in all the years before and after combined. Organized in 879 peasant groups, 31,527 families received 381,280 acres.[8] That was actually much less than the 120,000 families and the nearly million and a half acres INA had ambitiously hoped for. Still, at the peak of the mid-1970s land reform, peasant unions found the legal route responsive enough that they could sometimes refrain from promoting new land recoveries. This was the era in which INA officials might boldly tell influential landowners: negotiate a price or we'll take the land outright.

Unfortunately, by early 1975 when the government released a permanent version of its initial agrarian reform decree, political momentum was waning. And by the time specific regulations governing the formal law went into effect, the era of "populist" military reform had produced the Santa Clara–Los Horcones massacre that gave the peasant movement the martyrs it most often evokes to this day. On June 25 of that year, large landowners acting in collusion with military authorities in the Olancho province tortured and killed fourteen people, including two priests. Light sentences suggested that the military government was losing its commitment to agrarian reform.[9]

Any idea that "populist" military rule left a lasting commitment to structural change in favor of the nation's neediest is not the whole story. In the end, the legacy of that mid-1970s era mainly reinforced a two-pronged strategy that Honduran elites have long practiced. The two prongs are to tolerate pre-emptive reform, but repress those clamoring to quicken further the pace of change. During the 1980s any government effort to promote land redistribution was lethargic at best. At worst it unleashed new waves of repression, authoring disappearances and creating an environment that allowed landowner goons to attack and even kill peasants. In 1982, the first year of renewed civilian administration, the government distributed no land at all.[10] Four years later, Marcial Caballero, UNC general secretary, claimed that during the outgoing president's tenure the INA had denied eighty percent of peasant land requests. Only the peasants' own initiatives have kept land reform alive.

Changing the structures, soil up

Yet alive it is. Land reform may not fare well in the halls of the Honduran Congress, since Congress is filled with wealthy landowners. It may often get lost amid piles of paper and red tape in INA offices. It may never be more than a promptly forgotten campaign promise in the mouths of would-be presidents. And supporting it may simply be one more tactic in the military's arsenal of weapons for dominating civilian politics. But the peasants themselves are clear and committed to change: Year in and year out, they toil away at land reform in their own way. Some years the political climate favors a harvest of land transfers, and sometimes the harvest is meager. But working the land is always that way. Though "the government gives away nothing," as one peasant has said, "in Honduras, we are the agrarian reform."[11]

By learning to initiate change actively rather than fatalistically hanging back until the "powerful" act for them, the peasants are also changing the structure of Honduran society—in their own way, soil-upward. As one international development worker has reflected: What is structural change if not people taking control of their own lives, bettering prospects for their children, and learning grassroots participatory democracy for themselves? Honduran politicians could learn something from the peasants about justice and democracy. Someday, they may have to.

Another season in the cycle of change came in the spring of 1987. As planting season approached, official land reform policy was stalled, but peasant groups were on the move. On May 20 more than 20,000 peasants all over the country engaged in some two hundred recoveries. Nationally the need was obvious: A year and a half into its tenure, the administration in Tegucigalpa had redistributed virtually no land.[12]

To a group of 350 peasants "recovering" a large farm that day in the municipality of San Jerónimo, Comayagua, the need was more than obvious. What moved them was not newspaper reports about the administration's poor record on agrarian reform. As one landowner's cattle grazed peacefully and unharmed in a lush field that the members of the "Good Shepherd Group" hoped would soon feed their children instead, the peasants explained:[13] "The dogs of the rich wouldn't eat what we eat," they told a visiting foreigner. "If you came to visit us for three or four days, you'd starve because we'd be too ashamed to serve you the food we eat"—tortillas, beans, and salt, day after day. And without land, in a few months even that food would be short. "By July and August a lot of the peasant women get up in the morning and all they have to do is wash their hands. If there is sugar, it isn't enough for everyone to have with coffee. If we have any food, it is only enough for lunch or maybe supper."

By April they have used up any corn in store. As landless day laborers, they must wait until harvest comes in September for work. Local *truchas,* or tiny general stores, won't give them credit until then.

Given such conditions, even those who may once have feared involvement in anything resembling politics decide that their only hope for the future is to organize themselves with other peasants. The group's president is a case in point. He has been involved for only a year and a half. He says that if only work were steady he could get by as a day laborer earning a mere two dollars per day. But the best he can hope for is a week of work per month, and his family of four must live with others.

Still, his earlier fears of involvement with the movement may be all too well founded. He has been the group's president less than a month. Group members had occupied this same land three weeks earlier, only to have the military dislodge them. The soldiers ordered all the peasants to lie face down, some of them in cow manure. After kicking and beating them, the authorities took the group's entire executive committee to jail, where, seven weeks later, they still remained. In taking the place of a jailed group president, the new one has "had to do a lot of thinking." But he has seen the benefits for other groups that have organized and persisted.

The reason for persisting becomes all the more poignant when one walks a half-mile down the dusty dirt road to the well established "Sixth of November Cooperative." On November 6, 1980, 150 peasants first attempted to recover the land they now own and work. Two years later they were building the first of fifty-four small but comfortable cement block houses that now sit together in neat rows, and they were cultivating 350 acres of land.

What happened in the meantime, however, was twenty-four separate land recoveries! Twenty-three times the landowner called out the army to evict the settlers. Twenty-three times, they returned. That does not mean the struggle was easy. One man was shot and killed (not by the army but by paid agents of the landowner). And simply holding onto contested land takes scarce resources. Until the land was their own and they could harvest their own crops, they had few sources of income. They could hardly leave to seek out the temporary work they had once depended upon, lest they abandon their claim and lower the force of their numbers. Some of the peasant men even lost their wives due to the hardship, explained the group's former general secretary. There was so little to eat, some women left their husbands to seek income-generating work or to rejoin their families. Others, however, eventually joined their husbands on the "recovered" land, hoping to make a greater impression on authorities.[14]

Today, to the surprise of his visitors, the former leader of the cooperative prefers to talk about efforts to organize and manage the productive little community, rather than discuss the recoveries. Again and again he goes into a room off his shady porch to retrieve ordinary looking notebooks, seminar guides and manuals. The notebooks record years of committee minutes, co-op accounts, hours individual members had worked, and loans to respective families. The manuals are about bookkeeping, pest control, how to improve production, and how to conduct meetings. What the visiting foreigner may be slow to realize is that, to these peasants, these seemingly mundane matters represent control over their own lives and destinies. The co-op, for example, is no longer dependent on "*coyotes*," or middlemen, to market its products. Having learned both to confront a powerful landowner and to demystify basic mathematics, negotiating prices in the Tegucigalpa or San Pedro Sula markets is quite possible.

What the co-op leader most wants to talk about is how things have changed so much for the better. Three-fourths of the cooperative's land is divided into plots for individual households. Each family farms three or four sites so that all have some quality land near the river, some steeper land, and some poor land. They grow staples (corn, rice, beans) and vegetables. In addition, every family must contribute at least twenty days of work per year to community upkeep and farming of collective land. Most do more.

Traditionally, peasants are highly individualistic; at first many group members disdained working collectively, deriding the idea as "pure communism." But now, according to the former general secretary, "people like collective work so much they fight for the work!" A further incentive is that every day of work beyond the required quota means the family will have a greater share in profits and products at harvest time.

On the average, families now earn more than 3,000 dollars per year. That is ten times what they earned as landless day laborers.

Furthermore, the "Sixth of November Cooperative" has warehouses to store its own grains, so that members will not have to buy from others at high prices later in the year. But perhaps the most telling statistic is this: In the last few years, not one infant has died of malnutrition or disease.

With that sort of example just down the road, it is no wonder the landless peasants of "Good Shepherd" and indeed other groups all over Honduras persist in their struggle. Three weeks after the May 20, 1987 campaign of nationally coordinated recoveries, INA announced it would hand over from 37,000 to 50,000 acres, more than it had handed out during the administration's first year and a half combined.

The nonviolence of desperation: an assessment

While the legacy of 1970s Honduran reformism has been less than promised, peasant union leaders are not naive. They do not simply blame the military's loss of heart, as though the military and other elites were capable of more than the most halfhearted conversion to the interests of the poor. "We didn't swallow the hook of 'populism,' " claims Teófilo Trejos Pérez of the National Rural Workers Central (CNTC), the peasant bloc that is today probably most in touch with its grassroots and most militant. Rather, suggests Santos Ignacio Ramírez, another CNTC leader, the reasons for lost momentum lie as much at the peasants' own feet as at the elites': "The context was definitely favorable that year [1972-73]. If the peasants had been better trained and prepared, they would have recovered more and better land. But at that time, none of the existing organizations was prepared to take full advantage of the configuration of forces."

Even now, too many members and leaders of the peasant movement "think its force is in its friendship with military officials," says Victor Meza, director of the Honduras Documentation Center and a prominent social commentator in the country. Such a phenomenon could simply reflect the persistence of a trait in Latin American culture that trusts knowing the right people in authority as the way to get ahead. In fact, Meza continues, "the reverse is true: it is the military that needs the support of the peasants."

To some, including Meza, land recoveries actually seem to be part of the reason Honduras's peasants have not gone on to create a thoroughgoing movement for the kind of structural change that would institutionalize land reform. "The problem with the recoveries is that they are the highest expression of the peasants' consciousness," he laments. "The peasants organize, plan their land action, and get all excited, but once they've gotten their land, that is usually the end of their militancy." They have developed the strategy, he says, without realizing its potential significance for national politics.

That the folk tradition of peasant mobilization has become a permanent fixture of Honduran political scenery may be a sign of both its success and the limits of its success. The limits are clear: Like a heavy coffee drinker unable to go to work without a dose of caffeine, official mechanisms for land reform are unresponsive unless the peasants take action again and again. The system itself remains permanently sluggish.

Yet to the extent that the rural poor have broken with fatalism and despair, creating their own mechanism for change, the folk tradition is a victory. "Twenty years ago the peasants didn't want to take the land," says the CNTC's Trejos. "Everyone was afraid. But now they do it themselves and we don't find out until later." In the process they have established their political clout and they have organized. Though the powerful contrive to create and exploit divisions, the movement's strength and the number of cooperatives it has engendered are unimaginable in neighboring Guatemala and El Salvador, with their own cycles of military and civilian rule, and with their far greater levels of political repression.

That the nonviolence of desperation should have a mixed record is actually quite predictable. Total political and ethical visions do not consistently advise the peasants. But neither do they encumber them with ideological baggage. The power of their brand of nonviolence lies in having few illusions and instead, a single burning dream of enough work and food to feed one's children.

One might dream of greater dialogue and mutual learning between peasants and the other two main currents of active nonviolence: the tactical one rooted in political experience, and the ethical one rooted most often in religious conviction. The first stream might help peasants better perceive that their power does not lie in alliances with the so-called powerful. Rather, their power lies in the question their very landlessness evokes within the national conscience. The peasants and the fruit company workers have played a pivotal role in Honduran history. Their plight provides the sharpest reminder that the system is not working and could quickly collapse if those faring poorly by it would withdraw their consent.

In Roman Catholic Latin America the second, religious stream of nonviolence might help establish the cross of Jesus Christ yet more firmly as a symbol of liberating power rather than fatalistic defeat. As such, it could highlight the vision of change implicit in the fraternity, mutual aid, suffering service, and "relentless persistence" that peasant groups already practice intuitively. A corresponding vision of power could offer its own dynamic basis for studied distrust of those promises of change that rely on a military elite to promote and sponsor it.

But let there be no doubt. Nothing can replace the power of a movement rooted in the traditions and deepest aspirations of a people. When detached from that power, tactical nonviolence has seldom moved far beyond theory, and ethical pacifism has seldom moved far beyond creed.

Notes

1. Interview with Ovidio Flores, Comisión de Acción Social de la Iglesia Evangélica Menonita Hondureña; by author; San Pedro Sula, Honduras; November 20, 1986.

2. Mario Posas, *El Movimiento Campesino Hondureño*, Colección Cuadernos No. 2 (Tegucigalpa: Editorial Guaymuras, 1981), pp. 4-6.

3. Gene Sharp, *The Politics of Nonviolent Action*, three volumes in paperback: *Power and Struggle, The Methods of Nonviolent Action, The Dynamics of Nonviolent Action* (Boston: Extending Horizons Books, Porter Sargent Publishers, 1973).

4. Agrarian Census of 1952, cited in Posas, *Movimiento Campesino*, p. 12.

5. USAID Agricultural sector assessment, 1978, cited in Paul Glickman, "Honduras: Peasants orchestrate nationwide land grabs," *In These Times*, May 22-28, 1985, p. 10.

6. Statistics on infant mortality and malnutrition from the Instituto Nutricional para Centroamérica y Panamá (INCAP), based in Guatemala. INCAP placed infant mortality at 103 per 1,000 live births. A USAID Fiscal 1984 Congressional Presentation put the infant mortality figure as high as 118 per 1,000 live births. In the United States, the figure is 13.

7. Victor Meza, *Historia del Movimiento Obrero Hondureño*, Colección CODICES (Tegucigalpa: Editorial Guaymuras, 1980), pp. 97-98.

8. Instituto Nacional Agrario, "Resumen de datos generales del sector reformado," Tegucigalpa, 1978, p. 27; quoted by Douglas Kincaid, "The Peasant Movements Gain Momentum," *Honduras Update*, March 1985, p. 6.

9. For further details on the Santa Clara–Los Horcones massacre, see: Posas, *Movimiento Campesino*, pp. 33-34; and Penny Lernoux, *Cry of the People: The Struggle for Human Rights in Latin America—the Catholic Church in Conflict with U.S. Policy*, (Garden City, NY: Doubleday, 1980; reprinted with a new preface, Middlesex, England and New York: Penguin Books, 1982), pp. 107-114.

10. *El Tiempo*, December 22, 1982, cited by the Centro de Documentación de Honduras, *Conflictos Agrarios en Honduras: Cronologia {January 1982-January 1986}*, Serie Cronologias (Tegucigalpa: CEDOH, March 1986), p. 5.

11. Quoted in " 'We are the Agrarian Reform': Rural Politics and Agrarian Reform" in *Honduras: Portrait of a Captive Nation*, edited by Nancy Peckenham and Annie Street (New York: Praeger, 1985), p. 136.

12. "The Campesino Movement's May 20 Action: An interview with Medea Benjamin," *Honduras Update*, (June/July 1987), pp. 1-4.

13. The material through the end of the section is based on interviews with members of the Good Shepherd Group in the midst of their land recuperation, and with a member of the Sixth of November Cooperative; by author; Municipio San Gerónimo, Comayagua, Honduras; May 20, 1987.

14. For a fuller account of the peasant movement from the perspective of women involved see Elvia Alvarado, *Don't Be Afraid, Gringo: A Honduran Woman Speaks from the Heart*, translated and edited by Medea Benjamin. (San Francisco: Institute for Food and Development Policy, 1987).

For further reading

Alvarado, Elvia. *Don't Be Afraid, Gringo: A Honduran Woman Speaks from the Heart.* Translated and edited by Medea Benjamin. San Francisco: Institute for Food and Development Policy, 1987.

Lapper, Richard and James Painter. *Honduras: State for Sale.* London: Latin America Bureau, 1985.

Lernoux, Penny. *Cry of the People: the Struggle for Human Rights in Latin America—the Catholic Church in Conflict with U.S. Policy.* Garden City, NY: Doubleday, 1980; Reprinted with a new preface, Middlesex, England and New York: Penguin Books, 1982. [See especially pages 107-123.]

Peckenham, Nancy and Annie Street. *Honduras: Portrait of a Captive Nation.* New York: Praeger, 1985.

Rosenberg, Mark B. and Philip L. Shepherd. *Honduras Confronts Its Future: Contending Perspectives on Critical Issues.* Boulder, CO: L. Rienner Publishers, 1986.[See especially part 4, chapters 11-14, on "Agricultural Policy and Prospects."]

Sharp, Gene. *The Politics of Nonviolent Action.* Three volumes in paperback: *Power and Struggle, The Methods of Nonviolent Action, The Dynamics of Nonviolent Action.* Boston: Extending Horizons Books, Porter Sargent Publishers, 1973.

Argentina

FIVE

Introduction

In the 1970s, a wave of political violence overtook Argentina in stunning dimensions. A 1976 coup by the armed forces set off a reign of terror that included the first large-scale use of disappearances in South America. The military junta, under the leadership of General Jorge Videla, defended the repression as a necessary response to a guerrilla insurgency. Yet the swath the military cut through society did not discriminate neatly. Anyone who did not publicly support the junta might become a victim of its "dirty war."

In 1983, civilian government returned to power and soon appointed a National Commission on Disappeared Persons (CONADEP) to investigate. CONADEP documented 8,961 cases, including 172 children under the age of thirteen; and it estimated that the actual number of "disappeared" was probably a third higher. Human rights groups give estimates as high as 30,000. No more than a few hundred were guerrillas. And under Argentine and international law even they had a right to due process.

The CONADEP report characterized the dictatorship's terrorism as "infinitely worse than that which they were combatting." CONADEP said the actions were "far beyond the merely criminal": they fell into the "category of crimes against humanity." More than mere "excesses" were at stake, said the report, for "atrocities were carried out as an everyday, commonplace part of the repression."

The military's rule tended profoundly to corrupt all aspects of Argentine life. It resulted in international isolation and economic crisis. In 1982 it helped bring on the unsuccessful Malvinas/Falklands war as a last-ditch attempt at diversion.

Nevertheless, this story focuses not on these factors but on another and most unexpected challenge to the regime: the witness of the relatives, mostly mothers, of the "disappeared." In 1977, fourteen mothers gathered in sheer desperation to defend the lives of their "disappeared" loved ones. From that inauspicious beginning, the Madres de Plaza de Mayo (Mothers of Plaza de Mayo), grew to 3,000

At a protest of the Madres de Plaza de Mayo in Argentina, the disappearance of three high school students is marked by a pile of their clothing and personal belongings. The signs note their names, their ages and the dates they were "disappeared." Photo by Alicia Sanguinetti.

members from around the country. More importantly, they became the conscience of the Argentine people in the moment of their greatest trial.

Argentina's Mothers of Courage
Philip McManus

At 4:30 in the afternoon . . . a woman in tears comes out of the Interior Ministry and rushes into Marta's arms. "I can't take it any more," she says. "When I told them that my two sons disappeared four months ago, they said that I should have worried about them sooner. If they were abducted, it's because they were subversives. That I should have paid more attention to who their friends were and what they were reading. And that I should be happy that the authorities don't hold me accountable for not educating my sons correctly. They are monsters, Marta. We have to do something. I'm going with you."

Marta, who carries her fifty years gracefully, gives me a resolute look. "What more can I say? You heard her. In half an hour, for the first time in my life, I am going to disobey the law. . . . At 5:00 P.M. we are going to demonstrate in front of the Presidential Palace so that General Videla will finally agree to deal with the situation of

In the absence of a full accounting and the punishment of those responsible for massive human rights violations, for years the Madres have demanded the return *alive* of their loved ones. Photo by Alicia Sanguinetti.

our 'disappeared' ones. This is why I insisted that you should come. We also asked other members of the international press. And Argentine journalists as well, although without any illusions. It is crucial that the whole world hear our anguish and help us. Alone we are nothing. . . . "

The women begin to walk toward the Plaza de Mayo in small groups as though they are out for a stroll. Demonstrating in front of the Presidential Palace, without a doubt the most tightly guarded place in Buenos Aires . . . ! When the clock strikes 5:00, they gather together unhurriedly. Then two-by-two they begin to walk slowly around the Pirámide de Mayo, the monument in the center of the plaza. Many of them are wearing white scarves on their heads and each of them is carrying a carpenter's nail. "This is to remember the sacrifice of Christ nailed to the cross," one of them explains. "We each have our own Christ too, and we relive the sorrow of Mary. But they don't even let us try to console him with our presence. We too are Christians, the same as those who proclaim themselves the servants of Christianity, and yet torment us so. . . . "

Many passersby do not even notice. Others stop a second and ask, then quickly leave, avoiding a touchy topic. Some exchange a few words: "Yes, me too, I know a friend, someone in the office whose son disappeared. . . . "

Less than three minutes after the silent march begins, two carloads of police pull up to the curb. "What are you doing here?" they ask. "Don't you know that demonstrations are illegal?"

"We aren't demonstrating. We simply came to witness to our grief. They have taken our children. We ask the government to tell us where they are, what has happened to them."

"You should talk to the appropriate authorities," the official insists. "But you can't disturb the public order. If you persist, I will be obliged to have my men disperse you."

In spite of their fear, the voices of the mothers rise. "Aren't you ashamed of attacking defenseless mothers? You want us to leave. We do too. Give us back our children. Tell us what has happened to them. Don't you have children? Wouldn't you do the same as we if your son had disappeared?"

Faced with this explosion the official withdraws. He goes to his car, and the mothers continue their march. At 5:30 they stop. "That's enough for today. We'll meet again next Thursday at the same time. Try to get others to come. Be careful going home. We'll call each other to make sure we all get home safely. . . . "

Wearing their distinctive white scarves, the Madres display both the grief and grit that kept them going. Photo by Alicia Sanguinetti.

Later I meet with Marta. . . . She is trembling. Her voice is agitated. Yet she seemed so serene and confident in front of the police. "You can't imagine how scared I was when I saw them arrive. I wanted to hole up, to flee, to hide myself in my mother's skirt, like when I was little. I had to think about Luis, my son who has disappeared. I had to imagine him near me, in order to confront them. This gave me a courage like indignation. But I'm still trembling.

"What do you think? Do you believe that they will talk about us, that this will change things? Next week we will be many more. There are many mothers who agree with the idea . . . but who didn't dare come. We aren't activists. It's a difficult step for us. But now that we have dared to do it, I'm sure that many more will follow us. They will have to do something. General Videla will have to meet with us."

—from Jean-Pierre Bousquet, *Las Locas de la Plaza de Mayo*
[The Madwomen of the Plaza de Mayo][1]

A coup unlike any other

Argentina in the mid-1970s was a badly divided country facing grave economic and social problems. Isabel Perón had succeeded her husband Juan Perón as president upon his death. But her ineffectual leadership made most Argentines ready for a change. Political violence took the form of numerous paramilitary groups, representing a spectrum of right-wing extremists, to political parties, to unions, to leftist revolutionaries. Overshadowing all of these were the armed forces, which had moved in and out of power in Argentina since 1930 and now waited in the wings as the Perón government stumbled along.

On March 24, 1976, the military struck. A bloodless coup installed a military junta and pledged to restore order and stability to Argentine society. The popular response was largely relief; someone would now bring the chaotic situation under control. The press generally welcomed the coup and the military's "laudable moderation in words and actions." Among initial measures were a ban on political activity, a freeze on trade union funds, and the dismissal of judges and provincial governors. Under the circumstances most people accepted these as temporary expedients.

Only gradually did it become apparent that this was a coup unlike any other in Argentina's history. After a month in power, the junta decreed: "It is forbidden to report, comment on, or make reference to . . . subversive incidents, the appearance of bodies, and the deaths of subversive elements and/or members of the armed and security forces, unless these are announced by a high official source. This includes kidnappings and disappearances." During that month more than 120 people disappeared. By the end of the year, the number was over 1,400 and the average was 15 per day.

In the name of democracy and the defense of "Western, Christian civilization" the regime censored movies, plays, television, radio, and the press. It burned books. It prohibited Freudian psychology. It eliminated sociology, philosophy, and psychology majors in the universities. Thousands of professors lost their jobs. Many others were murdered.

Previous ·dictatorships had limited themselves to beating back unwelcome challenges to their authority. This time the military set itself a different task: the *extermination* of all subversive elements. Ominously, junta leader General Videla defined a subversive as "anyone who opposes the Argentine way of life." Two months after the coup, General Ibérico Saint Jean, military governor of Buenos Aires, elaborated: "First we will kill all the subversives; then we will kill their collaborators; then . . . their sympathizers, then . . . those who remain indifferent; and finally we will kill the timid."[2]

The disappearances followed a familiar pattern. Heavily armed men in civilian clothes pulled up to a home in their trademark Ford Falcons, broke down the door and dragged their victim out. Sometimes they also took a spouse, a child or another relative. The captors then took their victims to a clandestine jail for torture. Consistently, they looted the house; sometimes they later sold it. Disappearances were good business.

Professor Alfredo Bravo, president of a teachers' union, is one who survived to describe his ordeal. "His teeth were broken by hammers, he was half-drowned several times in baths of water, he was tortured with an electrical cattle prod by other prisoners and forced to torture them in his turn. Finally he was crucified upside down." Estrella Iglesias, a 31-year-old factory worker, survived only because she happened to hold Spanish citizenship. Once at the jail, her captors beat, stripped, and tied her to a table. "They began to torture me with applications of electric current to my genitals, breasts, toenails, mouth, and gums; stretching my arms, mostly my right arm until they dislocated it; putting rats on my face and between my legs."[3]

For the families whose loved ones were suddenly gone, "to disappear" became a transitive verb. There was a subject—a military gone berserk. And there was an object—those taken without warning, without trial, without leaving a trace, lost in a nether world between life and death. To say, "my son who was disappeared" reflected the families' special pain. He didn't vanish due to some unfathomable tragedy. He wasn't simply murdered. It was something worse, more horrible, almost unspeakable.

Initially night was the time for the military to "disappear" people. But over time they began to strike in broad daylight. The closely monitored press generally ignored such incidents. *La Opinión*, a Buenos

Aires daily, was a rare exception until its editor, Jacobo Timerman, was himself imprisoned and brutally tortured.[4] Human rights groups such as the Permanent Assembly for Human Rights collected data but found little opportunity for effective action. An extremely conservative hierarchy dominated the Catholic Church, one of the most powerful social forces in Argentina; it tended to support rather than challenge the dictatorship.

Family members of the "disappeared" began to search. At police stations and military bases the answer was always the same: "Not here." In the courts, judges routinely denied petitions for writs of habeas corpus. The junta leaders refused to meet with them. So did Cardinal Aramburu, the ranking official of the Catholic Church.

For years after the coup the junta denied that disappearances actually took place at all. If people were missing, they must have been subversives who had gone underground, fled the country or been killed in clashes with the army. Because the government controlled information very tightly the public generally knew little of the problem's size. While it was impossible to know nothing of the military's repression it was safer to ignore it. Besides, "they must have been involved in *something*." For many Argentines para-military violence of both the left and the right was a shock and a threat. They apparently were willing to tolerate official repression and restrictions as the necessary price of order.

From brick walls, to the Plaza

As the relatives of the "disappeared" made their lonely rounds in search of loved ones, they began to recognize each other. They talked, shared information, commiserated. Faced with nothing but brick walls, they decided to act. Their pain was already tearing them apart. What more did they have to lose? Perhaps a public challenge to the regime would force a response to their unanswered pleas.

So on Saturday, April 30, 1977 fourteen mothers whose children had been "disappeared" gathered bravely in the Plaza de Mayo. Only after they got there did they realize that Saturday was not exactly the best day to impress the officials, most of whom were relaxing at home. Someone suggested Friday, but that seemed unlucky. So they settled on Thursday. The Plaza was busier that day anyway, they agreed.

The next week there were twenty. The week after that, thirty. Slowly their presence grew. By June their numbers had grown to one hundred. Frustrated by the courts' rejection of their petitions for individual habeas corpus, they filed a collective petition on behalf of 159 missing persons.

Frequently the police harassed them, sometimes forcing them out of the Plaza at gun point as soon as they arrived. Sometimes they arrested the women and held them overnight. Still the movement grew, including not just mothers but also wives, grandmothers, sisters, and daughters of the "disappeared." And they acquired a name: Las Madres de Plaza de Mayo. Now conscious of the need to go beyond individual searches, their protests became a demand on behalf of all of the "disappeared."

On October 5, the Madres de Plaza de Mayo published a paid advertisement in *La Prensa,* a major daily. In it they listed 237 "disappeared persons" and requested an explanation from the government as to their whereabouts. The mother of each one of the 237 signed. Because of the military's pressure on the press, this was the first time that their message reached a mass audience. The government gave no response.

Meanwhile, the Madres were doing their own outreach. They circulated a petition throughout the country that listed 571 "disappeared" persons and 61 others detained without charges. The petition demanded an investigation of the disappearances and due process guarantees for those detained. The Madres insisted that supporters sign the petitions clearly and give their national identification numbers. They felt that people should take a small risk in order to confront the terror that held the nation in its grip.

On October 15, eight hundred Madres demonstrated while a small delegation representing them and other human rights groups delivered the petition—with 24,000 signatures. Police response was quick and violent. They surrounded the demonstrators, assaulted them with tear gas, and fired their weapons in the air. They then herded two to three hundred of the frightened Madres, most of them older women, into commandeered city buses and took them to jail for the night. The next day they released them, but not before extracting a good deal of information and issuing stern warnings that if the women continued their protests the authorities would treat them too as "enemies."

Clearly, the dictatorship was worried—and frustrated. The Madres' campaign was a model of nonviolent, fearless confrontation. The military decided to make an example of them.

The Madres conducted their affairs openly, even meetings at which they discussed strategy. New people were always coming to volunteer their help. Toward the end of 1977, Gustavo Niño, "an intelligent and pleasant" young man in his mid-twenties, showed up and said his brother had disappeared.[5] He appealed to the maternal instincts of the Madres and became a particular favorite of Azucena De Vicenti, a founder and guiding light of the Madres. At the Plaza de Mayo the two often walked arm-in-arm. In fact, Niño was a Naval officer whose real name was Alfredo Astiz. He has since become famous as one of the most brutal torturers of the dictatorship. He is believed to be responsible for the disappearance of hundreds of persons.

On December 8, 1977 Niño attended a meeting of the Madres in the Santa Cruz Church. The group was putting final touches on a paid ad with the headline, "For a Christmas of Peace, All We Ask Is the Truth." As ᴜne participant recalls, Niño "left a little after 8:00 P.M. when we were just finishing up. . . . I remember that Niño was very disappointed that Azucena wasn't there."[6] Shortly thereafter, as the Madres were leaving, a group of armed men in civilian clothes assaulted them. Ford Falcons were parked in the street. The men took nine of the women along with money they had collected for the ad. Among them was a French nun, Sister Alicia Domont, a tireless supporter of the Madres.

Undoubtedly Niño had identified who was to be taken and what they were wearing. The fact that Azucena De Vincenti was not there proved only a temporary setback. Two days later, in spite of the public outcry that resulted, Azucena, a second French nun and another member of the group were kidnapped. All twelve remain "disappeared" today.

The ad ran anyway, albeit in a smaller and less expensive form. And the following Thursday, forty of the Madres defied the regime and returned to the Plaza.

For its part, the military issued a statement on December 16 blaming the disappearances on "nihilistic subversion." The very same day, family members of the "disappeared" held a press conference in the Plaza. Four foreign journalists came. So did a much larger number of security personnel. Disregarding friends' advice to be prudent, the relatives publicly accused the dictatorship of responsibility: "They are gangsters. They kidnap us in order to muzzle us, but it won't work. . . . We want our sons, our husbands, our fathers. We don't ask more than the simple truth. But here that is a crime."

As the police moved in to break them up the women appealed to the press: "Tell the world about our situation, the Calvary which we are suffering. Our cries must be heard. We appeal to the conscience of the world. We need help!"[7]

The next day the French news agency AFP received a note purportedly from the two French nuns, saying that guerrillas of a group known as the Montoneros had kidnapped them and listing a series of demands as conditions for their release. Enclosed was a photo of them in front of a Montonero banner. The note was clearly a fabrication, and international outcry continued unabated. Yet the military steadfastly denied responsibility. Years later, survivors of the military's secret jails testified that they had seen the nuns in captivity. Before killing them, say witnesses, their captors tortured them so badly they could not stand up.

Despite savage repression the Madres continued their courageous struggle, marching weekly in the Plaza until the police forcibly dispersed them. In addition, they often intercepted foreign dignitaries at the statue of the Argentine Liberator, San Martín. The monument was an obligatory stop for official visitors. There the Madres presented them with white scarves with the names of the "disappeared," and requested that they ask the government for an accounting.

On July 1, 1978 the Madres marked the inauguration of the World Cup soccer championship with their customary procession. The World Cup was to be a carefully crafted propaganda extravaganza to project a favorable image of Argentina during its moment in the international spotlight. Under the watchful eye of a greatly expanded international press corps the police did not dare to move against the women. But two days later at a press conference a government spokesperson exploded in a rage at the "old women" who were spoiling the sporting event. "These crazy women are liars. They say anything to damage Argentina. It's your fault too. If the international press ignored them, they would quit their demonstrations." Two weeks later, one of the Madres present at the July 1 march disappeared.[8]

On December 21 the Madres mounted their biggest demonstration, demanding a response from the government before the end of the year. Nearly two thousand people gathered in the Plaza de Mayo while a delegation went inside the Presidential Palace to deliver their latest petition. The only answer: a request to come back next week. As the police moved to disperse the crowd there were forty arrests. The following Thursday officials again put them off. After that, a large force of police and military sealed off the Plaza each Thursday afternoon. The principal plaza of Argentina was closed to the public.

Facing down Argentina's "final solution"

Banning of all political activity; widespread, sometimes random arrest, torture, and disappearance of citizens; even the disappearance of some whose only crime was seeking their "disappeared" loved ones—the repression of the military dictatorship was relentless and all-encompassing. In its scope and systemic brutality, it had little to do with traditional army power grabs. Rather, it reflected the application of a National Security Doctrine that defined security in narrowly military terms, identified its enemy as "international communism" in the form of "left-wing terrorism," and sought to organize all social and political life around a paranoid world view. The Argentine military believed World War III had already begun and that given the softness of western democracies and their squeamishness about human rights, they themselves were the first line of defense.

To be sure, the military did face a guerrilla movement. Since the late 1960s, two groups, the Montoneros and the People's Revolutionary Army (ERP), had been responsible for the deaths of perhaps two thousand persons, mostly military or police personnel. Other victims included businessmen, the families of military officers, and some innocent bystanders. The guerrillas clearly shared responsibility for the climate of violence and lawlessness from which the coup and the dirty war emerged.

But by the end of 1976 military clashes with the guerrillas had virtually ceased. And in any case the military had cast a much wider net from the start. The military never touched the right-wing paramilitary groups who shared responsibility for the rising tide of violence. In contrast, an Air Force Academy pamphlet of the time depicts a "tree of subversion" linking everyone from the Montoneros to the hippies to the Lions Club in a de facto subversive Marxist conspiracy. All of this might be comical were its consequences not so real and so tragic.

The regime targeted lawyers, journalists, psychologists, and church activists for disappearance. Nearly one-third of the victims were workers or union organizers. Simply being young was cause for presumption of guilt. In the end, according to Jacobo Timerman, "the government of the armed forces eliminated thousands of individuals in Argentina who had no relation with subversion, but who (according to the military) formed part of, or represented, that world which they found intolerable and incomprehensible, and who hence constituted the enemy."[9]

The military tended to be anti-Semitic. In the secret jails the tormentors singled out Jews for especially harsh torture. Swastikas or photos of Hitler hung in some of the interrogation centers. Prisoners reported that their torturers had played tapes of Hitler's speeches or Nazi military marches as they went about their grim work. Indeed, the influence of Nazi ideology was no secret. During the dictatorship titles such as *The SS in Action, Maybe Hitler Was Right,* and *The Protocols of the Elders of Zion* sprang up in bookstores.

To the totalitarian mentality of the military the solution of choice was physical elimination, for it left no trace. Large scale disappearances were an alternative to the weaknesses the military had perceived in other strategies of repression. In Chile following General Pinochet's 1973 coup the undisguised murder of thousands of people had resulted in international isolation. In Argentina an earlier mass imprisonment gave way to an amnesty that contributed to the ranks of the guerrillas. This time all would be clean, quiet, and deadly efficient. Instead of martyrs only question marks would remain.

The thought and tactics of the dictatorship reflected a disturbing influence from the United States. Throughout the 1960s, in the aftermath of the Cuban revolution, the United States had promoted the Alliance for Progress which combined economic aid with counterinsurgency training for Latin American military forces. In 1963 Secretary of Defense Robert McNamara defined the focus of U.S. policy: "Our fundamental objective in Latin America is to help where necessary with the continuing development of the local military and paramilitary forces so that, in conjunction with the police and other security forces, they will be able to guarantee the necessary internal security."[10]

Since the 1960s the U.S. government had systematically expounded the National Security Doctrine through its School of the Americas training center for foreign military, then in Panama. Besides encouraging the authoritarian, conservative attitudes of their students, the U.S. instructors taught counterinsurgency tactics, including the methods and theory of torture. By the time of the 1976 coup, 600 Argentine officers had graduated from the school and had begun putting their lessons to work. Top military officials told one visiting U.S. human rights activist that "many persons in military custody were thrown out of helicopters into rivers and lakes, a tactic learned, they claimed, from the American experience in Vietnam."[11]

Clever, not crazy

While the repression raged on, important sectors of the society played along. Most newspapers continued to support the military, despite the disappearance of nearly 150 journalists. There is evidence that forty-one doctors were accomplices to the repression. Officially the Catholic Church condemned torture and incommunicado detention; twenty-one priests and religious, including two bishops, were "disappeared" or murdered. But the Church hierarchy had long maintained a close alliance with the military. Hence some priests and even bishops blessed the torturers, visited the secret jails, encouraged the prisoners to talk, and in some cases, attended torture sessions and executions. Archbishop Plaza referred to the Madres as "mothers of guerrillas" and declared that "there are no innocent victims in Argentina." Cardinal Aramburu called the Madres' behavior "anti-evangelical." On one occasion the police raided the cathedral at Aramburu's request in order to evict the Madres when they were beginning a hunger strike.[12]

In this climate, with fear and the explosion of violence from the right and the left numbing the public, the Madres sought to defend human dignity and struggle against the insanity that threatened to engulf them. Ironically this earned them the nickname "las locas de Plaza de Mayo"—the madwomen of Plaza de Mayo. In a sense it was crazy to confront the brutal dictatorship publicly. But the regime employed the term "madwomen" in a more insulting manner. One spokesperson claimed, for example, that "out of more than two hundred mothers, only twenty-five are legitimate. The rest are crazy. They're madwomen who don't even have children." As one Madre recalls, the *Buenos Aires Herald* picked up on the term but "transformed it into an expression with the almost tragic sense of a Greek chorus; 'the ones who have been made crazy by grief in the search for their "disappeared" children amidst the terror which rules Argentina.' "[13]

In practice, the Madres proved that they were much more clever than crazy. They employed a wide variety of creative nonviolent tactics to strengthen themselves internally and increase their impact. They supplemented their weekly marches, which gave them a voice in a land of official silence, with vigils, petition gathering, paid ads, prayer services, fasting, fund-raising for the needy among the families of the "disappeared," outreach throughout the country, foreign speaking tours, and meetings with visiting dignitaries. The Madres' foray into the international arena reflected the regime's vulnerability, given Argentine dependence on foreign aid and trade. International activism—monitoring, demonstrations of support, and fund-raising efforts of human rights groups and solidarity groups in Europe, Canada, the United States and elsewhere—was a continual thorn in the dictatorship's side. Some Madres believe they owe their lives to such international support.

In addition, U.S. President Jimmy Carter had made human rights a cornerstone of his administration's foreign policy.[14] Argentina was its test case, and the Carter administration passed the test with high marks. Madre Treasurer Juanita Pargament recalls, "We went nearly every day to the U.S. Embassy. The doors were open for us. . . . We had good meetings. They would tell us when officials were coming from abroad. . . . They even provided escorts for us after the kidnappings at the Santa Cruz Church."[15] In fact, Embassy personnel met with thousands who came to denounce human rights violations, compiling and analyzing statistics. The State Department severely criticized the dictatorship before Congress.

Shortly after Carter took office the U.S. government cut military aid to Argentina by forty percent. The following year it blocked a $270 million loan. In mid-1978 Vice President Walter Mondale met with General Videla and secured an agreement: Argentina would allow an Organization of American States (OAS) human rights delegation to visit; in exchange the United States would not press for a lower credit rating for Argentina in upcoming loan negotiations. Reportedly, the agreement was a turning point for the regime. Hoping for a favorable OAS report, Videla used the upcoming visit to pressure hard-liners; disappearances began to taper off.[16]

However since the regime's real concern was restoring its international image, less drastic measures against the Madres actually increased in order to keep them off the streets and away from journalists' cameras. When the OAS Commission on Human Rights finally arrived in September 1979, the military felt that it had the situation under control. The violent chaos of recent years had subsided. Even the "madwomen" had not been able to demonstrate all year.

But while the Madres had been quiet, they had not been quiescent. All year they had met secretly, mostly in one church. One Madre recalls, "In the middle of praying the rosary, María Adela would stand up and say, 'Well ladies, now we are going to do such and such' and then we would go on praying. In that way we kept ourselves informed, with great caution, because the repression was very strong."[17] In the weeks prior to the arrival of the OAS Commission, the Madres had been carefully preparing for its visit. The morning the Commission began to take testimony, a line of two thousand people extended for blocks outside the OAS office.

The national press gave prominent coverage to the Commission's visit—the first time major papers had acknowledged gross human rights violations in Argentina. The Madres took advantage of the opening to organize a demonstration in the Plaza de Mayo. The military countered with a clumsy attempt to link the Madres to the Montoneros by planting leaflet bombs in the Plaza. The Commission publicly denounced the maneuver.

After three weeks the Commission finished its investigation and returned home. But their findings had left the Madres with a deep and bitter ambivalence. For the first time, they had told their story fully and comprehensively. The Commission had talked to everybody, visited the secret jails, inspected the cemeteries. Yet none of the "disappeared" had appeared. "Is it possible," asked one of the Madres, "that men, who on top of everything call themselves Christian, have massacred so many people that they had at their mercy?"[18]

When published, the 266-page OAS Commission report listed details of dozens of cases and held the Argentine government responsible for massive human rights violations. Given the Commission's prestige the military could no longer deny the obvious. Instead the government defended the necessity of the dirty war and proclaimed its triumph to an increasingly unconvinced domestic and international public. As for possible international sanctions, Argentina's rulers asserted defiantly that "the Nuremberg Tribunals were only for the defeated."

During 1979 the Madres had only demonstrated twice in the Plaza de Mayo: when the OAS Commission visited and again just before Christmas. At the end of that most difficult year they decided that they would renew their weekly march, no matter what the cost. On

January 3 they did so, and their numbers caught the military off guard. So they paraded without incident, wearing their white scarves and carrying photographs of their loved ones.

The next week the police were out in force; but the tide had turned and the Madres marched on. They continued to face arrests and beatings, but never again did they give up their right to the Plaza they had claimed as their own. Soon other groups were also protesting frequently. By mid-1981 a general strike attracted the support of one million people. The military's power was waning.

The conscience of their people

The military regime managed to hang on until 1983, when the nation elected Raúl Alfonsín of the Radical Party to be president. It is difficult to know how much the Madres hastened the regime's demise. Economic crisis and the 1982 Malvinas/Falklands war with Great Britain surely contributed more to their departure than did exposure of human rights violations.

Yet it is clear that in the very spot where the dictatorship had successfully excluded every political party, labor union, and human rights group, the Madres had carved out a political space. They belied the military's belief that enough terror would silence everyone. From them others found the courage to do what the Madres had proven possible. The Madres challenged the Argentine people to deal with their plight rather than simply to look away.

Some criticized the Madres as too excitable, too confrontational, too shrill, and their judgments as too quick and ill-considered. Even with the civilian administration of President Alfonsín, the relationship between the government and the Madres degenerated into a kind of name calling. Under a great deal of pressure from the military Alfonsín made a calculated choice to prosecute former junta members but exonerate virtually all others. His Radical-dominated Congress in turn passed the corresponding legislation. For this Alfonsín drew strenuous criticism from many quarters, including human rights groups. However, this hardly made his government the dictatorship that Madres President Hebe Bonafini alleged it was.[19]

The fact was, the Madres were not schooled in the niceties or the wiles of politics; their experience with a most brutal government hardly encouraged them to learn or trust the precarious art of compromise. The Madres spoke and acted from their hearts. What is remarkable is that their hearts grew to include not only their own children, but all of the "disappeared." "I am doing this work to recover all our children," said Hebe Bonafini in a 1981 interview. "I do not know if I can still recover mine, but I know that there are many others who expect a lot from us."[20]

In fact, the Madres' hearts began to beat with the cause to which many of their children had dedicated themselves. The vast majority of the victims of the military's paranoia had no ties with the guerrillas. Many were not involved in politics at all. Yet most vulnerable to repression were those working peacefully and openly for social change. "Our sons and daughters," said Madres Treasurer Juanita Pargament, *were* "fighters, unselfish fighters, who gave the best that they had, their lives and their bodies." They had "fought" in ways that most democracies would take for granted or even applaud. "They didn't want anything for themselves. They went to the poor neighborhoods, to the churches. They taught literacy. They treated the sick, giving them medicines. This was their mission. They wanted a better country. This is why they were taken."[21] And it is also why the Madres' own vision has grown. Far from simply terrorizing them, the disappearance of their children radicalized and emboldened many parents who earlier had not shared their children's political views. "It is as if lions grew inside of me, and I am not afraid . . . ," said Hebe Bonafini.[22] In the newspaper they published, the Madres recalled their process of *concientización:*

> We had always been at home, busy only with the family. . . . When we went to look for our children we found a new world where everything was rotten. . . . We learned to put aside our self-centeredness, always being concerned with ourselves and with our families. . . . Now we began to really understand many things which our sons and daughters had told us and which, in those times, we did not want to accept and we could not imagine. The "disappeared" represented everyone and the struggle had to be everyone's struggle.[23]

The Madres paid dearly for their efforts. In addition to frequent detentions and beatings, many lost their jobs. Sometimes they were ridiculed. Former friends sometimes shunned them or more often were simply indifferent. The Argentine press ignored the women. The Plaza was closed to them for a year. Some of them were "disappeared." Others lost additional children to the repression. Above all they could never escape their inconsolable pain. As they described that pain in a 1980 statement, "Nothing can do more human harm than the pain of such long years of uncertainty—of simply not knowing. The passing days with their alternations of feeble, fading hope and hopeless depression cause a grave deterioration of spirit and body."[24]

Yet through it all they seemed to grow stronger and more tenacious—precisely because they united in action. Nora Cortinas explains, "Although I didn't realize it at the time, it was partly therapy, a way of dealing with so much pain. The Plaza is a reunion with our children. There is a spiritual and mental reinforcement." Emphasizing their politicization, former Madres Vice President Adela Antokoletz observes, "We decided to take to the streets; it was the streets that taught us. That was what gave us our political strength."[25]

In 1987, Juanita Pargament pointed to the fruit of their relentless persistence: "In the Plaza today, you heard when the people were shouting, 'The Plaza belongs to the Madres/And not to the *cobardes*' [cowards, i.e., the military]. The people chant this slogan because in reality we were out there by ourselves. . . . We protested for everybody, but we were by ourselves."[26] And it is true: The military has vacated the President's office; the Madres remain in the Plaza now identified so firmly with them.

Adolfo Pérez Esquivel, the 1980 Nobel Peace Laureate, was himself a victim of the dictatorship's prisons and torture centers. Speaking of the Madres, whom he served as adviser, he has said, "I always preferred to call them the Mothers of Courage since, in the face of the strong repression they suffered . . . they remained firm; weeping, but firm." Friar Antonio Puigjané, a Franciscan priest who accompanied the Madres in their struggle, believes that "they taught us the humble but sure and invincible path of popular struggle. An immense love in their hearts, a white scarf on their heads, and their feet determined never to stop. They are the terror of the murdering military! . . . " The impact of their resolute witness, said Puigjané, was nothing less than to have "spearheaded the struggle against the dictatorship. . . . They were always the most lucid and brave, the ones who wouldn't give an inch. . . . "[27]

Years after the military gave up the Presidential Palace, the Madres continue their relentless campaign. They have not slowed their invariably high level of activity. Since 1979, first the military and now the civilian government have tried to convince the Madres to acknowledge the death of their loved ones. Officials have offered death certificates, exhumation of mass graves, economic reparation, and even monuments. The Madres have steadfastly refused and have continued to campaign for their initial demand: "We want them back alive." If they are dead, reason the Madres, someone killed them and someone must be held accountable. True reconciliation must rest on justice.

The Madres continue to denounce human rights violations. They have also joined efforts such as opposition to austerity measures that hit the poor hardest, support for the labor movement in Argentina, and solidarity with Central America. But, as one Madre explains, there is always one central passion:

> Like all the mothers, I came to demonstrate to defend the life of my son. Today I can see further ahead. I don't want another mother, in this country or in any other, to have to live through what I have. Beyond my personal case is the basic principle of the systematic use of repression and state terrorism as a method of government which I must denounce and combat.[28]

Juanita Pargament elaborated: "We realize now that we will not get our children back. But we have a commitment: the other generations, the generations of children, of young people, of students who have a right to live in freedom, to dissent without being kidnapped, tortured, killed. This is why we are going to continue . . . to defend their name."[29]

Perhaps these statements provide the clue to the real legacy of the Madres: simple truths, stated in measured tones, carrying great moral authority. The Madres pricked the conscience of many in Argentina and abroad. They *became* the conscience of their people. And in so doing, they saved many from degradation and despair. They lit a candle in honor of human dignity and protected it with their lives.

For most of the Madres the first exposure to Gandhi was when the movie version of his life washed ashore, years after their worst trials. Yet in the best Gandhian tradition they had relentlessly proclaimed a simple but enormously powerful truth, holding fast to that truth against all adversity.

A group of the Madres de Plaza de Mayo is comforted by Mons. Jaime de Nevares, one of only four Argentine Roman Catholic bishops who clearly condemned the human rights violations of the Argentine military dictatorship. Photo by Alicia Sanguinetti.

And they still have not let go. The Madres themselves are still the targets of surveillance, telephone threats, burglaries, and other forms of harassment. Argentina is still struggling to free itself from vestiges of the dictatorship's social corruption. If it succeeds, Argentina will owe an enormous debt to these Mothers of Courage. Asked to look back and explain the significance of their struggle, Juanita Pargament replies, "To have learned that when a moral witness uplifts a country, truly it is a great merit. And our movement has achieved respect here and abroad precisely for this."[30]

Notes

1. Jean-Pierre Bousquet, *Las Locas de la Plaza de Mayo* (Buenos Aires: El Cid, 1984), pp. 45-49.
2. Quoted in John Simpson and Jana Bennett, *The Disappeared and the Mothers of the Plaza* (New York: St. Martin's Press, 1985), pp. 66 and 76.
3. Bravo account is from Simpson and Bennett, *The Disappeared*, p. 19; Iglesias account is from Paul Heath Hoeffel and Juan Montalvo, "Missing or Dead in Argentina," *New York Times Magazine*, October 21, 1979, pp. 5-6.
4. The *Buenos Aires Herald* was the most forthright in reporting on the situation. However, it was an English-language publication with a small circulation.
5. Simpson and Bennett, *The Disappeared*, p. 161.
6. Bousquet, p. 74.
7. Bousquet, p. 81.
8. Bousquet, p. 104.
9. Jacobo Timerman, *Prisoner Without a Name, Cell Without a Number* (New York: Vintage Books, 1981), p. 96. Timerman's book is a chilling analysis of contemporary totalitarianism, which, he observes, cannot explain what it seeks to build but sees with deadly clarity what it wishes to annihilate. To illustrate he quotes a military official, and goes on to comment: " 'Argentina has three main enemies: Karl Marx, because he tried to destroy the Christian concept of society; Sigmund Freud, because he tried to destroy the Christian concept of family; and Albert Einstein, because he tried to destroy the Christian concept of time and space.' For any moderately civilized individual, this statement reveals a clear desire to revert to the society of the Middle Ages. It is a form of rejection of modern society, and of attempts to understand the contradictions of the contemporary age. For a totalitarian mind, there are no existing contradictions to justify a pluralist, tolerant society. Nothing exists but enemies or friends.
   "For a Jew, the description put forth by a military ideologue as to the nature of Argentina's main enemies is like the appearance of an ancient ghost, since the figures chosen to illustrate the enemy are three Jews. . . . " (p. 130.)
10. Servicio Paz y Justicia. *La Represión en la Argentina*. Pamphlet. (Buenos Aires, n.d.).
11. Paul Heath Hoeffel and Juan Montalvo, "Missing or Dead in Argentina," *New York Times Magazine*, October 21, 1979, p. 5.
Perhaps the most troubling contribution of the United States to the Argentine experience of totalitarianism was the example of its ultimate weapon against totalitarianism: the atomic bomb. The bomb was developed in a perceived race with the Germans, dropped on the Japanese, and utilized as a graphic warning to the Soviets. Its lessons, writ not in a book but on the stage of history, are in the eye of the beholder. In a speech to retired military officers in 1987, Brigadier Major (Ret.) Federico Alsogaray defended the dirty war by reference to the use of the atomic bomb. "The human rights violated in Nagasaki and Hiroshima saved the human rights of the West." Indeed, if the killing of hundreds of thousands of civilians is an acceptable

cost in the name of "democracy" or "freedom," there is a certain irony in criticizing the killing of 10-20,000 in supposed defense of the same values. However, it is inevitable that in such a world, democracy and freedom will increasingly come to be viewed as luxuries. See "Militares retirados exaltan la lucha contra la subversión," in the Argentine daily *Clarín*, July 7, 1987, p. 12.

12. The best source of documentation on the role of the Catholic Church under the military dictatorship is Emilio F. Mignone, *Church and Dictatorship* (Maryknoll, N.Y.: Orbis Books, 1988).

13. Quote of government spokesman from Hoeffel and Montalvo, p. 7; *Buenos Aires Herald* quote from *Boletín Informativo de la Asociación Latinoamericana para los Derechos Humanos*, "Un desaparecido fluctua entre la realidad de la vida y la irrealidad de la muerte," January 1982, p. 21.

14. The Carter Administration's treatment of the Argentine junta stood in stark contrast to that of its predecessor. On June 10, 1976, then-Secretary of State Henry Kissinger met with the junta's Foreign Minister, Admiral César Guzzetti. The U.S. Ambassador to Argentina, Robert Hill, had urged Kissinger to press the junta on the escalating violations of human rights. Instead, Kissinger simply told Guzzetti that Argentina should "clean up the problem" before the new U.S. Congress convened in January 1977. As Ambassador Hill saw it, according to a State Department memorandum, "Kissinger gave the Argentines the green light." See Martin Edwin Anderson, "Kissinger and the 'Dirty War'," *The Nation*, October 31, 1987, pp. 477-80.

15. Interview with Juanita Pargament, by author, Buenos Aires, July 1987.

16. Concerning loan cutoff, see Simpson and Bennett, p. 272. Upon assuming office in 1981, the Reagan administration quickly substituted terrorism for human rights as its central foreign policy concern. Yet the state terrorism of its chosen allies was pointedly ignored. In the case of Argentina the administration easily accommodated itself to what one official described as the "more robust approach" to internal security of the dictatorship. See Simpson and Bennett, p. 314.

17. Interview with Hebe Bonafini and María Adela Antokoletz, by César Chelala, M.D., New York, July 1981. Unpublished.

18. Bousquet, p. 161.

19. Kevin Noblet, "Argentine Mothers' Undying Memories," *Sacramento Bee*, November 30, 1986, p. D5.

20. Interview with Bonafini and Antokoletz.

21. Interview with Pargament.

22. Interview with Pargament; interview with Bonafini and Antokoletz.

23. *Madres de Plaza de Mayo* (monthly newspaper) No. 3, p. 15.

24. Adolfo Pérez Esquivel, *Christ in a Poncho* (Maryknoll: Orbis, 1983), p. 44.

25. Cortinas quote from Noblet, p. D5; Antokoletz quote from Simpson and Bennett, p. 169.

26. Interview with Pargament.

27. Pérez Esquivel quote from Bousquet, pp. 11-12; Antonio Puigjané, quote from an unpublished, undated letter.

28. Bousquet, p. 182.

29. Interview with Pargament.

30. Interview with Pargament.

For further reading

Bousquet, Jean-Pierre. *Las Locas de la Plaza de Mayo*. Buenos Aires: El Cid, 1984.

Hoeffel, Paul Heath and Montalvo, Juan. "Missing or Dead in Argentina," *New York Times Magazine*, October 21, 1979.

Mignone, Emilio F. *Church and Dictatorship*. Maryknoll, N.Y.: Orbis Books, 1988.

Pérez Esquivel, Adolfo. *Christ in a Poncho*. Maryknoll, N.Y.: Orbis, 1983.

Simpson, John and Bennett, Jana. *The Disappeared and the Mothers of the Plaza.* New
    York: St. Martin's Press, 1985.
Timerman, Jacobo. *Prisoner Without a Name, Cell Without a Number.* New York: Vintage
    Books, 1981.

Uruguay

SIX

Introduction

Uruguay is a small country of three million people in the Southern Cone of South America. Its population is highly literate and largely urban. In the 1970s it was one of a number of Latin American countries that fell victim to military dictatorships grounded in the repressive, quasi-fascist National Security Doctrine.

For several years after a 1973 coup d'etat, no one challenged the military. This was largely due to the repressive nature of the regime, which some analysts regard as the most totalitarian in the recent history of Latin America. Censorship was widespread, the regime had categorized the entire population according to its perception of each citizen's politics, and at one time or another the strong arm of the military swept up one out of every fifty Uruguayans.

Under such conditions, developing organized opposition was no small feat. When a small human rights group formed, it was taking a bold step. Yet it was hardly a serious threat, at least not at first. This chapter is the story of how that small group became a powerful force for change. It is also the story of the resilience of the human spirit, the reawakening of long dormant hope. In the Uruguayan people, that newly animated spirit burst forth precisely at one of Uruguay's darkest hours.

Finally, this chapter is the story of what active nonviolence may mean in the aftermath of a dictatorship. Human rights groups and other movements for social change in Latin America have sometimes found themselves struggling to redefine their roles in post-dictatorship eras. For a long, dangerous, and intense period they have had little choice but to define themselves mainly by what they are against.

In the new era their situation is more nebulous. Though the military, which once united a people in opposition, is now off center stage, it is not out of the picture. Furthermore, democracy may return in its formal trappings, but remain limited because some are more equal than others. The new task is to insist on a full range of human rights, including not only due process of law and freedom of speech or assembly, but also employment, shelter, and health care. And the ongoing task is to remind society that the best way to protect human rights is for all citizens to recognize and make a commitment to those rights. After all, it is the people, not the government, who must ultimately protect those rights.

Police arrest a demonstrator during a protest demanding freedom for political prisoners and the return alive of the disappeared. Photo by Cyro Giambruno, courtesy of Servicio Paz y Justicia/Uruguay.

Nonviolent Resistance and the Pedagogy of Human Rights
Katherine Roberts

For fifteen days Father Luis Pérez Aguirre and two friends had been fasting. Theirs was a simple act of prayer and reflection, but it had prompted a frenzied response from the government. The military dictatorship that ruled Uruguay had blockaded the site of the fast, the modest office of Servicio Paz y Justicia (Service for Peace and Justice), and was holding its own kind of round-the-clock vigil. Lights, water, and telephone were cut. The building was sealed off. The government censored any mention in the media of the action by the priest and his friends.

Yet word of their fast had spread like wildfire through the capital city of Montevideo and beyond. At noon each day and again each evening, hundreds of people had gathered for a vigil in front of the office, staying until the police drove them away.

Now it was the last day of the fast, August 25, 1983. To conclude their action the fasters had called for an hour of national reflection from 7:00 to 8:00 P.M. They had asked all Uruguayans to reflect on their personal responsibility in the face of the violence and repression throughout the country. People were asked to turn off their lights as a silent protest. Pérez Aguirre remembers the moment:

> At 8:00 P.M. the entire city went dark. Everything was silent. It was like a desert; a very impressive experience. Then at 8:15 the *caceroleada* [banging of pots and pans in protest] began. Soon everyone was doing it. We were still cut off by the police. But we could look out the window. When we began to hear the noise, it was very moving because it was spontaneous on the part of the people after their reflection. You can't imagine! A city of one and a half million people, everyone banging their pots. It was incredible. 8:15 P.M. on August 25, 1983. I'll never forget it.
>
> And the military men were in their trucks, shining their lights up on the houses, which were still dark, shining them all around. But they couldn't arrest anyone. We saw it from the window. They wanted to do something, to identify someone, but there was nothing they could do. . . .[1]

The regime

From 1973 to 1985, the people of Uruguay endured one of the most repressive dictatorships in Latin America. Numerous organizations mobilized against military rule during the final years of the dictatorship. These included women's groups, families of political prisoners and the "disappeared," housing advocates, unions, cultural organizations, and political parties. One such group, the Service for Peace and Justice (SERPAJ), grew from a small number of activists to become a national human rights movement.[2] Founded in the early 1980s in a bold challenge to the military, SERPAJ/Uruguay came to symbolize Uruguayan society's conscience in its demands for an end to violence and a return to democracy.

Uruguay was once known as the Switzerland of South America. Its population is largely European in origin, and it had enjoyed a century of political stability with social and economic reform, a large middle class, and an influential organized labor movement. Because European immigrants escaping both political and religious authoritarianism heavily influenced its history, Uruguay is a highly secularized society.

The foundations of Uruguay's political stability rested upon an export economy of beef and wool, which prospered until the mid-1950s. At that time, the economy nearly collapsed as prices for its agro-exports fell dramatically on the world market. Subsequent state economic policies failed to check what was for most Uruguayans a declining standard of living. By the late 1960s the result was social unrest, economic stagnation, and political instability. These conditions led in turn to growing social mobilization, strikes in all economic sectors, and, beginning in the early 1960s, the first urban guerrilla movement in Uruguay's history.

Uruguay's traditional institutions proved incapable of confronting the country's mounting political, economic, and social crises. So the military began intervening in government and eventually took over the state in a June 1973 coup d'etat. Under the pretext of combatting the guerrilla movement, which the armed forces had in fact summarily dismantled even before the takeover, the military asserted its role as absolute authority.

Until 1985, Uruguay suffered a repressive military rule similar to those that swept Argentina, Brazil, and Chile in the 1960s and 70s. The ideological base for these regimes was the U.S.-exported National Security Doctrine. The doctrine essentially defined popular demands for social, economic, and political reform as externally controlled communist subversion. The armed forces virtually declared war on their own populations in the name of "national security."

The violence and the capacity of the armed forces to penetrate and repress all sectors of society instilled deep fear among Uruguayan citizens. By the mid-1970s, the country had the highest number of political prisoners per capita in the world. Estimates suggest that military repression in the form of arrest, detention or torture directly affected one out of every fifty Uruguayans.[3] From a country of just under three million people, well over 200,000 fled into exile.[4]

More than 150 Uruguayans disappeared both inside and outside the country, including pregnant women and ten children. The collaboration among the military regimes of Argentina, Brazil, Chile, Paraguay, and Uruguay in their effort to root out "subversives" is startling: more than three-quarters of the missing Uruguayans disappeared in Argentina with the active complicity of the Argentine military. The case of former Uruguayan political prisoner Sara Méndez is a good example:

> My child's name is Simón Antonio Riguelo. He was born June 22, 1976 in Buenos Aires. When Simón was born there were already disappearances of Uruguayans in Argentina . . . twelve had disappeared. In addition to the twelve, another six had appeared dead; Gutiérrez Ruíz [former Congressional representative] and Zelmar Michelini [former head of the Uruguayan Senate] were the most representative figures.
>
> I was arrested when Simón was twenty days old. The armed forces, dressed in civilian clothing, arrested me and took me to a secret jail. Simón remained with them; they would not let me take him or leave him with a neighbor.
>
> During the thirteen days I was detained in Argentina I had no news of my child. Nor was I informed of him during my detention in Uruguay after being moved to a jail there. I was in Punta de Rieles [women's prison] for four and a half years.
>
> When my family was finally able to visit me in prison, I realized they did not have my child. . . .
>
> The steps I could take in my search from prison were of course few and futile, due to the isolating conditions of being a prisoner, being impeded from all communication. . . .
>
> My family began the search from the beginning. At first they had looked for me and my child . . . later they continued actions for him here and in Argentina, without results. . . .
>
> Upon my release I took charge of the search. Possible avenues for the search are few. . . . [5]

The most penetrating tool of the dictatorship's repression was its systematic categorization of all Uruguayan citizens. Because of the country's small population, half of which is concentrated in the capital city of Montevideo, the military handily registered, documented, and placed every Uruguayan into category A, B or C, according to the junta's definition of the individual's level of subversiveness. Officials considered an individual in category A among the least suspect of citizens; category B was a borderline category; and an individual in category C was supposedly a subversive. One's category often depended upon an arbitrary decision. The military placed Uruguayans in the subversive category who might have signed a petition in the 1960s calling for normalization of relations with Cuba or who had appeared at one of a number of political rallies. This then restricted their capacity to find a job, travel outside or even inside the country, or carry out any public transactions that required personal identification. Thousands of Uruguayans lost their jobs, particularly in the public sector, the country's largest employer.

The dictatorship practiced some of the harshest controls of the press and media in Latin America.[6] It closed twenty-eight newspapers and magazines, spanning most shades of the political spectrum and including church publications. It frequently arrested, tortured, and exiled editors or other journalists.

The regime also strictly curtailed freedom of assembly, defining "assembly" as a gathering of two or more persons. Virtually every social activity required government permission:

> Public events, assemblies (of social, cultural, professional, sports, and cooperative institutions, businesses, mutual medical aid societies, etc., even in certain cases religious organizations when they go beyond the mere exercise of worship on their own premises), elections, benefits, conferences, cultural, and artistic events, tributes (to living or dead persons, to be held on sites or at cemeteries, monuments, etc.), processions, including sports parades, scientific, technical, and other congresses. . . .[7]

In November 1980, in keeping with a timetable the military had set, the government held a plebiscite to vote upon a draft constitution and a one-candidate presidential election for the following year. It was a constitution designed to maintain military authority over future governments in areas of "national security," broadly defined. The military launched a major media campaign to convince Uruguayans to vote "Yes" on the new constitution. Ads stated that to vote "No" would mean support for "terrorists, Marxists, and all those who do not love their country. . . ."[8] The country had one month to study the plebiscite, and the military granted limited public debate while it simultaneously arrested political leaders who urged a "No" vote.

Despite the military campaign, Uruguayans chose to vote "No" by a margin of fifty-seven to forty-three percent, with an eighty-seven percent turnout.[9] Behind the closed doors of homes throughout the country, Uruguayans rejoiced. For the first time in eight years, the people of Uruguay could share in a knowledge of their collective wish for a return to true political democracy. As one Uruguayan described it, "The repression, the fear, and the self-censorship had been so strong over the years that the people didn't talk among themselves, and it was very common to have companions at work or at school and not know what they thought, whether they were with the military or not.

It was like temporarily opening the floodgates."[10] There are numerous accounts of tears of gladness among friends, smiles exchanged among strangers on a bus, and winks at one another as word of the plebiscite's outcome spread by word of mouth.

While its defeat clearly stunned the dictatorship, the military junta violently renewed its crackdown on all political activity. The government set a new agenda of gradual negotiations between the military and a limited number of political leaders. Political prisoners remained in jail under horrendous conditions; censorship of the press concerning politics and human rights continued; and Uruguayans retained their A, B, and C categories. From 1973 to 1983, no one in the country publicly printed a single word on the torture daily taking place in Uruguayan prisons or on the fact that Uruguayans had disappeared.

The tiny band

It was in this context that in 1981, on a farm for abandoned children outside of Montevideo, Jesuit priest Luis Pérez Aguirre and a small Christian-based group formed SER-PAJ, the first human rights group in the country.

Throughout the years of the dictatorship, Pérez Aguirre had repeatedly demonstrated his courage and capacity to influence various sectors of Uruguayan society through his writings and his work with young people. Pérez Aguirre's La Huella, an orphan community he founded during the dictatorship, had come to be known as an alternative model of human relations. It starkly contrasted with the kinds of

Father Luiz Pérez Aguirre, SERPAJ/ Uruguay. Photo courtesy of Servicio Paz y Justicia/Uruguay.

human interaction that the National Security ideology condoned. La Huella favored the weak and abandoned, established communal property, combined manual work with technical and intellectual activities, and divided work roles according to the talents of each community member rather than according to an imposed structural hierarchy. As a community, La Huella committed itself to active nonviolence. As such, it reflected the belief of Pérez Aguirre and the founders of SERPAJ that people must come together to challenge the violence inherent in today's society.

"When our society is structurally rooted in economic, political, and cultural inequality," wrote Pérez Aguirre, "when it operates based on competition among ourselves and exploitation of some by others, when the dissatisfaction and frustration of the majority is considered a mere demand of the market, when what is 'normal' is economic crime, the abuse of power by officials . . . , when we pretend to preserve peace while preparing ourselves for war, when we live without time to think about what we do, to communicate, to love . . . then living among one another is based on an explosive established violence. . . ."[11]

A broader, Latin America-wide SERPAJ network founded in 1974 has based its work on a similar belief that the most poor and oppressed of the continent must challenge structural violence through active nonviolent participation. In 1980, SERPAJ/Latin America's coordinator, Adolfo Pérez Esquivel, received the Nobel Peace Prize for his work. At a time of great repression, Pérez Esquivel offered Pérez Aguirre and his companions the international strength and support necessary to found SERPAJ/Uruguay.

"I remember," said Pérez Aguirre, "how I went about burdened, anguished by the publicly 'taboo' or 'unmentionable' issues muzzling the truth and information all over the country. I was concerned not only for the poor and forsaken social sectors, but also for the unemployed, the destitute, the prisoners, and their families, the 'disappeared.' . . . I was concerned for the lack of 'space' for the defense of basic liberties and human rights in Uruguay. I remember understanding   this   as   an   enormous   challenge   to   our imagination. . . ."[12] Given a certain international visibility, SERPAJ began to elaborate a strategy of action, to establish an organizational base, and to broaden its network of contacts.

Martha Delgado, a young literacy teacher, describes how she came to be a founder of SERPAJ:

> For some time I had known that I wanted to work at a popular level. I came from a middle-class family, had always lived in relatively comfortable neighborhoods . . . , and felt a disquieting desire linked to my Christian faith to opt for a more radical commitment to the Uruguayan majority. Together with my friend Mirta we began to search for a way to integrate ourselves. . . .
> Mirta and I began literacy work in one of the largest poor neighborhoods in Montevideo. It opened another world for us, an entirely different perspective. We began to question our own values, lifestyles. It changed our lives.
> We began to discover other people doing the same. . . . young people, Christians, trying to propose an alternative of participation and commitment in a country that was paralyzed, where any kind of popular movement had been undermined. . . .

We visited La Huella and began to work there on weekends to be with the children, washing clothes, cooking or whatever. We got to know Pérez Aguirre at the time they were first talking about the idea of SERPAJ. . . . He placed us in his confidence. It was a time when we had no idea if SERPAJ could work or if it would last. We were very excited to be able to participate. . . .

At the same time, we began to talk about the ideas of SERPAJ with others we could trust, asking them what they thought. To our surprise, the general reaction was one of fear, or that SERPAJ could never survive, or that we would all be thrown in jail. We thought that there .would be many who would want to participate, but no. . . . So the group started with about fifteen lay people and priests, and very few women, three of us. [13]

Theoretically, the members' ecclesiastical ties gave SERPAJ a certain protection within the country. But official bodies of the church were unwilling to support the group's existence or activities. "The military was somewhat confused about our exact relationship to the church," Pérez Aguirre says, "which aided us until the church publicly separated itself from our actions during the (1983) fast."[14] Nonetheless, a small community of nuns gave SERPAJ two rooms of a house in Montevideo, where the group would operate until it was banned in August 1983.

In the classic style of active nonviolence, SERPAJ's strategy relied on a refusal to play by—and a determination to abolish—the dictatorship's "rules of the game." For example, a basic element of the National Security Doctrine is absolute control over information, since it translates into power that must never be "in the hands of the enemy." SERPAJ confronted this notion by proclaiming the truth about the regime, and by doing so as publicly as possible. The group used channels such as a bulletins, religious commemorations, and the limited press coverage Adolfo Pérez Esquivel received in his visits to Uruguay until the government barred his entry in 1983. SERPAJ took full advantage of international contacts, as Pérez Aguirre traveled to Europe and the United States to meet with government officials, human rights agencies, and others, impressing upon them the horrors of the dictatorship and the urgency of international support for Uruguayan victims of repression.

SERPAJ asserted that societal violence is not limited to the physical brutality and bloodshed that the dictatorship was inflicting—that it is also structural. Hence, SERPAJ organized itself into departments that addressed the rights of workers, of the socially marginalized, and of the illiterate, as well as those of political prisoners, the "disappeared," and the relatives of victims of civil and political human rights abuses.

SERPAJ helped to revitalize labor unions that the dictatorship had severely weakened or destroyed, and it organized soup kitchens for the unemployed. SERPAJ worked with groups of families who had been thrown out of their homes, some of whom the government had forced to live under horrible conditions in an abandoned warehouse. It gathered a group of lawyers, social workers, and psychologists to serve individuals and groups in need of housing, health care, and work.

Still, SERPAJ's best known work was in its defense of political prisoners and the "disappeared." Together with families of jailed men and women, SERPAJ prepared packages of food and essential items for the prisoners, raised transportation money for the limited visits that prison officials allowed families, organized small silent marches without banners on behalf of those in jail, and printed updates about the prisoners and prison conditions for international circulation. SERPAJ printed leaflets on an offset printer and then smeared them with kerosene to make them appear mimeographed and therefore harder to trace.

One of SERPAJ's most difficult tasks was the drafting of a location map of the political prisoners. In a country where the government refused even to recognize the category of political prisoners, SERPAJ attempted to map out cell by cell, floor by floor, who in fact the authorities were holding. For this, members relied on individual reports of visits to the jails. The group worked to discover what prisoners needed immediate medical attention and told the international community. It provided initial support to the Families of Political Prisoners and the Disappeared, and it organized European and U.S. meetings and speaking tours for families of Uruguayan human rights victims. In June 1982, the human rights group sent a letter to military president Alvarez signed by more than 300 mothers of political prisoners asking for the freedom of their children.

While the military tried to silence SERPAJ, often by arresting and torturing Pérez Aguirre and others, both spontaneous and organized protest—within and outside the country—was challenging the junta's repressive actions. Uruguayans expressed their opposition to continued military rule in creative nonviolent ways. They used social protest songs and theater, neighborhood soup kitchens, symbols such as Picasso's dove, hands raised in peace signs, and hand-clapping in a certain rhythm. They sang the national hymn with accent on a phrase warning "Tyrants, tremble." And they even developed a way of speaking based on double meanings, unfinished words, and cryptic gestures.

National and international pressure for the generals' exit steadily mounted. In November 1982, political parties held internal elections. By the beginning of 1983, the military initiated negotiations with selected political party leaders.

Yet, inside and outside the prisons, it was business as usual. In June 1983, the authorities arrested and tortured a group of young people; the young women were raped. The families of the victims came to SERPAJ, which issued a public denunciation and sent it to the radio and the press. For thirteen of the relatives the horror of what had happened to their loved ones was greater than their well-founded fear of retribution. So they personally signed the denunciation. On the strength of such personal testimony the Uruguayan press published the allegations of torture and abuse for the first time since the military coup. One paper editorialized that the government should either publicly disprove the charges or punish the guilty.

Unable to do either, the regime responded in the only way it knew: It suspended the dialogue with the political parties and on August 2 issued a far-reaching decree. All public political activity was prohibited, as was publication of all political news. The military that had so recently begun attempting a controlled democratic transition had only succeeded in exposing its own hypocrisy.

The fast

The public was outraged. On August 6, despite the government's ban on political activity, Uruguayans held a mass protest. Eighty-three people were arrested and two were critically wounded.

SERPAJ, searching for a way to end the political impasse and regain the initiative without risking lives in continued street protest, devised the idea of a fast. SERPAJ members felt that a show of force in the streets at that moment would achieve only limited participation and would play into the military's strategy of terrorizing the population.

On the other hand, a fast could create new possibilities. Rather than a hunger strike with a set of rigid demands aimed at the dictatorship, the fast would invite the Uruguayan people to define their response to a national crisis. SERPAJ planned the fast to last fifteen days and issued a call for a National Day of Reflection at its conclusion on the country's day of independence. The group asked all Uruguayans to reflect on three questions: "What have I done for my country? What can I do now? What can I do for my fellow citizens?"

"To fast," said the people of SERPAJ, "is to share hunger for a time and to listen to our hearts to feel the suffering of the malnourished and unloved. Our fast is a symbol of the strength of a people who suffer but who will not give in, who create alternatives, acting always in a peaceful spirit."[15]

Uruguay's highly secularized society offered no precedent for such a fast with its religious overtones. Furthermore, with activity so tightly controlled, spreading the "call" was problematic. Pérez Aguirre remembers:

> I was convinced that depending on word of mouth would work
> well because we had confronted a similar situation in the 1980

plebiscite campaign. The Uruguayan people had a certain training for this. But people said to me, 'Look, with censorship the way it is now, it will be very difficult to get the word out in a few days.' But it all got out. For example, the media couldn't report on it, in spite of the fact that it began to have a tremendous impact. . . . So one paper that ran a report, and was censored, responded by cutting the page in half. When the paper came out with a page cut, people said 'Something's going on here,' and began to ask around. And so it set off a chain reaction . . . and it just got worse for the military. They couldn't control anything, in spite of the censorship. Things were happening very quickly. Finally the Minister of the Interior [responsible for internal security] was obliged to go on radio and TV and accuse us of subversive activities, and, in doing so, to recognize our fast. . . . It couldn't be hidden any longer.[16]

The fast began on August 11. Participating with Pérez Aguirre were another priest, Jorge Osorio, and Methodist pastor Ademar Olivera. The military had never confronted a protest of this kind, and for the first four days it remained puzzled over how to respond. A dramatic impact was quickly apparent. Union and political party leaders, religious and lay people, students, social organization members, young people and old, all gathered in front of the SERPAJ office to show support. In fact, unprecedented coordination of support among all opposition sectors was one of the most important and lasting results of the fast. At the same time, telegrams from around the world flowed in to support the peaceful protest.

After four days police surrounded the fast site, cut the building off from electricity, telephones, and water, prohibited all but medical personnel from entering, and arrested hundreds of supporters gathered outside. SERPAJ's international coordinator, Adolfo Pérez Esquivel flew to Uruguay to support the fasters but officials would not let him into the country. Police carried off supporters by the truck and busload. But as they arrested people, more arrived.

The fast ended on August 25 with the evening of silent national reflection, darkness, and the thunderous "caceroleada" of banging pots and pans. The success of the protest was stunning. It had reversed the political paralysis of August 6. There was no question that the SERPAJ initiative was a watershed event. In its aftermath, a massive national movement for the overthrow of the dictatorship emerged.

Analyzing the military's response, Pérez Aguirre has observed, "What happens is that . . . there is inertia. They are so confident in the control they have that they don't coordinate their actions with the rapidly changing situation. . . . So we took advantage. We took advantage, but it put us in a very difficult situation. We didn't know what was going to happen. . . . "

On August 31, 1983, the military declared SERPAJ illegal,

ransacked the SERPAJ offices, and carried off all of the group's files and equipment. Yet the momentum of the popular mobilization had escaped the junta's control. Behind the scenes, the small SERPAJ group continued its efforts. It assisted in the formation of an Uruguayan Human Rights Commission, consisting of prominent leaders from across the political and social spectrum. Marches and *caceroleadas* took place each month, and on November 27, 1983, more than 400,000 Uruguayans participated in the largest national protest in Uruguayan history, demanding respect for human rights and a return to democracy. In January and June of the following year the people staged two successful general strikes. On August 4, 1984, the Families of Political Prisoners and the Disappeared held a massive demonstration for the "disappeared."

Together with the families of the human rights victims, SERPAJ had come to symbolize the country's challenge to military-wrought violence. This small group of fifteen people had achieved a unique place of respect. It served as society's conscience and played an important role in unifying opposition to the regime. As a result SERPAJ was invited to join an opposition negotiating table with leaders representing hundreds of thousands of political party, trade union, and student federation members. SERPAJ pressed opposition leaders to commit themselves to a transition to democracy based on a platform of: (1) freedom for all political prisoners; (2) the return of the "disappeared"; (3) the return of Uruguayan exiles; (4) the restoration of jobs for all those who lost their positions for political reasons; (5) the lifting of the bans against a large number of people, parties, and social and cultural organizations; (6) trials in civilian courts of all responsible for crimes against humanity; and (7) the dismantling of the repressive state apparatus.

A pattern developed in 1984—mobilization, followed by negotiation, renewed mobilization, and continued talks for democratic elections. In November 1984, Uruguayans participated in national elections for the first time in eleven years. While the government restricted the elections by excluding various leaders from the process, Uruguayans were euphoric that the dictatorship had finally ended.

The aftermath

The initial triumph of returning to civilian rule, however, soon gave way to a painful economic and political reality. Foreign debt, unemployment, inflation, and severely deteriorating social services continued to plague the country.[17] Then in December 1986 the very leaders who had signed accords committing themselves to bringing to justice those responsible for grave human rights violations caved in to pressure from the discredited but unvanquished armed forces. A "law of impunity" was passed that effectively granted a broad amnesty to the military. While the cases of the "disappeared" were not included, the law placed their investigation in the hands of a military prosecutor, thus giving the military responsibility over the investigation of itself. The prosecutor eventually closed all such cases for "lack of evidence."

For SERPAJ, the Uruguay of today presents fundamental new challenges. In the aftermath of dictatorship the role of active nonviolence is different, but no less essential. Some of those tortured, including Pérez Aguirre, have come face to face with their torturers in the streets of Montevideo. This has forced them to deal in a personal way with sometimes conflicting demands of truth, justice, and reconciliation. Pérez Aguirre recalls:

> . . . I told him I forgave him. It's a personal, internal process that I went through, from profound Christian conviction. It's not a simple process. It takes a lot of internal effort. You need a strong conviction of the power of pardoning—the power of love and reconciliation—and how it affects the other person. But it has to be true reconciliation. And it's something I have to do—the state can't do it for me. If there should be a truth-telling, I'm sure people would find ways of pardoning most torturers. We have a tradition of mercy.[18]

This same challenge prompted SERPAJ to join a national campaign to repeal the 1986 law of impunity. SERPAJ and others asserted that allowing immunity and anonymity for those who tortured, murdered, and "disappeared" others provided no safeguards to prevent a recurrence of crimes. Full democracy and true national reconciliation are impossible, SERPAJ maintained, when the government covers up and excuses such crimes, offers no answers to victims of abuse or their families, and provides no equality or full recourse under the law. Together with leading political, social, and cultural figures and organizations, SERPAJ formed the National Pro-Referendum Commission.

Uruguay's Constitution permits a referendum on laws passed by parliament, provided that twenty-five percent of the voters sign a petition for it. Undaunted by the enormous challenge (this would be the equivalent of 40 million signatures in the United States), a coalition of human rights, union, political party, and religious groups undertook a successful petition drive. The Uruguayan government attempted to thwart the effort at every turn, publicly discrediting it and arbitrarily rejecting tens of thousands of signatures. In spite of such efforts the referendum finally reached the ballot in April 1989.

In the end, the Uruguayan people upheld the amnesty law by a fifty-seven to forty-three percent margin. No doubt some supported the military's claim that their "dirty war" was necessary and therefore justifiable. Many observers felt that a larger number succumbed to the military-encouraged fear that repealing the law might return Uruguay to the chaos of the past. Nonetheless, the campaign served as a powerful statement about the political and moral costs of accepting government by crime and abuse in the name of preserving the rule of law.

SERPAJ has investigated and documented hundreds of cases of human rights abuse under the dictatorship. The group hopes judicial officials will use this work in the future. Meanwhile, it has published the documentation as testimony to the darkest period in Uruguayan history.[19]

In the eyes of its country, SERPAJ is still the organization that challenged the military dictatorship on its violent abuses of civil and political human rights. Yet SERPAJ defines human rights in the broadest sense of the term—as social and economic as well as political and civil rights. The group has undertaken a major educational campaign grounded in the United Nations Universal Declaration of Human Rights, which includes the right to life, health, shelter, work, rest, education, and participation as well as to that of political freedom and civil liberties.

SERPAJ believes that the prevention and elimination of human rights violations can only take place through active human rights education. Writing in 1985, Pérez Aguirre and Father Juan José Mosca argued, "The governments that pursue the Doctrine of National Security tried to make the whole nation forget the rights to which they were entitled. A whole generation of young people was brought up in complete ignorance of these matters. No educational courses exist which include the study of basic human rights."[20]

SERPAJ has worked steadily to fill the gap by elaborating teaching materials and workshops. Mosca and Pérez Aguirre contributed a major foundational work, *Derechos Humanos: Pautas Para Una Educación Liberadora* [Human Rights: Standards for a Liberating Education]. The book is a theoretical and methodological tool that other groups throughout Latin America are now using. With SERPAJ assistance a team of high school teachers has developed human rights curricula for courses in biology, sociology, philosophy, history, and literature.

The human rights activists hold workshops in schools, youth organizations or union headquarters, hospitals, neighborhoods, and other sites. Through active participation, members of the workshops begin to think through their understanding of human rights and to devise collective strategies for transforming concrete problems they face in their places of work or study, and in their homes and neighborhoods. Workshop leaders seldom use the term "nonviolence." The focus is simply on themes like participation, democracy, justice, and peace. As in most of Latin America, the word "nonviolence" is not familiar and too easily suggests a negative or passive attitude. Yet the strategies that workshop participants discuss are those of active nonviolence.

During the workshops SERPAJ teams teach by a variety of techniques, including games, role plays, audiovisuals, photographs, and small group exercises. Through evaluation both within the workshops and among the SERPAJ team members, SERPAJ continues to develop and improve the workshop process.

Just as the education workshops reflect a constant process of adjusting, redefining, and clarifying goals, so too does the work of SERPAJ in Uruguay. SERPAJ organizes its work into two general and related areas. The first area is focused on what SERPAJ terms *"verdad y justicia"* [truth and justice]—full disclosure and accountability for those responsible for grave human rights violations. SERPAJ believes that a truly democratic Uruguay is impossible without truth and justice as its foundations. The second area is SERPAJ's work with human rights education. "We are convinced," write members of SERPAJ, "that only through active human rights education can we confront . . . [the] origin and causes of torture, genocide, racial and religious discrimination, poverty, and the dreadful hunger of the majority of the world's population."[21]

After more than a decade of military repression a deep-rooted fear of collaborating with SERPAJ continues. The current government enhances this fear by condemning SERPAJ's demands for redress of the dictatorship's human rights violations. Nevertheless, as past activities such as its 1983 fast demonstrate, SERPAJ has the capacity to coordinate across various social, political, and economic lines, and to create and expand networks of people committed to continued social change. The unique history and evolution of SERPAJ is a valuable lesson to all groups involved in movements for democracy and fundamental human rights.

Notes

1. Interview with Luis Pérez Aguirre, S.J.; by Philip McManus; Montevideo, Uruguay; July 13, 1987.
2. The Uruguayan chapter of SERPAJ is one among an international network of groups promoting nonviolent social change in some eleven Latin American countries.
3. SERPAJ, written materials and interviews. This is also the standard figure according to Amnesty International.
4. The standard estimate for the number of Uruguayans who went into exile is 200,000. Amnesty International estimates that approximately half of these left because of political repression, while the other half left the country for economic as much as political reasons.
5. Testimony of Sara Méndez in *Desaparecidos: Los Niños*, publisher unnamed.
6. For a good general description of this period, including aspects such as press censorship, see Americas Watch, *With Friends Like These: The Americas Watch Report*

on Human Rights and U.S. Policy in Latin America (New York: Pantheon Books, 1985), pp. 80-81.

7. Ibid., p. 82.

8. Ibid.

9. Charles Gillespie, "Uruguay's Transition from Collegial Military-Technocratic Rule," in Guillermo O'Donnell, Phillepe Schmitter, and Laurence Whitehead, eds., *Transitions from Authoritarian Rule: Latin America* (Baltimore: Johns Hopkins University Press, 1986), p. 181.

10. Interview with Martha Delgado, by author, July 1987.

11. Pérez Aguirre, "Predicaciones Acerca de la Violencia: Carta abierta a los violentos que se ignoran." Unpublished.

12. Pérez Aguirre, memo, "El Servicio Paz Y Justicia/Uruguay."

13. Delgado interview.

14. Pérez Aguirre interview.

15. Paz y Justicia, 1, (August-September 1985), p. 4.

16. Pérez Aguirre interview.

17. Economic consequences of military rule involved a sixteen percent decline in overall economic growth, a foreign debt of $5 billion, a fifty percent loss of purchasing power between 1968 and 1984, and loss of twenty percent of the work force to exile or emigration. Lawrence Weschler, "The Great Exception," *The New Yorker*, April 10, 1989, passim.

18. Ibid. p. 95.

19. Francisco Bustamante, ed., *Uruguay: Nunca Más*, Montevideo: Servicio Paz y Justicia/Uruguay, 1989.

20. Juan José Mosca & Luis Pérez Aguirre, *Derechos Humanos: Pautas Para Una Educación Liberadora*, Montevideo: Servicio Paz y Justicia, introduction.

21. Ibid.

For further reading

Americas Watch, *With Friends Like These: The Americas Watch Report on Human Rights and U.S. Policy in Latin America*. New York: Pantheon Books, 1985.

Bustamante, Francisco, ed. *Uruguay: Nunca Más*. Montevideo: Servicio Paz y Justicia/ Uruguay, 1989.

Handelman, Howard. "Labor-Industrial Conflict and the Collapse of Uruguayan Democracy," in the *Journal of Inter-American Studies and World Affairs* 23 (November 1981): pp. 371-94.

Mosca, Juan José and Luis Pérez Aguirre. *Derechos Humanos: Pautas Para Una Educación Liberadora*. Montevideo, 1985.

Weinstein, Martin. *Uruguay: Democracy at the Crossroads*. Boulder: Westview Press, 1988.

Weschler, Lawrence. "The Great Exception." *The New Yorker*, April 3 and April 10, 1989.

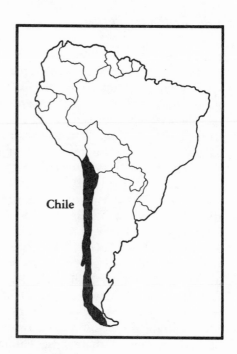

Chile

SEVEN

Introduction

The military coup d'état that rocked Chile in 1973 shattered one of the strongest democratic traditions in the Americas. In presidential elections in 1970 Salvador Allende, a socialist, had succeeded a centrist Christian Democrat elected in 1964—who in turn had succeeded a conservative elected in 1958. The tradition stretched back 150 years. Democracy in action.

The military dictatorship that seized power in 1973 battered Chilean democracy but did not manage to snuff it out. This chapter tells how the roots of popular participation survived and even deepened in spite of the dictatorship. Democracy survived in urban neighborhoods where people gathered together, discussed their problems, and acted to resolve them. It also found new life in the streets, which the people eventually reclaimed through concerted nonviolent action.

Salvador Allende's election in 1970 reflected the growing strength of socialist political parties and labor unions in Chile as well as the success of the "popular front" strategy of the Popular Unity coalition

117

that he led. The "Chilean road to socialism" held out the prospect of far-reaching social reform without the travail of revolutionary violence.

However, the destabilization efforts of powerful elements of Chilean society and of U.S.-based corporations and the CIA took a heavy toll on Allende's efforts to implement socialism within the limits of the Chilean constitution. When Allende's Popular Unity coalition scored substantial gains in midterm congressional elections of 1973,[1] destabilization efforts gave way to coup plotting.

On September 11, 1973, the armed forces struck, bombing and then attacking *La Moneda,* the presidential palace. President Allende died in the attack. While many accepted or even welcomed the coup as a temporary expedient that would bring relief from growing turmoil, few expected the level of bloodletting that accompanied it. Many politicians and other government supporters managed to secure asylum and escaped to a harsh life in exile. Others were not so fortunate. In Santiago, the military rounded up 10,000 Chileans and held them in a soccer stadium. Many were tortured and executed. The U.S. embassy estimated the death toll nationally at 5,000, while other figures range as high as tens of thousands. The extent of the carnage shook the Chilean people's very sense of being as a civilized, democratic nation.

In the years that followed, ruthless repression continued. Between 1973 and 1989, 768 people were "disappeared" by the security forces and were never heard from again. The National Coordination of Human Rights Organizations estimates the regime locked up 500,000 people in prisons or concentration camps. Torture was routine.

The military replaced the Popular Unity economic model with the radical free enterprise model of U.S. economist Milton Friedman and his colleagues, known as the "Chicago Boys." Friedman's "trickle down" approach left many of the Chilean poor dying of thirst. By the mid-1980s, in poor neighborhoods, as many as seventy-four percent of the families were undernourished and unemployment reached sixty percent. Between 1973 and 1985, the number of unemployed increased well over five times (by 566 percent).

While by the late 1980s macroeconomic indicators had improved, only the wealthiest 20 percent of the population benefited. The standard of living of the popular classes continued to be significantly lower than during the Allende years.

Throughout this period the poor struggled to organize, but their efforts ran counter to the military dictatorship's policy of proscribing, destroying, or at least controlling social and political organizations. A 1988 Amnesty International report painted a grim picture of death threats, kidnappings, and torture of government opponents often by clandestine groups linked to the security forces. The report noted: "Anyone perceived as critical of government practices risks harassment and thousands live with the uncertainty of possible abuse."[2]

In addition to selective attacks aimed at undermining social organizing, the poor were repeatedly victims of indiscriminate attacks. *Allanamientos,* military raids on poor neighborhoods, were a favorite technique of the regime. On November 10, 1984, in a typical example, the military invaded the Silva Henríquez neighborhood in Santiago. A human rights activist reported that: "Supported by tanks, helicopters, and armored vehicles, they surrounded and then entered the settlement. They conducted house-to-house searches, destroyed property— including a community clinic—and beat up many people. All men over the age of fifteen were forced from their homes into air force buses. Several thousand were arrested and released after questioning. At least 153, including a number of community leaders, were banished without trial to a military 're-education camp' in the northern town of Pisagua."[3]

In spite of such repression, popular organizations grew dramatically in number and strength in the last years of the dictatorship. This growth reflected the desperate need as well as the political skill of the poor, who in large numbers adapted but not did conform to life under the dictatorship. Such popular organizing efforts also received help from social development and human rights organizations committed to establishing democracy based on the full participation of all.

One such organization is Servicio Paz y Justicia (SERPAJ).[4] Since 1977 it has worked throughout Chile to defend human rights and to promote the empowerment of popular organizations. Rooted in a holistic understanding of active nonviolence, SERPAJ engages in popular education, the building of base-level organizations, and social mobilization as an expression of a commitment to "active participation in the liberation struggle of our people."[5]

While denouncing the anti-democratic character of the military regime and its outrages against human dignity, SERPAJ is committed to more than a simple change in rulers. Only as the "marginalized majority" actively participates in a rebuilding of the social fabric will removal of the dictator lead to real democracy.

In "A Proposal for Active Nonviolence,"[6] Fernando Aliaga, one of the founders of SERPAJ, has argued that the struggle of elites— whether they be a revolutionary vanguard or the leaders of the established political parties—simply postpones the rightful role of the people as social actors. Such postponement only furthers their dispossession and manipulation. Additionally, the institutional violence from which the poor suffer extends far beyond military repression. Only a change in the social and economic structures of the society will overcome it. Hence the principal task is to organize and consolidate base-level initiatives, which Aliaga calls the "signs" of popular liberation.

In the dual struggle both to build up a new order and to denounce and actively resist the old, SERPAJ finds that active nonviolence creates a right relationship between ends and means. "In this long night of pain and rebellion," writes Aliaga, "those who struggle for justice have realized the inextricable connection between their decision to defy the tyrant and the will to establish a new society which will *never again* permit such outrages. Hence the fundamental principle of consistency of ends and means is established, precisely so that there will never again be a system that uses whatever means it chooses to keep itself in power."[7]

In this chapter, written at the end of 1988, the coordinators of the SERPAJ chapter in Antofagasta discuss practical, base-level organizing. They share both the obstacles and the achievements of several years of dedicated work. At this writing, the end of the dictatorship is in sight. Yet the degree to which real participatory democracy will take its place remains to be seen. This will depend to a significant degree on the strength of the sorts of popular organizations described here. Amid the repression and the brutality of the dictatorship, they have already proven themselves dynamic and resilient. They stand today as a testimony to what one observer has called "the ultimate failure" of the regime: "the survival of all the major political movements and groups entrenched in Chilean politics since the 1930s and the creation of new groups in the face of state terrorism and institutionalized repression."[8]

Police use water cannons to spray demonstrators protesting torture in Chile. Dirty sewer water or water with dangerous chemicals is often used. Photo courtesy of SERPAJ/Chile.

Cultural Action for Liberation in Chile
Blanca Yáñez Berríos and Omar Williams López

Antofagasta is a port city of 200,000, sitting at the edge of the semi-arid desert of northern Chile. Since the last century, its lifeline has been the region's copper and nitrate mines. Digging the earth, its mine workers have carved its history. But the military dictatorship of General Augusto Pinochet, which came to power in a ruthless, bloody coup in 1973, has taken away many of their hard-won gains and severely undermined their right to organize.

Police arrest a demonstrator at a protest against torture in Chile. Photo courtesy of SERPAJ/Chile.

The mine workers have not been the only ones to lose. Under the dictatorship, thirty-two percent of all Chilean families do not earn enough for adequate food. Since 1969, this index of extreme poverty has more than tripled. In the midst of this suffering, and despite continual repression, popular resistance has grown increasingly strong.

Direct action: women re-take the streets

Among those seizing the initiative at the neighborhood level are women's groups, which have struggled to defend life through bold and creative organizing. Their efforts include everything from economic alternatives addressing basic needs (communal soup kitchens, food banks, household gardens) to mass protests publicly denouncing the regime and its continual violations of human rights.

In 1987, the regional government in Antofagasta prohibited the public celebration of May Day, the International Day of the Worker, and announced that it would only allow official events of the regime. Responding to the order on April 30, a group of two hundred women staged a *mitín relámpago*, or lightning action.[9] For ten minutes we held up a canvas banner on which we had written: "The Women Demand That He Go!" It was a clear call for General Augusto Pinochet to step down. We handed out leaflets and threw them into the air. We chanted slogans such as "Women demand democracy and freedom!" and "We want to live in a country without Pinochet and without the C.N.I.!" (the secret police). The action took place in a central location where there is always a lot of foot traffic. It lasted only ten minutes, which was the time we estimated we had before the police would arrive. Once we completed the action, we all withdrew quickly in pairs, ducking into stores and markets.

Three poorly dressed men followed one group of three pairs. One of the men appeared to be a bootblack. As they followed, they pulled out walkie-talkies to call the police. Our *compañeras* tried to get into a taxi in order to get away, but their pursuers quickly arrested them. A police car arrived and took them to the police station where they were detained and interrogated for several hours. Eventually the police released them with citations to appear in court on charges of creating a public disturbance. At the same time that the police detained the six women, others arrived at the demonstration site and tore down the banner. They were unable to arrest anyone else since by then we had mixed in with the other passersby, and they could not tell who had participated.

We felt the action was a success. We had achieved our objectives, reclaiming a public place for expression of our demand for freedom and democracy, and successfully demonstrating that women are a political and moral force in a small and highly militarized city.

Organizing a lightning action

Organizing this nonviolent lightning action involved several stages. First the Women's Program of Servicio Paz y Justicia (SERPAJ) in Antofagasta and the Women's Democratic Coordinating Committee formed an action team. This team recruited women from other groups. With this group of twenty we defined the following phases of the action:

1. Planning the action

We discussed what we wanted to do and defined the following objectives:

a. To organize a women's action in order to show the public that we women will not be accomplices of the dictatorship.

b. To demonstrate our strength and our capacity for organization in the face of the prohibition of non-official May Day celebrations.

c. To raise public awareness about the outrages against human rights.

d. To demonstrate to the political parties that women want and are capable of real participation in all aspects of their lives: family, social organizations, political parties, etc.

e. To improve on previous actions by creating a style at once joyful and disciplined, so that more women would overcome their fear and join us.

We defined the form and the type of the action. We chose a lightning action in order to reduce the risks for those participating, to awaken sympathy on the part of the people, to motivate others to join us in future actions, and to make the police feel outwitted by a group of women. Given the *macho* mentality of the police, this is a way of challenging their sense of being all powerful.

We chose the most appropriate spot, as well as an alternative in case the police got word of our plans. We also fixed the day and the time. We agreed on the chants we would use and the wording of our banner. We organized a team to make the banner.

We also set up a communication network, woman to woman, with a great deal of attention to security. A day before the action we went over the list of women who would participate, and we gave out final instructions. Before that they had known only the type of action, the day, and the time. On the last day we communicated the place. We also named group leaders and gave them three responsibilities: to communicate instructions, to keep a close watch on security, and to let the others know if anyone in their group was arrested.

2. The action

By previous agreement, three of us initiated the action with hand-clapping to attract the attention of people walking by. The others, scattered around the area, immediately gathered together. We unfurled the banner and read it aloud three times. Then we hung it up and distributed the leaflets. As a closing, we shouted chants and then quickly dispersed.

Everyone followed our security precautions except the six *compañeras* who left together, thus making it more easy to identify and arrest them.

Afterward, all of the group leaders met at a previously selected place in order to check on each other, to do an initial evaluation, to take legal action to free the detained, and to advise their families.

3. Evaluating the action

Three days later we met for a more thorough evaluation of the various phases, tasks, and responsibilities connected with the action. This permitted us to correct mistakes, which in this type of action must be held to an absolute minimum.

We also shared our feelings. Most common among them were: fear (which all felt in different ways and in different parts of our bodies); anxiety; nervousness; and a feeling of responsibility for the *compañera* next to us. We also felt we were part of a highly cohesive group. We felt each other's strong and heroic support. We felt a powerful bond of solidarity. We shared the anger, the sorrow, and the impotence we experienced with the arrests. But above all we shared the joy of feeling alive, struggling for deeply held values, defending life, being committed to attaining justice.

A lightning protest blocks traffic in Santiago, Chile. Photo courtesy of SERPAJ/ Chile.

Organizing within the popular sectors: building nonviolent struggle

It is important to note that a long process of working with popular organizations preceded this action and all of its attendant risks. That process is part of a larger social development strategy in the northern region.

The local SERPAJ group in Antofagasta has been working since 1981 amid difficult conditions for the popular movement. The military coup d'état of 1973 and the subsequent policy of social control led to an extensive dismantling of social and political organizations. The regime has imposed controls on the mass media. It has censured violators through fines, suspension of publication, and even violence. The military dictates the content of education. It appoints educational administrators, even down to the directors of rural primary schools, all of whom are Pinochet supporters. The aim is to implant an authoritarian culture based on obedience and hierarchy, where loyalty is defined as submission.

Because of its mining reserves and its proximity to the northern border, the Antofagasta region has strategic importance. There is a large military presence, and since the largest mine is nationalized, employment depends primarily on the state. This makes it all the more difficult to mobilize the labor movement and redress economic, social, and political grievances.

As always, it is the popular sectors, the poor, and the working class of our city who suffer the most in terms of unemployment, social neglect, and political and cultural control. SERPAJ prioritizes work with those sectors. We have undertaken an educational process that takes into account the high degree of marginality and the low level of formal education of these groups. Hence our methodology is popular education, a dynamic education/action process aimed at addressing basic needs while developing a critical consciousness of one's social, political, and cultural reality. Popular education enables people to reclaim their own authentic values, to reconstruct the social fabric of their lives, and to become agents of both personal and social transformation.

At the neighborhood level, the women are the most likely ones to get involved. Because the neighborhood is viewed culturally as an extension of the house and the family, it is more difficult to organize the men. When the man comes home, he seeks rest and a chance to restore his strength for work. For many decades his avenues for participation have generally been unions, political parties, or regional sports leagues. So he seldom participates in neighborhood organizations.

The woman's life revolves more around the neighborhood, and she is the one who must continually confront the lack of basic necessities: potable water, sewage systems, playgrounds for the children, paved roads, schools and social centers, telephones, emergency clinics. So, we have found, she is more likely to participate in an educational program.

1. Phase of making contact, gaining acceptance

This phase lasted around three months. We chose the shantytowns[10] with the greatest socioeconomic need and began to organize. We had to deal with the problem that the shantytowns had been guinea pigs for different groups such as churches, social scientists at the universities, and social agencies of the regime. None of these had developed a process together with the people. When they experienced difficulties in organizing, they said it was because the people were lazy and irresponsible. As a result, the people had a negative self-image and had grown accustomed to paternalistic assistance programs. This made our work more difficult.

As a first step, we initiated a free milk program. This enabled us to make contact with those who were most interested in becoming organized. Funds for milk came from an international organization. Our staff handled the first distribution. For the second, we organized committees of the people from the neighborhood. After that, the committees directed the distribution while our staff organized meetings on health, nutrition, and community organizing. The people gradually accepted us, and we began to work on the issues of greatest concern to them.

2. Work phase—basic elements for a group or organization

When the first groups formed in the shantytowns, we realized that the majority of those involved had no concept of the basic elements of organization: planning an action, the action itself, and evaluation of what happened. We felt an urgent need to deal with this, because the people did not apply these concepts to their personal lives either. The harshness of the daily struggle for survival, along with the authoritarian culture of the regime, left little space for reflection. As a result, the people were not critically conscious of their behavior, of the behavior of others or, much less, of the system and the dictatorship. The majority saw unemployment and its consequences as a problem of personal inadequacy; they did not connect it to the economic policies of the dictatorship. This reflected a sort of magical consciousness about cause and effect, and a fatalistic vision of the future. It led to discouragement and a sense of impotence about the potential for transforming the situation.

We began to apply the three elements of organization (planning, action, and evaluation) to all the tasks the groups undertook—everything from meetings to political action in the shantytown. After these steps became an established practice among the groups, we began to use thematic discussions and workshops to help participants reflect on their personal lives.

The activities in this phase were rich in both quantity and quality. They included fundraising, a sewage system project, and a large public protest against the suspension of a children's milk program. We all experienced qualitative growth in our vision, our commitment, and our critical consciousness. This phase lasted around one year, at which time the process became, for most groups, an instinctive practice. Based on this initial experience, we produced a pamphlet entitled "Planning and Evaluation of Community Actions," which we give to other social organizations in the training courses we offer.

3. Interaction with other organizations

It was also necessary to link up the groups from the poor neighborhoods so that they could work together. We set up a coordinating committee made up of two people elected by each group plus the SERPAJ team. The coordinating committee meets weekly to plan and evaluate the educational programs. As a representative body, the committee is able to decide when and how the groups will work together, and how to make best use of available resources.

Each year the base-level groups and SERPAJ meet to prioritize activities in the following areas:

Personal growth of the participants; support for their process of becoming critically conscious and empowered persons.

Manual skills training workshops, which last two months.

Initiatives in popular economics for meeting basic needs. Examples include community soup kitchens, food banks, and community gardens that raise vegetables for the soup kitchens.

Organizational skill-sharing and leadership development activities: schools for community organizers, workshops for women on subjects such as human rights, political education, and popular theology.

Community development activities, which involve large numbers of people, including children, youth, and adults who are not part of the groups. Examples include: Christmas parties for the children; voluntary work projects to fix up houses or clean the streets; other recreational and educational activities for children and adults, such as summer camps. These activities are a means of demonstrating the value of the organizations to the community.

In this phase of work, the object is group formation related to specific needs of the people and the organization. We try to ensure that this is a comprehensive formation and that it is not just for those involved in the groups but also for the entire neighborhood. We promote a sense of identity within the poor sectors and an appreciation for the role of the popular sectors in the history of the Chilean people. Among the themes we have used are: I Am Part of a People, The Family in Chile: Human Rights and Daily Life, The Capitalist System in Latin America, Community Soup Kitchens and the Economic System, The Fundamental Rights of the Human Person, and Nonviolence as a Means of Struggle of the Chilean People.

4. Tying the coordinating committee to the popular movement

In this last phase the base-level neighborhood groups, represented by the coordinating committee, link up with the larger popular movement (labor unions, human rights groups, organizations of women, students, etc.). Through such networking, we act as a leaven within the popular movement and help solidify the choice of active nonviolence in the struggle against the dictatorship. Our strategy for this phase includes:

Local workshops in a number of northern cities offering training to three distinct sectors: women's groups, human rights groups, neighborhood and popular education groups.

Annual regional gatherings of the networks with which we work to evaluate the work in the region as a whole.

Broad-based regional conventions around specific concerns. In 1988 we held the first of these for women's groups. Its purpose was to bring together representatives of diverse organizations working on similar issues in order to evaluate the struggle from a larger, longer term perspective and to undertake shared projects or campaigns. For example, the gathering evaluated the development of women's organizations during the military dictatorship and offered projections for the movement during the period of transition to a democratic Chile. A gathering of shantytown dwellers will be the next such gathering.

Mass actions aimed at public education in relation to the October 1988 plebiscite on the continued rule of General Augusto Pinochet. This phase of work was aimed at developing the popular movement, which suffered under the repression and social control of the dictatorship.

This entire process of our work as SERPAJ in Antofagasta reflects our commitment to the social development of our region. We believe that with the support and guidance of popular participation, and with adequate economic resources, such efforts can be of great significance in the struggle to build a democratic Chile. For the people, the opportunity to discover themselves as persons—assuming their responsibilities and asserting their rights to provide for their families, to resolve their own problems, and to struggle for change in an organized manner—is an occasion of profound cultural change. For Chile, such opportunity is the light of a new day.

Nonviolence and the struggle for survival

For the poorest sectors of our people, the struggle for survival has been hard and debilitating. Thousands of Chilean families daily spend more than half of their time simply trying to find something to eat. The children wash cars or beg for food in the wealthier neighborhoods. The mothers wash clothes, sweep streets, or, if they are lucky, work as maids in private homes. The young girls have to take the mother's place in the house, assuming responsibility for taking care of the other children, cleaning, washing, and so on. As a result they usually have to quit school. The fathers do whatever work they can find, usually part-time at a miserable wage inadequate to cover even the most basic necessities.

Because of this reality, our nonviolent organizing work has included popular economic initiatives. These have been quite diverse. Examples include:

People's bakeries: Several families organize to make bread for themselves and for sale in the community.

Family gardens: A small area in the backyards of the mostly makeshift cardboard houses is set aside. In this little piece of land, people grow greens and other vegetables for home consumption. This has been a good experience, but in our desert region the water distribution system is inadequate and favors the wealthy. The gardens have not been very successful since we only have water every other day, and then only for five hours at a time. Obviously the people use it first for consumption and washing clothes. As a result, it is not always possible to water the gardens.

Food banks: We have a small warehouse from which we sell food to community soup kitchens at reduced prices. A team elected from the various groups administers it.

Community garden: We acquired a piece of land thanks to the support of an international solidarity organization. The parcel supplies vegetables for the soup kitchens of the various groups, which use about half of the produce. The family that works the land sells the rest locally.

Community soup kitchens: Found throughout Chile, these "*ollas comunes*" (literally, "common or shared pots") are self-help projects that neighborhood women organize to benefit their families and their communities. Daily they provide a hearty, affordable, nutritious meal. The women are organized into teams of three which take turns cooking for all of the families. Each team cooks about once a week.

The *ollas comunes* sell the meals to shantytown dwellers at the lowest possible price. Each ration costs sixteen cents. That is, six people can eat for a dollar. It is the most complete meal the budget will allow. In fact, it is much more than one could otherwise buy for a dollar, which is just about enough for a box of tea, a pound of sugar, and two pounds of bread.

The rations are handed out and the families return home to eat them. This practice dignifies the life of the family since family members need not separate to seek their own food individually.

SERPAJ supports these organizations in three ways: publicizing and promoting their experiences as a means of confronting the pangs of hunger; assisting each organization until it can manage the many aspects of the community soup kitchens; and providing initial funding to get started.

The organizational phases of the community soup kitchens are:

a. Analysis with the women in need; raising consciousness about how they feed their children and about the consequences of malnutrition.

b. Planning; defining together the objectives, the distribution of tasks, the schedule, the menu, and so on.

c. An information campaign directed at the rest of the neighborhood in order to promote participation in the program. (If more than a hundred rations are sold, those who do the cooking get the rations for their families for only four cents.)

d. Ongoing consultation in order to minimize any problems.

e. Training in basic accounting so that the groups can manage expenses and income and make a small profit. The groups keep a daily record of sales, the number of meals prepared, and all income and expenses.

Popular economic initiatives for survival such as these produce various positive results. To begin with, they confront the problem of hunger in an organized manner. Participants build trust in one another and in the organization. The experiences show that the contributions of everyone in the group are essential. We are able to overcome the paternalism and the dependency that otherwise degrade both the one who gives and the one who receives.

At the same time, these projects dramatize the fact that the problem is not an individual one but rather a general one, that national economic policy and the hard reality of daily life are closely connected. People go beyond living the effects of hunger and malnutrition to a conscious effort to examine the causes.

The people of the shantytowns also gain a greater degree of participation in the decisions affecting their lives. In the Chile of Pinochet, only the businesspeople and financiers have real participation. Pinochet's Chile denies working people their rightful place in the search for economic solutions in the face of a weak economy, skewed priorities, and widespread unmet human needs. We believe that popular economic initiatives are essential because they enable the people to have a voice as an important sector of the society. They provide a platform from which to struggle for full participation.

Through this nonviolent struggle, the people exercise their fundamental right to life in a country where survival is a basic challenge. Such experiences will continue to multiply until the poor family has won the right to work and to a just, livable wage.

Nonviolence and social mobilization

One of the fundamental challenges to active nonviolence is to demonstrate that it is capable of creating real social transformation. To be an effective means of struggle it must enable the people to discover and demonstrate their political power in the building of a society of justice and peace. Nonviolent resistance has been an important element in the political struggle against the Pinochet dictatorship. It has shown its strength in a great variety of ways.

Servicio Paz y Justicia actively promotes such expressions throughout Chile. Since its founding in 1977, SERPAJ/Chile has been a voice of conscience, denouncing the regime's brutality and the structural injustice that it protects. SERPAJ has built a national network of regional groups in eleven Chilean cities. The work of the regional groups, as our work in Antofagasta illustrates, nurtures a sense of dignity and empowerment. The regional SERPAJ groups accompany local groups, many of which SERPAJ helped start, as they struggle to define their identity, participate in the popular movement, and relate to but not be co-opted by the political parties.

Today only a minority understand and explicitly accept the strategy of active nonviolence. However, this work and the extensive networking that takes place among the regional groups and the popular organizations with which they work contribute to the building of a broad national movement and strengthen the capacity for sustained nonviolent resistance.

Throughout the country, the national office of SERPAJ offers workshops on themes such as nonviolence, democracy, and human rights. Thousands of people participate each year. SERPAJ has also helped organize a number of important national campaigns. Examples include the 1978 campaign "What Have You Done with Your Brother?" in support of a prolonged hunger strike by family members of those the regime has "disappeared"; a campaign to prevent an outbreak of war over a border dispute between Chile and Argentina in that same year; massive national protests in the mid-1980s;[11] and the anti-Pinochet campaign leading up to the 1988 plebiscite.

Acts of public, nonviolent denunciation, such as the 1978 hunger strike, gave nonviolence a specific meaning for increasing numbers of Chileans. Originally it simply meant an active denunciation of injustice. In the process of successive campaigns, which increasingly challenged the legitimacy of the regime, that meaning grew to include a broad strategy of confrontation involving many different groups and a decentralized, highly efficient communication system.

During the early 1980s an economic crisis raised unemployment levels and threatened the survival of many businesses. In 1983, trade union leaders joined together to call for national protests. At this point SERPAJ played a key role by offering "Nonviolence Schools," intensive training programs in nonviolent action. Many of the participants were neighborhood leaders from the shantytowns. Alongside the "Nonviolence Schools" SERPAJ organized neighborhood committees that planned local nonviolent actions. A larger "Creativity Committee" was also an important source of inspiration and organization. Initiated by

SERPAJ, it included members of many different groups. The committee shared reports, heard proposals, and developed plans for actions aimed at expanding the protests while maintaining their nonviolent character.

During the successive protests, people discovered many creative forms of resistance. Women protested hunger and unemployment by blocking checkout lines at supermarkets with their shopping carts full of groceries. Young people organized marches. Shantytown dwellers took over vacant land. There were innumerable street protests.

The Creativity Committee had some initial discussions on a nonviolent strategy that would start with public demonstrations and lead, step by step, to conditions making the country ungovernable, thus forcing the regime to step down. One criticism of the national protests was that there was insufficient planning and training to effectively undermine the regime through such a strategy. The protests ended amid increasingly violent repression by the security forces, which took many lives.

One of the lasting benefits of the protests was practical experience. Evaluation among neighborhood leaders followed each protest. This proved to be an important element in building the movement and strengthening the network of autonomous local committees. One dramatic result was a national "March for Life" in 1984. Throughout the country there were coordinated, disciplined actions. Participation of social, political and religious organizations reached a new level.

Any dictatorship requires the cooperation, whether voluntary or involuntary, of a large part of the population. Collective withdrawal of this cooperation causes a crisis and a definitive break in the dictatorship's domination. Therefore, we have argued, massive civil disobedience is an unavoidable moral imperative. However, such a definitive break does not happen all at once nor all in one place. It must be the culmination of a long process of creating "free spaces," such as popular organization, economic alternatives which promote self-reliance and public protest. These spaces are crucial steps in the progressive liberation of a critically conscious people. This strategy changes the focus of politics from a concept of power centralized in military might and political parties to cultural action that rebuilds the social fabric. It gives the poor majority its full voice in articulating its own values and defining its own future.

Certain principles are crucial to such a long-term strategy. Among them are: to ensure that any proposal will deepen and broaden public awareness and involvement; to never confront the adversary where the adversary is strongest, nor to allow the adversary to take the initiative; to focus the conflict on its political causes (e.g., the lack of democracy) rather than its "public order" symptoms, by putting democracy into practice through disciplined, nonviolent action; in the midst of the conflict, to create a certain tension that makes the status quo unviable and makes some sort of resolution necessary.

Another principle that is both political and ethical is that we insist on means that are consistent with our ends. At the practical level, this means choosing immediate objectives that are realizable given the current stage and resources of the struggle. The action itself must also allow participants to experience the long-term goals they seek, such as democracy and freedom. Finally, we must recognize that we will create a nonviolent society only through nonviolent means.

In addition to a well developed strategy, a successful movement requires that large numbers of activists receive training in nonviolence. In order to do that, the "Nonviolence Schools" SERPAJ offers incorporate elements of both formation and training. Participants study the economic, legal, psychological, and social conditions of the conflict. They discuss the history and practice of nonviolence. Trainers use techniques that ensure that all participate and set aside time for personal reflection as well. Participants may also learn the basic logistical and practical skills of organizing a campaign.

Nonviolent training techniques include role plays, quick decision-making exercises, strategy games, and discussion and practice of techniques that develop the inner strength of the person to confront fear and resist the violence or torture of the "forces of order."[12]

Our triumph has begun

In the months leading up to the October 1988 yes-or-no plebiscite on Pinochet's rule, the national SERPAJ office anticipated a polarized and repressive election climate and expanded its efforts in nonviolence training. The hundreds of people who participated in diverse parts of the country also received training in special tasks: supporting the opposition's poll watchers (who were present at every polling place), developing mechanisms for the quick dissemination of information, and planning for the possible need for mass mobilization in the critical hours and days after the vote. We recognized that the opposition could win in mobilizing at the polls but lose at mobilizing in the streets— something that has always been crucial for defending the rights of the poor.[13]

One of our greatest challenges during the plebiscite campaign was to nurture the conviction in the Chilean people that after fifteen years of unyielding dictatorship, change was indeed possible and that standing up for change—even simply voting for it—was worth the risk. The process, though long and arduous, was ultimately successful. An unprecedented seven and one-half million people registered to vote.

As the opposition's campaign picked up momentum and the regime
relaxed restrictions on public gatherings in the last weeks of the
campaign, many thousands demonstrated. A march starting
simultaneously from the northern and southern ends of the country
proceeded through all of the most important cities of Chile, shouting
a joyful "No!" to Pinochet. The shout proclaimed that we want no
more violence and no more darkness. We showed that we are a people
with dignity. Women and men of all ages joined the caravans. We
did so with determination and with great hope, with the strength of
those who have reason on their side.

In the end, Pinochet's apparatus of repression, his police, and his
control of the means of communication were of no use to him because
they failed to intimidate the people. When the march converged on
Santiago, we were 100,000 Chileans who, joining hands, formed a
human "Chain for Peace" that stretched 78 kilometers around the city.

After that march of joy, all doubt was gone. The "No" to Pinochet
was the voice of the majority, as we proved at the polls on that beautiful
fifth of October 1988. It was very moving to see a whole people,
dressed in their best clothes, dressed for a celebration, waiting peacefully
with heads up and hearts beating with excitement for their chance to
vote for change. This was our triumph, the triumph of the people,
organized in political parties, social and labor organizations, Christian
base communities, and neighborhood groups. Our triumph was that
we began to dismantle the dictatorship without bullets, without
violence.[14]

Translated from Spanish by Philip McManus

Notes

1. Popular Unity's 36.2 percent plurality in 1970 grew to 44 percent in 1973.
2. Quoted in *Southern Cone Report,* September 8, 1988, p 1.
3. Virginia M. Bouvier, "Church-State Conflict Soars in Chile," January 1985,
unpublished. Bouvier is a former Senior Associate of the Washington Office on Latin
America.
4. One of eleven national chapters of the Latin America-wide network.
5. SERPAJ, "Acta de Identidad."
6. Fernando Aliaga, "Una Propuesta de No Violencia Activa" [A Proposal for Active
Nonviolence], SERPAJ/Chile document, December 1983.
7. Fernando Aliaga, "No-Violencia Activa: Estrategia Democrática" [Active
Nonviolence: A Democratic Strategy], SERPAJ, October 1985, p. 4.
8. Brian Loveman, "Government and regime succession in Chile," *Third World
Quarterly* 10, January 1988, p. 280.
9. "Lightning actions" have become a hallmark of popular resistance in Chile. For
virtually the entire rule of the military dictatorship in Chile, nonviolent direct actions
have been, by definition, actions of civil disobedience. Given the regime's brutal
repression, including beating, imprisonment, and torture, participation can carry a
serious risk to the physical and mental integrity—or even to the lives—of those

involved. Lightning actions are well organized demonstrations that last long enough to make a clear public statement but usually end quickly enough to avoid arrest.

10. "Shantytown" refers to a poor neighborhood where the houses are usually nothing more than shelters of cardboard, metal and other discarded materials, with a dirt floor and just a bit of wood or tin for a roof; sometimes they do not even have a bathroom. For the people living in them, a "real" house remains a dream.

11. Broad-based, multifaceted protests that swept Chile and rocked the regime.

12. During the national protests, a number of workshops focused specifically on dealing with fear. For a fuller description of the theory and objectives of nonviolence preparation, see Appendix B: "Preparing for Nonviolence."

13. SERPAJ is a respected voice in opposition political circles. In addition to the nonviolence trainings, SERPAJ was also a consistent and effective voice for unity of opposition forces during the plebiscite campaign. One cost of that stand was a fire-bombing of the home of a SERPAJ leader in Valparaiso.

14. The October 1988 plebiscite called for a yes-or-no vote on the continued rule of General Augusto Pinochet. Opposition forces demonstrated a strong show of unity by successfully launching a massive registration drive, a number of major demonstrations, and a sophisticated poll-watching strategy that made large-scale fraud virtually impossible. This effort overcame the regime's advantages—control of the media, repression of voter registration and other opposition efforts, etc. The result was a fifty-five percent to forty-three percent defeat for Pinochet.

As important as the victory of 1988 was, the building of a demoracy is a long process. The 1980 constitution, written by the military, allowed Pinochet to stay as commander of the armed forces even after civilian opposition leader Patricio Aylwin was elected president and took office in March 1990. A variety of other constitutional provisions are designed to preserve the autonomy of the armed forces and the key role they have assumed in Chilean politics. While some changes in the constitution were approved by a popular vote in 1989, many anti-democratic elements remain.

Tensions between the unrepentant armed forces and the democratic opposition will not easily be resolved. But as former SERPAJ National Coordinator Domingo Namuncura noted during the 1988 campaign, " . . . no dictatorship abandons power simply as a result of the mathematical majority of the votes. It goes when the mobilized people defend their vote and demand the effective recognition of their sovereignty." See Domingo Namuncura, "Escuela de la No Violencia: Un Entrenamiento para Promover la Vida," *Paz y Justicia*, No. 55, August 1988, p. 9.

For further reading

Allende, Isabel. *The House of the Spirits*. New York: Alfred Knopf, 1985.

Feinberg, Richard. *The Triumph of Allende: Chile's Legal Revolution*. New York: New American Library, 1977. ·

Loveman, Brian. *Chile—The Legacy of Hispanic Capitalism*. New York: Oxford University Press, 1988.

Stallings, Barbara. *Class Conflict and Economic Development in Chile, 1958-1973*. Stanford, CA: Stanford University Press, 1978.

Timerman, Jacobo. *Chile: Death in the South*. New York: Alfred Knopf, 1987.

Valenzuela, J. Samuel and Valenzuela, Arturo. *Military Rule in Chile: Dicatatorship and Oppositions*. Baltimore: Johns Hopkins University Press, 1986.

EIGHT

Introduction

Most of the stories in this book focus on action—strikes, demonstrations, marches, land takeovers . . . —but such actions do not spring forth out of thin air. In any successful nonviolent campaign they are always the result of two things: organization and *conscientización,* the process of coming to a critical awareness of one's place in the world and one's potential as a maker of history and not just its object.

This chapter is a story of sowing seeds. With its origins in some of the most remote and inaccessible corners of the Peruvian Andes, it tells of the slow and laborious process of working with the resources and abilities of an oppressed but undefeated people. Solidarity, a core value in the culture of the people of the Andes, becomes the basis of building organization and rooting it in a critical consciousness of the need for and possibility of change.

Examples of revolutionary demagoguery and totalitarianism are evidence that just as movements do not emerge spontaneously, neither does democracy. Democracy must be carefully nurtured in the process of building a new society step by step, day by day, in the shell of the old. This chapter describes experiences of proto-democracy. They are the solid roots that a mighty movement needs in order to grow.

The chapter focuses not on the political organizing of a labor union, a human rights group or the landless but on the pastoral ministry of the church. In this case it is the Roman Catholic Church. In a situation of extreme necessity no church can divorce its work from organizing for change. The chapter details how some sectors of the Peruvian Catholic Church have realized that fact and applied it concretely.

The vast majority of Latin American people share the Christian faith. That faith provides much of the vision and sustenance for the long, difficult process of creating peace as the fruit of justice. To understand Latin America today and the broad liberation movement in the region, one must understand this dynamic relationship between faith and politics.

The cultural context that the chapter describes is not pacifist in the strict sense of the word. Nor is nonviolence a frequent topic of discussion in San Ignacio, Chachapoyas or Puno. Moreover, since this chapter was written, the increase in the revolutionary violence by Sendero Luminoso (Shining Path) guerillas has hampered the work in these communities. Nonetheless, the traditional values of classic nonviolence are present here. Dialogue, love, speaking truth to power, a willingness to risk and to suffer on behalf of others without recourse to violence—all these deeply permeate these experiences. This is due to an extraordinary confluence of indigenous traditions of solidarity and the people's Christian faith, rooted in a liberation perspective. The point where the two meet is the community. Therein lies the strength and the hope of "*los de abajo,*" those at the bottom.

Peru: Furrows of Peace in a Blood-stained Land
Edmundo León y León and Oscar Aliaga-Abanto

Peace is always a gift of God, but it depends also on us. And the keys for peace are in our hands. It depends on us to know how to be able to use them to open all of the doors.   John Paul II

They wanted to build a highway right through our *chacras* [tiny farms]. We do not have much land and what we have is of poor

This chapter originally appeared in a different form in the Peruvian magazine, *Paz: Tarea de Todos*, 1:Nos. 2-3 (January-April 1987), pp. 12-19.

quality. We and our families live on what little we plant. One day they came to destroy our fields with a bulldozer so we stood up and opposed them. As a result, on the following days the police came and threatened to shoot us.

We protested to the assistant governor of the province of Cutervo, but he said he had orders from the Ministry of Transportation and that he had to comply. To prevent this outrage, we organized. Around the clock the men and the women took turns guarding our fields. In spite of our opposition, they were able to destroy the *chacras* of some of our *compañeros*.

A lawyer friend confirmed what we felt to be right: that no one can take away or destroy our lands arbitrarily. First the government must formally expropriate them and then pay us a fair price in advance. This had not happened. The law was on our side so we decided also to use the law in our struggle. A committee from our community went to meet with the departmental authorities in Cajamarca. Other leaders went to Lima to speak with the Director General of Roads. We also had contact with the Ministry of the Presidency. They listened to our arguments and the legal principles that supported us, and promised to help us.

However, in our village, called Allanga Baja, engineers and machine operators continued to come and destroy our lands. So we decided on more drastic measures. Men and women together, we sat down in front of the bulldozer. In spite of the fact that they had the help of hundreds of police they had to stop their machines. We were ready to die in order to defend our land. It is all we have in this world.

For no reason a judge ordered that eleven of our *compañeros* be detained. Just for defending our rights! Finally with the help of the church we got them freed.

Some weeks later, we went to Cajamarca and began a suit. Thanks to that the government reversed itself and abandoned the project. More than thirty peasant families saved their way of life, and we strengthened our peasant organization.

The most important thing we got from this experience was the conviction that if we had struggled individually we would never have gotten anything. The key was that all of us organized to defend what is to us the source of life, our land. And ever since, right up to today, we have maintained our organization. Moved by our Christian spirit we collectively have come to another conviction: the impulse to defend life is absolutely fundamental. Rooted in it, we must continue to seek peace as the fruit of justice.

—Testimony of a Peruvian peasant

In recent years in Peru a wide variety of peasant organizations have sprung up. They represent a search for alternatives to the present political, social, economic, and ethical situation. This organizational work is also emerging as a way to confront the steadily worsening political violence in the country, which is aggravating the existing conditions of poverty and injustice. The task is to sow the seeds of a new, more fraternal and more democratic society where, as the peasant said, peace becomes the fruit of social justice. In recent decades the

Peruvian Indians find solidarity and hope in the suffering of
Jesus. Photo courtesy of *Paz: Tarea de Todos.*

Peruvian Catholic Church has given special help to this effort among poor peasants in the mountains of the Andean region of the country.

Misery and injustice: structural violence

The situation in the rural areas of Peru is complex and difficult to describe. Tremendous ethnic and cultural differences, racism, and unjust socio-economic structures conspire against the largely Indian population. The immediate victim is the peasant, especially in the mountains. The net result has been poverty; lack of government services; cultural oppression, with the exclusion of the Quechua language and other Andean traditions from the areas of education, public administration and development; and the marginalization of a large percentage of the nation's Indians.

In 1981 the rural population of Peru was 5,917,814 out of a total of 17,005,210 (34.8 percent). A large portion of that rural population lives in seven of the poorer departments: Amazonas, Apurimac, Ayachucho, Cajamarca, Cusco, Huancavélica, and Puno. Taken together these seven represent twenty-five percent of the national population but produce only nine percent of the Gross Domestic Product. The average amount of land under cultivation per inhabitant is only .57 acres. In 1987 the average life expectancy ranged from 47.6 years (Huancavélica) to 58.5 (Amazonas). Both figures represent a slight *decline* from 1979 figures.

The following table lists some other critical indicators of health and welfare:[1]

	Number of inhabitants per doctor (1981)	Infant mortality (per 1000 live births) (1979)	Percentage of urban homes with water, electricity, and sewers (1981)
Amazonas	25,456	96	15.1
Apurimac	29,395	124	9.4
Ayachucho	16,779	128	14.0
Cajamarca	18,027	95	33.4
Cusco	5,904	139	24.7
Huancavélica	28,899	142	10.8
Puno	12,717	125	27.5

Summary executions, torture, disintegration: death through armed violence

The situation demonstrated by the above data is similar in many of the other seventeen departments. Moreover, since 1980 the peasants in many of the mountainous regions of the country have faced another form of violence, a violence which has cast a permanent shadow of worry, despair, and death. This is the unjustifiable cruelty of the Maoist group Sendero Luminoso. The group's authoritarian strategy is to organize small, armed contingents of terrorists who fan ancient resentments that go all the way back to the barbarity of the colonial period.[2] They urge the peasant masses to join them in making war. War, they say, is the key to their liberation.

Many of the Sendero Luminoso attacks have been in rural areas. In most of their innumerable acts of *ajusticiamiento* (summary political execution), torture, and *coacciones*[3] of entire villages, the victims have been peasants.

The state has answered this violence with an equally authoritarian and cruel response. Torture is common. The inhuman practice of forced disappearance has claimed more than two thousand victims. Using many peasant villages as pawns for confronting the Sendero Luminoso, the military has imposed tight control.[4] A great many such communities have been destroyed or forced to move. Thousands of people have had to flee to urban centers or into the jungle. By 1988 the war had cost some ten thousand lives, mostly of innocent peasants.

The political violence is closely related to long-standing poverty and at first occurred mainly in a few mountainous departments (Apurimac, Ayacucho, and Huancavélica). Today it extends through almost the entire country. In the absence of structural reforms the influence of Sendero Luminoso has grown substantially.

In the jungle departments, especially San Martín and Huanuco, there is also the violence of the drug traffic. In the last few years that traffic has brought many more deaths. Here too the victim is most often the peasant, the poor person of the countryside, the forgotten one of our society.

Constructing peace in the countryside: the vitality of peasant organizations

Still, the countryside is not all terror and death. Rural Peruvians also possess an immense vitality, which finds expression in a multitude of organizations. Throughout the length and breadth of the country these organizations, representing men, women, and youth, have struggled to defend life and build strength and unity. Gradually the peasants are setting forth an alternative vision of the countryside and of society, a vision of justice, democracy, and freedom. Although their organizations are still young, widely separated, and lacking a common strategy, they have great potential in today's Peru. The modern world seeks to absorb them even as it undermines their economy and values. But through their organizations Peruvian peasants are reinforcing the traditional give-and-take and solidarity of the Andean indigenous communities.

Our central point is simply this: Amid waves of violence rolling across the country, the rural areas are witnessing the birth of important experiences and creative initiatives in the search for peace. While efforts to build organization, foster democracy, and promote new values are crucial, real peace will come only with a broad redistribution of wealth and privilege together with the creation of alternative patterns in human, social, and political relations.

In all Latin America, Peru is among those countries with the greatest number of rural organizations. There are approximately five thousand peasant communities. Two large peasant organizations are active—the Confederación Campesina del Peru (CCP) and the Confederación Nacional Agraria (CNA). But the peasant movement is broader than these formal entities.

Some organizations are ancestral. The peasant communities themselves meet, work in common, and defend their rights. Through their rituals and feast days they express their faith, their culture, and their sense of life. Other organizations have emerged in the last three decades. In addition to these groups, the people are undertaking many projects for their economic and social development, such as marketing associations, communal stores, and community farming projects.

In the last ten years *rondas campesinas,* or peasant patrols, are another form of organization. Initiated mainly to prevent crime in the rural communities (especially cattle rustling), they have begun to have a very significant impact in the Peruvian countryside. Their main method is nightly patrols of community lands in which adult men take rotating shifts. They also serve as community self-defense organizations. In addition to the regular patrols, the *rondas campesinas* have developed a well-organized system of justice to identify and punish offenders. It is a system that is outside of—and represents an alternative to—that of the government.

In this sense they administer justice in a broader form, in accordance with their traditions, norms, and customs. As such they represent a very important experience of democracy, both socially and juridically. Through the *rondas campesinas,* the values and culture of the Andean peasants are put into practice. *Ronderos* have testified:

> The *ronda* is involved in everything. We have built the school . . . and the health clinic and have worked to get a doctor here. . . . We also have organized communal work crews. If the irrigation canals have to be cleaned the *ronda* is there, organizing and calling people together. . . . Before it was more difficult. Some didn't want to join in. Now, everyone respects the *ronda*; it has authority. And that's why we have also been able to resolve a number of disputes about

property lines. There have been cases in court for five or six years, paying the lawyers all the time, and the *ronda* has been able to resolve them in one day, with no money.

Punishment for those caught stealing is likely to be mandatory participation in the *rondas* and labor for the community. Cases of repeat offenders may call for another response:

> There was one *compañero* whom we had to punish several times. So we asked ourselves why he continued stealing. . . . We investigated and discovered that he had many children and he wasn't able to finish building his house. Because he was busy with all that, he couldn't care for his fields very well. So once a month he would steal an animal to make ends meet. Once the *ronda* started it made matters worse. It was more difficult to steal and then when he got caught and had to work, he had even less time to work his fields. So the *ronda* got together and went to help him finish his house. . . . Now it has been a year and he isn't stealing. In fact, he is now a good *rondero* himself.[6]

Cultural organizations also play an important role. Hundreds of peasant radio correspondents work throughout the country.[7] Labor federations and non-governmental development agencies have mobilized many rural residents for peasant drawing and painting contests. There is a network of rural libraries in Cajamarca and a movement of peasant technical advisers in San Ignacio.

So we see that in the countryside there are elements of both life and of death. Distinct projects provide alternatives and seek to establish themselves in the lives of the rural poor.

The church: weaving a fabric of life in the countryside

Over the last 30 years, the Peruvian Catholic Church, faithful to its commitment and preferential option for the poor, has been developing a *ministry of accompaniment* in the countryside. This has meant getting physically and culturally close to the problems of this exploited people, sharing in their pain and their joy. It has also meant persistent effort to preserve indigenous languages, traditions, and values.

The primary actors in this ministry are the thousands of catechists who fulfill a variety of functions in their communities. Their experience demonstrates that as animators of faith they act out of a liberating, Christian commitment. From that basis they are constructing life-giving alternatives for their families, their communities, and their peoples. Bit by bit they build for the nation as a whole. Through their structures of coordination the catechists gather to discuss their problems, make decisions, and plan joint projects. In this way the perspective of "*los de abajo,*" those at the bottom, becomes a presence in history where for centuries it has been ignored.

Along with these catechists there are many Christian men and women who also root their work in a liberation perspective and unite their efforts to those of the popular organizations. They are technical advisers; members of Christian youth groups; members of the *"rondas campesinas"*; leaders of peasant communities, labor unions, and peasant federations; and so on. These Christians have come to understand that they have a responsibility to their community, their country, their church, and their God. Without confusing the two they work to be and to build the church, even as they serve the autonomous popular organizations.

The proposal that the church makes to the peasants is not political in the strict sense of political parties or organizations. But without a doubt the church communicates elements and criteria of what a new society should be, with a new way of relating and a new attitude toward one's neighbors. These spring forth from the message of fraternity and justice that is at the heart of the gospel. Meanwhile the same attitude of respect for the dignity and liberation of the flesh-and-blood person rejects the manipulative populism seen in some politicians. And it rejects any sort of violent terrorism.

At the heart of the church's work is the affirmation that since the Christian communities and the thousands of rural peasant groups are saying *yes to life* every day, they are witnesses for peace. This is enormously important for the task of evangelization and also for the development of a national identity and vision.

To illustrate, we would like to describe three cases of the Catholic Church's work in the countryside. They have several points in common: all take place in remote corners of the country, all are organized by religious groups, and each reflects a history of at least ten years. They also share a common education in the faith and a shared liberation perspective on building the church and the Kingdom of God. The fundamental basis of this work is solidarity, a characteristic value of the ancient Andean tradition.

San Ignacio: catechesis and evangelization

For more than thirty years the Jesuits have worked with catechists in the Vicariate of Jaén, in the northern department of Cajamarca; in the parish of San Ignacio, they have worked for fifteen years. From their work has come a network in which clergy and laity share pastoral ministry. The peasants and each little village have become actively aware of what it means to belong to the church. For many years it has been possible to maintain a group of around 250 catechists. They have established ties with even the smallest and most remote settlements of the parish.[8]

Each parish is divided into zones with catechists grouped according to zone. Each zone has one delegate. A local assembly democratically elects each delegate, selecting on the basis of his or her daily behavior and Christian practice. The delegates are responsible for encouraging and coordinating the work of their local *compañeros*. The catechists in turn can count on the backing and confidence of their villages.

Hence the catechists are usually the authentic leaders of their communities—as respected and as well recognized as the local political authorities. They are people with a religious task, continually and deeply preoccupied with their community's problems. Most of these problems are due to lack of governmental support. Catechists promote an integral approach to health, develop alternatives to improve production, attempt to improve respect for the role of women, and help create and strengthen many different social organizations.

In the specifically religious area, catechists organize persons highly committed to the work of the church into Bible study groups. The groups meet weekly to pray the rosary, read and discuss passages from the Bible, and analyze local and national problems. The catechists also conduct Sunday liturgy and prepare people for baptism, marriage, and first communion. With the great size of parishes and quantity of communities, parish priests visit each one only once or twice a year. So the role of the catechists is crucial.

In San Ignacio, the central activity of peasants is cultivating coffee. Standards of living and the very survival of a large percentage of peasants depend on this crop. Catechists have helped organize technical training in farming and ranching. To participate in the courses the people must meet three conditions: (1) communities must choose trainees; (2) they must set aside at least one-half hectare (1.2 acres) for communal work in order to share with others the skills they have learned; and (3) they must organize a committee dedicated to improving production and addressing other community needs.

Catechists have also made rural people more and more aware of the need for organization. This awareness has been crucial for the *rondas campesinas* in San Ignacio. In contrast to similar groups in other parts of the country, they are not limited to defending justice for the peasants and organizing the community. In the last few years the state has eliminated its support to cooperatives in marketing coffee abroad and credit policies have been inadequate. The peasants have also faced unstable prices for coffee on the international market. So in San Ignacio the *rondas* are increasingly concerned with the cultivation and marketing of coffee. In order to deal with this situation the pastoral ministry in San Ignacio has been directly involved in developing strategies for marketing outside of traditional channels. At the same time it has helped create a greater consciousness of the exploitation of peasants and of the structural mechanisms of oppression that characterize capitalism.

Chachapoyas: health care as a task of evangelization

Ten years ago, a group of Carmelite sisters in Chachapoyas, in the northern department of Amazonas, initiated a program of health care and preventive health education. This program is the central element in their ministry, a means of addressing the difficult living conditions of the people. Step by step, year by year, their work has developed in this impoverished area whose mountains and rivers present major obstacles to any such effort. There are now more than a hundred trained health promoters, and an even larger number of communities have organized health committees. Among the hundreds of men and women on these committees one observes a new and steadily developing vision of their community, region, and country. And that vision of the small teams has spilled over into larger groups.

Today health promoters make periodic visits to even the smallest, most remote villages. Sometimes on foot, sometimes on horseback, they promote traditional natural medicine with the support of modern medicine. Through these visits they seek to encourage broad participation in the task of community health care.

Each community that has its own health promoter organizes to identify high-risk groups such as children and pregnant women. Helping the promoters identify the most needy sectors are health committees, a community assembly (similar to a town meeting), or other entities, such as mothers' clubs (for the pregnant women) and the local schools (in the case of the children). The target groups are offered preventive health education courses. Local midwives participate in prenatal care programs.

Promoters also work to identify the most serious problems of these groups—malnutrition and toxemia among pregnant women; diarrhea and respiratory disease among children. Along with their care for the sick they compile data such as the time a sickness occurs and how it develops. These data are useful for preventive health care. For example, they enable health workers to identify children who need vaccination. Promoters then organize periodic vaccination campaigns.

Although this strategy is relatively new the communities show a great deal of interest. The health data permit better appraisal and follow-up of health problems with a minimal investment of time and money. They are also useful when leaders want to pressure government authorities to provide greater attention to health problems. For instance, in response to such efforts, the Agriculture Ministry has established programs to improve crops and nutritional practices. Communities have also begun trying to get authorities to improve drinking water and sanitation.

Through their experience promoters and community members are coming to understand health care in an increasingly integral manner. On the one hand they see it as the responsibility of both the individual and the community; on the other hand it is a right which ought to be demanded of the government, whose services are completely nonexistent in most of the communities.

Of course the health promoters, who work on a strictly volunteer basis, have not been able to eliminate health problems. But undoubtedly they have been able to reduce the level of suffering and death and have helped develop a critical consciousness of the situation. They have taken up the challenge to promote the gospel, to live the faith, and to struggle for life as committed participants amid the suffering of their people. And as these forgotten Peruvians have worked together in groups, their sense of identity has grown.

Puno: The struggle for land and the defense of life

Since the 1950s, the Diocese of Puno has witnessed the development of what is now known as the Movimiento de Animadores Campesinos Cristianos (MACC, Movement of Christian Peasant Activists). As its name implies, MACC is an organization of Christian peasant leaders and change agents. While the political inclinations of its members vary, members share an awareness that their task is to promote the gospel and build peace among the people. This presupposes a commitment to their families, communities, labor organizations, and political parties. Meanwhile because they identify with the church they assume responsibility for many of their communities' religious activities. This holistic perspective explains why some of the leaders of MACC are municipal authorities, leaders of their peasant federations or organizers of community work projects, while others work in more pastoral roles.

MACC has established various committees covering such areas as human rights, the role of women, training, and culture. With about eighteen hundred members, this Christian movement is active in four provinces of the department of Puno, in Peru's southeast. The members in each parish nominate delegates who together form a steering committee.

Over the last five years the movement has taken on increasingly concrete tasks. For example they have struggled for the democratic restructuring of land tenure and worked at problems of drought and flooding. They have reflected together and proposed alternatives in the face of armed terrorist violence and the violence of the security forces.

The struggle for land is really a struggle to recover what was taken away centuries ago. A 1969 agrarian reform law did not resolve this

In the Peruvian Andes, popular education empowers Indian women. Photo courtesy of *Paz: Tarea de Todos.*

problem. Although it established government-run enterprises which benefited a limited number of families, it ignored traditional peasant communities. Those communities, which include the great majority of the population in Puno, were the original property owners.

The land struggle re-emerged in the 1970s. In 1985 presidential candidate Alán García promised to address the problem. He was elected, and immediately the struggle heated up. During his administration there were a number of land takeovers or "recoveries" as the peasants call them. Some of the recoveries had the support of Agriculture Ministry rulings that were never actually implemented. Yet the land struggle has led to a climate of fear and repression and the death of numerous peasant leaders. The strong presence of Sendero Luminoso in the region has heightened tension as Sendero has attempted to polarize the situation.

The Catholic Church, and especially the members of MACC, have been very much a part of the land struggle. Christians of the region have taken part in various land takeovers and in negotiations with government authorities. They are aware that their Christian faith demands that they struggle continuously for justice, peace, and human rights. They recognize that in their case, this means being fully present in the struggle to recover the *Pachamama,* as the Quechua call their mother earth.

Some final reflections

The three experiences described here are important examples of education, *conscientización*, and democratization. But to us they are, above all, significant advances in the task of promoting the gospel and building faith in the rural areas. We clearly see the hand of the God of Life stretching out to the forgotten ones of this world, to those in our country who do not count. A people saddened by the pain they have gone through for so long are also bursting with the joy of an event that occurred twenty centuries ago: the resurrection of Jesus, the gift and the promise of the Kingdom. The loaves multiplied for the masses simultaneously satisfy their hunger for God and bread. To remember the resurrection is to contribute to the sowing of life, with the stubborn hope that the peace being built in ministries like those we have described may one day extend to all the men and women of this country.

These experiences of church have taken root in the religiosity, the solidarity, and the reciprocity of the Andean world. They give that world a larger perspective while maximizing the level of commitment and unity of the rural communities to which the church has drawn close. In other words, the church has recognized and embraced that key idea of the Latin American Bishops Conference of Puebla, the "evangelizing potential of the poor."[9]

The two essential characteristics of this work have been the special value it has placed on the cultural roots of the indigenous people and secondly, its respect for the dignity of the person, which have found expression in active solidarity with the struggles and joys of these, the poorest of this country.

With this attitude of profound respect for the peasants, the church is breaking down its older image of God as a faraway, punishing God who meets us only after we die. This new perspective is teaching the peasants an attitude of commitment to the here and now. It is encouraging them to be the creators of their own history rather than always being objects of oppressive forces seemingly beyond their control.

The people are recovering their self-confidence and their faith in the God of Life, which finds expression in love for the land. As Monsignor Vallejos, the former Archbishop of Cusco who was very close to the poor, used to say, "The land is the place of fraternity where the peasants are able to make the solidarity they share a reality in all of its fullness."

Of course there are also challenges in the peasant ministry that have not been resolved. For example pastoral agents need to understand the peasant worldview better. There are also various problems among the committed laity. Commitment to their families may not keep pace with their group commitment, resulting in neglect of spouse or children. A sense of responsibility toward the community may sometimes express itself in domineering or overly bureaucratic attitudes. Nonetheless, these experiences clearly express the vitality of the poor. In the midst of their limitations they are building on their own initiatives and building peace in this country so marked by violence. The hope created by these projects of popular education and evangelization constitutes an important source of strength amid Peru's widespread climate of skepticism.

Land, fraternity, and a holistic view of reality—as peasant groups rescue all these they rescue a peasant spirituality. Their spirituality is an expression of a popular religiosity, and it is a crucial liberating element in the countryside. Experiences of church are the heart and soul of the struggle for peace in the Peruvian countryside. Committed individuals, working always in an organized manner, confront all the forms of death that threaten their communities while creating the possibility that their people may live life in its fullness.

These are experiences of peace because they seek to establish justice as a basis of social organization, community, and democracy. The men and women involved are agents of peace because they are confident that they will build a better tomorrow. Each day they are doing just that by creating new alternatives to overcome their society's obstacles to peace.

Translated from Spanish by Philip McManus

Notes

1. These and the preceding statistics are based on Consejo Nacional de Población, *Peru: Guía demográfica y socio-económica* (Lima, 1985); and Ibid., *Indicadores demográficos y socio-económicos: Peru, 1987* (Lima, 1987).

2. The Spanish conquest of Peru produced a tremendous confrontation with the indigenous people who at that time were part of the Inca Empire. At a great social and cultural cost the Spanish destroyed the Empire itself. However, the indigenous population continued to resist attempts to suppress their culture. During the colonial period and the history of the Peruvian republic, the Spanish and the dominant classes have not been able to fully consolidate a nation-state. Instead there has been constant tension and a traumatized history along with the unmitigated oppression of the Indians, all of which has served as a base on which Sendero Luminoso has built its struggle.

3. In this context *"coacciones"* refers to the imposition of a strict regimen governing social behavior, mandatory work projects, obligatory contributions of food, lodging, and money, and an absolute code of silence vis-à-vis the authorities regarding the presence of guerrillas in the communities. Violations may be punishable by death.

4. In Peru, the peasant community is the social, political, economic, and cultural structure of the inhabitants of the rural areas, especially in the Andes. The inheritor of the pre-Hispanic cultures, they have developed in the greatest numbers and strength in the Andes, based on ties of blood, tradition, and culture as well as ownership of land. These organizations have legal recognition and the government guarantees their autonomy.

5. The establishment of the republic in the last century left intact the feudal structure of land tenure and a constantly tense situation of confrontation between the big landowners and the peasants who worked in a form of servitude. Especially since the end of the 1950s, peasant movements have emerged organizing numerous acts of protest. The redistribution of land and abolition of all forms of servitude have been their central mobilizing thrust. The first stage of this process ended with the Agrarian Reform of 1969 under the government of General Velasco (who nonetheless was unable to eliminate the problems of the rural areas). The mobilization continues today, but now the central demand is simply the right to life, a right that is sadly not secure for many Peruvians.

6. "Organización Popular y Educación," *Paz: Tarea de Todos*, 2, June-August 1988, pp. 52-53. The *rondas campesinas* are found principally in the northern part of the country. They should not be confused with other groups found further south, which the government also calls *rondas campesinas*, but which are really para-military groups. The military and police use the latter as shock troops in their counterinsurgency campaign.

7. The correspondents are community members who assume the essential responsibility of local coordination of classes transmitted over the radio to remote rural areas. In one such program alone, there were eight hundred correspondents, each with his or her own class, each specially trained for this task. Some of them go on to help set up additional groups. Others assist in the production of parts of the radio programs themselves.

8. As is typical in much of the Peruvian Andes, these settlements are spread over an immense area, are often unreachable by road, and have very little contact with the rest of the country.

9. Puebla Final Document, article 1147.

For further reading

Aliaga, Oscar. "Puno: Campesinos recuperan tierras." *Andenes*, 38 (May-June 1987); pp. 4-6. Published by Servicios Educativos Rurales, Lima.

Cotler, Julio. *Clases, Estado y Nación en el Perú*. Lima: Instituto de Estudios Peruanos, 1978.

Degregori, Carlos Iván. *Sendero Luminoso*, vol. 1: *Los hondos y mortales desencuentros*, 2: *Lucha armada y utopía autoritaria*. 5th ed., Lima: Instituto de Estudios Peruanos, 1987. Documents nos. 4 and 6.

Guillet, David. *Agrarian Reform and Peasant Economy in Southern Peru*. Columbia, MO: University of Missouri Press, 1979.

Isbell, Billie Jean. "Languages of Domination and Rebellion in Highland Peru," in *Social Education* 49:2 (1985); p. 119-121.

Mariétegui, José Carlos. *Seven Interpretative Essays on the Peruvian Reality*. Austin: University of Texas Press, 1971.

McClintock, Cynthia. "Peru's Sendero Luminoso: Origins and Trajectory," in Susan Eckstein (ed.) *Power and Protest: Latin American Social Movements*. Berkeley: University of California Press, 1989; p. 61-101.

Miller, Rory (ed.). *Region and Class in Modern Peruvian History*. Liverpool: University of Liverpool Institute of Latin American Studies, 1987.

Reid, Michael. *Peru: Paths to Poverty*. London: Latin America Bureau, 1985.

Life in the Peruvian Andes is a constant struggle for survival. Photo courtesy of *Paz: Tarea de Todos.*

Nicaragua

NINE

Introduction

Throughout the 1980s, no situation in the hemisphere provoked and drew more heated emotions in the United States than did Nicaragua's.

On July 19, 1979, a wide cross section of the Nicaraguan people succeeded in throwing off the rule of one of Latin America's most durable dictatorships, the Somoza dynasty. Shaping the popular uprising was the Sandinista Front for National Liberation (FSLN). Shaping the FSLN were nineteen years of revolutionary trial and error, listening and learning. The FSLN had begun as a tiny, doctrinaire band of guerrillas much like many other short-lived Latin American leftist groups. Most such groups have proven more successful at providing a pretext for right wing repression than at threatening it. But those nineteen years of listening and learning had increasingly changed the FSLN into a pluralistic movement—responsive enough to the sentiments of the populace to rewrite basic Marxist tenets concerning religion and to adopt approaches to land reform and Third World development that were both revolutionary and pragmatic.

153

Throughout Latin America, both inside and outside Nicaragua, the Sandinista revolution brought cheers and euphoria. The early years of revolutionary government brought dramatic improvements in the lives of poor Nicaraguans. During five months in 1980 a massive crusade reduced overall illiteracy from 52 to 13 percent.[1] Infant mortality plunged from 121 per thousand live births in 1978 under Somoza, to 63 in 1987.[2] By 1985, more than 120,000 families had gained land through agrarian reform.[3]

Even within the U.S. government there were officials who showed a certain openness; after a long fight, the administration of President Jimmy Carter convinced Congress to approve a substantial aid package to the battered Central American country. As the decade of the 1980s dawned, however, euphoria gave way to polarized political debate. And all too quickly, polarized debate gave way to an ugly war. Ronald Reagan was in the White House and the "Reagan Doctrine" took over: support "freedom fighters" to "roll back Soviet influence" anywhere in the world, especially in "our back yard."

The administration's policy toward Nicaragua was to bleed the country into submission, or, as Reagan put it, to make the Sandinistas "cry uncle." An opposition army, the contras, emerged, created largely by the U.S. Central Intelligence Agency (CIA). But the contras could not mount a real threat to the military or the government. Nor, given a leadership all too often drawn from Somoza's old National Guard, could they offer a clear and credible political alternative. What the contras could do, however, was wreak havoc on the civilian population and on economic targets. Meanwhile, a U.S. trade boycott undermined the economy. And some questionable economic decisions by the Sandinistas probably undercut social programs further, while the costs of financing the war surely did. By the mid-1980s, improvements in social services were beginning to stall.

At the same time, the very language that President Reagan and his administration used to describe the effort was itself destructive. His polarizing language imposed acute dilemmas on analysts, both in North and Latin America, who sought to maintain a balanced view of the unfolding revolution and to make any criticisms of the Sandinistas into a constructive force. For example, as the young government's policies toward the indigenous peoples of the Atlantic Coast moved from generally bumbling to sometimes criminal, many commentators felt caught between forthrightly voicing their concern at the risk of abetting Reagan's cause, or appearing to be blindly ideological in support for Nicaragua.

This dilemma could easily have ground North Americans committed to nonviolence into the dust of factionalism. What their attitude should be toward Third World "wars of liberation" and the violence of the desperate poor has sometimes been a point of heated, yet futilely theoretical, debate. When detached and academic, that debate prompted the disdainful invective of Nicaragua's colorful poet-priest, Ernesto Cardenal, who railed against "stupid pacifists." Fortunately, however, some of North America's nonviolent activists forged a more promising approach. They lived not only with the complexities of revolutionary Nicaragua, but above all, with the Nicaraguans, putting love into risky practice on their behalf. Combined with vigorous efforts back home to oppose U.S. policy, these initiatives presented the Reagan administration with a formidable obstacle.

Meanwhile the Nicaraguan people, though increasingly tired of war and crises as the decade wore on, did not let the vise of U.S. aggression on one side, and their own perceived need to militarize on the other, squeeze all creativity from them. Though few Nicaraguans felt they had the luxury of scaling back the option of armed military defense, they turned to every imaginable nonviolent means—diplomatic, legal, political, and even nonviolent theology—in order to dig trenches of self defense. This is the story that Paul Jeffrey tells.

It is a story unfinished. Jeffrey had scarcely completed this chapter, when Nicaraguan President Daniel Ortega was making new, unilateral initiatives to unloose the deadlocked Esquipulas II (or "Arias Plan") peace accord between Central America's five presidents. Since its signing in August 1987 that agreement seemed to offer the best hope for peace in Central America. Greater reliance on moral suasion and a willingness to take the first step—both elements of active nonviolence—seemed to guide Nicaragua's highest official.

In March 1988 the Sandinista leadership took a step it had vowed never to take. It opened a dialogue with contra leaders. Results were mixed, and at the official level, negotiations eventually broke down. But at the grassroots level, in many areas of the countryside, efforts for dialogue continued. During a cease-fire period, new life persisted in local and regional reconciliation commissions tentatively begun in the wake of Esquipulas II. Often headed by Roman Catholic Delegates of the Word or evangelical pastors, a significant number of these groups carried out a creative and patient witness in the midst of a lengthening, brutal war. In many ways their courageous work symbolizes the unwillingness of people at the base—the very people who suffer first-hand the ravages of war—to wait for their political leaders to negotiate peace. Supported by the Sandinistas, the groups encouraged acceptance of the government's amnesty and guaranteed protection to ex-contra combatants. They fostered face-to-face dialogue between enemy military units; dozens of encounters took place where government troops and contra soldiers shared cigarettes and family news and discussed the prospects for peace.

It would turn out to be an important precedent. In February of 1990, in compliance with the Esquipulas Accords, the Sandinista-led government held national elections. Although the FSLN had won similar elections in 1984, by 1990 war and economic disintegration had taken their toll. The Sandinistas lost. UNO, a diverse coalition of fourteen opposition parties—some with connections to the contras—won. If national reconciliation was possible in the aftermath of the elections, it was largely because grassroots reconciliation had already begun.

It was also possible because the power of the Nicaraguan poor and the Sandinista social revolution were now established facts. Some Nicaraguans surely found it easier to vote for UNO's presidential candidate Violeta de Chamorro because she promised to dismantle military conscription, for example, but *not* to dismantle social gains such as land reform.

Increasingly throughout the 1980s active nonviolence became an integral part of the Nicaraguan people's defense. As Nicaragua struggles to rebuild, it will continue to do so. The seeds, and now the saplings, remain.

In Nicaragua disabled war veterans joined the two-week, 200-mile *Via Crucis* from the Honduran border to the capital to "touch the heart of God" with Nicaragua's cry for peace. The sign reads: "We are marching from Jalapa with the God of Peace and Life." February, 1986. Photo by Paul Jeffrey.

Nicaragua:
Planting Seeds of Nonviolence
in the Midst of War

Paul Jeffrey

Gregorio Martínez clearly remembers his days with Sandino. Now almost eighty years old, his eyes still flash in the tropical sunlight as he recounts his years with the man whose struggle and ideas inspire Nicaraguans on their course into the future.

In 1923, when he was only thirteen years old, Martínez joined up with Augusto C. Sandino's ragtag band of soldiers. For the next several years he trekked through Nicaragua's mountainous northern provinces waging guerrilla war against a foreign army that occupied his country—the U.S. Marines. Injured in his leg during a battle at El Jícaro, he still limps slightly as he hikes the rugged roads and trails of his native mountains. Today, the peasant describes with considerable zest and pride his adventures against the "Yánquis." Pointing with a gnarled hand at the nearby pine-covered hills as he relives a skirmish that took place there, he recalls an earthy comment General Sandino once made to him. Six decades later, Gregorio Martínez laughs.

The old, leather-faced, one-time guerrilla, still relishing a sixty-year-old joke about enemy "bastards," might seem an unlikely creator of an authentic Nicaraguan nonviolence. Yet nonviolence emerges from unlikely places in revolutionary Nicaragua. Gregorio Martínez now walks in its vanguard.

Early in 1986, during Lent, Gregorio Martínez continued his struggle against foreign aggression. But now his method was different from that of Sandino. Beginning in Jalapa, near the country's northern border with Honduras, he joined with thousands of other pilgrims in a fifteen-day Via Crucis ("Way of the Cross"), a religious procession recalling the sufferings of Christ on his last day. From the cool northern mountains where Martínez had fought with Sandino, the Via Crucis wound more than two hundred miles south to the sprawling and sweltering capital of Managua. Thousands of people left their villages or urban shacks to march a mile, or for several days, of the Via Crucis. Each day as they commemorated the suffering of their Savior in one of the traditional Stations of the Cross they recalled how their sisters and brothers had also suffered. Marching past the sites of massacres and ambushes the pilgrims prayed and sang. They hoped to "touch the heart of God" with Nicaragua's cry for peace.

The story of Gregorio Martínez is in some ways typical for Nicaragua. Martínez is a deeply religious man. For the last twenty years he has been a Delegate of the Word, a Roman Catholic lay pastor. He is also a refugee within his own country, having fled his home in San Pablo de Murra when U.S.-backed counterrevolutionaries, known as contras, stepped up their activity in the area during 1984. Since then he has been living with his wife in La Estancia, a resettlement cooperative nestled in a rich valley just west of Jalapa.

Martínez set off on the procession with only the clothes he was wearing and a gourd for water strung over his shoulder. If he had money in his pocket, it was nothing more than a few devalued *córdobas*. When asked how far he was walking, he simply said, in the manner of the Latin American poor: "To Managua, God willing."

The old man was clear about why he was marching. "The contras have already killed eight of my grandchildren," he said. "And now I've got three sons and five grandchildren in *la defensa*. I'm walking for them, so that they, and all of us, can have peace."[4]

On February 28, two weeks after he began, Gregorio Martínez entered Managua with twenty thousand people walking behind him. As they reached the end of the *Via Crucis*, he was at the head of the pilgrimage, in a place of honor, still limping.

A gospel insurrection

The long walk that brought Martínez to Managua was one expression of a newly emerged nonviolent movement for peace among Nicaraguan Christians. Begun in 1985 with a month-long fast by Nicaragua's foreign minister, Father Miguel D'Escoto, the "Evangelical Insurrection" had spread through the Christian base communities and the ranks of poor and faithful Catholics. They found in the movement an authentic Christian response to the growing aggression against their country by the United States and what many Nicaraguans see as its proxy army, the contras.

D'Escoto's decision to fast in 1985 grew out of his unique position as both a Maryknoll priest and a high government official. As a Christian he had proposed specific nonviolent actions over the years, actions for priests and other religious leaders in his country to undertake against injustice and for social change. But Nicaragua's Roman Catholic hierarchy had turned a deaf ear. A disciple of Gandhi and Martin Luther King, Jr., D'Escoto struggled to find practical responses that would incarnate his desire for social justice and his belief in nonviolence. In the late 1970s he became a member of "The Twelve," a group of leading Nicaraguan public figures who formed a visible political opposition to Somoza.

Although D'Escoto never took up arms, he had supported the Sandinista Front for National Liberation (FSLN). Feverishly he worked to convince world public opinion of the Somoza government's repressive nature and of the FSLN's legitimacy. Following the July 1979 triumph of the Nicaraguan revolution the new government named him its foreign minister.

As the principal architect of foreign policy in a country that rapidly drew the ire and the organized violence of the United States, D'Escoto worked on several fronts for peace, even as his country simultaneously prepared for war. As young Nicaraguans went to the mountains to die fighting the contras D'Escoto went to the capitals of the world to exert all his diplomatic leverage against the Reagan administration. He was also the chief proponent of a suit Nicaragua brought before the International Court of Justice. In June 1986, the justices of that court, the world's highest, ruled overwhelmingly that the U.S. war against Nicaragua was illegal.

D'Escoto called these efforts the "military, diplomatic, and legal trenches" of Nicaragua's resistance to foreign aggression. With his 1985 fast, he also proclaimed the opening of a "theological trench" in the struggle. It was to be a realm of action where Christians, through prayer and fasting, could make a unique and nonviolent contribution to defending the lives of their people and the sovereignty of their country. With the *Via Crucis* the following Lent, D'Escoto sought to broaden the Evangelical Insurrection through an action in which many could participate.

The Maryknoll priest believed nonviolence to be the essence of the Evangelical Insurrection. He chose to call it an "insurrection" because, he said, "Christians together, uniting, can rise up in rebellion against injustice, against oppression, against foreign intervention, against whatever prevents people from relating as brothers and sisters." He used the word "evangelical," he told an interviewer, because "this uprising, this protest, uses a different arsenal, with weapons different from the traditional, conventional weapons that the world has always used. The weapons of the gospel, the weapons that our Lord wants us to use, are nonviolent weapons. The most obvious ones are fasting, prayer, and walking."[5]

D'Escoto, a rather rotund cleric until his fast, intended the actions of the Evangelical Insurrection to appeal to several parties. First of all, he described the *Via Crucis* as an attempt "to cry out to heaven" about the aggression Nicaragua's poor were suffering, and to "touch the heart of God." The Catholics—and a handful of Protestants—who joined the fast or walked part of the *Via Crucis,* saw their action as embodied prayer, calling on God to respond to their appeal for peace. The activities also aimed to "touch the heart of Pharaoh," biblical imagery for the President of the United States, whom many participants saw as the head of an "empire" violently imposing its will on the small and poor Central American country. Those who fasted and walked for peace prayed that their sacrifice would move U.S. citizens to new levels of commitment in their resistance to U.S. policy.

As D'Escoto pointed out during the *Via Crucis*, the crucifixion of

The mostly peasant marchers filled the road during the *Via Crucis*, part of the ongoing Evangelical Insurrection. February, 1986. Photo by Paul Dix.

Jesus was possible only because the empire and the religious hierarchy of Palestine were in collusion. So D'Escoto drew attention to the Roman Catholic bishops of Nicaragua who had refused, at least as a group, to denounce contra atrocities and U.S. backing of the terrorists. He and others prayed that their bishops would respond to the suffering of their people and break their complicity of silence with the empire. One bishop, Rubén López Ardón, did pray with the pilgrims and gave them his blessing when they passed through Estelí. But the rest of

the hierarchy kept silent and stayed away despite repeated invitations to join. During the final evening's mass in Managua, in a controversial homily, D'Escoto denounced the country's highest Catholic leader, Cardinal Miguel Obando y Bravo. To D'Escoto, Obando y Bravo's pro-contra activities had made him a "traitor to the people of God."

Clearly in some ways the pilgrimage and D'Escoto's words widened rifts within the Roman Catholic church. In his 1985 fast, D'Escoto had called people of faith to "a moment of definition" in which, no longer hiding from the socio-political conflict whirling around them, they would make direct contributions to the struggle to stop the aggression and achieve peace. Yet an important theme for the walkers was reconciliation. During the *Via Crucis,* especially while visiting war-torn villages near the Honduran border, D'Escoto issued an invitation to peasants who had joined the counterrevolution. He called on these "deceived peasants" to accept the government's amnesty and come home to live securely in their communities. At various times he publicly prayed for the contras.

Those who struggled in the "theological trench" did not see their nonviolent work as the only option for Nicaraguans interested in resisting the violence of the empire. Indeed, they felt their action was complementary to the military defense of their country. Delegations of soldiers came to visit the fasting D'Escoto; walkers on the *Via Crucis* waved and cheered as trucks full of government soldiers rolled past on dusty northern roads.

D'Escoto was clear, however, that the long-term project of the Evangelical Insurrection was a completely nonviolent means of resisting aggression. As he walked the second day of the *Via Crucis,* he told an interviewer:

> At this present time, because nonviolent struggle is something that has not been developed, its role is to complement conventional methods to defend our sovereignty, independence, and right to life. But in due time nonviolence will replace the old, violent methods. We must remember that in spite of all this theology about the just war, about tyrannicide and all that, violence is simply not Christian. We must never proclaim it as if it emanates from the gospel. Violence is only a concession of the gospel to a world in transition.
>
> But the transition will come only if we begin to use nonviolent means to replace the violent means that the world has already known. In Nicaragua this transition has already begun. More and more you see our people responding to this call to bury wars forever, to opt for God's methods. In the eyes of the world, God's methods may appear ridiculous, feeble, weak, or unimpressive. But we have faith—our people in Nicaragua have faith—that because these are the methods that God wants people to use, God's force will be behind our walking, our praying, our fasting. And God will make up the difference. Eventually, through this prayer and sacrifice, the walls of Jericho will fall.[6]

Indeed the strength of the Evangelical Insurrection was precisely in its apparent weakness: its basis in the unarmed power of the poor and the powerless. The moral witness, the truth-force, of the poor who answered the call to pray, fast, and walk proved to be a powerful evangelizing force. As a result, a new spirit of clarity and rededication emerged in Nicaragua. And expressions of international solidarity poured in from North America, Europe, and elsewhere in Latin America. In the U.S., thousands fasted, prayed, and demonstrated against U.S. policy. The example of Nicaraguan Christians inspired churches and other faith-based organizations in the U.S. to condemn relentlessly the immorality of U.S. intervention. U.S. government officials acknowledged these efforts as one of their greatest impediments to carrying out the war.

Centered not in the Foreign Ministry but in the Christian base communities, the Evangelical Insurrection continued. At the beginning of 1987, however, leaders of the nonviolent movement were witnessing a new attempt at dialogue by the Catholic bishops and the Sandinista government. With a tentative détente emerging from that dialogue, the movement's leaders decided not to plan any major public activities that might jeopardize the progress the two sides of the dialogue might make.

The leaders also felt a need to reconnect with the roots of their faith. So during Lent 1987 they went on a retreat, joining with leaders of the base communities from throughout the country for a week of focus on their "personal relationship with Jesus Christ." D'Escoto and other leaders felt it important not to forget that Christian faith was the central motivation of their movement. The participants came out of the retreat with a new commitment to a process of "re-evangelization" in their communities. As many of the Christian base community leaders had become leaders of Sandinista popular organizations before or at the time of the 1979 triumph, they had filled their time with the myriad tasks of national reconstruction and defense. Meanwhile, there had been a waning of the ongoing and intentional reflection that had led to their social and political commitment in the first place. And, given the hierarchy's public opposition to the revolutionary process, many observers had noted the Catholic Church's declining appeal to the young. To call backsliding activists back into the fold and to reach out to young people turned off by the bishops, the evangelical insurrectionists planned a new program of evangelism.

This interest in what many considered the province of the more traditional or pious believers surprised some observers. But this circle of progressive Catholics, whose members had given much of their life—and many lives—to overthrow the Somoza dynasty and bring about a political order that would mean justice for the poor, was only

keeping in contact with its
roots. It was from the Bible
and their relationship to
Christ that their activism
had sprung. In order to expand their nonviolent
movement, they would
have to bring others to
drink from the same
springs that had sustained
their revolutionary faith.

Watering scattered seeds

The activists of the
Evangelical Insurrection
were not the first Nicaraguans to engage in nonviolent activity aimed at liberating the country from
repression, foreign or domestic. Earlier champions
of nonviolence were iso-
lated individuals, however.
Many paid for their labors
with their lives. Bishop

Miguel D'Escoto, Catholic priest and
Foreign Minister of Nicaragua, finds a moment of quiet reflection during the two-
week, 200-mile *Via Crucis*. February, 1986.
Photo by Paul Dix.

Antonio Valdivieso, for example, the third bishop of León, suffered
assassination in 1550 at the hands of wealthy landowners for his steadfast
defense of indigenous peoples' rights.

In the popular insurrection that overthrew the forty-five-year-old
Somoza family dynasty over 400 years later, many thousands of people
participated without firing weapons. They organized and carried out
strikes, work stoppages, marches, international protests, and rearguard
activities such as piling paving stones to form street corner barricades
that protected both civilians and fighters from the advance of Somoza's
National Guard. In fact, a large majority of the hundreds of thousands
of Nicaraguans who participated in the insurrection did so through
means that were nonviolent, or at least unarmed. This component of
the popular insurrection was almost indistinguishable from the armed
struggle. Observers may debate whether it qualified as nonviolent.
But such unarmed activity, albeit in support of Somoza's violent
overthrow, was all that was available to most Nicaraguans. There was
no person or group ready to mobilize their energies in a coordinated
campaign of nonviolent protest.

What the Evangelical Insurrection did was to marshal formally, for the first time, the energies of people interested in nonviolent alternatives. It organized them as a full and mature partner in the far-reaching struggle against imperialism. And, while the "theological trench" is currently just one of the Nicaraguan people's means of self-defense, those who struggle there believe that, in time, it must and will become the primary means of a poor people's struggle finally to be free.

Among Protestants, who compose about one-sixth of Nicaragua's population, some traditions of nonviolence had existed in Nicaragua. But their potential for developing any national movement or consensus regarding the efficacy of organized nonviolent struggle was slight. The Mennonites, a "historic peace church," had begun mission work in the country only a decade before the 1979 triumph; their numbers were growing but still small.

The Moravians, who have many nonviolent elements in their history, were largely isolated from political developments of the capital due to being rooted in the Miskito and other indigenous populations of the distant Atlantic Coast. By 1985 when D'Escoto began his fast, only a few Miskitos were thinking of nonviolence. The insensitive and sometimes criminal manner in which the Sandinistas related to the predominantly Moravian Miskito Indians during the revolution's early years had provoked many Miskitos to begin an armed resistance quite separate from that of the contras.

Nonetheless, a few Mennonites and Moravians were wrestling with issues of nonviolence. For the Mennonites, with pacifist traditions stretching back to the sixteenth-century Anabaptists, the revolution and U.S.-backed counterrevolution gave an opportunity to apply their pacifism in a context of violence, oppression, and social change that bore some resemblance to the one that had spawned their church. It was an opportunity to take their theological heritage seriously. But, in the judgment of some Mennonites, they failed the test.

"We have a history, and a philosophy, of nonviolence," says Verónica Argueda, a twenty-seven-year-old Mennonite leader, "but this hasn't moved to the level of our ethics." Some young Mennonites joined the armed struggle against the Somoza dynasty, but Argueda says they did so because there was no consensus or leadership for a nonviolent national struggle. She claims the young people "were able to participate in the struggle without buying into all the ideological values."[7]

In 1983, four years after the revolution's triumph, the nation was facing a growing aggression from the CIA and its contra army. In response the Nicaraguan government instituted an obligatory military draft for young men. A number of Mennonite youth received exemptions from service or arranged ad hoc forms of "alternative service" as the result of initial dialogue between the government and denominational or ecumenical leaders. However because the arrangements were informal, regional authorities were able to apply them differently or not at all. Some Mennonite youth fled the country or hid out, and a small number served jail sentences for refusing to carry arms.[8]

Meanwhile a few Mennonite youths proposed an alternative. Motivating them to do so was a desire that their pacifism take visible form in the context of the country and time in which they lived. Another motivation was a government decision in 1984 to quit granting exemptions. These young people suggested that youth brigades form to carry out tasks important for national reconstruction and defense of the civilian population. Though the leadership of the Mennonite denominations in Nicaragua was leery of forging too close a relationship with any government, especially one under siege, some young people suggested picking coffee in dangerous zones or even clearing mines from harbors or civilian roads. According to Argueda the government was open to their suggestion initially but church leaders turned down the idea. "They had the idea that 'alternative service' would be easy," Argueda says of church leaders. "We young people were willing to risk, to move our beliefs from the level of theory to practice," she says, "but the leadership didn't catch on. We lost a historic opportunity."[9]

The Evangelical Insurrection inspired young pacifists like Argueda. They began organizing educational campaigns within their churches to help twentieth-century Nicaraguan Anabaptists search for a theological stance consistent with both their history and their context. "We are a new church here, and we can't go on living off the experiences of European Mennonites so many years ago," said one young Mennonite. "We've got to define what it means to be a Nicaraguan Mennonite."

For other Protestants in Nicaragua, the ongoing violence of the war and the example set by their Catholic brothers and sisters in the Evangelical Insurrection created a climate that has moved even conservative evangelicals to speak out publicly against the war. In mid-1986, a year after Father D'Escoto's fast, a majority of the country's Protestant denominations, organized in CEPAD,[10] the Nicaraguan evangelical church council, began a Campaign of Fasting and Prayer for Peace and Justice in Nicaragua that lasted several months. The campaign brought together Protestants of different traditions, including some very conservative ones, for a series of prayer vigils in small communities and larger cities. It culminated in an all-night vigil in Managua in October 1986, in which over 10,000 Christians, most of them Pentecostals, prayed energetically for peace. As one CEPAD leader observed, it was especially significant because of "the humble people of the countryside who traveled so far to be here. These are the people who are suffering the war and their desire for peace is a testimony to all of us."

A lamb's war for reconciliation

As the Sandinista Revolution arrived on Nicaragua's Atlantic Coast following the July 1979 triumph over the Somoza dictatorship, the largely Moravian population of Miskitos, blacks, and other indigenous groups looked with suspicion at this latest product from "the Spanish," as people of the Atlantic Coast call western Nicaraguans to this day. The young Sandinistas—conquering heroes on the other side of the mountains—could not understand the easterners' lack of enthusiasm toward their revolutionary project. Centuries of isolation, mistrust, and racism quickly joined with post-insurrection upheaval to produce an escalating conflict between cultures. That conflict soon became a war.

The Miskitos were in the heart of the war. And wherever the Miskitos were, there was the Moravian church. Indeed, former Moravian pastors provided a disproportionately large segment of the leadership among armed indigenous groups fighting against the government. Whatever trust they might once have placed in their church's teaching of nonviolence and peaceful methods of reconciliation, some Moravians apparently forgot it as they headed to the bush to take up arms.

But other Moravians stayed faithful both to their people and their traditions of nonviolence. The suffering that the Sandinista government had inflicted on the indigenous people moved them no less, but it moved them not to the CIA, but to the prophetic and suffering servant of Isaiah. Their witness has given powerful new meaning to the emblem of the Moravian Church throughout the world, which declares: "Our Lamb Has Conquered, Let Us Follow Him."

The Reverend Norman Bent is one of these people.[11] In January of 1982 the government called Bent, then a Moravian pastor in Puerto Cabezas, along with fellow pastor Fernando Colomer, to Managua for a meeting with Sandinista officials. The two went, only to find themselves placed under arrest. After five days of protests from their bishop and ecumenical church leaders, the government released Bent and Colomer but refused to let them return to the Atlantic Coast. Bent and Colomer were popular leaders in the Moravian community on the Atlantic Coast and the government was afraid they would soon follow the path of other Miskito leaders to the ranks of the counterrevolution. By bringing them to the capital the government hoped to preempt such a move.

With the two pastors in Managua, Sandinista leaders got a better look at them and slowly realized they might have made a mistake. Although Bent and Colomer—because of their unrelenting belief in the power of dialogue—were not afraid to criticize the government for its repeated mistakes in dealing with the indigenous minorities, neither were they willing to lend themselves to the CIA-directed military campaign.

At the end of 1982 the government restored their freedom to travel to the Atlantic Coast, but Bent and Colomer remained in Managua. They traveled regularly to the Coast, but their main ministry turned to the growing Miskito population in Managua. Many of their parishioners had come to the capital because family members were in Managua prisons. Others were refugees from warfare or forced relocation. Both Bent and Colomer remained ready to criticize the government for shortcomings in its Atlantic Coast policy, but they believed that honest dialogue remained preferable to the military solutions both sides frequently pursued.

One day almost a year after Bent's detention, Comandante William Ramírez, a top Sandinista leader who was Administrative Governor of the Atlantic Coast, asked the pastor to come to his office. (Colomer was out of the country at the time.) On behalf of the entire government Ramírez apologized to Bent for the treatment to which he had been subjected. In their emotional encounter Bent told Ramírez, "I have already forgiven you." The two men shared a tearful embrace.

The forgiveness that marked Norman Bent's prophetic contribution to a genuinely Nicaraguan understanding of nonviolence was to become a central element in the tasks of reconciliation and reconstruction that Atlantic Coast communities faced in the years that followed. Several Moravian pastors, whom the government had jailed but released under a December 1983 amnesty, returned to their pulpits to proclaim forgiveness as the key to reconciliation. They demanded an end to the war. Earlier that year, a special assembly of the Moravian Church had hotly debated, but finally approved, a focus on peacemaking as a ministry of the entire church. Slowly but steadily the descendants of a tradition with its roots in the fifteenth-century Czech reformation found themselves speaking and acting in the role of peacemaker amid cultural and ethnic communities torn apart by war and mistrust.

As both government officials and Miskitos came to understand the integrity of the peacemakers, the influence of Moravian leaders spread. In 1985 they finally convinced the Nicaraguan government to allow the return of Miskito communities to the Coco River from which it had expelled them several years earlier. There they began a feverish work of supporting refugees willing to repatriate and encouraging others to join them. In mid-1987, together with other leaders both Catholic and Protestant along the Coco River, Moravians organized teams of pastors to travel the river offering encouragement to returnees and taking needed relief supplies to remote communities. The unarmed teams often came under fire from indigenous insurgents and faced constant harassment and threats from these as well as Honduran troops.

The active involvement of Moravians contributed to the process of grassroots consultation and legislation that moved the nation toward granting governmental autonomy to the Atlantic Coast, with the approval of the autonomy statute in 1987. Norman Bent was able to declare with satisfaction that year that the whole church had taken on "a general peace offensive." It seemed that the Moravians in Nicaragua were finally coming to grips with the pacifist aspects of their roots.

Indeed, as Central America struggled to make reconciliation a reality in the aftermath of the August 7, 1987 signing of regional peace accords in Esquipulas, Guatemala, both warring Indians and the Nicaraguan government asked leaders of the Moravian Church, along with CEPAD, to mediate their bitter conflict. Almost two years of church-mediated dialogue led to a ceasefire and in September 1989, the final return from exile of the coast's indigenous leaders.[12]

In the fertile ground of forgiveness and solidarity

The climate of post-1979 Nicaragua nourished a fertile soil for the sprouting of the Evangelical Insurrection and the growth of other strains of nonviolent practice. The triumphant Sandinistas had adamantly insisted on "generosity in victory."

That policy had broken the historical tendency of long oppressed peoples to reap vengeance as their revolutions take power. In the days and weeks following the 1979 insurrection, Sandinista leaders had striven mightily—and, with few exceptions, successfully—to keep lower-level cadres from personally settling accounts with those who had mistreated them. Indeed, one of the Sandinistas' first acts of government was to eliminate the death penalty.

A telling story began circulating a few days into revolutionary rule. Even if apocryphal the mere fact that it circulated suggests the kind of revolution many Nicaraguans expected and that the Sandinistas, at their best, hoped to engender.

The story goes like this: Comandante Tomás Borge was in Managua reviewing treatment of captured ex-members of Somoza's National Guard when he spotted one of the officers responsible for his wife's torture, rape, and murder only a few months before. Borge, the only surviving member among the FSLN's founders, had himself suffered torture while in prison during the mid-1970s. Now he was the new Minister of Interior. When Borge pulled the man out of line, the defrocked official undoubtedly feared orders to shoot him on the spot. Instead, according to the account, Borge told him, "My revenge will be to pardon you."

A kind of international cross-fertilization further strengthened the nascent sprouts of nonviolence growing in Nicaragua's own soil. The revolution beckoned thousands of the struggling republic's sympathizers to journey from their homes in Europe, North America, and other parts of Latin America. They came to live in Nicaragua, share the journey of Nicaragua's people, and make their own contributions to the country's reconstruction. The development of nonviolent programs aimed at ending outside aggression was one such contribution.

Most notable was a U.S.-based group called Witness for Peace (WFP). Formed in 1983 after a large contingent of North American Christians noted a reduction of contra violence in a border area during a visit they made, WFP grew to become a major component of U.S. citizens' opposition to their country's policies in Nicaragua and Central America. Motivated by religious conviction, WFP maintained an active presence in the war zones of Nicaragua, bringing U.S. citizens there for both short and long periods. By living and praying with their Nicaraguan sisters and brothers suffering from the war, then returning to tell their stories and provide systematic documentation of the violence, WFP members sought to make the human cost of the war more visible back in the United States.

In November 1984 Witness for Peace carried out one of its most dramatic actions. The Reagan administration was attempting to distract media attention from Nicaragua's national elections, which international observers had acclaimed as relatively fair and clean. The United States claimed that Soviet MIG fighter jets were on the way to Nicaragua. The Pentagon overflew the country with SR-71 "Blackbird" reconnaissance planes whose sonic booms reminded Nicaraguans that the empire to the north could level their homes and snuff out their lives at a moment's notice, U.S. warships prowled up and down the coastline.

WFP volunteers watched anxiety build among the people and felt their own frustration and anger. Out of a mixture of helplessness and hopefulness, they decided to meet the U.S. ships of war with a message of peace. On November 10, twenty WFP members, along with numerous journalists, sailed in an old fishing boat to within a mile of a U.S. frigate off the Pacific coast. With banners and a megaphone they beseeched it to leave Nicaragua in peace. As the fishing boat approached, the frigate turned and headed out to sea. Whether or not the U.S. navy crew heard the message, it did reach millions of U.S. citizens via the evening news.

Nicaraguans heard the North Americans' message of peace on the radio and read about it on the front page of the newspaper. It was the first time that Witness for Peace had achieved a high level of visibility in Nicaragua beyond the regional towns and villages where its volunteers were present. To many it was a compelling demonstration of nonviolent action. At an ecumenical service closing a two-week vigil at the port of Corinto, the Baptist pastor Ernesto Córdova of the Baptist Seminary in Managua told a packed crowd, "True, the little boat did not have the firepower, but it had the power of love, the power of justice, and the power of God. And the weakness of God is stronger than the power of human might."

While the daily activities of WFP volunteers did not draw the same attention as such highly visible ones as the frigate encounter, they were no less important. When a delegation went to the town of El Cua shortly after a contra land mine killed thirty-four people traveling in a truck, there were no journalists there to report their presence. But the group's willingness to risk traveling the dangerous road, and the solidarity they brought to that grieving community, made a deep impression on the people. Word of their loving witness spread through the mountains.

Countless other conversations with suffering Nicaraguans, soldiers, FSLN officials, church people, and even contras whom WFP volunteers encountered in the mountains challenged them to relate their nonviolent ideals to the stark facts of Nicaraguan reality. In turn the Nicaraguans, after seeing their deeds, were more interested in the ideas of those who accepted the risks of nonviolent action.

In December 1983, as troops fought on the road between Ocotal and Jalapa, the first short-term WFP delegation was delayed. When the road was again open the Nicaraguan military sent soldiers to accompany the WFP delegation with an armed escort. In keeping with a WFP covenant the group tactfully and gratefully refused the escort, something that completely surprised the soldiers. The WFP decision was without precedent. But it won the soldiers' respect.

As time went on and long-term WFP volunteers integrated themselves into community and parish life, opportunities arose for their nonviolence to merge seamlessly with homegrown Nicaraguan nonviolence. On one occasion two WFP volunteers were accompanying Father Enrique Blandón and twenty Nicaraguan Delegates of the Word on pastoral visits to outlying communities in the parish of Waslala, Matagalpa. They were in the town of Yaro when they learned that a contra group had kidnapped the parish's other priest, Ubaldo Gervasoni, while he was on a similar trip. The entire team, along with some twenty-five peasants who had arrived early for a worship service, decided to march to the farm where the contras were holding Father Gervasoni captive.

When the group arrived and urged the contras to release him, hours of discussion ensued. Father Blandón and the internationals challenged the contras to live up to claims they were fighting for human rights and religious liberty. The Nicaraguan peasants' silent witness to the exchange was equally powerful. Eventually the overwhelmed young contra leader who had led the kidnapping and feared to disobey orders by releasing his captive, actually asked Father Blandón what to do. "If you are democratic," responded the priest with a gesture toward the watchful peasants, "why don't you ask the people what they think?" The vote of the group, which had already walked several hours at risk to liberate Father Gervasoni, was no surprise. By the following morning the priest was free.

D'Escoto himself, as he fasted and walked to launch the Evangelical Insurrection, attested to the importance of Witness for Peace for himself and others interested in developing an authentic Nicaraguan nonviolence. Indeed, the involvement of North Americans in Witness for Peace, traveling to the suffering, striving Central American country, came to symbolize the world attention that was focused on the valiant country of barely three million people. Nicaragua's struggle to free itself from foreign empires and domestic elites had inspired sympathetic supporters in every corner of the globe to launch nonviolent campaigns of solidarity with the beleaguered people.

*   *   *

Prior to 1979, few people in the United States knew where Nicaragua was. Yet as the people of Nicaragua rose up to throw off a brutal dictatorship supported by a foreign power, their country became a meeting ground for the forces of history and a focal point of national and international resistance to the designs of empire. The experiment, still under siege, is far from finished. But as a revolution among revolutions it has proven full of innovations. Among them are its many lessons for the continuing development of a Latin American praxis of nonviolence.

Notes

1. "Education for Change: A Report on the Nicaraguan Literacy Crusade," *Interracial Books for Children Bulletin* 12 (1981). In *Nicaragua, Unfinished Revolution: The New Nicaragua Reader*, pp. 418-21, edited by Peter Rosset and John Vandenmeer (New York: Grove Press, 1986).

2. Richard M. Garfield and Eugenio Taboadas, "Health Services Reforms in Revolutionary Nicaragua," *American Journal of Public Health* 74 (1984).

3. David Kaimowitz, "Nicaragua's Agrarian Reform: Six Years Later," in Rosset and Vandenmeer, pp. 392-93.

4. Interview with Gregorio Martínez, by author, along route of *Via Crucis*, February 1986.

5. Interview with Miguel D'Escoto, by author, along route of *Via Crucis*, February 1986. See Paul Jeffrey, "Miguel D'Escoto: Preaching an Evangelical Revolution," *The Other Side*, June 1986, pp. 12-17.

6. D'Escoto interview.
7. Interview with Verónica Argueda, by author, Managua, November 1986.
8. See *Revolution and Nonviolence in a War-Torn Region: A Central America Organizing Packet* (New York: War Resisters League, 1988); and Gerald Schlabach, "Revolutionary Nicaragua: Military Service, Conscientious Objection and Nation-building," *The Role of the Church in Society: An International Perspective,* Urbane Peachey, ed. (Carol Stream, Illinois: International Mennonite Peace Committee, 1988.), pp. 61-66.
9. Argueda interview.
10. Formerly CEPAD stood for Comité Evangélico Pro-Ayuda al Desarrollo (Evangelical Committee for Development Aid), reflecting its roots in the recovery efforts after the devastating 1972 earthquake that leveled much of Managua. Today it continues to undertake a wide variety of development projects throughout Nicaragua. However in 1989 its name was changed to Consejo de Iglesias Evangélicas Pro-Alianza Denominacional, reflecting its actual role as a council of churches. The same acronym is still used. The official English translation is the Council of Evangelical Churches of Nicaragua.
11. See chapter 12, "To Accept the Enemy as a Challenge: The Ministry of Reconciliation," by Norman Bent.
12. The mediation team benefited from the valuable assistance of John Paul Lederach, a specialist in conflict resolution. The experience of Lederach, a Mennonite from the U.S., demonstrates that such work carries its peculiar risks. He was injured along with two Nicaraguan members of the mediating team in a 1988 melee between government sympathizers and Indian supporters in Puerto Cabezas on the Atlantic Coast. Earlier his family had gone into hiding for a period following the disclosure of a plot, evidently hatched by the CIA, to kidnap Lederach's daughter in Costa Rica.

For further reading

Berrigan, Daniel. *Steadfastness of the Saints: A Journal of Peace and War in Central and North America.* Maryknoll: Orbis Books, 1985; Melbourne Australia: Dove Communications, 1985.
Cabestrero, Teofilo. "Miguel D'Escoto, Foreign Minister." In *Ministers of God, Ministers of the People: Testimonies of Faith from Nicaragua,* Maryknoll, N.Y.: Orbis Books; London: Zed Press, 1983, p. 91-127.
Close, David H. *Nicaragua: Politics, Economics, and Society.* London and New York: Pinter Publishers, 1988.
Collins, Joseph. *Nicaragua: What Difference Could a Revolution Make? Food and Farming in the New Nicaragua.* New York: Grove Press, 1986.
D'Escoto, Miguel. "The Power of the Cross." *Catholic Worker* (February 1979), pp. 1-2, 6.
————. "An Unfinished Canvas: Building a new Nicaragua." *Sojourners* (March 1983), pp. 14-18.
Heyward, Carter. *Revolutionary Forgiveness: Feminist Reflections on Nicaragua.* Maryknoll, NY: Orbis Books, 1987.
O'Brien, Conor Cruise. "God and Man in Nicaragua." *The Atlantic Monthly* (August 1986), pp. 50-72.
Rooper, Alison. *Fragile Victory: A Nicaraguan Community at War.* London: Weidenfeld and Nicolson, 1987.
Schlabach, Gerald. "Bringing Change Through Prayer." *Fellowship* (November 1987), pp. 5-6.
————. "Revolutionary Nicaragua: Military Service, Conscientious Objection and Nation-building." *The Role of the Church in Society: An International Perspective,* pp. 51-70. Edited by Urbane Peachey. Carol Stream, Illinois: International Mennonite Peace Committee, Mennonite World Conference [465 Gundersen Drive, Suite 200, Carol Stream, IL 60188], 1988.
War Resisters League. *Revolution and Nonviolence in a War-Torn Region: A Central America Organizing Packet.* New York: War Resisters League [339 Lafayette Street, New York, NY 10012], 1988.

Brazil

TEN

Introduction

Brazil is the size of the continental United States and comparable in wealth of material resources. It is the world's top exporter of coffee, orange juice, and soybeans. It is the number one sugar producer, and the third largest grower of corn. It has vast areas of good agricultural land.

Yet two-thirds of Brazil's 145 million people go hungry.[1] Poverty has been increasing. One thousand children die every day, mostly of hunger-related causes. Seven million children—more than twice the total population of Nicaragua—are abandoned and live on the streets because their families cannot provide for them.

If redistributed, Brazil's arable land would provide livelihood for all the landless poor in Brazil today. Landlessness is a major cause of their poverty, as ownership of land is concentrated for large-scale agriculture. A mere one percent of landowners controls forty-eight percent of the arable land. In the past two decades, they have pushed more than 24 million small farmers off their land.

Dispossessed farmers have migrated to urban areas, swelling the *favelas* (shantytowns) that surround every city. They arrive in desperate need of work but without urban skills. Fierce competition for the few jobs that exist drives wages down and allows employers to impose brutal conditions. Brazil's inequities are increasing as the poor carry the burden of repaying the nation's $116 billion foreign debt.

In the 1970s, U.S. commercial banks urged the military government to borrow large sums of money at low but fluctuating rates of interest. The dictatorship spent little of the money on socially useful projects. As interest rates increased in the 1980s, the debt mushroomed. Brazil grew increasingly vulnerable before the International Monetary Fund (IMF) and the World Bank. The U.S.-dominated World Bank has played a major role in promoting a shift from small-scale food production to large-scale, high-tech, cash-crop agriculture. It is this shift that has cost millions of peasants their land.

U.S.-based transnational corporations continue to profit from the destruction of the Amazon rain forest and the construction of hydroelectric dams that are disastrous to the environment as well as to local inhabitants. In submitting to IMF and World Bank conditions, the Brazilian government continues to pursue policies that favor the banks but run counter to the desperate needs of its own population. Acute and rising social tensions have been the result.

Foreigners have helped determine Brazilians' fate before. The United States has had a very strong presence in recent Brazilian history. In 1964 the CIA and the U.S. ambassador played critical roles in a military coup that unseated a populist government and established the military regime. Not until 1985 did twenty-one years of dictatorship come to an end. But the "New Republic" inaugurated under President José Sarney has mostly been window-dressing. Extreme structural violence in the form of malnutrition, unemployment, and landlessness is still the primary fact of life for most Brazilians.

In 1985, shortly after Sarney's accession to power, the Ministry of Agrarian Reform proposed a National Agrarian Reform Plan. The plan promised to redistribute some of the vast areas of idle land held for speculation. But President Sarney's government, beholden to large landholders, insisted nine times that the Ministry revise the plan. Each revision was weaker until the plan was but a token effort to deal with the nation's gravest problem. Even so, the landowners resisted strongly, creating the right-wing Rural Democratic Union (UDR), which has grown in two years to 230,000 members.

In October 1987, shortly after the events that this chapter describes, a presidential decree added loopholes and exemptions that pulled most of the remaining teeth from the Agrarian Reform Plan. Finally, in the fall of 1988, Brazil's Constitutional Convention gave the *coup de grace* by approving an article on land reform that was even more favorable to large landowners than a land reform law the military dictatorship had once approved.

Still, despite the failure of the Sarney government to enforce its Agrarian Reform Plan, the plan's very existence has had a far-reaching effect on the landless poor. It has kindled their hopes, focused their aspirations, and helped strengthen a national Movement of Landless Rural Workers (known popularly as *Sem Terra*). By the beginning of 1989, an estimated 9,700 families in the movement were living in thirty-five separate encampments, occupying land they claim is rightfully theirs.

As the landless grow in the strength of their mass organization, the landowners have been forming private militias. In the past several years, hired thugs have murdered hundreds of peasant leaders, as well as lawyers, priests, nuns, and trade union officials supporting the peasants. One may count the cases that have come to justice on the fingers of one hand.

And yet, with a dogged faith the landless persist in their struggle. In the chapter that follows, Judith Hurley tells of her encounter with that struggle and that faith.

A Brazilian peasant with the tools of the trade. Competition from corporate agribusiness has made the peasants' life harder, forcing many to migrate to the cities. Among those who stay, the struggle for land reform is intense. Wealthy landowners hire private militias. Tens of thousands of landless families have banded together to occupy unused private and public land. They claim that "Land is for people, not for profit." Photo by Mev Puleo.

Posseiros, untitled small farmers, demonstrate before the state governor's office in João Pessoa, Brazil. Their banner reflects the cleverness and creativity that, even amid desperation, have given such strength to their struggle. Implementation of agrarian reform under the government agency, INCRA (Instituto Nacional de Colonização e Reforma Agrária), has been widely perceived as a farce. The word *"vulgo"* (alias) refers to the popular name for INCRA listed above: "National Institute *Against* Agrarian Reform." *"Vulgo"* also means "masses" and is used with *"incravado,"* a play on words combining the acronym INCRA, with the Portuguese word for "enslaved," i.e., "Under INCRA, the masses are enslaved." A spokesperson said, "We can no longer accept the government's lack of response to our appeals when the wave of violence against farm workers is rising." The *posseiros* successfully pressed for a meeting with a governor the day this photo was taken. Photo by Mev Puleo.

Peasant women, children and men create temporary homes out of black plastic tents during an occupation of the main plaza in João Pessoa, Brazil demanding land for the landless. The governor's palace in the background provides a stark contrast. One percent of the landowners owns half of the agricultural land in Brazil. Much of it lies idle. Photo by Mev Puleo.

Peasants who immigrate to the cities squat on vacant lands, building shantytowns which now ring every Brazilian city. Their black, plastic tents make an easy target for the bulldozers of the police. Photo by Mev Puleo.

The number of homeless in Brazil, which includes seven million children, is growing. This young person sleeps on a park bench surrounded by the high rises of São Paulo. Photo by Mev Puleo.

Maria Piaui, in her seventies, is raising her three great grandchildren. Sixty percent of the population of Brazil are descendants of Africans brought to Brazil as slaves. There is a strong Black Consciousness movement in Brazil. Photo by Mev Puleo.

The relentless persistence of base-level movements in Latin America as well as international solidarity increase the possibilities for a full life for this peasant child. Photo by Mev Puleo.

All photos in this essay were taken by Mev Puleo, a U.S. photographer and writer, during a 1987 visit to Brazil sponsored by Project Abraço: North Americans in Solidarity with the People of Brazil.

Brazil: A Troubled Journey to the Promised Land

Judith Hurley

Abraço is the Portuguese word for embrace. An *abraço* is the Brazilians' universal mode of greeting one another. Yet only rarely does the embrace stretch across the sharp divisions of class, land ownership, and social power in Brazil. Likewise, only rarely does a sector enjoying clout and prestige embrace the cause of the poor, the landless, and the marginal.

One powerful sector, however, has embraced the cause of the poor. It is the contemporary Roman Catholic Church. Long allied with the nation's ruling elites, in the last twenty-five years the church has instead chosen a "preferential option for the poor." In practice this has meant an enormous commitment of people and resources to empowering the poor at the base of society. From 1964 through 1985, during twenty-one years of brutal repression under a military dictatorship, the church was the only institution powerful enough to continue the pursuit of justice.

Vital to the church's action has been the formation of over 100,000 Christian base communities. These are small groups of neighbors from rural areas or urban slums. They meet, reflect on their situation in light of the Bible and the church's call for social justice, and then work together, often in small ways, to better their lives. The energy for this work comes from *"conscientização,"* a term that Brazilian educator Paulo Freire popularized.[2] The mass media, textbooks, and traditional religion disseminate a view of reality that attributes poverty to laziness or lack of ability. *Conscientização* consists of breaking through this view of reality to the individual's own experience of day-to-day reality. The face-to-face meetings that are the lifeblood of the Christian base communities encourage all participants to speak their truth, which the community then validates. A new vision of reality, a new understanding of the forces at work in society, emerges from the sharing of individual experiences. Beyond that, the act of speaking out, of having one's experience heard and validated, is profoundly empowering.

The church's role in the base communities has been to facilitate the process of *conscientização* by providing meeting places and group "animators." Experiences in the base communities over the past twenty years have built the social analysis, self-confidence, and organizational skills necessary to confront the powerful groups who presently control Brazilian society. The base communities have been the backbone of the people's struggle for land.

In 1975 the church founded a Pastoral Commission on Land (CPT), which has lawyers, organizers, and agricultural technicians working out of regional and diocesan offices throughout Brazil. The CPT coordinates the church's land-related activities, represents organized groups of rural poor in land-related legal cases, and cooperates with rural labor unions and popular movements on a wide range of activities.

In 1984, inspired by the wonderful warmth and vitality among Brazil's poor despite their suffering, I started Project Abraço. My hope was to inspire support in the United States for the struggles of the Brazilian people. Often, solidarity movements in the United States arise in response to massive armed conflicts. Perhaps, I hoped, it might be possible this time to arouse support for the Brazilian struggle during its present, nonviolent stage. I also hoped to bring into U.S. movements for social change a spark of inspiration from the extraordinary strengths of the Brazilian popular movement.

In the intervening years the confrontation between Brazil's landless poor and its wealthy elite has intensified. As the landless have become better organized they have employed a wide range of nonviolent tactics: lawsuits, demonstrations, religious ceremonies, fasts, vigils, marches, pilgrimages, funerals, and memorial services, and—most recently and most significantly—long-term occupations of public and private land involving tens of thousands of people. But the landowners, supported by the state's military police,[3] have met this creative and resolute struggle with ever increasing violence.

During the summer of 1987 I had the opportunity to visit several sites that represent various stages of the struggle for land: Cruz Alta, Erexim, Fazenda Annoni, and Nova Ronda Alta, all in the southernmost state of Rio Grande do Sul; and the northern and northeastern states of Goiás, Maranhão, and Paraíba. Following are excerpts from the journal I kept during the trip. They describe the content—and attempt to convey the feeling—of the popular movement at one moment in its long and difficult struggle.

The cutting edge of conflict

July 20, 1987. Cruz Alta, Rio Grande do Sul. When Luis Carlos, from the *Movimento dos Sem Terra,* or Movement of the Landless, came for me at 5:15 this morning I had no idea what to expect. Now, after a nine hour bus trip, I am relieved to be at this large, clean, pleasant pastoral center that belongs to the diocese and is run by a wonderful group of Dominican nuns. Despite its calm and peaceful appearance, this center is battle headquarters for an action that is at the leading edge of the land struggle in Brazil.

Until two days ago 1,500 landless families had been camped out at

Fazenda Annoni (a *fazenda* is a large private landholding), 150 kilometers from here. They were waiting to be settled on the land in accordance with provisions of the 1985 National Land Reform Plan that was then in effect. Now 330 of the 1,500 families have occupied Fazenda São Juvenal. In both cases the government had expropriated the land on the grounds that it was idle. But the owner of Fazenda São Juvenal, who is grazing one head of cattle for every fifteen acres, has challenged the expropriation and the case is stuck in the courts like virtually every other attempt at expropriation throughout Brazil.

Two hundred families managed to enter the *fazenda* before the occupation was discovered. The landowner, with support from the military police, prevented the remaining 130 families from getting inside. Instead, they have camped out on the shoulder of the road. Although it is a public road the military police have closed it off with barricades, isolating the families and leaving them without water or food. Those controlling the barricades have allowed a few media people inside, but otherwise the families are incommunicado except for a system of signal flags.

When I go out to the barricade this afternoon I am very touched to see the "all's well" flag flying none too jauntily in the downpour, looking very small at a mile's distance. I try unsuccessfully to gain entry as a foreign journalist. It is a gloomy scene. The military police are busy securing their tent against the rain. They have a huge bonfire going and are barbecuing a side of beef that the landowner has given them. Two dozen neighbors sympathetic to the cause of the landless, gauchos huddling in their long ponchos, stand around in the road discussing the situation. I hear one offer his land as an alternate encampment should the occupiers be forced out. This is the third day of the occupation.

Tonight, on the evening news, we learn that the group at the side of the road, which has been digging a well since its arrival, has struck water.

Over the past two days, the owner of Fazenda São Juvenal has mobilized the support of the state chapter of the UDR, or "Rural Democratic Union." The UDR is a powerful organization of landowners that has sprung up in the last couple of years in response to the pressure for land reform. It seems that dozens of armed UDR members, with their hired gunmen, are meeting at this very moment in the main house of the *fazenda*. The atmosphere is very tense with the threat of violence. The local bishop has made a public statement of support for the occupiers. The nuns express their concern by cooking up huge cauldrons of hearty soup to feed the Sem Terra members and sympathizers who keep arriving. It is now about 11:00 P.M. and it looks as though the coordinating committee will be meeting through the night.

Darcy's history lesson

I met Darcy Maschio at the Sem Terra office three days ago. With his broken teeth and rough clothes, I mistook him for a "simple peasant." So much for stereotypes. He turned out to be the leader of the occupation. He cut a very dramatic figure in his long black poncho. The door to the tiny 9'x 9' room that serves as the coordinating office was open to the street. Anyone could walk right in or shoot at the occupants. There was an endless stream of people. The phone rang constantly. Periodically Darcy had to leave for meetings with the bishop or the governor or the lawyers, but somehow he found a half-hour to meet with me. Between sips from his *chimarrão* (a gourd filled with bitter *mate* tea, sipped through a silver straw) he gave me a briefing on the background of this occupation:

Up until the 1960s, small landowners known as *colonos* farmed this area in the north of Rio Grande do Sul. They were immigrants of Polish, German, and Italian descent. They produced the staples of the Brazilian diet—rice, corn, and black beans.

Starting in the 1960s and increasingly in the 1970s the Brazilian government, with the strong backing of international lending institutions, began to offer incentives for the production of wheat and soy for export. Government policy made capital for expansion available to the large landowners, while denying small landowners the credit they needed to keep going. The government set prices for corn, rice, and black beans well below the actual cost of production, according to Darcy. Intending to create an abundant source of cheap labor for industry, as well as to make land available for export crops, the government mounted a propaganda campaign, talking up the cities as centers of opportunity. As a result of all these pressures, many small farmers sold out. There was a massive redistribution of land into the hands of the large landowners.

Hearing of the miserable fate that actually befell those who went to the cities or took part in the government's colonization plans in the Amazon, the smallholders who remained were determined to stick it out. But as their children came to maturity they could not indefinitely subdivide the small parcels of land they held. In 1978, having nowhere else to go, about 300 of these landless families occupied public land in Ronda Alta. They eventually gained title to the land. In the next few years, more and more groups adopted the strategy of land occupation, enduring tremendous hardships. Many of those who persisted for years, despite military harassment, did succeed in getting land. Out of these occupations came the Movement of the Landless, which was formalized in 1983. By 1985, there were Sem Terra groups in thirty-three localities.

In the 1970s, the building of the Rio Passo Fundo Dam on the Uruguay River displaced thousands of families, who received neither indemnification nor new land. These families attempted to claim Fazenda Annoni, a large piece of privately owned, unused land, which the government had expropriated for their use. Ten years later their case was still in the courts. The end of the military dictatorship in 1985 and the beginning of the "New Republic" spurred new efforts. According to Darcy the would-be settlers made hundreds of visits to government offices. Finally, on October 29, 1985, 1,500 families occupied Fazenda Annoni. Darcy and his family were among them.

For four months the military surrounded them. On February 28, 1986 the smallholders occupied the offices of the national land reform agency, INCRA, in the state capital of Porto Alegre. The minister signed a document stating that by April 30 the government would redistribute over 85,000 acres of land to the 1,500 families. The ministry did not carry out the promise.

On May first, fifty families camped out in front of INCRA. On May 27, 250 people started a *romaria*, or religious pilgrimage, from Fazenda Annoni to Porto Alegre. It was a twenty-eight day, 450 kilometer march. When they arrived the government distributed only 9,500 acres instead of the promised 85,000. Outraged, the smallholders occupied the state legislature grounds for three months. The government responded by allocating another 19,000 acres, at Fazenda São Juvenal, here in Cruz Alta. But following the act of expropriation the landowner took his case to court, and no exchange of land took place. So on September 24, 1986 the smallholders gave INCRA an ultimatum: If you don't give it to us, we'll go there and take it. On November 29, 1986 the families attempted to leave Fazenda Annoni for São Juvenal, but 2,000 military police stopped them. Finally, on Saturday of this week, the promised occupation took place.

According to the provisions of the National Land Reform Act, Darcy concluded, the government was to have settled 3,500 families on expropriated land in Rio Grande do Sul during 1986. In fact, it did not settle a single family. In 1987 it was to have settled 7,300 families, but by the end of July it had settled only 200, all of them in response to the pressure of land occupations.

"Our strength is in our organization"

July 22, 1987. Erexim, Rio Grande do Sul. During the last few days I have experienced the realities of the land struggle in its various phases and moods. Right now, I am in Erexim, in the extreme north of the state. I arrived here a couple of hours ago after a bizarre bus trip. I sat next to a talkative, young, upper-class woman who was excited about meeting a North American. She chattered away to me about the Paris theater scene (her mother is an actress) and skiing in Argentina. After what I've encountered these past few days, I found it hard to be civil to her, though she is not personally responsible for the class differences.

My hotel room is directly opposite the Union of Rural Workers of Erexim. Painted in large letters across the front of the building is its slogan, *"nossa força está na organização"*—our strength is in our organization. People in this area are struggling against plans to build more dams on the Uruguay River.

I had left Cruz Alta yesterday morning with a heavy heart, haunted by images of unarmed groups of children, women, and men camped out in the cold and rain, facing brutal bands of armed landowners and gunmen on horseback. The landowners' determination to use violence is no secret. In the last few years they have murdered hundreds of people in the land struggle. Lately they have been organizing private militias, luring soldiers away from the army by offering three times as much pay as the government. Both soldiers and gunmen come largely from the same class of desperate, landless peasants as the people they are hired to fight.

At Fazenda Annoni, the largest land occupation in Brazil

The driver who had taken me to Fazenda Annoni yesterday is quite taciturn during the three hour trip from Cruz Alta. He may not be happy, on such a momentous day, to be spending his time chauffeuring a *norteamericana*. He does become more animated as we actually get near Annoni. As we skid along the deeply gouged mud road, he points out memorable sites—where the military police had set up a barricade for several months, where the encampment's first martyrs had died. One of the martyrs, Roselli Correa da Silva, was a leader of the encampment. Her child was the first to be born here, a symbol of hope. A car presumed to be associated with the landowner or the UDR had run down and killed both mother and child. As usual the case was never investigated.

Later I see posters with photos of Roselli and her child in almost every home I enter. The violence of the landowners, up to a point at least, seems to be counterproductive. There is a strong and self-fulfilling conviction that "the blood of the martyrs fertilizes the land."

I am taken first to the "Holandes," a *fazenda* that had belonged to a Dutchman. Thirty-two families from Fazenda Annoni had been resettled there three months earlier. In contrast with Cruz Alta, the mood at the "Holandes" is extremely upbeat. Fields are already green with their first crop of wheat. The government, in a rare instance of fulfilling the land reform law, actually provided families with the infrastructure necessary to get started. The settlers exude pride and satisfaction as they show me their new truck and shiny new red tractor. Almost everything still needs doing; of the thirty-two families, twenty-nine are still living in makeshift housing in the outbuildings. Yet the people's joy and gratitude are obvious.

The three families who share the one real house on the *fazenda* give me lunch and then take me around to meet the women. I feel a particular rapport with one woman, Anita, about my age (fifty). Her dirt-floored, plastic-walled room in the big barn is particularly spotless, with a cloth and flowers on the table. The flowers seem a sign of triumph, indicating that the people have moved beyond bare survival.

In the afternoon, a couple from the "Holandes" take me to Fazenda Annoni itself. This is a huge *fazenda*, miles on a side. The encampment is bleak, with black plastic shacks outlined against the wintry landscape. The wind is blowing and everyone is indoors except for some pigs and chickens. When I arrive, only women are in the camp—women and their sad, sickly children. It always takes me a while, in such a situation, to become fully present as I struggle to face the fact that a group of young women and children, who so much deserve a good life, should be living in such miserable circumstances. But of course, that is my view of their situation, and their own is very different. They tell me proudly of their history, what they have endured, their hopes, and their communal accomplishments. They show me a communal bread oven they have just completed. A number of the men are working nearby, constructing a new school that the government has finally agreed to finance. A woman from the encampment will be employed there as a teacher.

As the afternoon wears on, we move to the one dwelling that is made of wood instead of plastic and has a floor raised above the mud. Although it is roughly framed, with big gaps between the boards, in this context it seems positively luxurious. This dwelling houses a big communal cookstove, a gift of the church. A huge pot dominates the stove with nothing, apparently, to put into it. The women disperse to their respective shacks and, just as in the old folk tale, "Stone Soup," each returns with something: a can of lard, a bag of rice, a chicken, vegetables from their communal garden, two loaves of bread. Soon there is the reassuring sound of food sizzling.

Husbands return, one by one, and lean against the walls. There is only one unbroken chair and I am sitting in it. The conversation focuses entirely on the situation of their companions at Cruz Alta. A couple of the men had driven into town earlier to phone the pastoral center at Cruz Alta. They learned that the landowners did, in fact, attack the encampment inside the *fazenda,* shooting over the heads of the occupiers. Miraculously, no one was hurt.

As we talk, further news comes crackling over a beat-up radio. The military police have expelled the occupiers and at this very moment are bringing them back to Fazenda Annoni by bus. The mood in the room is divided. There is frustration and rage at the government for siding with the landowners. But there is also eagerness for the return of their friends. People eat sparingly, saving most of the stew for their returning neighbors.

Hours pass, many more hours than are necessary for the journey, and there is no sign of their companions. The conversation turns to violence. A number of voices say, "If they're going to shoot at us, they had better know that next time *we'll* go armed!" I wonder whether this comes out of the emotion of the moment or whether they mean it seriously. The Sem Terra movement is basically nonviolent, as a result of both the religious formation of so many members and their pragmatism. But it is not pacifist in a strict sense.

The evening ends with the fate of the people's friends still unknown. The men open the door repeatedly to look for the lights of a bus, but the landscape is utterly dark. Morosely, people drift off to their shacks. They don't have flashlights, so the husband from the wooden house guides them with what seems to be the only kerosene lamp in the camp. I am invited to sleep in the wooden house, on an extra mattress stored under the couple's bed. I am glad that, against advice to travel lightly, I have brought my sleeping bag; now I can convincingly refuse the couple's offer of their only quilt. It is another very cold night, with the temperature near freezing.

When we awaken the next morning, the comrades from Cruz Alta still have not returned. Everyone is irritable with suspense and uncertainty. I am driven to the nearby town of Sarandi to visit with the parish priest whose support has been so crucial in enabling the occupiers to hang on. But he is out, and although we wait around for a couple of hours he does not return. Newspaper clippings and photographs of the occupation cover the walls in the sitting room of the parish building. Especially prominent is the *romaria,* the long march to the capital. Also prominent in many photos is the big cross that has become the symbol of the occupation. Draping the cross is a white streamer for each martyr who has died since the occupation began.

As we get back into the car Osmar, the driver, pulls a Bible out of the glove compartment and waves it at me. He thumps it on the dashboard, exclaiming vehemently that the Bible is all that is necessary for the struggle; any other learning or political theory is superfluous. I am a little taken aback, not sure whether my questions and remarks this morning seemed to imply otherwise. This is quite possible; my faith is so much less than theirs. More likely, this gesture represents Osmar's affirmation, on this discouraging day, that despite the power of the forces aligned against them, they have all that they really need in order to win in the long run—God is on their side.

Nova Ronda Alta, image of the possible

We travel a few kilometers to Nova Ronda Alta. I have heard much about this place already. It is a Cinderella story for the landless throughout Brazil. The ten families who are now settled at Nova Ronda Alta were part of an earlier occupation of Fazenda Annoni. For three years they endured the cold, dirt, illness, and harassment. Finally this piece of land was their reward.

Nova Ronda Alta is very impressive. As an outsider I am tempted to describe it in utopian terms. Clearly the community is serving the land struggle as an invaluable model of what is both possible and worth seeking. Through their common hardships over such a long period of time the families have developed not only deep bonds with one another but also much experience and skill at working collectively. Many people come here to learn from this model of community. In anticipation of getting land of their own, the group from Fazenda Annoni with whom I spent last night has developed a charter modeled on the one from Nova Ronda Alta.

At Nova Ronda Alta, a full-sized soccer field dominates the landscape. It was the first thing they built upon arrival, a tribute to their playfulness even under extreme stress. Half of the families already have real cement and brick houses. The other half live in rough wooden shacks, stockpiling building materials and awaiting their turn. One of the ten men is a carpenter. The group has released him from other work so he can build houses full-time.

Farming here is extremely diversified. The families raise products both for home use and for market—wheat, corn, rice, beans, beef and dairy cattle, pigs, chicken, bees, vegetables, fruit, even medicinal herbs. They seem well aware of conservation issues and have developed a direct marketing system in the city. They also seem to be making real efforts toward the equality of men and women, while acknowledging the different contributions each has to make to the life of the farm. In determining work loads they have made generous provision for each person to travel and participate in political meetings off the farm. They are conscious of the significance of their achievement and committed to supporting the struggle of others for land.

The Nova Ronda Alta community has its own school in which all of the families participate, and has designed the curriculum around the values and activities of the community. Communal worship is a source of unity, discipline, and inspiration. Faith guides this as well as all of the communities I have visited.

Moving the structures of power, inch by inch

July 25, 1987. Porto Alegre, Rio Grande do Sul. I am at the airport, trying to get a flight back to São Paulo, struggling to keep up with events of the last two days that have unfolded at a quickly accelerating pace.

The day after the authorities expelled them from Fazenda São Juvenal, the 'militants' did in fact return home to Fazenda Annoni. There they immediately convened an assembly to decide how to respond to the landowners' violence. The group has determined to demonstrate its resolve by mounting another land occupation this very weekend. To judge from the coverage even in the mainstream press and on television where the "invasion" and its aftermath continue to be top news, public sympathy is strongly on the side of the occupiers.[4] There is widespread agreement that land reform is the most urgent priority for Brazil. Given plans for further "invasions," the state governor, who just a few days ago sanctioned use of the military police to expel the occupiers, apparently feels compelled to moderate the extremely tense situation somehow. Armed bands of landowners are determined to hold the line against expropriation. Equally resolute Sem Terra groups are determined to push forward the agenda of land reform. Confrontation could be explosive.

At a meeting here in the capital yesterday the governor asked for a three-week moratorium on "invasions" while he "searches for public lands" on which to resettle the 1,500 families of Fazenda Annoni. The Sem Terra groups accepted, despite the government's long history of bad faith. There seems little doubt that the escalation of tension between the landless and the landowners has pushed the struggle to a new stage. The landless have said all along that their fight ultimately is not with the landowners but with the government, which is responsible for carrying out the land reform law.

The high level of political consciousness and organization here in the South was evident yesterday at a demonstration in Erexim. Several thousand farmers turned out from the surrounding areas despite roadblocks erected to stop them. Their major demand was for a halt in construction of dams on the Uruguay River or for secure guarantees of adequate compensation and resettlement of those displaced. The demonstration was an open-air working meeting the likes of which I had never seen in the United States. The crowd voted to move the demonstration first to the Bank of Brazil, which had been closed for the occasion, and then to Eletrosul, the utility company that is building the dams. At both places, delegations representing each community succeeded in crossing police lines to meet with management representatives.

While the delegation was inside Eletrosul, the crowd outside carried on a vigorous debate. Many of the farmers had come carrying their long-handled hoes, which they raised in the air to punctuate their shouts of approval. Should participants stage a sit-in and refuse to leave until the president of the company appeared to answer their demands? Or, since he was in another state at the moment, should they be content to issue an ultimatum stating that they would return, in force, if he did not satisfy their demands within a certain number of days? The crowd split fairly evenly at first, but in the end decided on an ultimatum.

The archbishop and the nonviolent struggle of Alagamar

August 2, 1987. João Pessoa, Paraíba. I have spent the morning with Dom José Maria Pires, the archbishop of João Pessoa. I had long known of Dom José's reputation as a leading proponent of nonviolence in Brazil. He is indeed a remarkable man, with an extraordinarily lucid mind that seems to illuminate effortlessly whatever it comes to rest upon. He possesses a notable tranquility of bearing, which I take to emerge from his depth of faith and conviction.

I came here to discuss a well-known struggle of the peasants at nearby Alagamar, which began in 1976 and lasted several years. By law, some 600 families of tenant farmers were entitled to assume ownership of the land they were working when the owner died without leaving heirs. Many had worked the land for generations, while renting from the landlord. The government, however, sold the land to wealthy, absentee landowners. Seeking to maximize profit, they began to plant sugar cane and graze cattle.

When the peasants asserted their rights and refused to move, the new owners attempted to drive them off by force. They repeatedly let cattle loose wherever the peasants began to cultivate, or sent in armed men to pull up their crops. They hired other poor peasants to come in and plant sugar cane for them. They convinced the local government to back them and spread rumors that outside agitators were inciting the peasants. The authorities sent police to break up meetings between farmers, sympathetic neighbors, and church representatives.

The farmers met the landowners' efforts with determined resistance of their own. They witnessed the destruction of their crops without retaliating, then turned around and planted on some other part of the tract. Often they spent night and day in long vigils, guarding their fields with only sticks to drive off the cattle. At one dramatic point, when the authorities arrested eight of the farmers for frightening cattle, the other ninety-six went along to the prison and demanded that they too be arrested. The spontaneous pressure tactic brought release for those imprisoned.

Not all persisted in the long struggle. But in time, the families who did—about half of the original number—got title to their land.

The struggle at Alagamar was especially notable because despite the landowners' use of violence against their property there were no deaths during all the years of intense struggle. The landowners destroyed crops, fences, and buildings. They hired gunmen who shot up some of the houses and threatened worse. Yet after many years, only one person had been wounded. According to Dom José, Alagamar is the best example in Brazilian history of a struggle in which the people have consciously and continuously embraced active nonviolence as a strategy and a guiding moral principle.

I arrive for my meeting with Dom José full of questions. Frankly, I want reassurance from him that justice is attainable through nonviolent means. The dynamism of the struggle I have seen in the South has inspired elation. But news from other parts of the country is depressing. I had also visited Maranhão, a state in northern Brazil, and had seen evidence of the landowners' increasing violence and organization. It seems as if, in the North, everyone involved in organizing the peasants is getting killed. Meanwhile the landowners are not only arming themselves to the teeth but are even using the nonviolent struggle's own tactics against the people. To protest expropriations, UDR members have staged tractor blockades of public highways. Now they are threatening that if the government enforces land reform, they will withdraw their deposits and boycott the banks.

As Dom José describes what happened at Alagamar, it becomes clear that the struggle there benefited greatly from the support system available here in nearby João Pessoa. The church did not organize or lead the struggle but did provide valuable assistance. Early on, Dom José wrote a pastoral letter in support of the peasants, and had it distributed to every church in the diocese. The support of public opinion, the media, lawyers, labor unions, and the academic community contributed to the struggle's success. Dom José's own charisma, prestige, and commitment to active nonviolence—together with the power, influence, and resources of the church he represents— were critical throughout. He does not tell me this directly, of course, but it is obvious in other accounts. When all other church representatives were barred from Alagamar, he and Archbishop Hélder Câmara personally entered the area and helped drive away cattle with wooden sticks.

Of course, the enthusiasm and loyalty of this support network responded directly to the quality of the struggle that the Alagamar peasants initiated and waged. Dom José emphasizes that the community was particularly outstanding in its level of collective activities and development as a Christian base community. But not uniquely so. The entire Sem Terra movement and its struggle for land has grown from local experiences of building community.

Dom José suggests one reason why the movement in Maranhão is so much less developed than those either in the South or here in the Northeast. Many of those involved in the North are recent migrants, part of the government-encouraged wave of colonization. They lack the bonds and skills of community life that take years to create. Maranhão is a frontier state, where it is difficult to communicate and generate support.

Gospel nonviolence: the message of "liberating moral pressure"

I question Dom José about the source of the idea of nonviolence here in Brazil. In 1968, Dom Hélder Câmara, Archbishop of Recife, called a meeting during which forty bishops committed themselves to a campaign of "liberating moral pressure." Dom Hélder was very conscious of the work of Gandhi and King. But Dom José downplays the importance of the recent genealogy of nonviolence, and even of the word itself. What we are calling nonviolence, he says, is simply living out the teachings of the gospel. It is a commitment to respect the sacredness of each person, whatever his or her role in society, while maintaining a resolute determination to overcome all forms of domination.

Whatever the term, this gospel nonviolence is central to the people's land struggles in Brazil. Often unstated, it is nonetheless so pervasive that it defines not only the methods the people use in their struggle but the struggle's goals. Arthur Powers, who has worked in rural Brazilian communities for many years as a lay missionary with the Franciscan and Maryknoll orders, has noted that "what is occurring here is not fundamentally reform or revolution but *transformation*." Change begins within groups themselves, where "justice, love, and unity become concrete values." The people's attitude toward their oppressors suggests the depth of this transformation. To them, the rich are "wayward siblings," he says. Certainly they feel anger as they recognize that the greed of the wealthy is the cause of their poverty. "But more than anger, they express humor about the wealthy (whose greed they see as ridiculous) and pity for them." Powers tells of the time "a pastoral worker lightly suggested that it would be nice if a

Brazilian bishops Dom José Maria Pires (with glasses) and Dom Hélder Câmara (facing on the right) join hands with peasants of Alagamar after driving cattle loosed by wealthy landowners out of the peasants' fields. January 5, 1980. Photo courtesy of Diocese of João Pessoa.

certain corrupt official's airplane fell out of the sky." The same *posseiros* (small untitled landholders) who were trying to take over the official's land gently rebuked her.[5]

A similar spirit appears in the "Five Commandments of Nonviolence" that emerged from the Alagamar struggle. They rhyme in Portuguese: "Never kill; never wound, in deed or in word; always be alert; always remain united; always disobey the orders of His Excellency [the state governor] which would destroy us."

Supporting the struggle from the northern hemisphere

Despite the difficulties of the present situation, Dom José is optimistic about the long-term prospects for change: "The people are becoming more organized every day," he assures me, "more conscious of their power and of their obligation to participate. They are becoming a group that is conscious of itself." And as Dom José points out, this awareness and organization is powerful: "Among the cases in this region in which the people have made a firm option for active nonviolence, not a single struggle that I know of has been lost."

The poor in Brazil have a mythic sense of their own struggle, derived from the Biblical tradition that unites them so powerfully. One young woman involved in both the land movement and a Christian base community puts it this way: "The Bible isn't just about the past, it's happening today. If we place the Bible in our reality, we see that the power of Jesus' time is like our state today—and Pharaoh isn't that different from our large landowners!"[6] Identifying themselves with God's people, the Brazilian poor see themselves reenacting the Exodus. Their faith in the reality of the kingdom of God empowers them enormously for it enables them to believe in a future in which justice will be realized here on Earth. While desperation pushes them from behind, hope pulls them forward—a combination of forces that leads to powerful and sustained acts of resistance. The framework of their thinking builds on the polarities of justice and oppression. While gospel ideas of love and sharing prevail in the Christian base communities, to do God's will also means to fight for justice against oppression.

The poor and their allies profoundly cherish the nonviolence of the gospel and value their new brotherhood and sisterhood. They also widely understand and uphold the value of tactical nonviolence as a method. Old Testament images of the God of Justice standing beside the chosen people and striking down their enemies contribute powerfully to their willingness to refrain from retaliating themselves.

Ultimately, whether the struggle is violent or nonviolent depends on us more than we realize. The way that people in North America and Europe can best support nonviolence in Brazil is to act now, before unbearable pressures push the poor to take up arms. People in North America and Europe have a crucial role to play in confronting the structural violence that is driving the poor in some parts of Latin America toward extreme measures. Brazilian power holders also bear responsibility, but the power centers of the Northern Hemisphere consistently buttress the ruling elites in countries like Brazil. Our governments and corporations are exacting repayment of the debt at the cost of millions of human lives.[7] Our governments, through the projects they support, continue to redistribute wealth *away* from the poor to the rich at a moment in history when that process has become intolerable. The World Bank finances the dams on the Uruguay River that the farmers in Erexim are protesting. It also funded the agribusiness firm that had forced peasants I met in Maranhão off their land. We must use the power we have as citizens to stop the bleeding of the Third World. Key institutions like the World Bank are sensitive to public opinion. Furthermore, North American and European public opinion has a significant impact on the Brazilian ruling class.

The respective situations of the poor in Brazil and of advocates for social change in countries in the North offer different possibilities for action. The poor in Brazil are exploring their possibilities with extraordinary energy and creativity. But they do not have the resources, access to travel and information, or possibilities for communication that we have.

While the poor fight large landowners, local banks, and utility companies, their voices cannot easily reach the powerful institutions in Washington and New York which are often primary decision makers. On the other hand, few of us in comfortable situations in North America are hardy or resilient enough to carry out the long marches, occupations, and other actions that the Brazilian poor have come to take for granted. But we are in a position to affect our governments, the World Bank, International Monetary Fund, and other powerful institutions.

Discerning without sentimentality what is possible, what is appropriate, and what is the responsibility of each of us, may we join in a common struggle for liberation.

Notes

1. Between 1961 and 1963 the Brazilian Institute of Economics, with the help of the U.S. Department of Agriculture, surveyed the homes of Brazilians and concluded that 27 million (one-third of the population) suffered from malnutrition. Recently the Institute of Economic and Social Planning, an agency of the Ministry of Planning, estimated that by 1984, 86 million Brazilians (two-thirds of the population) were starving.

2. The term "*conscientização*" was coined at the Higher Institute of Brazilian Studies (ISEB), a think tank in Rio de Janeiro. It gained wide usage as a result of the far-reaching impact of Freire's work in adult literacy education. Elsewhere in this book, we use the Spanish form "*conscientización*" which is more common throughout Latin America except in Portuguese-speaking Brazil. [Eds.]

3. Following Brazil's 1964 coup d'état the military dictatorship created a new police force, separate from the civil police, but certainly meant to intervene in civil affairs. This *policia militar* should not be confused with the military police or MPs in other countries, which serve internal functions on military facilities.

4. Brazilian mainstream media and right-wing sectors consistently refer to the land actions of the rural poor with the somewhat pejorative term "invasions," while the settlers prefer to speak of "occupations" or rightful expropriations.

5. Arthur Powers, "The Great Brazilian Land Grab," *Commonweal*, May 8, 1987.

6. Interview with Antônia Lima Barros; by Mev Puleo, Associate of Project Abraço; Liberdáde, Para, Brazil; 1987. Unpublished.

7. UNICEF's "State of the World's Children 1989," reports that at least half a million children died the previous year as a direct result of "the slowing down or reversal of the development process in the 1980s." UNICEF singles out the international debt crisis, which erupted in 1982, as a key cause of this startling reversal. UNICEF, *The State of the World's Children, 1989* (New York: Oxford University Press, 1989), p. 1.

For further reading

Boff, Clodovis. *Feet-on-the-Ground Theology*. Maryknoll, N.Y.: Orbis Books, 1987.
Boff, Leonardo and Clodovis Boff. *Introducing Liberation Theology*. Maryknoll, N.Y.: Orbis Books, 1967.

Branford, Sue, and Oriel Glock. *The Last Frontier: Fighting Over Land in the Amazon.* London: Zed Press, 1985.
Freire, Paulo. *Education for Critical Consciousness.* New York: Continuum, 1973.
Galeano, Eduardo H. *Open Veins of Latin America: Five Centuries of the Pillage of a Continent.* New York: Monthly Review Press, 1973.

II
TESTIMONIES

Ecuador

ELEVEN

Introduction

Las Lomas is a shantytown of squatters perched on a piece of municipal land a stone's throw from downtown Guayaquil. The material wealth evident elsewhere in this port town, the largest city in Ecuador, is absent in Las Lomas. The sounds of children, pigs, and chickens compete with the blare of radios from within the bamboo shacks. The deeply rutted dirt streets wind to and fro, hinting at the haphazard origins of this now crowded community. At first glance, life in Las Lomas seems highly precarious. But a conversation with Nelsa Curbelo and Yanín Espinoza reveals another side of the community.

Nelsa is a former Catholic nun. For several years she was the National Coordinator of the Servicio Paz y Justicia (SERPAJ) chapter in Ecuador. In 1990 she was elected General Coordinator of the international SERPAJ network. Originally from Uruguay, she has lived many years in Ecuador. Her work has drawn her ever closer to the poor and for several years she has lived in a flimsy but well-kept shack that doubles as a community chapel for Las Lomas. As part of her work with

SERPAJ, she publishes a newsletter entitled *Buenas Nuevas* ("Good News"), which chronicles the struggles of the people and shows other signs of hope in news stories from around the world.

Yanín Espinoza, twenty-six, grew up in a poor neighborhood of Guayaquil. Through her activity in Christian youth organizations she developed a critical perspective on the world around her, along with leadership qualities and a faith-based commitment to work to change that world. She is coordinator of the Casa de la Juventud ("Youth House") in Las Lomas and is active with SERPAJ.

The Las Lomas that Nelsa and Yanín describe through the lens of their work is a community laying a foundation and building upward. After years of struggle, the community's cooperative has secured title to the land and is in the process of building new, permanent housing. Weekly assemblies are an exercise in direct democracy. Residents debate issues openly and fully; all have voice and vote. It is a community with a sense of a future. And while economic development is a clear priority, the social development of the community and its members is no less central.

The work in Las Lomas illustrates practical applications of active nonviolence to the problems of a Latin American slum—promoting solidarity and a sense of purpose with teenage gang members, assisting women to become fuller participants in the community, developing nonviolent alternatives that address both immediate problems and the long-term need for structural change. As is true in a wide variety of settings, *conscientización*, popular education, and organization are the key building blocks of change.

In June of 1987 Philip McManus conducted this interview in Nelsa's kitchen as she prepared a delicious vegetarian meal. Over the sound of roosters, street vendors, the conversation of next-door neighbors, and the ever present music, Nelsa and Yanín discussed their work and their vision.

Nelsa Curbelo, Guayaquil, Ecuador, 1987. Photo by Philip McManus.

Yanín Espinosa, 1988. Photo courtesy of *Sioux County Capital-Democrat.*

Ecuador: Good News in the Barrio
Nelsa Curbelo and Yanín Espinoza

Philip McManus: How long have you lived in the barrio of Las Lomas?
Yanín Espinoza: Three years.
Nelsa Curbelo: I'm going on six.
Espinoza: She's been living in the parish eleven years and six here in Las Lomas barrio.

I work specifically with youth, teenagers. Many don't have an adequate family situation. They practically live on the streets. And they grow up with all the problems of psychological and social maladjustment. So to a point they are also aggressive. And they lack motivation. It is difficult to get them involved with parish youth activities. It's a lot easier for them to talk about sports. Most of them are unemployed.

McManus: Even when they look for work, they don't find it?
Espinoza: They look for occasional work, and many don't even find that. A few have gotten used to not looking at all.

McManus: They don't go to school either?
Espinoza: After they finish primary school, it is very difficult to continue.

McManus: Why?

Curbelo: It is very expensive.

Espinoza: And they don't have adequate motivation to study.

McManus: What is expensive?

Curbelo: Books, notebooks, materials.

Espinoza: They also pay expensive registration fees. And bus fares, every day. And sometimes they don't h⌐ve even one *sucre* a day.

McManus: To go to school, you have to pay a registration fee?

Espinoza: Yes, for primary school you have to pay up to a thousand *sucres* [about $5.50].

McManus: Each semester?

Espinoza: No, one time. In secondary school it is worse. The registration fees are three to five thousand *sucres* [$17 to $28]. Even for those who get the minimum wage of twelve thousand *sucres* [$67] a month, it is difficult to pay. Those who only have occasional work don't have even twelve thousand sucres a month. To pay five thousand sucres to register just one child is almost half a [month's] salary, and then there are the other children. So this is a big reason why many kids don't go to school.

Then there is the problem that they aren't motivated to study. They aren't prepared to struggle and confront this difficult situation. So they allow themselves to be overcome—kids sixteen or seventeen years old practically defeated. They allow themselves to be overcome and they get used to making a little money once in a while with occasional work. Or they get permanent work, hard physical labor, and they don't have energy for anything else.

Apart from this they develop a certain aggressiveness that comes out among themselves. They are friends, but if they have the opportunity to cut each other down, they insult or even beat each other. During play one puts his foot in front of the other and trips him. Or gives him a kick from behind. In spite of being friends and just doing it for fun, it's still aggressive.

When we first started seeing youth gangs, about five years ago, the kids in this barrio also started to organize themselves in little groups.

McManus: Before that there weren't any gangs?

Espinoza: No, not here, not as gangs. There were delinquents or thieves, but each one acted on his own.

One of the bad things is that a gang will go as a group to the movies to see violent shows like *Rocky* and *Rambo,* all of that. Inside the theater they create a disturbance. Then they leave the theater together, the whole group thinking and feeling the same.

Curbelo: And all their names . . . they use the English word "the." "The" Apaches, "the" Murcielagos [Bats], "the" Rambos.

Espinoza: Or the Buffalos. The Buffalos were university students. It is easier for them to be in a group. To be in a group means to do whatever they please. It is to play, to hurt each other, to say bad words, to insult each other. The most valuable part of it for them is to be together. To go home means to confront problems, their parents fighting or whatever. The situation makes them apathetic. Their only ambition seems to be to buy a pair of stylish running shoes or some dark glasses or to party. The only ambition of their lives seems to be to make money.

Curbelo: Something else is that they have learned how to make guns from water pipe. They showed me how they do it. They put grease in the pipes to make them slick, then put buckshot and a fuse at one end, and then shoot. They can kill with them. Here no one has been killed yet, but in other barrios some have been.

Espinoza: Within Ecuador, Guayaquil is the city with the most problems. For example, these gangs. They are looking for a way to escape reality and have turned into hoodlums—robbing, using drugs, oftentimes even killing.

McManus: What kind of drugs do they use?

Espinoza: Marijuana, contact cement. Contact cement is the cheapest.

Curbelo: It's the drug for those who don't have anything else. They put it in milk. You see little kids, eight years old, sitting in the street taking contact cement.

Espinoza: You can imagine that they grow up with limited physical and intellectual capacities for confronting the problems of living in society. So to a certain extent our work is to get them out of their cynicism. To get them to react, to grapple with new ideals, so that they want to live in a deeper way.

McManus: And for you as a woman, is working with them a problem?

Espinoza: It is more difficult.

McManus: That isn't apparent. You seem to be very comfortable working with them, and they with you. There is a good atmosphere, isn't there?

Espinoza: At this point it is easier. At first it was very hard for me. In the barrio where I used to live, it was easy. There everybody knew me. I grew up there. I didn't have any problem speaking with anyone.

But in this barrio, no. They had to get to know me. Here the machismo is very strong. Before I came a man had been working with the group here. When I first arrived the group totally rejected me because I was a woman. They couldn't accept a woman leading an organization; it went against their machismo. So they began to punish me a great deal, to find ways to reject me. It was kind of hard. I had to start over from zero; I couldn't build on anything that had already been done here.

McManus: The Catholic parish supports you?

Espinoza: Yes.

Anyway, in December 1984 the gangs began to have confrontations.

For a pretext they made something up, like saying that so-and-so insulted the other group. But that was just a pretext to throw rocks at each other. So taking advantage of Christmas preparations, the celebration of Advent, we called the leaders of all these groups together.

McManus: Whom you already knew?

Espinoza: Right, they all live in the barrio. So we identified the leaders and went to look for them on the corners where they hung out, or in their houses. And we invited them to the meeting.

McManus: Why did you choose Christmas time?

Espinoza: For one thing, it was a way of sensitizing them; also we have Christmas *posadas* here. Each day the families of the barrio—youth, children, and adults—go with Joseph and Mary to seek hospitality in a home, like before the first Christmas. A family will receive them and lead a reflection on a Bible reading, then everyone sings and the children sing Christmas carols. The next day everyone goes and another family receives them with a different reflection.

Curbelo: It was a great opportunity for fights between different barrios. While all of the people were walking along, some threw rocks and others responded and the scene became a battlefield! It was the perfect opportunity for a confrontation.

Espinoza: We had seen this situation before; so we had to find a way to change it. We got together to talk—Nelsa, Padre Pepe Gómez, and myself—and decided to have a meeting with them. We didn't call everyone, just the leaders. But a whole platoon came. They all came. We spoke to them and asked them to say their names and also their nicknames. When we asked their nicknames they smiled. It was a matter of pride to say, "They call me 'Scarface'," so to them it was a lot of fun. They laughed and kidded each other in a friendly way.

After this we asked them why they had formed groups. Some said, for example, "Because I like to dance, and we dance very well." Others said, "Because we like to be together; we are a group of friends who like to get drunk together." They said some outrageous things in a rebellious and joking way—and some heavy things, too. To seem more macho, tougher, they were even a bit grotesque. But at the same time, they were defensive.

Then we asked them their ages and where they lived. We already knew where they lived but we wanted to call attention to it. And we asked them how the life of each one was. Or in other words, how the life of the youth in the barrio is. We were drawing out from them all of the things they had in common.

Then we led a reflection with them, talking about how they all live in the same barrio, they were all youth, their families had known each other for many years, they had seen each other grow up, and the like, and that they all had the same problems. Then we asked them if by chance they were rich. We were trying to get them to look at why they hurt each other, why they separated themselves from each other. And it was really good because as a result of that first meeting they decided that they should do some activities together. They decided that it was fine for each person to be in a group, but that the groups had to look for beneficial, positive things to do, and organize themselves for good things. So, for example, we said to them, "You have the opportunity to do what you like. But it should be what everyone likes, not just what is good for one group—positive things that don't ruin the lives of others."

The first thing we did was hold a sports tournament. This was fantastic! Then for New Year's we invited them to participate in a meeting in Alcedo, where the whole barrio goes to join in artistic presentations. It occurred to us to take them there so that they could see and participate in a different sort of activity. It was terrible for the *compañeros* of Alcedo: they knew we were coming but they didn't expect who it was that actually came. When they were arriving, the folks from Alcedo created an uproar. [She laughs] Padre Pepe was there. He almost had a heart attack, because we didn't expect the reaction from the *compañeros* there. They shouted and yelled and made a lot of noise. The person in charge had to calm them down, which was difficult. When the group finally joined in the activities they liked it—a lot.

McManus: This was a beginning; but afterwards the problem of the gangs continued?

Espinoza: Right; this didn't resolve it.

In March of 1985 we organized a weekend camp-out with seventy youth. They went to a campground and participated in activities together—like cooking together, playing together, learning to be disciplined about a schedule. At camp they all had to get up at the same time. They had time for prayer together, for singing together, for reflecting together as a group. For them that was hard. [She laughs] They weren't accustomed to meetings.

The first night was horrible! They were ready to make the whole thing fall apart. We had five or six sleeping in each tent, so it was pretty uncomfortable for those who wanted to sleep. Some suffered a lot because the troublemakers were picking fights, farting, and carrying on, trying to cause problems. They made up bird noises and wouldn't let anyone sleep. They talked, laughed, hit each other, pushed each other. It was a terrible night. We didn't sleep either.

McManus: Where were you?

Espinoza: In Ballenitas. It's on the beach, two and a half hours from here. Then the following day early in the morning one of them escaped. And that morning we had to send three of the worst behaved home.

We hadn't had a decent sleep and Nelsa had to accompany the three. But that was the rule of the campground. If someone misbehaved, he had to leave. So to follow through and to set an example for the others we had to send three back.

They couldn't have liquor or weapons there either. They didn't have weapons—but liquor, yes. We had to take bottles from them. Also, they wanted to bring tape players, but those weren't allowed either. The objective was that they use the things available in nature, without drugs, without distractions, so that they could focus on each other.

Curbelo: When the time came for introductions the leaders of the gangs didn't want to speak. They were trembling because they didn't know how to speak to a group. The most aggressive, the toughest, the ones with the most weapons were the ones who hid in a tent and didn't want to come out. They were embarrassed to say to the others, "My name is such-and-such, I live in such-and-such a place." Scared stiff! Their insecurity was amazing.

Espinoza: This was a lesson for us, a remarkable experience, no? To see the weaknesses of the teenagers. When we had the first meeting, since I didn't know them very well, I was very nervous. But after that camp-out I knew them a lot better. After that we could have a more personal relationship, with more trust, more friendship. After that we knew what language to use with them. Yes, that too.

So, to sum up a bit, there have been ups and downs, good things and not-so-good things, for various reasons. Many of the youth have changed their way of living. Or to put it in the most concrete terms, some don't take drugs now. Others, just a few, use drugs less. Others don't steal. Others are now working, or at least they have looked for work. Still others are trying to study. (We'll have to see how far they get. They don't have much persistence. They don't have relentless persistence!) [She laughs] And a few continue participating in the groups we work with. That is, some have had changes in their lives but now they don't continue in our groups. For them to reorganize their lives is very difficult. If they have to work and also study and at the same time to go to meetings, for them it is asking too much.

Curbelo: But they do maintain a relationship. Now they have seen something else.

Espinoza: Now they have seen something new. Now they choose between the good and the bad. So their lives are more normal. The task for us now is that they learn to do more things. Not just to work and to study but also to continue reflecting, to continue analyzing their lives, to continue focusing on their lives, to deepen their faith commitment, to continue grappling with their faith and their lives, to continue putting into practice a struggle, a life, the construction of something new, something more communitarian.

Curbelo: Here the organization began with the youth. But there were the mothers of the barrio also. The women's groups have another, very rich history of organizing. It is parallel to and at the same time converges with the story of the youth. The women are the ones who organized the barrio to deal with the problems here.

Espinoza: They support the youth. For example, they organize neighborhood watches—women, the mothers of the families. They organize watches at Christmas for the *posadas.* Or on other predetermined dates they do the same and continue doing so in their own way. For example, say there is a group of teenagers over here. The mothers come and sit themselves down, taking turns. Then when any trouble starts, they call the other mothers, and they all come and stop the kids and question them.

Curbelo: The neighborhood patrols are a response to the need to cut down on assaults and other types of abuse. It is a coordinated effort.

Another thing we haven't mentioned is our cottage industry program. There is a community workshop to provide employment, which the Central Bank supports and where people are learning skills. Twenty-one youth are in this program.

The women have also started a community workshop. So when they sell crafts, they sell together, the women and the youth of the barrio.

The women have contributed to the barrio in other ways. They were able to kick the sale of liquor out of the barrio. It took two years of digging in, putting themselves in front of the bars at night, sitting there, trying to stop them from selling. It is tremendous. A *tremendous* struggle!

Espinoza: Three months ago, there was a confrontation between the youth of this barrio and a gang from a nearby neighborhood. It was a shock for us to see them begin to fight again after two, almost three years. So to deal with the situation we called an assembly of all the barrio youth, both men and women. The young women weren't involved in the problem, but here we try to have the women integrate with the men. So we got together and analyzed the violence that had taken place, very concretely. Among the things the guys said was that they had not wanted a fight, they didn't like the aggression because it damaged friendships and hurt them physically and spiritually. It was amazing that after three years they talked like that. Sometimes you don't know what a capacity they have for analysis. In that meeting they were even talking about the effect of television and the movies. And all about the gangs. It was incredible.

Curbelo: Plus the lack of work. They also said they wanted to be more macho—that they fought for women. And that there wasn't any reason for it but it was because of the limitations of their situation: no work, nothing to do. They spoke very clearly.

Espinoza: So in this way we can evaluate the effect of our work. At that meeting we discovered that they no longer live just to live. Now they analyze their lives. And furthermore, they are integrating their faith into their lives.

Now the youth meet weekly. They plan their activities, then go out and do them. For example, now they are working with younger kids, to help them grow up in a different way. This is part of a group commitment.

Recently we have begun to work with them on education in active nonviolence. We have organized and held workshops, or seminars as some call them, on active nonviolence.

Curbelo: We hold them every night for a week, here and in the other barrio.

McManus: Do you have materials you use for the seminars?

Espinoza: There are a variety of ways of doing it. We can use audio-visuals. We work together as a group. First we get them to do an analysis and then we feed it back to them. We use socio-drama also. But almost always we try to start with group reflection, then presentations. Then we analyze nonviolence in its various aspects.

Curbelo: We have a workshop outline for this. We always begin by analyzing the violences that the people see around them. What are the causes? Then we deal with possible responses.

McManus: When you speak of these violences, do you also speak of structural violence?

Curbelo: Structural violence is always the first to come out; almost never personal violence.

McManus: How does it come out? In what form?

Curbelo: That it is the result of a lack of work, that the government doesn't support the people, that the social classes are divided, that the foreign debt has to be paid. . . .

McManus: Even the foreign debt?

*Curbelo: Sí!*Oooh! They understand that very well. They discuss all of this but hardly ever call themselves into question. Almost never.

Espinoza: The youth do talk about the gang fights, the fights between friends. But they always refer to a big group; they never look inside themselves.

Curbelo: In the middle class and the upper-middle class they always start with themselves. . . .

Espinoza: It will be "because we are selfish, because we don't help each other. . . . "

Curbelo: In the poor classes, in the poor barrios, first they analyze the violence that results from the lack of work, because the government doesn't offer support, because of the foreign debt, because of the marginalization of women, because of the struggle between social classes. It is always more structural. And almost never do they ask what they themselves have to do with all this. You have to push, you have to try a second time, for them to begin to see that we are responsible too, that we help maintain this situation—that through our way of being and acting we are sustaining this, we are a pillar of this injustice.

The women also have been involved in nonviolence workshops. It is extraordinary, especially since some are illiterate. One of them says, "But the eternal debt, why do we have to keep paying it eternally?" At first I thought that she said that because she didn't know the right word—*external* debt.[1] So I said, "No, it is not that it is eternal." But the only thing she didn't know was how much we owed per person.

McManus: How much is it?

Curbelo: It is almost eighty thousand *sucres* [about $450] per person. I told her how much it is. So she said, "But our problem is that nobody pays us. We work and nobody pays us. We don't cost the government anything. And we have to pay when we give birth to our children in the hospital. But if somebody paid us, instead of paying the foreign debt, then we would be able to face our situation and deal with it. And everything that we do has value. By not paying us they say it doesn't have value. But our work also has value. If we stopped functioning, it would paralyze the country. So we do have value."

You can see that they are very *conscientizadas.* It is the women who have gotten the whole barrio moving. Each week there is an assembly of the barrio to deal with problems. For example we had a problem with water. The Catholic university above us ran all its rainwater through here. To separate the University from the barrio they had built a big wall, which you can see over there; and they left an opening through it for the water to run off. They didn't want us to be here, because we are the poor. Everyone was saying, "The university is responsible." The women said, "No, we are also culpable, because we let the university send the runoff through here. So we are also accomplices. And being accomplices, we have to do something." So they went up to the university and spoke with the dean and with many others. The university had to invest millions to divert the water in another direction.

Later the same thing happened with the bars.

This coming Monday night the barrio assembly will take up the question of whether the guard patrols in the barrio should carry arms.[2]

McManus: And this is a small group of women?

Curbelo: There are twenty. I used to meet together with them too, but now they meet on their own. They publish a newsletter, and they print it. Those who don't know how to write dictate to their daughters. It's really wonderful. The newsletter is called *Caminemos* ("Let's Walk").

In it, for example, they write, "In front of the house of so-and-so there is a lot of garbage." Things like that, no? And they put the person's first name and last name. So the people read it and then clean up. And in the next newsletter: "Now that place is clean. And now there is going to be a *minga* [a community workday] on such-and-such a date." They publish educational materials and their reflections on what is going on. It is very, very interesting. But all in their own way, in their own language.

Some people call them "busybodies," "idle women," and other names. But in the barrio assemblies they were successful at getting majority votes against the bars. Three times they voted on the issue and each time they won a majority. Now the bars are swept out. Nobody sells liquor.

I have this documented—what everybody said, how they said it, their manner—in a booklet I made with little drawings. And now, as a history, we are going to do another one with drawings of the women and their efforts. The people will buy it and read it. In this way they recover their history, which we believe is very important. It is all dated: "On such-and-such a date, this was done and that was done. . . . " We are rescuing their experience, giving it value, and returning it to them.

We have opted for a long-range commitment to education. We don't believe we can do anything worthwhile in terms of active nonviolence without first having at least three years of preparation among the people. We need a broad formation. And given the situation in the country, we must do this work at the organizational level: unions, barrio groups, etc. Perhaps after that we can take on broader tasks. But we think we have a lot of work to do at the base level. So, very modestly, according to our means, we are pushing forward. That is to say, we have opted clearly for everything that is involved in education within the context of active nonviolence.

McManus: Are you worried that there might be repression? You were telling me earlier about some influential people who are saying that the development of human rights groups in Ecuador has contributed to the emergence of gangs— that the authorities could deal with them more effectively if human rights considerations didn't constrain them.

Curbelo: The authorities have come looking for me here. And in Machala and Belao, where other groups work with SERPAJ, they arrested one person. Also, they were going to expel the priest there from the country.

On Good Friday there was a demonstration in Machala. The people carried a huge crucifix showing how Christ is crucified today. It was beautiful. They carried this enormous cross and on it were the words: "foreign debt," "injustice," everything that is crucifying the people today. So they were accused of being communists.

Belao is a peasant area. They had a procession of the Stations of the Cross there also. Later the authorities said that the priest, who is a North American, is a communist. They have petitioned the bishop to kick him out of the parish and the Minister of Government to expel him from the country. The problem is that because he is a North American such action would create a mess with the U.S. Consulate. The consulate protects its people. Still, now he can't live in the city; he has to live in the rural areas with the peasants.

The people here also had a procession of the Stations of the Cross on Good Friday. We recorded it and are thinking about publishing it as a booklet, because it belongs to them, no? It was very beautiful. During the Stations of the Cross they talked about how Jesus was—not about how he fell down and that sort of thing, but how Jesus pardoned his enemies, how he organized the people, how Jesus always spoke the truth. They chose a Bible reading and reflected on it.

In these reflections you can see how the people understand the stories. For example, in Alcedo they talked about how Jesus shared the loaves with the people. They noted that it was the loaves the people already had that permitted him to do the miracle. He needed the two loaves and the fish that they had. They said that when each one shares of what one has there is enough for everyone. And then later they said that since there were many people, they sat them down in groups of fifty. In other words the community must always be a small group because in that way they can get organized. And so on. It was *beautiful,* really beautiful.

How did they put it? They said they had to organize themselves in small groups so they could know each other, so they could know each other's names. And in that way there is enough and even more than enough. After this kind of discussion the question always arises: "And we? What are we doing in our community?" It was very special.

Translated from Spanish by Philip McManus

Notes

1. In Spanish, the term for the foreign debt is *"deuda externa."* The substitution of the adjective *"eterna"* (eternal) for *"externa"* is based not only on the fact that they sound alike but also on the experience that the foreign debt *is* eternal, i.e., that it is experienced by the people as a source of unending suffering and that it is simply impossible to pay.

2. The assembly subsequently decided against allowing the neighborhood patrols to carry arms, believing that it would contribute to violence and that the number of persons in the patrols was their greatest strength and security. [Eds.]

For further reading

Corkill, David and Cubitt, David. *Ecuador: Fragile Democracy.* London: Latin America Bureau, 1988.

Hurtado, Oswaldo. *Political Power in Ecuador.* Albuquerque: University of New Mexico Press, 1980.

Thomson, Moritz. *Living Poor: A Peace Corps Chronicle.* Seattle: University of Washington Press, 1969.

Nicaragua

TWELVE

Introduction

Not only Roman Catholic but also other Christian traditions have enriched the struggle for justice and peace in Latin America. As Paul Jeffrey points out in Chapter Nine, the Moravian Church in Nicaragua drew on its sometimes neglected peace heritage as it struggled for reconciliation between the Sandinista government and the indigenous peoples of Nicaragua's Atlantic Coast during the 1980s.

The Rev. Norman Bent has played an important role in both his church's mediation efforts in that regard and in its own recommitment to peace and justice. In August 1986 he delivered the following speech to a consultation on strategies for peacemaking, held in Honduras under the sponsorship of the Mennonite Central Committee. Though ostensibly speaking about the strategy of conflict resolution, Bent also articulated a spirituality of suffering service that has inspired others both within his own church and far beyond it.

Bent was born in 1939 in the village of Tasba Pouni, on the shore of the Caribbean, about forty miles north of Bluefields. His father was of Jamaican descent; his mother was a Miskito Indian. In 1963 and 1970 he studied at the Latin American Biblical Seminary in Costa Rica, where he came into contact with liberation theology.

While serving his first parish in the mining town of La Rosita, Bent felt compelled to put into practice his growing social concern. He discovered by listening to his parishioners that the U.S.-based mining company not only underpaid its workers and offered them no benefits, it also promptly dismissed those who became ill with the lung disease silicosis. Together with a handful of other pastors he began to urge the Moravian Church to demand justice for the poor of eastern Nicaragua, particularly fellow Indians.

Eventually the church named Bent director of its program for development. Projects included farming and fishing cooperatives, literacy, and health. In 1980 the Moravian development program would participate in the national literacy campaign that won the young Sandinista government worldwide acclaim for lowering Nicaragua's rate of illiteracy from fifty to thirteen percent. During the mid-1970s Bent's role in the church's social ministry brought him into regular contact with leaders of a new Indian liberation movement. That movement drew the suspicion and harassment of the Somoza dictatorship. In the first year or two of the Sandinista revolution it seemed to offer a way for Miskito, Sumo, and Rama Indians to participate in the effort to rebuild and restructure the Nicaraguan nation. However, as Sandinista policy toward the indigenous peoples proved first paternalistic, then heavy-handed, some leaders of this Indian liberation movement formed an armed insurgency against the Sandinistas.

Bent's years of contact with those same Indian leaders made him an object of Sandinista suspicion as the national government's relationship with the Coast deteriorated and the Indian insurgency began mounting attacks. Bent's account of his detention and patient rebuilding of relationships with the Sandinista government is part of the chapter that follows. Eventually his relations with leaders on both sides of the confrontation placed him in a position to work with other Moravian leaders for a mutually beneficial reconciliation.

That position, and that work, have certainly brought pain. In 1983, when the Sandinistas had barely begun to turn around their Atlantic Coast policy, and when fellow Moravian Church leaders had only just begun to heed the call to work actively for peace, Bent told an interviewer: "The revolutionary [Sandinista] leadership does not trust me because I am a church leader of the Indian people. Neither am I trusted by my own people, because of my revolutionary approach to interpreting the Scripture. So you see where I am: I am the meat of the sandwich."[1]

In the field of conflict resolution, some have observed that the efforts of the Moravian Church of Nicaragua and of individuals like Rev. Bent make a unique case study. Rarely, they say, is a party to a conflict able to play the role of mediator. Yet that observation may underestimate the role that deep spiritual roots and a yearning for peace can play. Those qualities are evident here in a commitment to persist—to persist in that tight space between two apparent adversaries, amid misunderstanding and against frequent setbacks—for the sake of the Nicaraguan poor of all ethnic groups.

Rev. Norman Bent, Managua, Nicaragua, 1986. Photo by Joetta Handrich.

To Accept the Enemy as a Challenge
The Ministry of Reconciliation
Norman Bent

The fundamental reason for reconciliation is at the center of the gospel message that the angels announced—"Glory to God in the highest, and on earth peace, good will toward all people." Society is in serious conflict first with its Creator, and as a result, has conflicts between people and between peoples. The angels announced that through the incarnation of Christ God was intervening in the process of human history in favor of peace for human society.

The conflict that biblical history describes is ancient. Since the fall of humanity we have lived in constant conflict with God. We have practiced disobedience in diverse forms, we have done our own will, and we have made few efforts toward the total harmony of society. Instead, we have created major conflicts among ourselves as we have sought to fulfill our own very personal interests, rather than collective ones. What the gospel offers and expects here is clear: good will. In this phrase lies our best hope for finding solutions to our conflicts and achieving peace. Herein lies our hope for the power to enjoy God's total salvation, which is the final liberation of all humanity, the building of God's Reign in its fullness.

This phrase, "good will," contains the entire technique and strategy of nonviolent struggle. We need good will to recognize and acknowledge conflict in the first place. Second, we need good will to accept the enemy as a challenge. I say this from my own experience. Third, we need good will to accept our role as part of the conflict—not becoming its victims but instead helping create solutions. And fourth, we need good will in order to establish clear objectives at all levels— global, international, national, and local. Above all, we need good will to struggle honorably.

Good will to recognize the conflict

Let's look at some elements in one way of struggling, the strategy of mediating conflicts. Keeping in mind the phrase "good will," we must first of all create conditions that allow everyone involved to recognize the conflict. Without recognizing the conflict we will hardly accept working at the conflict and seeking solutions. Therefore, the role of the mediator is not so much to solve conflicts as it is to create conditions wherein conflicting parties can discover each other and discover their own solutions within the conflict.

We need to help create a certain atmosphere: the parties to the conflict must come to see the counterproductive nature of competition, coercion, bad faith maneuvers, and violence. They must come to see that it will be more fruitful to establish, together, a mechanism for solving the problem in the long run rather than the short. Then the parties must discover those elements they must deal with to solve the conflict cooperatively. The mediator's role here is to insist firmly that each party articulate its concerns even in the face of opposing views. Otherwise the strongest will simply win the battle. Furthermore, relevant information about the conflict must be available and we must help create the resources that the parties will need in order to resolve the conflict. In sum, recognizing the conflict, and helping those involved to recognize it, means creating a forum that will allow cooperative work toward a solution.

Here I would like to mention our own experiences in Nicaragua. Historically, Atlantic and Pacific Coast Nicaraguans have mistrusted each other. Therefore much of the Nicaraguan Moravian Church's energy as a mediator has gone into creating the atmosphere and the forum for dialogue. We have struggled to help the Sandinistas see that however much the United States and the CIA have manipulated the Atlantic Coast conflict, the situation is first of all a result of the government's own mistakes. At the same time we have struggled to help the Indian resistance see that their interests do not coincide with those of the CIA and the Pacific-based Hispanic contra leaders. These efforts have sometimes provoked misunderstanding and accusations from both sides. But our own need to explain ourselves has often provided key opportunities to help each side recognize the conflict's true nature. After all, it is by staying inside Nicaragua on one hand, yet remaining loyal to the concerns of our own indigenous people on the other, that we have won the respect of both sides.

Atlantic-Pacific mistrust has a long and tragic history. To begin with it was not Spain but rather the British who first came to the Atlantic Coast of Nicaragua. Following British colonialism we suffered internal colonialism. This division has contributed to a historical racism in Nicaragua, a racism that is part of our problem today, a racism between the Pacific Nicaraguan and the Atlantic Nicaraguan, divided as they are by mountains and distinct cultures. On the Atlantic side, most of our population is Protestant; on the Pacific, most of the population is Roman Catholic. And on the Atlantic we speak diverse languages.

It is racism that has created mistrust. Those of us on the Atlantic side mistrust any human being who comes speaking Spanish. Although superficially we may seem to be listening, in the background we are asking ourselves, "Could this fellow really be telling the truth?" Because of our history the Spanish-speaking *ladinos* will go home and we'll doubt what they have said. A North American *gringo* will get a much better hearing. It is the *ladinos* who are the historical, cultural enemy. For them there is only suspicion. Even if you come with the best intentions of helping, what you say in Spanish will turn into so much theory that will be lost with the years. It won't make any sense within the cultural life of the people. Of course, if you say it in Miskito, then yes, it will make sense.

Even as the Sandinista National Liberation Front (FSLN) was taking power, the Catholic priest in Puerto Cabezas and I were trying to promote an atmosphere of reconciliation. On July 17, 1979, the day Somoza fled the country, the military colonel in Puerto Cabezas invited the local Catholic priest and me to a meeting, along with two prominent community leaders known to sympathize with the Sandinistas. The colonel wanted to negotiate a transfer of power with them. We as church leaders were to serve as witnesses that if an agreement were reached, the [Somocista] National Guard stationed in town would not fight. The Guards agreed to turn over their weapons to the church if the Sandinistas would not attack them when they took control. We negotiated for a day and a half, through the night, without sleeping, and the Guards turned themselves over to the church. On July 19th, then, the whole town turned out for a service of thanksgiving. The town—several thousand people—pardoned the Guard. We as church leaders proclaimed a time of forgiveness and rebuilding. We then asked them to train a couple of local fellows as interim police, to protect the city from possible looting. We made contact with the Sandinistas via radio, and a week later they came in.

But the attitudes and immaturity of the first Sandinista officials who arrived did not bode well. With so many things for the new national government to do, the Atlantic Coast did not seem so important. The Sandinistas sent young kids out to run the town, twenty or at most twenty-five years old. They were *ladinos* who had never been to the Atlantic Coast before. They were inexperienced, anti-Protestant, not very well educated, somewhat hateful racially, and of course they didn't speak anything but Spanish. So the troubles began. For example, in our negotiations we had promised the colonel that he would be safe. After the insurrection, then, he actually stayed, settled, and began cooperating with the revolution. But one of the young Sandinistas had known him as a torturer in another part of the country. Even though the Managua government had decreed an end to the death penalty, the young Sandinista in Puerto Cabezas ordered the ex-colonel shot. The government did eventually try the young man who gave the orders, and I think he is still in jail. But the incident didn't do much to instill confidence among our people, who had committed themselves to reconciliation.

Over the next two years we church leaders kept telling the Sandinistas, "Look, you have to change this leadership here. These guys are making trouble. You have to understand. You have to work with the people. Let the people participate. You just can't rebuild this country like a bully." But they just did not understand. It took too long to change their imposed leaders. What the FSLN did was try to bring the Atlantic Coast into the national life for the first time. You can imagine what happened. They had no theoretical understanding of our cultures, no technique, no experience. So as Tomás Borge[2] himself admits, "We entered the Atlantic Coast with too much revolutionary vision, too little understanding, and very little love or even tact. The Indian continued to be our enemy, and we pushed the Indian right into the hands of our real, much greater enemy, the CIA."

Given those errors, the Moravian Church as a whole began to play a key mediation role. Our church's position is unique for Protestant churches in Latin America in the first place, since about eighty percent of the Miskitos are Moravians. Historically, the church was more involved in education, health, and development on the East Coast than was the central government. And the Indian people have a special respect for their pastors.

As Indian-Sandinista relations disintegrated I tried to use my position as a pastor to convince the young East Coast [indigenous] leader Steadman Fagoth that nonviolence was the approach to take. He was too violent and I discovered that. He needed strong leadership, people to help him understand that he was too violent. I felt that by standing alongside and instructing him I had some possibility of helping him. Many times he came to my house to talk. I remember one evening. A Sandinista soldier had shot a young Indian out of personal, individual conflict. Steadman had taken the body of the young man into the central park of Puerto Cabezas. And I had gone there because he was really blowing the army apart verbally. I went and said that the church too was concerned by the state of violence, that the incident needed a careful investigation and that the army should punish the soldier. But I pleaded that we did not need this barrier Steadman was erecting. So he came over later to say that he had appreciated my public stand. On the other hand, he felt maybe I was too hard on him—that I was pushing him too hard for alternate ways of dealing with the conflict.

Such incidents moved me even deeper into searching for alternatives. I too could see the army's repeated mistakes, and it became necessary for someone to talk to them. When both my pastoral responsibility and the church's social responsibility are on me, I have a double responsibility to focus on a problem. So I began to speak out on both sides—to the local Sandinista leadership and to the Miskito Indian leadership. Perhaps I spoke a little more to the Indian leadership at first because at the time I had more access to them. They knew—even Steadman knew—I was speaking as a pastor. I made it clear that I wasn't interested in any political power, that my role was to be a reconciler.

In 1981 and 1982, the government tried to respond to a military situation in purely military terms. Eventually it did what the United States did in Vietnam and what the Guatemalan government has done in its own country. It used military tactics and evacuated the indigenous population from war zones in order to concentrate them in areas it considered secure. To try to justify this military situation before international opinion the government sent its Atlantic Coast delegate to meet me as I returned from a World Council of Churches meeting in Ecuador. "The government would like you to stay here in Managua eleven days and represent us at a United Nations seminar on racism," he explained. "I have your wife's permission." I accepted the invitation but I was not about to wash the government's face [whitewash the government's record] and say there was no racial problem in Nicaragua, when there was.

When the meeting in Managua was over I went back to the Atlantic Coast and found that there was warfare in a community called San Carlos. This was late 1981. In what was later called "Red Christmas," disaffected leaders mobilized hundreds of Indians in the community for the first time. This situation seriously affected the Moravian Church since most Indians belong to it. In mid-1982, the Catholic Church publicly made a pronouncement condemning the Sandinistas, which only augmented the violence between the various parties. However, the bishop of the Moravian Church had a press conference in Managua and called for a struggle of national reconciliation, as well as international reconciliation among indigenous peoples.

At the same time, the bishop also called for an emergency synod of his own church. There he insisted that the church take a mature position and that it struggle as a people of reconciliation. It took three days of heavy discussion and review of church history. The Moravian Church historically stands up for peace, out of its own experience when early Moravians faced terrible persecution. We church leaders reminded the church of the Moravian missionaries who had come to Nicaragua and had trouble with both Sandino and the Somoza government, but yet had always been ready to forgive and serve. In the end the Moravian Church authorized the bishop to choose a group of church leaders to cooperate with him and be an official delegation at the reconciliation process.

Two long years later the Sandinistas recognized that they had made mistakes and needed to accept the challenge of seeking reconciliation with the indigenous people. One result was their proposal to initiate a process for giving autonomy to the Atlantic Coast. That would mean East Coast people governing the East Coast themselves according to patterns and policies appropriate to our cultures. The process for creating the autonomous government took over a year, but the process itself provided a forum, as Indian communities assembled throughout the region to name representatives, debate the proposal, and suggest their own ideas.

So then, the mediator first of all needs to create the proper atmosphere, and the forum, in order to be able to mediate.

Good will to accept the enemy as a challenge

Secondly, there is the challenge of mediation itself. The will to accept the enemy as a challenge is one of the most positive steps in mediation. The mediator, in a sense, becomes one more participant in the conflict. He emerges from his environment and may see the other two parties as his enemy, but he nonetheless takes them as a challenge, in order to help them play more constructive roles within the conflict. The mediator then becomes a reconciling agent.

In 1982, on the 17th of January, a representative of Comandante Tomás Borge brought me a letter which Borge had signed. The letter invited me to a meeting in Managua to discuss the problems on the Atlantic Coast and the warfare that had erupted in 1981. A large number of Indians had already joined the counter-revolutionary struggle, which favored the U.S. government. War was already at the borders. Comandante Borge invited me because I lived on the Atlantic Coast and, along with my fellow pastor Fernando Colomer, was playing a leadership role among the communities there.

Fernando and I both flew to Managua. For the first time in my life a revolutionary *comandante* received us at the international airport in Managua and drove us in a bulletproof, air-conditioned Mercedes Benz, with police escort in front and behind. At that moment I felt like one of the highest ranking statesmen in Nicaragua!

They took us to an office in an air-conditioned government building. The *comandante* asked, "How's everything on the Coast?"

"Well, it's still there," I replied.

"Okay, we're glad you guys are here, because we're going to dialogue about the problem. I'll let the others know you are here for the meeting. In the meantime, here are two beds."

And sure enough, there were two fine beds in an air-conditioned room. "For now, why don't you get some rest," the officer said. He left at 5:00 P.M., and at 6:00, they brought us some food and we ate. It was good food.

But for five days no one came to meet with us! After a while Fernando started getting a little nervous and he told me, "Look here! My heart is thumping like crazy."

Meanwhile, we could go out to bathe, and we ate three fine meals a day. Once I asked the soldier who brought us food, "Do you eat the same food?"

"No," he said, "it's only for the officers."

After five days the *comandante* finally came again and said to us, "We made a mistake, but for your own good it would be better if you two didn't go back to the coast. Stay here in Managua, don't go anywhere else, because we want to guarantee your safety."

After a week of our absence, the bishop came to ask the authorities what had happened to us. They told him, "Look, we were afraid that, given their leadership roles, these two brothers would cross over into Honduras and join up with the counter-revolution. Or, on the other hand, because of the mistakes we have made there on the coast, they might lead the Atlantic population in a popular uprising against the army and force us to turn the Atlantic Coast into a sea of blood."

Now their first fear, our going to the counter-revolution, didn't interest us. And the second didn't either, because of our own spirit of nonviolence. Yes, the indigenous people wanted to support the Indian insurgency. The people were at the very edge of popular violence, ready to confront the army's machine guns with rocks and stones. And if we two had returned to the Coast, simply getting off the plane would have brought a massive reception, which the army would have taken as a threat. The bloodbath could have begun. I remember how the situation forced me to reflect very hard about what the moment demanded, to look at Nicaragua, and to see how I could contribute. I again chose to play the role of mediator.

One year after the government released me from detention I received an invitation to meet with Comandante William Ramírez, the top government official for the East Coast. We talked about various things, but he especially wanted to ask me to forgive the government for the mistakes made in bringing Fernando and me to Managua. I said, "William, there was no reason for you to ask forgiveness, because my Christian spirit has told me that I had to forgive my enemy and love him more than ever."

Ramírez stood up from behind his desk and for a moment I was actually afraid that he was becoming violent at me. But then he embraced me and we both cried, shedding tears for the joy of being able to reconcile with each other and forgive one another. We both made promises that as Nicaraguans it was our responsibility to work toward reconciliation on the East Coast, to work toward peace, and to look for an end to the conflict there. Though as a government they were admitting their mistakes, they hoped that the church and church leaders would support their work in trying to correct those mistakes.

But, he was my enemy! I had to accept the challenge, the challenge of seeing the Sandinistas as my enemy—yet working with the Sandinistas to find solutions to the conflict on the Coast.

And I also had to see my own people, the indigenous people of which I am a part, as my enemy and as a challenge. Why? In order to struggle as a mediator between both of them and win them over.

Yesterday I received a phone call [here at the conference center in Honduras]. I went to the phone a little surprised and uncertain. The person on the other end asked, "Are you the Reverend Norman Bent?"

"Yes."

So he spoke to me in Miskito: "*Pasin, nahki yamni sma?*" *Pasin* is a word that comes from English, because when the missionaries came here they called themselves "Parson." "*Yamni*" is the way we translate "shalom" or blessing. "*Pasin nahki yamni sma?*" was his way of asking, "are you well?"

So I responded, "*Ao, yamni sna,*" yes, I have shalom. "*Man ka nahki sma?*" Are you well, do you have shalom?

And he told me, "*Diera kum kum mapara yamni sna.*" In some things I have shalom.

So then I asked him, "Tell me, who are you anyway?" And he identified himself as *comandante* so-and-so, a commander in the Indian insurgency. He had called to ask me to take some money and some medicine to his family back in Nicaragua. Once he wouldn't speak to me. Once he had orders to kill me. Comandante "Ráfaga," one of the first Indian leaders to negotiate a separate cease-fire with the Sandinistas, once showed me a letter. It was a list of names; the armed Indian resistance had direct orders to eliminate certain people inside Nicaragua. My name was number four.[3]

So as a mediator I discovered that my role was in the middle of both sides and I had to look at both sides as enemy because both sides mistrusted my role. But at the same time I loved both sides because both sides were Nicaraguans. On one hand there was love because, as we say, "the blood runs through our veins." Being an indigenous person I felt closer to that side, the group of Nicaraguans who have suffered most. On the other hand, I also saw the other side as Nicaraguan brothers and sisters who were struggling for a dream, a dream that we all want to be a part of, a dream for a more just society. I believed that these people, who were trying to be leaders of this dream, were people who needed some support. And I accepted them as a challenge as an enemy.

But the question then became, how are we going to fight? Do I face them with anger and hate, or do I face them with love and forgiveness? Here is where I realized that I had to fight by loving them, by being willing to forgive them, while at the same time demanding prophetic justice from them for the people, and demanding pastoral understanding from my people for *their* enemy.

I could not forget for a moment that I was a part of the people. Yet to play the role of a mediator I had to forget that I was also victim, and become a neutral person instead. I reminded the people that I knew suffering; I have cried many times for their pain, for their hard life. But I closed my eyes at that and said, you *have* to forgive. What about the oppressor, in this case the Sandinistas? They are not an oppressor who willingly did what they did. Maybe they had good intentions but they made terrible mistakes. So I looked at the Sandinistas and I said, "All right, you people want to do good, but you don't know how to go about it." I said, "You *have* to forgive us, ask for forgiveness, and try to overcome the mistakes that you made."

Until I was able to think of each side as a challenge, I was not able to really mediate between them.

Good will to be part of the conflict, without being its victim

At other points in the mediation process, one needs the will to avoid becoming a victim to the conflict. If one feels that the enemy is more powerful, it is hard to avoid a victim mentality. One needs to feel just as powerful as the enemy, not to increase the violence, but to be able to contribute positively to the search for solutions. If we as indigenous people of the Atlantic had let ourselves feel like victims we would have lost the battle.

I have repeatedly preached on this in my church. The Sandinistas have committed many errors and continue to do so in some individual cases. But I tell my people that we never need to feel like victims of these errors. Rather, we must feel equally powerful in order to help avoid a breakdown in the Nicaraguan process. As part of the conflict we have accepted the fact that we have a very special role to play. Our role as a member of the conflict and as mediators is to influence the environment so that the parties in conflict may adopt the attitudes necessary for peace. Positive attitudes are very important. We need them ourselves.

Good will to establish clear objectives

To summarize let me mention one more element of the process, based once again on the phrase from the sacred text, "good will." Our efforts should have global objectives as well as specific national and local ones.

The simple fact that we have recognized the conflict, accepted being part of it, and sought to mediate the conflict in favor of peaceful solutions, should imply that we have clear objectives—certain reasons for mediating. When our bishop invited us to be agents of reconciliation, the Moravian Church in Nicaragua had to define its objectives clearly. Among these objectives was the objective of justice. The unjust structures have to change. Justice continues to be at the center of the gospel message. Ultimately, justice is the goal of our mediation for peace.

When the Sandinistas told me I would not be able to leave Managua I didn't become bitter. And when they lifted that restriction after three months, then allowed me to travel abroad and finally back to the Atlantic Coast, I didn't abandon Nicaragua. I never stopped being a revolutionary.

I never stopped supporting the revolution but I never stopped criticizing it strongly wherever there were criticisms to make. Why? For me, the Nicaraguan revolution itself is one more objective, an international one, for it gives hope to the poor in Latin America. It is a hope for peoples everywhere on the path to development. That is why I could not stop contributing to this revolution. I did not want to see it lost due to human errors. The hope of the poor is a global objective. And once the revolution's errors are corrected, it still offers hope to my Indian brothers and sisters, for they are among the poorest of all Nicaraguans.

The ministry of reconciliation continues

Today we are about to become the only ones in Latin America to have a federated state within a national state, thanks to the autonomy that will soon go into effect. However, if our indigenous brothers in combat through armed struggle do not participate in the autonomy process, there will be no autonomy. Even if Nicaragua's legislature proclaims it a thousand times, there will be no autonomy. We need their dynamic participation.

Secondly, until all of us *costeños* [coastal people] participate conscientiously in the autonomy process, there won't be autonomy either. Within the autonomous state the struggle may be between different ethnic groups. That is already happening in the southeastern part of Honduras between the two insurgent groups Kisán and Misura— Indians killing Indians. For us, autonomy means the creation of another problem, which will demand even more work. We need maturity as well as prophetic and pastoral responsibility to achieve national reconciliation.

Translated from Spanish by Gerald Schlabach

Notes

1. "Bordering on Reconciliation," interview with the Rev. Norman Bent in *Sojourners,* March 1983, p. 27.
2. Tomás Borge is the only surviving member of the FSLN founders, and in the early years of the revolution was among the nine *comandantes* in the FSLN's National Directorate as well as Nicaragua's Minister of the Interior.
3. Almost two years after this speech Bent met Steadman Fagoth in Miami and was told that he also had received orders to kill Bent and other church leaders. At that time Fagoth also asked for forgiveness.

For further reading

Interview with Rev. Norman Bent. "Bordering on Reconciliation." *Sojourners* (March 1983), pp. 24-28.
Dozier, Craig L. *Nicaragua's Mosquito Shore: The Years of British and American Presence.* University, AL: University of Alabama Press, 1985.
Helms, Mary W. *ASANG: Adaptations to Culture Contact in a Miskito Community.* Gainesville, FL: University of Florida Press, 1971.

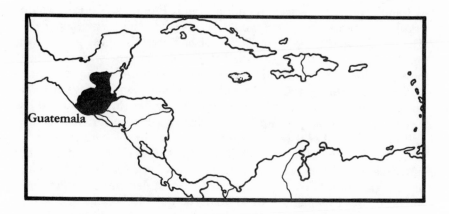

THIRTEEN

Introduction

Nineteen eighty-six was supposed to be "the year of democracy" in Guatemala. For the first time since 1954, when the CIA masterminded a coup to overthrow ten years of reformist government, clean, fair elections had produced a civilian president: Vinicio Cerezo.

But Guatemala could hardly rebuild something approaching government by and for its people without confronting the issue of land. Reflecting on the relationship between wealth, power, and land, Thomas Jefferson once expressed doubt that democracy could endure in the young United States unless it remained a nation of mostly mid-sized landholdings. In Guatemala, however, land tenure has long been highly skewed. A mere two percent of all landowners control sixty-seven percent of the arable land, forcing nine out of ten families to live on parcels too small or too steep for even their own subsistence. A 1984 U.S. Government Country Study of Guatemala concluded that "Probably no country in Latin America has fewer people owning so

225

much of the country's farmland."[1] Moreover in Guatemalan politics the very mention of land reform is anathema.

Candidate Cerezo had promised, and President Cerezo would regularly repeat, that there would be no land reform in Guatemala. Though the young Christian Democrat had been the most progressive man on the late 1985 election ballot, land reform was what had provoked the 1954 coup and ushered in an almost uninterrupted string of military regimes that were ruthless, bloody, and always fiercely conservative. Cerezo clearly feared jeopardizing his government and its weak democratic momentum by alienating the alliance of rich oligarchs and military men still holding so much power in the country.

So it took a fiery Catholic priest, Father Andrés Girón, to speak the unspeakable. With a peculiar mixture of prophetic zeal, ego, bravado, and pragmatism, Girón organized the National Association of Peasants for Land, or "Pro-Tierra." In so doing he quickly became one of the most controversial individuals in all Guatemala. While Girón's charismatic leadership is an important strength of the movement it is also a serious vulnerability.

As early as 1979, during one of Guatemala's most repressive periods ever, Girón had organized a march to "Stop the Repression and Bloodshed" in northern Guatemala. As a seminarian in Missouri during the 1960s Girón had been active in the U.S. civil rights movement. Circumstances in Guatemala were even more brutal than those facing black people in the United States during the 1960s, yet Girón retained the dream of confronting racism and exploitation in his own country through the power of nonviolence. The repression did not stop, but neither did Girón.

Thousands of leaders of popular and community organizations were being killed, "disappeared," tortured or exiled; among them were priests and religious. If groups and leaders survived at all it was by keeping a low profile. But in 1983, as the military promised a return to democracy and a small political opening appeared, Girón was one of the first popular organizers to drive a wedge into that opening. Taking advantage of his status as priest he organized a massive two-week "March for Peace" across the Guatemalan countryside and through the capital. Seven hundred and fifty of his parishioners walked the entire 280 miles from Tiquisate to Esquipulas, home of the nation's most sacred shrine. Along the way well-wishers swelled the march. There were as many as 20,000 on some stretches.

It was a third march in February 1986 that formally launched the peasant land movement, a "Hunger March" beginning in Girón's parish on the agriculturally rich southern coastlands and ending at the steps of the National Palace. Fifteen thousand Guatemalans made the hundred-mile journey. It was less than two months into the "year of democracy." Soon Girón was uttering the forbidden call for far-reaching agrarian reform, though technically his organization was simply requesting government help and credit in buying land. With upward of 100,000 members in the "Pro-Tierra" movement (and perhaps an equal number in nine other smaller organizations) no one could dismiss Girón's words as one more homily to forget upon leaving mass.

Initially, the Cerezo government promised to help peasants in the movement buy several large farms. But soon the president began backing off as he reacted to right-wing fears of "opening the floodgates." In April 1987, in order to regain momentum, Girón led a fast and occupation of the plaza in front of the National Palace. Three thousand people joined him and pledged to stay there without eating until Cerezo personally met with them. They demanded a written promise that the government would clear the last obstacles to the acquisition of the farms it had promised them. They politely refused the pleas of government officials for them to direct their pressure somewhere else. Finally after four days Cerezo came out of the Palace to meet with them and deliver the requested letter. A week later they had papers for the land.

The charisma and controversy that surrounded Father Girón sent shivers down the spines of large landowners. They considered him a demagogue capable of unleashing massive popular unrest. As one observer wrote, "Even the state facilitation of land purchases would upset the existing balance of power, politicize the peasants, and make cheap, docile labor more difficult to recruit."[2]

The measure of Girón's controversy is that he troubles progressive sectors as well. Decisions in the movement, notes the Central American Historical Institute, "are made top down, with the [Pro-Tierra] Association's success resting on Girón's charisma and wisdom."[3] In the interview that follows Girón talks about his efforts to develop new leaders. He states his intention to step aside when that is feasible. But people in key positions often find it difficult to recognize when that time has come. Even without meaning to, they can impede new leadership by identifying the movement too narrowly with their own efforts.

Furthermore, some have pointed out that if Girón merely proposes policies that help peasants buy land, the process will barely keep up with rural population growth. In late 1987, after intense organizing and protest action, the movement had succeeded in winning government help in purchasing a mere seven farms, benefiting seven thousand families. And it was not a case of government bureaucracy slowing the pace. The program was right on schedule, but its goal was to aid only 18,000 families over two years. By the government's own figures, that would be a mere 4.4 percent of the nation's 405,000 landless families, too few to keep pace with rural population growth.[4]

In December 1987 there began a new chapter in the struggle for land reform. Dozens of peasant organizations from all over the country united to form a National Peasant Confederation. The confederation issued an explicit call for land reform. Girón hosted the new organization's first meetings, and it named him one of its leaders.

Then, in February 1988 Guatemala's Roman Catholic bishops issued an unprecedented pastoral letter calling for land reform. For the first time the bishops publicly linked the plight of the peasants to "Guatemala's sinful and obsolete social structures." The document, entitled "Clamor for Land," urged that land reform take place through existing legal channels and cautioned against violent confrontations.[5]

Whatever the achievements of the new confederation, and however cautious most of the Catholic hierarchy remained, Girón and his Pro-Tierra movement had at least succeeded in uncapping the bottle. Land reform spilled once again into the national discourse. Even the government's most modest and palliative efforts, and even cautious approaches like the one the bishops were recommending, had large landowners up in arms.

Girón himself claims to be aware of weaknesses in the movement and in his proposals. In the following interview, which Gerald Schlabach conducted in March 1987 at Girón's parsonage among the plantations of Guatemala's southern coast, he talked frankly about the movement's shortcomings. Meanwhile the struggle continues and it remains to be seen whether or not Girón's leadership style proves in the long run to be more of an asset or a liability.

Uncapping the Bottle
Father Andrés Girón and
the Clamor for Land in Guatemala

Gerald Schlabach: Given the fact that popular organizations have been so cruelly repressed in Guatemala, I assume that you have felt the figure of a priest was necessary to legitimize or even create anew some space for popular action.

Andrés Girón: I was talking one day with certain people, especially people within the government who are a little more to the left. They told me, "Father, they killed all our best leaders, people in whom we had placed a lot of hope. You have come to fill the vacuum."

A priest still has credibility among the people. The peasants know that the priest will not lie to them and will not manipulate them. So yes, a lot has to do with the fact that I am a priest. And also the fact that my convictions didn't just emerge this year or last year—I have had them all my life. Throughout my life here, my life as a pastor, I have always been concerned for Guatemala. The documents from Vatican II, Medellín, Puebla,[6] the theology of liberation—these have all helped free us from some very erroneous concepts of what it means to be a priest. We

Father Andrés Girón with his seminarians in Tiquisate, Guatemala, 1988. Photo by Philip McManus.

used to be like the church waiters, producing the sacraments and dispensing them. But the sacraments are to be lived out in the unity of the people, no? If not, then the sacraments don't make any sense. One can talk about *agape* [self-giving love], or the Eucharist, and you know that your brother has nothing, nothing to eat. But the Lord invites us to his table to share, no?

They have called me a big-mouth priest, they have called me—well, you name it. They call me a communist. They say I've taken the place that should have gone to a layman. But I too am a citizen. I am a Guatemalan. I feel what is happening to the people. I live here, with the people. You know, I really spend very little time here in this parsonage. I spend a lot of time in the countryside. Once the harvests begin I am up at five to work in the fields—celebrate a mass with my seminary students, who are peasants themselves, and then out to the fields to work the land.

So sure, they're afraid of us. There is a fear about this priest, who "broke all the laws of the church," starting to meddle by working with his people. I hope to God that one day there will be more peasants leading this movement. I'll return to my normal life, working for the gospel within the communities. For me, that is my role, my work, no? Don't think it is easy being up in public view. It is better to carry on down below.

Schlabach: What is the attitude of the bishops toward your participation in the movement?

Girón: The Catholic Church has always been wishy washy, no? We have nice documents, all about social justice and a lot of other things. But at the moment of confrontation—the hour of decision, the time to take a strong stand and act concretely—the church excuses itself from what is happening. I am not going to do that. So the church looks on me with reserve. I have problems with my bishop. He would like me to leave here, and is already talking about limiting my functions.

The problem is that I do not work for the hierarchical church. I work for the people of God. And that is something very different. If the hierarchical church takes away my functions, the people will give them to me. I depend on the people, not the hierarchical church. No kidding. And theologically, I'm correct. I'm not committing any doctrinal error against the church. "The People of God," we say. Well, what the people of God says, for me, that is the Lord. I'm going to go with the people. The hierarchical church doesn't want to lose its status. There are still a lot of bishops who see themselves as lords, with their huge rings and their gold crosses and all their other things. I do believe that the church is holy. But we do have some very serious problems. They want to take the seminary away from me, the seminary for young peasants. Listen, they radicalize you. Just like the Lord Jesus. The Lord Jesus began with a lot of prudence, but you can see him becoming more and more imprudent until the moment comes when he kicks the pharisees and the robbers from the temple.

Schlabach: I would like to return to what you said about your desire to leave the movement one day so that the peasants themselves have complete leadership. How are you preparing for that day?

Girón: We have various projects at the moment. We have projects planned for the coming months, beginning with education for leaders, movement leaders only, some 200 of them. Right now I am needed in the movement. A single person should not be necessary, because that person can always be removed. Forgive me, but right now, I am needed. When I see that I am no longer needed, that we have our own leaders who are efficient and capable, our own leaders who are conscious of the Guatemala problem, I'll retire from the movement. Automatically, I'll retire. I've had enough. It's a headache, a real pain. You can't imagine the pressures I have, day in and day out—pressures from peasants who want funds, and I don't have any; pressures from people who want a solution this minute and can I help them? I'm not a technician, I'm a priest! What am I supposed to do? I'm telling you, sometimes I don't go to bed until three in the morning, to be awakened at five. But, I still haven't lost my sense of joy—that is very important—and my optimism that we will overcome. I know that we are going to overcome.

Schlabach: What kind of preparation are these leaders receiving?

Girón: Right now, awareness of our reality, no? What is the reality of our country? A lot of them don't know how to read: ninety percent of our peasant population, those who are in our movement, don't know how to read or write. So it isn't easy. The rich can easily manipulate them. We want to produce leaders who can take the message directly to their own people and make them conscious that we should change all this. Education is basic, for us. Without education, this movement won't go on.

Schlabach: Now, you personally have certain convictions about nonviolence. To what degree are these generalized within the movement? Are you trying to promote a nonviolent consciousness?

Girón: We are promoting it. We are teaching it to our people, teaching that there are better methods and paths to follow in order to achieve things, no? One of the most important concerns is to teach about specific nonviolent acts. And we are doing so. I am training all the leaders about how to work in the case of a land invasion, what to do if there are soldiers, how we would need to defend ourselves without taking up arms. It is very important. We have shared a lot about the theology of nonviolence, and I have been studying further. We believe that nonviolence is the most appropriate way of creating this movement. I look at it in a somewhat charismatic way.

Schlabach: In what sense?

Girón: I know that I have a charismatic image in Guatemala, no? Some look at me as Judas, and some, well, the other way. There are some who detest me, but there are many people who love me for the fact that I am a priest and for the fact that I am trying to see how to help the poor.

So a charismatic leadership is important. It is what the politicians do not have. That is why they are so afraid. Just now we have been receiving strong threats from the Secret Anti-communist Army [death squad]. They say it doesn't exist, but of course it exists.

And then there is the high and lofty pressure from subversive groups. They believe that change comes from the end of a machine gun. But look at Nicaragua: it has gone from a revolution that the people made in hope to a counter-revolution. How many years of chaos and death and destruction have they endured? I believe that Nicaragua should be left to be itself. But I wouldn't want to be in Nicaragua, in the position of the Nicaraguan people. It is a victim of the repression of American capitalism.

Schlabach: Forgive me for asking, but obviously it won't be the first time you have thought about this: If you are "disappeared" or exiled, what happens to the movement?

Girón: The movement is an established fact. My problem is: How deep are its convictions, you know? Because in this movement there are a lot of different interests at play, like in any movement. There are economic interests. What is the interest that moves me? Well, since I am a priest, my convictions about justice move me. We believe in a Jesus of justice. I don't know to what point it would continue strongly without me, or whether it might disappear with me. That is one of our biggest problems. We still need more capability and more conviction—and I mean conviction to the bone. But we did start the seminary, the peasant seminary that we have here. So we hope to mold some new leaders within two or three years.[7]

But now, right now, if you are talking about leaders with the means to take my place, it is hard. I have to be honest. There is no one who can take my place directly. The charismatic factor in the movement— and I say that because a movement like this is charismatic—is crucial. I have to play that role. And if those in power remove a movement's charismatic leader, it will be very hard for a layperson to carry on.

We are asking priests, members of religious orders and Protestant pastors to help out, to take a stand also, so that I'm not the only leader. Because that *isn't* healthy. The organization is not just Catholic, after all. We have Protestants, Evangelicals—we have all sorts of people in the movement. And that gives us credibility. Look, the problem of factionalism that exists in our countries is so great, with these Fundamentalist sects and Pentecostals who love a God who is so very far off, you know, not a God incarnate, involved with the people and their problems, living in the midst of that people. I have called upon Protestant pastors and said, "Let's talk together! After all, your people are poor too. Of whom are we preaching, if not the same Jesus? If we believe in a pastoral ministry we have to be with that people, not outside the people." I want my action to be Christian. Don't call me Catholic, call me Christian. If they really had Jesus' concepts, they would have joined the nonviolent struggle, don't you think?

If something happens to me right now, I have my doubts. Because the movement is still very young to retain its momentum—it is still very dangerous. The advisers I have must always work from the shadows. Honestly, there is a lot of fear of being a leader in Guatemala these days.

Schlabach: You were talking just now about the mixed interests that exist in any movement. Have you and the movement received criticism from the left as well? I read a quotation from someone who said that to simply buy land is a tranquilizer, which sounds like a criticism from the left.

Girón: Well, it's true, no? To buy land is to tranquilize a social pressure. I understand that perfectly. But in political terms, it is much more acceptable than if I say "agrarian reform." So we have to have our tactics. I know that the government is incapable of buying land for all of Guatemala's peasants. But it can open the valves to the beginning of agrarian reform. I know, it is a dilemma. The landowners hear of our interest in buying their land and they jack the price way up. So a campaign to buy land is really not the best. In the end, we won't have any choice but to invade the land. The landowners don't like the idea of peasants buying the land, but they won't pay them enough to live decently as farm laborers. If they would just pay decent wages! So this is a problem. Will we have the economic capacity to buy in Guatemala, if seventy-five percent of the arable land is in the hands of 1.1 percent of the land barons? That is why, in the end, there is no answer other than an aggressive land reform. And Vinicio [Cerezo, Guatemala's president] won't do it. We need someone who is gutsy enough to do it and at the same time maintain [social] equilibrium. But who?

Schlabach: So what really are the prospects for an agrarian reform?

Girón: A political movement. Tell me what else there is! How are we going to go to Congress to reform the law? Who will truly represent the people? Who claims to represent them now? The folks that the oligarchs themselves put in place. So there won't be agrarian reform if this movement doesn't turn into a political movement. And that is the politicians' terrible fear. Of course it already *is* a political movement. From the moment you start asking for land it is a political theme— eminently political. But they are terribly afraid that it will turn into a political party, because if this movement is transformed into a party, no one will be able to stop us—in Congress, or at the presidential level. So instead, they are trying to do away with us by wearing us down. They are trying to wear us down economically; the bureaucracy is wicked.

Schlabach: From a distance, however, one could analyze the movement politically and say perhaps it is serving as a counterweight to create a balance of power in Guatemala: Vinicio's hands are tied by the military and so, in order for the Christian Democrats to achieve their objectives, more or less, they need a counterweight. And so perhaps that is what you are giving them.

Girón: But it isn't true, eh? It's just not. And even if it were, as you supposed, a counterweight, if that brings well-being to people, don't you think it would be worthwhile? There is plenty of politics around here already. But what matters is the people, the people of God. The politicians don't matter. How are we going to feed our people? How will we provide them a decent life as human beings?

Schlabach: Yes, of course. I wasn't saying that would be a bad strategy; I'm just trying to discern what the movement's strategy is.

Girón: Have you gotten it yet?
Schlabach: I think so. To have a movement in favor of the people's well-being, and to . . .
Girón: And to stand tall. That is why we don't accept politicians of any type. Some have offered. People have offered us money, too, to quit. But this thing won't quit. The light that we have given off, at the national level, has created a terrible conflict. It has awakened something that was asleep, or that had been told to go to sleep. It has awakened all over the country! You can't imagine—everywhere you go people are asking for land. It is a terrible pressure, for the government. And as far as I'm concerned, that is good, very healthy. Because the land issue has blossomed in this year of democracy, or so-called democracy. It has blossomed in a way that is without precedent.
Schlabach: After being suppressed for thirty years, right?
Girón: And it has been my role to uncap it. What am I supposed to do? Why has the Lord placed me in this position? I certainly didn't go looking for so many problems! But now I have to sustain things. And I'm doing everything I can to do so, to sustain the movement. It is hard. To sustain its morale. It's hard and discouraging.

But agrarian reform—it simply has to happen. That's a fact, an unavoidable fact that stares you in the face. I have told the president himself: "You are a hypocrite and a liar." I said it just like that, clear and simple. "You are a manipulator. You don't care about anything except your power. But the people gave you power so that you would help the people, not so you would become God." And I say the same thing to cabinet ministers, rich oligarchs, military men—just as forcefully. That is why they look at me and say, "This guy isn't afraid of anything!" Well I'm not. I believe we are in the hands of God.

But to sustain the morale of a whole movement—that is hard. I have had to present signs of hope, of resurrection. After all, resurrection is what gives sense to the life of Jesus. Otherwise, he came in vain. And the resurrection is the people's most powerful hope. We have to increase it. I don't mean the resurrection of a certain position of privilege, nor flesh and bones, but the resurrection of a spirit, a spirit that hopes, a spirit who says *"papá"* to our Father God. And *"mamá"* to our beloved earth.

The unity of the earth and the Spirit of God—we can't undo it. That's why when the bishops tell me, "You have to dedicate yourself to your ministry as a priest"—well, what is that ministry? What is it? People leave mass and we say, "The Lord is with you." But I don't feel that presence when people are hungry.

The other day I was speaking on the multiplication of the bread, you know? And the bishop comes up to me afterward and says, "This teaching is errant." So I said to him, "Look, I honestly don't believe that the Lord Jesus multiplied bread, say, like magic, the way a magician pulls a rabbit out of a hat! I believe that the Lord spoke to the hearts of men and women, with their bread stored away in their packs, and they reached in and shared. I believe this miracle is a lot deeper than the act of pulling bread out of a basket. Jesus spoke to them: "You with your nice little packs, you have bread, and you must share with those who have none."

That's what we're trying to get the rich to do, no? We are not condemning them. But we are telling them that their ways and actions are wrong, that they have brought hunger and created elites in Guatemala, elites that . . . why, there are people here in Guatemala who live better than people in Europe, and a thousand times better than people in the United States! While others are dying of hunger! Thousands of thousands. Things are very, very shaky.

I was at a forum one day last year, a "forum on land issues." It is easy to preach to your own community, you know, because they listen to you. It's wonderful. But at that forum there were 500 landowners looking at me with hate in their eyes, and I mean hate. "Well, now it is the priest's turn to present his point of view." What could I come up with? I took the Bible in one hand, and I talked about Zacchaeus.[8] Everybody moaned! Well, I was telling them that they too were plunderers. In my other hand, I took a scale. On one side of the balance I put a huge bone, picked clean. On the other, a piece of meat. And I said: "This is what we are coming to. Meat here, bone here. Throw a little in this direction, and we will be brothers."

I crushed them and all their arguments, simply with the truth, the truth of Jesus. I didn't come with statistics. Everyone else came loaded with statistics, with careful studies, but not I. I came only with the tools that the Lord has given me, the word of God, and of justice— represented by the balance: "This is what Guatemala has become. Bones here, meat here. You are eating well, gentlemen. Put a little meat on these bones, and we will all eat, there will be peace, and our country won't go down the drain. Do you want to lose out, or do you want . . . ?" And no one asked me a single question! No one could, because they couldn't question the truth.

We are convinced of the truth, and we are going to keep working.

Translated from Spanish by Gerald Schlabach

Notes

1. Quoted in "Land Reform: Once Again in View," *OSGUA Newsletter* [of The Organization In Solidarity With The People of Guatemala], February 1987, p. 1.

2. Center for Study of Americas, *CENSA's Strategic Report* 8, December 1986, p. 8. (CENSA, 2288 Fulton St., Suite 103, Berkeley, CA 94704.)

3. "Fr. Girón and the Land Movement in Guatemala Today," Central American Historical Institute *Update,* 6, August 27, 1987.

4. "Fr. Girón and the Land Movement in Guatemala Today," Central American Historical Institute *Update,* 6, August 27, 1987.

5. Available in English in the *ICCHRLA Newsletter 1988 no. 4.* Inter-Church Committee on Human Rights in Latin America (ICCHRLA, Suite 201, 40 St. Clair Ave. East, Toronto, Ontario, Canada, M4T 1M9).

6. Convened by Pope John XXIII in 1962 and lasting until 1965, the Second Ecumenical Council of Roman Catholic Bishops, or Vatican II, sought to renew the church spiritually in the context of the modern world. At meetings in Medellín, Colombia in 1968 and Puebla, Mexico in 1979 Latin American bishops have sought to apply the social teachings of Vatican II specifically to the needs of Latin America. [Eds.]

7. Two months after this interview, part of the seminary was firebombed and destroyed. [Eds.]

8. Luke 19:1-10 recounts Jesus' encounter with the diminutive tax collector, Zacchaeus. His fellow Jews would have hated him, like all in his profession, for getting rich through collaboration with the Roman occupation forces. Upon encountering Jesus' concern for him as a person, and its implied offer of forgiveness, Zacchaeus announced that he would restore all his illegal gains fourfold. In the original Spanish of this interview, Father Girón made use of an inherent word play: the name *"Zaqueo"* sounds very much like *"saqueador,"* a person who sacks, plunders, or exploits. [Eds.]

For further reading

Bermúdez, Fernando. *Death and Resurrection in Guatemala.* Maryknoll, N.Y.: Orbis Books, 1986.

Handy, Jim. *Gift of the Devil: A History of Guatemala.* Boston: South End Press, 1984.

Immerman, Richard H. *The CIA in Guatemala: The Foreign Policy of Intervention.* Austin: University of Texas Press, 1982.

Melville, Thomas and Marjorie. *Guatemala: The Politics of Land Ownership.* New York: The Free Press, 1971.

Menchu, Rigoberta. *I, Rigoberta Menchu: An Indian Woman in Guatemala.* London: Verso, 1984.

LATIN AMERICA

● = cities mentioned in the book

SCALE:
⊢————⊣
= 520 Miles

FOURTEEN

Introduction

Adolfo Pérez Esquivel is an unusual mix: an artist become an activist. Born in Buenos Aires, Argentina in 1931, Pérez Esquivel showed an early inclination toward art. After finishing his studies at several art schools, he developed a reputation as a fine sculptor and painter. Like many struggling artists, he made ends meet not only by making art but also by teaching it in various Argentine schools and universities for twenty-five years.

Pérez Esquivel also developed an early interest in nonviolence as an expression of his Christian faith. In the 1960s, that interest led to a series of contacts which he describes in this interview; they changed his life forever. At the time these contacts formed a very loose-knit network of individuals interested in the prospects of nonviolence as a force for liberation. He was a key influence in changing it into an international organization with chapters in eleven countries. The organization, Servicio Paz y Justicia en América Latina (Service for Peace and Justice in Latin America, or SERPAJ), was formally founded under his leadership in 1974. He served as its General Coordinator until 1986. Today he is the Honorary President of SERPAJ.

SERPAJ works at the side of the poor and marginalized throughout Latin America. Its struggle is the defense of the human person and of the rights of the people to their own identity, to self-determination, and to a dignified life where access to basic human necessities is not a privilege reserved for the few, but a right for all.

He sees nonviolence as a wide range of struggles, some small, some large, "based on the proposition that the individual comes to a realization of one's real strength in the very process of confronting the powers-that-be . . . The organizational and decision-making forms that arise in these struggles enable people to believe in the possibility of controlling their own lives."[1] In 1977 the Argentine military dictatorship arrested Pérez Esquivel and imprisoned him for fourteen months, with an additional fourteen months of modified house arrest. An international campaign to make his case more visible brought his nomination for the Nobel Peace Prize. Much to the surprise of just about everyone—not least of all the Argentine dictatorship—he was named Nobel Peace Laureate for 1980. This is not to say that either he or the movement on whose behalf he accepted the award were undeserving. The sort of self-sacrifice, commitment, and relentless nonviolent struggle that he represents is what makes for true peacemaking. But for one far removed from the centers of power and fame to gain worldwide recognition was refreshingly unusual.

In this interview, which Philip McManus conducted in Buenos Aires in July 1987, Adolfo Pérez Esquivel assesses the struggle for liberation in the light of his own experience. He talks about the strengths and limitations of active nonviolence, its history in Latin America, and the difference he sees between its First World and Third World applications. Above all he asserts the pivotal role of discovering our own humanity. For the poor, the oppressor, even the torturer, authentic recognition of one's own personhood is the key to social relationships that acknowledge the personhood of all. Thus true liberation must liberate both person and politics.

To Discover Our Humanity

Adolfo Pérez Esquivel

Philip McManus: Can you tell us something about your personal history and how you became interested and involved in active nonviolence?

Adolfo Pérez Esquivel: My concern for nonviolence began when I was

Argentine Nobel Peace Laureate Adolfo Pérez Esquivel (holding cross) leads the first march to protest the widespread disappearances in Ayacucho, Peru; April, 1984. Photo courtesy of Servicio Paz y Justicia/Peru.

young, for several reasons. First, I rediscovered the power of the gospel. My upbringing had been religious, but it was very systematized, very formal—more of a religious culture than a religious formation. With time I began to understand more deeply the gospel's power, and I also discovered the struggles of a man called Mahatma Gandhi. I was always impressed by Gandhi's saying he had found the strength of nonviolence in the ancient sacred books of India and in the Sermon on the Mount. One of the fundamental books that Gandhi always had with him was the Bible, along with the sacred books of his country, the Upanishads, and others.

Many Christians who were friends of Gandhi asked him why he wasn't a Christian. He replied that he would be a Christian the day that he saw Christians living the teachings of their teacher. He asked very clearly for one thing: consistency between what we say and what we do. Of course in a violent society like ours you have to reflect on what nonviolence means; it is not simply being opposed to [physical] violence. There is a violence that is structural. And there is also personal, psychological, and spiritual violence. One must begin the task of discovering the "why" of the violence. The fact is that the societies in which we live are violent in their roots, in their education, in their culture.

When studying history one sees that what is taught is always the history of violence. We were never taught history from the point of view of the people. Instead we learned about heroes of war. But I believe that the world exists not because of violence but rather because human beings have the capacity to survive.

McManus: In the United States, applying nonviolence means something very different from applying nonviolence in Latin America, especially in the light of the dictatorships that have ruled many Latin American countries. So we need to know a little about your experience. What was your work before the dictatorship put you in jail?

Pérez Esquivel: I was a professor in the architecture college of the university, in arts schools, and in some teachers' training institutes. We began to work with student movements and with base-level groups in the neighborhoods, supporting development projects in marginalized areas.

McManus: As part of SERPAJ in those days?

Pérez Esquivel: No, more as neighborhood projects. Later SERPAJ formed, through the work of defending human rights in the face of so much violence—both from the armed forces and the police, and from the guerrillas. We had to make decisions and resist the rising tide of violence.

McManus: Why did the dictatorship arrest you?

Pérez Esquivel: Well, they never gave me a reason. They never interrogated me. I was under arrest for twenty-eight months—fourteen months in prison, fourteen months of closely controlled conditional release. I couldn't leave my neighborhood.

But we know why. It was because of our struggle in defense of human rights, for raising our voice against all the injustice, for accompanying those who were being attacked. But since these are not crimes they couldn't really accuse me of anything.

McManus: They never filed charges?

Pérez Esquivel: No; no, because they couldn't. They simply said that it was for security. That was one of their favorite lines. But of course we carry on the same work today.

McManus: What was it like in prison?

Pérez Esquivel: Well, it was very hard. But in the midst of it all one must begin to put into practice what one says one has learned. We weren't allowed to do anything—anything at all. For me, prayer and meditation helped a lot, as I tried to keep my mind calm.

McManus: Did you have a Bible?

Pérez Esquivel: No, it was prohibited as subversive material. One time some friends tried to bring me a Bible and they were all detained as subversives. The military men called themselves Catholics and defenders of Western, Christian civilization—but the Bible is subversive!

Anyway the experience was very hard. I was tortured for five days.

McManus: When were you arrested?

Pérez Esquivel: I was arrested on the fourth of April, 1977, the anniversary of the assassination of Martin Luther King, Jr. They took me to the federal police headquarters. For thirty-two days I was held in "the tubes." "The tubes" are cells about the size of this desk: one meter by 1.8 meters. From there they took me to the prison in La Plata where I stayed for fourteen months.

McManus: And all of this time you did not know when they might release you?

Pérez Esquivel: No, I had no idea because there had been no trial, there was no sentence, there hadn't been anything. However, there was a lot of international pressure. I often think about how, in the midst of all the difficulties, I at least had this possibility of people who were helping me. There were many people there—peasants, workers—who didn't have anybody to help them. It was horrible! So later we began to organize on their behalf.

McManus: How were you finally able to get out? Was it because of the solidarity campaign on your behalf?

Pérez Esquivel: Yes, because of the international campaign. The authorities freed me when the World Cup soccer championship was being played here in Argentina [July 1978]. There was a lot of international pressure, so they gave me a conditional release.

McManus: Do you think that through that experience you learned anything about nonviolence?

Pérez Esquivel: Yes, I think I learned several things. One is the capacity to resist. Another is that even in prison we must always maintain a spirit of struggle. Another is to know that in spite of being shut up in jail, if we have a spirit of freedom we can be free. Another thing is, put into practice everything that gives you control over yourself—meditation, relaxation, yoga, conscious breathing.

McManus: You have said that through all of the experience you never felt hatred for your tormentors.

Pérez Esquivel: No, I remembered that in the Gospels Jesus says, "Lord, forgive them for they don't know what they are doing." I thought, "But these people *do* know what they are doing, because the way they torture is scientific. They have doctors, they have psychologists, they have guards. They have electric prods, gas, cold showers, beatings, rubber hoses." But over time I began to understand what it is that they don't know. They don't know that they are persons. And they don't know that the one they are torturing is *their* brother. They do it as though it were just a job, like typing a report or painting a house. They have lost their capacity to be persons. I think that torture destroys a torturer much more quickly than it does the victim, because the torturer *self*-destructs. He loses all sensibility, all sense of life. So for him, the only thing that is left is destruction—he ends up destroying himself.

You can see this if you talk to them. After I got out, while the dictatorship was still in power, some of the torturers used to visit me at times. I talked with them.

McManus: They came here to talk?

Pérez Esquivel: Yes, they were afraid about what might happen to them. They were people who were totally lost—psychically and spiritually destroyed.

Anyway, yes one does learn many things in prison. And one comes out strengthened by the experience, with a better understanding of reality.

McManus: One can see that in Latin America people generally seek to avoid violence in their efforts to make change. Quite apart from this, one also encounters an appreciation of what we call active nonviolence as a positive force for change. What are the historical and cultural roots of this understanding in Latin America?

Pérez Esquivel: In Latin America, long before Gandhi, there were nonviolent struggles. The indigenous people are actively nonviolent. And their social structure is nonviolent too, even with their ups and downs and the problems of being marginalized and exploited communities. Think about the fact that after five hundred years the communities still exist, still survive. Some survive in bad conditions, some in better conditions, but they show the capacity to resist through nonviolent means. We see this continually. Traveling through Latin America one begins to discover the wisdom in the people. We think we have just recently discovered that wisdom; but we must take care. They have long known the methods of nonviolent struggle. It is just that they have used it as a way to survive, not to try to overturn a whole system.

But Latin American nonviolence has other origins as well, especially among intellectuals. It has roots in the experience in Europe and also in the influence of Mahatma Gandhi, Martin Luther King, Jr., and others such as Jean and Hildegard Goss-Mayr.[2] In recent times the Goss-Mayrs were among the first to promote nonviolence in Latin America through networking among many groups. They were the first who began the work that eventually resulted in what is now the Service for Peace and Justice in Latin America, or SERPAJ. They began from a gospel perspective even as they delved into the methodology of the Gandhian struggle. They began to help Dom Hélder Câmara[3] and Mário Carvalho de Jesus[4] in Brazil.

Dom Hélder Câmara is like a son of theirs. When he was auxiliary bishop in Rio de Janeiro in the 1960s, they began to explain to him what the strength of nonviolence is all about. Before that he had used nonviolence almost intuitively. What Hildegard and Jean did was give him a clearer understanding of nonviolence and its history, showing him the possibilities and the capacity of nonviolence and its power in all of society and in individuals.

I first had contact with Jean and Hildegard many years ago. I read a report of theirs and then we had a long correspondence and later a long friendship. They began to visit Argentina and got to know us and our work. Another person who was a friend of mine was Lanzo del Vasto of the Community of the Ark in France, who also visited here.

McManus: When was this?

Pérez Esquivel: Oh, about twenty-five years ago, about the same time that Jean and Hildegard came. He was a disciple of Gandhi, and worked a lot with Vinoba Bhave in the movement to secure land donations [in India]. Here in Argentina many groups of the Ark formed—nonviolent but with a communal life, working the earth, making handicrafts. For many years we ourselves belonged to the Community of the Ark.

McManus: To return to the present, do you see differences between how Latin Americans understand nonviolence and how North Americans or Europeans understand it?

Pérez Esquivel: There are differences and I believe they are root differences, not just differences of form. With regard to principles, such as the ethical principle of giving respect to one's neighbor, we are all in agreement. I believe that the differences that exist are historical and conceptual. For example, for Gandhi nonviolence was not only getting the English out of India. That's why his conception is so close to that of Latin America. He said that getting the English out of India was only the first step; the liberation of India would not be achieved until the last of the Untouchables had the same rights as the Brahmins. So he was speaking of a much deeper liberation.

In the United States and Europe there are important, serious nonviolent movements, but many of them aim more at modifying an unjust situation or conflict than at changing a structure. For example, the Martin Luther King, Jr. movement, with all of its importance for his black brothers and sisters, aimed at securing recognition of civil rights. King didn't really challenge the system.

McManus: Not at first . . .

Pérez Esquivel: Yes. . . . There was injustice, a conflict, but within the framework of the U.S. system. In Latin America we find ourselves in a process of liberation. We do call into question the system and the structures, the life to which we are subjected because we are dependent countries, exploited countries, shaped by the major international interests.

McManus: Then what does liberation mean?

Pérez Esquivel: We think of liberation holistically. It isn't only the resolution of a conflict; it is also a liberation of the social, the economic, and the political. And of the spiritual. One must understand that Latin America is a continent where religiosity is part of life itself. It is not incidental. The Latin American being is a deeply religious being. Maybe that's why I feel so close to the spirituality of Gandhi, who achieved a balance between the spiritual and the social, political, and economic.

This explains some of the difference in social movements. Many movements think economic life is the central issue, that overcoming the economic problems will solve the social problems. This is a utopia—more of a utopia than nonviolence. We aim for a change in the social structures, but also for the liberation of the person. I have said many times that the first step in the whole process of liberation is for men and women to realize that they are people. If they never discover themselves as people they will never know what liberation is. From that point we can open the doors to liberation, because then a person will recognize others as equals. And, logically, as people of faith we will recognize our neighbors as our brothers and sisters and as children of God.

McManus: I'd like to raise another matter. On the one hand, as you pointed out, some say that the way to achieve liberation is by resolving economic problems. There is another view that proposes democracy as the means to achieve liberation. That is to say, it focuses the struggle for liberation on the struggle for democracy, especially in the context of the dictatorships here in Latin America. How do you see the relationship between the struggle for liberation and the struggle for democratization of a country or society?

Pérez Esquivel: The democracy we have known in Latin America, with the division of the three powers of government (executive, legislative, and judicial) and with regular elections to choose representatives, is what we call "formal democracy," not real democracy. In a formal democracy one seeks to protect the status quo of the society with different levels of representation, but not to make changes. There is no possibility of changing the system itself.

In Latin America there is no equality of rights nor equality of possibilities. We see the great marginality that misery causes. We see hunger, malnutrition, and the lack of possibilities for the poorest, most needy sectors. It's a little like the case I mentioned before—the Untouchables that Gandhi pointed out so well.

Real democracies are participatory democracies, with the same rights and the same obligations for all. They also include redistribution of goods. They do not allow wealth to be monopolized under the pretext of democracy, leaving the few to benefit at the expense of the many.

As long as we have that kind of inequality, we don't really have democracy. Capitalism is not democracy. This is very clear. So when we speak of democracies in Latin America, I believe that the Latin American peoples are moving day by day toward a socialization of the structures. For example, the experience of the base communities, the cooperatives, the neighborhood organizations, and others.

McManus: What do you mean by socialization?

Pérez Esquivel: Socialization doesn't mean Soviet socialism nor simply following any other pattern. Rather it will grow out of the needs of the people themselves. This will really mean strengthening a true democratic process with full participation of the different sectors.

McManus: You spoke before of religious faith as a key support in the struggle for liberation. One hears much about the theology of liberation. To what degree—in theory and in practice—has the theology of liberation had an impact as a support for armed struggle, and to what degree has it had an impact in promoting nonviolent struggle in Latin America?

Pérez Esquivel: A theologian friend of mine told me that theologians can't write or make theology if there is no one to "do" the theology. Theology is not theoretical reflection. A theology arises from a praxis [an ongoing dynamic process of action and reflection]. This is fundamental. If not, it isn't theology; it's a theory.

After the Second Vatican Council [1962-65] and after the [Latin American bishops'] meeting in Medellín in 1968, there was a re-visioning of the attitude of how to assume a commitment to the process of liberation of the people. This happened principally in the Catholic Church but also in the evangelical churches.

Religion had been used to dominate, not liberate. But the gospel is liberating. In it one finds the greatest song of liberation—in the mouth of a woman, Mary of Nazareth. It's not in the mouth of a man. It is not in the mouth of a brave and powerful warrior. I find this important. God puts the greatest song of liberation, the Magnificat, into the mouth of a humble woman who suffered persecution, exile, fears (Luke 1:46-55).

So one begins to see the real meaning of liberation from the perspective of the gospel. Through a commitment of faith and what I was saying about recognizing one's brother as an equal, as a child of God, many Christians have begun to assume the commitment of freeing themselves from the structures, to build the kingdom of God and God's justice, to seek liberation. It is as much spiritual liberation as social, political, and economic liberation. And it is always *within* a historical situation. Not outside, not disconnected.

In this situation, the people don't choose violence. They have been submerged in violence. People who have come to the point of desperation resort to meeting that oppressive violence in any way possible. That's how armed struggles arise in many Latin American countries—some with success, many failures. We see the armed struggle in the Cuban revolution, in the present Nicaraguan revolution. We see that the people resort to armed struggle, but that is not what they seek.

At the same time, parallel to this in Latin America, there are also many nonviolent struggles—a great chain of them across the whole Latin American continent. However, because of the cultural mentality of violence, very little is said of those nonviolent struggles. We could go on talking for hours and hours about all the struggles in Latin America, but I can point out some to you.

There are the struggles for human rights. I believe all the struggles in Latin America translate into struggles for the defense of human rights. Like here in Argentina, what the Mothers of Plaza de Mayo have done.[5] They continue with their actions, with their struggle, which we accompany. And the Grandmothers of Plaza de Mayo work to recover the children who were kidnapped and "disappeared."

Other organizations have also arisen as social responses to this grave situation under the dictatorships. Just now a very interesting nonviolent struggle is arising in Paraguay, out of the experience of a peasant community struggling against the dictatorship of General Stroessner. There is also a nonviolent struggle in Chile, with the people mobilizing to confront the tragedy of the dictatorship of Pinochet.[6] There was one in Uruguay with SERPAJ, which Luis Pérez Aguirre and others led. They managed to motivate actions that led to the modification of the socio-political situation of Uruguay, even to regaining a democratic process.[7]

We could go on and talk of Brazil—not only of São Paulo, with better known struggles like the one at the PERUS factory,[8] but also of Alagamar in the northeast, where the peasants, with the support of some of the bishops, are struggling for their land and confronting violence with nonviolent means.[9] I believe this is very important, very significant.

Other organizations stage land takeovers in the urban areas where they establish what we here call "settlements." The people take over lands that belong to the government or are abandoned and begin to do the work of organization, of laying out streets, of setting up schools, of doing community service, of praying and reflecting.

These are all nonviolent struggles of the people. And then there are the thousands of base communities.

McManus: In all of this, what attraction does nonviolence have for the marginalized?

Pérez Esquivel: Dom Hélder Câmara used to say that nonviolence is the weapon of the poor. What is attractive is that it enables organization, joining together in action, and reducing risks through collective actions. (This doesn't mean that the poor aren't going to be repressed, only that the risks are less.) Nonviolence makes it possible to respond to aggression and to repression in a way that is original—with an alternative totally distinct from the game of the aggressor. One of the positive things to understand, and which the people are understanding more and more, is that you don't have to confront the aggressor on his own turf. The people, the poor, must select the field of struggle and act from a position of strength.

McManus: What is the strength of the people?

Pérez Esquivel: Their numbers, their organization, their collective actions, their solidarity and mutual support, the development of what we might call a chain of solidarity and resistance. There are many elements.

But I think we still have not advanced in the political dimension of nonviolent struggle. All nonviolent movements must seriously consider this. Up to now we have not gone beyond acts of recovery. Isn't that so? There is a conflict and there is the nonviolent action to overcome that conflict. There is aggression against Nicaragua so people react with campaigns, international mobilizations, marches, the sending of aid. It's a form of pressure. But we must seek a political dimension of nonviolence that we have not explored deeply enough.

Most of the time when people talk of nonviolence, they talk about street action, about confrontation with the police. But the issue goes beyond the police to the system. Nonviolence means work in education, in health, in the environment, in economics—a nonviolent economics, because the economy we now have is very violent. We lack alternatives that expand the social, political, economic, and technological horizons of nonviolence to their fullest extent. It is necessary to begin to have a much more holistic vision of how nonviolence can liberate.

McManus: In other words, you mean we should not just propose a new society but also start to construct it, not wait until political power is achieved but begin the task now.

Pérez Esquivel: That is the difference. We have to begin it from the micro and move to the macro. There are stages. We can't expect that we are going to change everything from the top down; change will never come that way. No, we must work in health care, in education with children, in energy alternatives, in the means of production, in the training of professionals and technicians.

McManus: But at the same time you propose to work in national politics?

Pérez Esquivel: Of course, because it's the only way to make a real change in the structures. If you don't have the political and transforming dimension, things end up in the same place. They move a little but then they settle back again.

That's why what Gandhi says is so important when he speaks of the Untouchables. He speaks to the root of the problem. Here we say, "Yes, we're going to get rid of the dictatorship in Argentina." We did manage to get rid of the dictatorship. But now we see that in some respects things are getting back as they were. They move a little but they come back to the same place.

To synthesize, I believe we need to understand the structural origins of violence, the response nonviolence can offer, and the alternatives that can make a new, liberated society a reality.

McManus: In a moment of confrontation, of crisis, the behavior of the people has a great deal of impact on what happens. You already mentioned the case of Argentina. Activists in Chile also have told me that as they look back they are critical of the massive protests of 1983 and 1984, which overall were very nonviolent but which were lacking in various respects, including organization. How is it possible to tap into the potential you refer to in order really to achieve structural change?

Pérez Esquivel: To begin with, we say that when the message is clear the people will be there. We have had marches and demonstrations here of 120,000 people, even more. But again, to use nonviolence as a real social alternative, not just as a means to confront a conflict, you have to see its political potential.

One thing is information; that's a first step. Without information you don't know what to do. At a deeper level I would say that education is the highest priority. A young person needs formation. Then comes the stage of organization. After that the next step is conquering spaces of power. You have to go stage by stage. This does not mean that the organizers direct the whole process. Rather it is to say that in order to achieve our objectives we have to recognize distinct levels. That's why I say we must explore nonviolence at all levels: in education, in the social, in the political, in the economic, in the preservation of the environment.

And we must analyze history. I believe that nonviolence has much to do and much to offer, just as it has much left to discover. We still don't know the full potential of nonviolent struggle. We have found that nonviolent struggle is effective to the extent that the people understand it and join together to take it up. It is effective when their collective actions develop the capacity of resistance, of solidarity, of pressure, of protest, but also of proposals, of alternatives.

Once in a while individual initiatives may be effective, if they aim at moving the people as a whole. I support some isolated, testimonial acts of nonviolence. But these are not going to change the system. Real change will happen only when the people have their objectives clear and have a critical consciousness of their responsibility to create liberating change. I believe that nonviolent struggle is what enables people to be fully aware as they participate. A good example is the process of reflection and action within the base communities in Latin America. For me the base communities are the seed of a wholly new social vision. And it is a nonviolent vision.

When we talk about nonviolence, we have to also speak about the relationship to power. Nonviolent struggle seeks to reinstate more horizontal social relations. People in power should place themselves on the same level as others, because it is not necessary that one be more than another. I think that the nonviolent movement must deepen its reflection on the meaning of power as a means of service. The one who has a higher position should be the servant of the most lowly. And this is the teaching of Gandhi. Gandhi made himself an Untouchable.

McManus: Now we are talking not just about a new society but also of building a new culture.

Pérez Esquivel: Right, a new culture. We must begin to see this— what sort of relations power implies, how nonviolent struggle may achieve power. The aim of a socio-political process is to achieve power, to gain the capacity to make decisions. But so often what happens is that small groups take power and the rest stay at the bottom. The people are always made to believe that they don't have any capacity to exercise power. But a people *is* power. And a people that begins to discover its power can begin to control its own life.

McManus: In the midst of this process, what is the role of SERPAJ in Latin America?

Pérez Esquivel: SERPAJ is growing according to the needs. Up to now its growth has been steady with some ups and downs, at times with difficulties. But it is making a concrete contribution. We never wanted to make a great super-structural organization for everyone to join because we know that's no good. Instead we sought a work that responds to the needs in each place. So if we look from where SERPAJ is now, and then glance back at our past, we see quite a significant advance. It has grown a lot in many countries and many new SERPAJ chapters have arisen. I think that not only in the present but also in the future, SERPAJ will maintain its identity as a support for the poorest and neediest sectors, committed to nonviolence and to an ecumenical spirit.

McManus: On another theme, within the movement for structural change in Latin America, how do you see the role of international solidarity between Latin America and the United States or other developed countries?

Pérez Esquivel: We view such solidarity as highly positive, not just with the United States. I believe that it is due to solidarity around the world, and to nonviolent struggle, that the Reagan administration has not invaded Nicaragua. To a great degree, it is because of this continuous pressure. Within the United States solidarity is now growing. Perhaps it has grown less than in the European countries, but it is growing rapidly now. Solidarity within the United States has achieved many things. You see this in the solidarity with Central America. You see it with groups that supported our struggles during the dictatorship, offering denunciations, political pressure, and concrete solidarity. You see this also in the support for the Chilean people.

McManus: Besides talking about what has already happened, we can look ahead to future possibilities. In Latin America one clearly sees the intervention of the developed world, especially that of the United States. The International Monetary Fund is one example and the U.S. military intervention is perhaps the clearest example. In view of the diverse forms of intervention, what do you see as the responsibility of the U.S. people in the present situation?

Pérez Esquivel: I travel frequently to the United States—at least every year—and I find some things positive and some things negative. Ten or fifteen years ago, when I went to the United States and spoke about Latin America and of the problems of our people, it was a bit like talking about Martians. My U.S. listeners understood nothing. Now I think there is a better understanding. And there is active solidarity and a greater awareness of their responsibility with the peoples of Latin America.

I believe that the people of the United States are disinformed or at least badly informed. It is crucial that they know what is really going on in Latin America as a result of the policies of their government—and that they assume responsibility for modifying those policies.

McManus: Finally, in this long struggle, do you ever get tired? Do you lose hope or do you feel depressed?

Pérez Esquivel: No. I know that the struggle must travel the paths of the people and that it is long. At times one gets distressed at not seeing problems resolved more quickly. Some things distress me but not because I lose hope—hope is the motor of life. I do get distressed when I see right now how many politicians here in Argentina, for example, apparently have not learned anything from the suffering of the people, from so many deaths, from so much destruction, persecution, rape, and children kidnapped and "disappeared." And how today they commit the same errors that they committed before, as though they have no capacity to change or see things from another perspective. That today they negotiate with the same persons who murdered thousands. That they are interested in nothing more than promoting their own political interests, without regard to what happened to the people. This distresses me. I am distressed also that the military is not capable of recognizing its errors. All these barbarous actions, and still they stick to a very sinister ideology.

It also distresses me that all of this makes it difficult to move ahead in building a real democratic process. Democracy is not an absolute, it is a path. In a society that we want to make viable, we have to make democracy real.

On the other hand, we also need to see the signs of hope. One can't help but see hope if one looks at the level of organization among the neediest sectors. In spite of everything the people don't lose their smiles or their joy. Every morning, the sun rises. So I think that there are positive factors.

McManus: This is what gives you encouragement . . . ?

Pérez Esquivel: Right; that, and seeing so many people working for change. I am also encouraged to see that in other countries—like the United States, Europe, Canada—the people are becoming more and more aware of their responsibility with the countries of the Third World. Increased communication is helping the peoples of the industrialized countries to understand their situation better. I think that solidarity grows more than one may think. It is like a network, a fabric that is continually being woven. And too, it is like a tree that always bears its fruits.

Translated from Spanish by Philip McManus

Notes

1. Juan José Mosca and Luis Pérez Aguirre, *Derechos Humanos: Pautas para una Educación Liberadora* (Montevideo: Servicio Paz y Justicia, 1985) pp. 414-15.
2. Jean Goss, who is French, and his Austrian wife, Hildegard Goss-Mayr, have worked for many years in Europe, Latin America, the Philippines, and elsewhere as field secretaries for the International Fellowship of Reconciliation (IFOR). They are currently Honorary Presidents of IFOR.
3. Now the retired Archbishop of Recife in Brazil's impoverished Northeast, Dom Hélder is one of the most prominent Latin American proponents of nonviolence.
4. See Chapter 2, "Firmeza Permanente: Labor Holds the Line in Brazil."
5. See Chapter 5, "Argentina's Mothers of Courage."
6. See Chapter 7, "Chile: Cultural Action for Liberation."
7. See Chapter 6, "Uruguay: Nonviolent Resistance and the Pedagogy of Human Rights."
8. See Chapter 2, "Firmeza Permanente: Labor Holds the Line in Brazil."
9. See Chapter 10, "Brazil: A Troubled Journey to the Promised Land."

For further reading

Câmara, Hélder. *The Desert is Fertile.* Maryknoll, N.Y.: Orbis, 1981.
Goss-Mayr, Jean and Hildegard. *Otra Revolución: La Violencia de los No-Violentos* [Another Revolution: The Violence of the Nonviolent]. Barcelona: Editorial Fontanella, 1973.
Muñoz, Carlos, Creuza Maciel and Carmen de Souza. *Reseña Histórica del SERPAJ-AL: ¿Una Alternativa Revolucionária?* [Historical Review of SERPAJ-AL: A Revolutionary Alternative?] Rio de Janeiro: SERPAJ-AL, 1986.
Pérez Esquivel, Adolfo. *Christ in a Poncho.* Maryknoll, N.Y.: Orbis, 1983.

EPILOGUE

More Than One Task
North American Nonviolence
and Latin American Liberation Struggle
Gerald Schlabach

"The challenge is not between status quo and change; it is between violent change and peaceful change." So reflected Latin America's Roman Catholic bishops as they gathered in Medellín, Colombia in 1968.[1]

Historians and journalists as well as activists and policymakers have largely ignored the stories of nonviolent change in Latin America. In this book we have tried to rescue such stories. Still, the desperation that may finally lead some to take up arms remains part of the picture.

So does the reputation of "liberation" struggles and "liberation" theology for turning finally to armed revolution. They remain there because the challenge that the bishops voiced in 1968 remains.

Will change be violent or peaceful? Even as the question persists there comes another: Who decides? It is true that when our government and our lifestyle have shackled Latin Americans, we North Americans have no moral right to advise, much less judge, the means they use to break the fetters. In that case our task is first to listen and then to speak out in North America and to change ourselves.

Yet that course may have its own trap. We may get the idea that since the injustices in Latin America have deep roots in Washington, New York, and other First World power centers, we and our choices will in fact decide the fate of Latin America or the Third World. We may think we alone are to decide whether change there must be violent or may be peaceful. Is that not just one more kind of backhanded imperialism, one more way to deprive Latin Americans of their own history and their role as its creators from bottom up? Certainly there is the risk that we will miss important cues that come from Latin American popular movements, cues that might help us strengthen their efforts and enlighten our own.

Let there be no mistake. We must humbly listen and learn in Latin America, and we must speak out boldly in North America. But the truth is that we have both more to listen to, and more to say, than we may think.

The first task: to hear the cry

The place was a tribal village in the Asian nation of the Philippines, but it could have been one of many places in Latin America. After all, Latin American and Filipino history share the legacy of Spanish then U.S. domination. Their cultures share the imprint of Roman Catholicism. In both places centuries-old feudalism has lately made an unholy union with modern transnational corporations. That union has estranged peoples from land in order to plunder both.

A group of Filipinos and a North American friend of mine, Earl Martin, had gone to that village to mourn with the Kalinga people after the assassination of one of their tribal leaders. That leader had organized and voiced his people's opposition to a government dam project. Funded by the World Bank, the project promised to flood not only their homes but the rice paddies and terraces they had lovingly built over generations. The authorities' reply had been a late night knock on the leader's door, then bullets.

On each of the three evenings that Earl, a North American pacifist, spent in the village, sympathetic visitors of another kind also showed up to share the mourning. They were guerrillas from the New People's Army. The situation led to long talks around campfires late into each night. By the third night, according to Earl, "the exchange had become fairly honest, sometimes painfully so." Yet trust was developing as well. Around 2:00 A.M. on the last night Earl felt he could respectfully broach the question that troubles many of his fellow North American pacifists. "Many of us struggle with the question of using arms, the question of armed violence. Help me understand what you think about that. How does the use of arms affect the radical social change that we seek? Might it be possible to achieve a more just and compassionate society with nonviolent means?"

The response, Earl recounts, "exploded with more force than an M-16: 'Why is it we always hear the question of nonviolence from Americans? Americans, who barged in and stole our country from us just when we succeeded in kicking out the Spanish colonists! Americans, who incinerated women and children in the villages of Vietnam with napalm! Americans, who maintain an economic world order that takes food from our children in order to over-fatten the rich in their own country! And now it is Americans who come and ask us why we are violent?' "[2]

In the course of their conversations the Filipino who confronted Earl acknowledged that there were different kinds of North Americans. He knew that Earl's primary identity was with a faith community, not with the nation where he happened to be born. Further, Earl was now endeavoring to identify with poor Filipinos and to speak for them. But the poignant outcry of desperate, suffering people in the Third World is enough to make North American pacifists shy about their nonviolence. Clearly we must get our own North American house in order, or show that we are doing all we can toward that end, before we have the right to enter any discussion on the relative merits of violence and nonviolence in Third World liberation movements. And that is no small order.

The words of Jesus come to mind: "Do not judge, or you too will be judged. . . . You hypocrite, first take the plank out of your own eye, and maybe then you will see clearly to remove the speck from your brother's eye" (Matthew 5:1-5). After all, armed guerrilla groups in the Third World sometimes hold innocent noncombatants hostage, but superpower stockpiles hold all of humanity hostage to nuclear terror. Washington decries revolutionary threats to regional stability in places like Central America while destabilizing governments not to its liking and fueling arms races all over the Third World with its military aid. Meanwhile the centers of financial, military and political power in the First World tolerate, undergird, and profit from the most insidious violence of all—the economic violence of hunger, illiteracy, indebtedness, and landlessness. If such institutionalized violence gives rise to armed opposition, we should not be surprised. Certainly the injustice they confront is more profound and insidious than that which prompted our own American Revolution.

With a plank so big, it is no surprise that some North American pacifists wonder if they will *ever* dare to comment about merits of revolutionary violence versus revolutionary nonviolence in Latin America and the Third World.

But are we really listening?

On the way to solidarity with Latin America I have heard the voice of other friends too. Gilberto Aguirre is executive director of the Council of Evangelical Churches of Nicaragua, known by its Spanish acronym, CEPAD. Founded six years before the insurrection that launched the Sandinista revolution, the agency has served as a shop in which the country's Protestant churches have hammered out the role to take within Nicaragua's revolutionary process and in carrying out their commitment to serve the poor. My work in Nicaragua took me into Gilberto's office regularly, but we usually spent most of our time reflecting together on the challenges facing our nations and our churches at a time when U.S. intervention was growing ever more vicious, Nicaragua was polarizing, and the national economy was coming apart. Fortunately, international solidarity was growing too, and U.S. churches and Christian efforts such as Witness for Peace[3] were becoming a major obstacle to President Reagan's anti-Nicaraguan crusade. Aguirre was grateful and increasingly impressed with the power of active nonviolence.

However Aguirre often received questions about the participation of Christians in the Sandinista insurrection, the military defense, and the revolutionary process. When such questions came from representatives of historic peace churches such as my own or from activists in the North American peace movement, Aguirre had a blunt yet heartfelt reply: "Where were you when we needed you most?" Quite a while before a Sandinista victory looked inevitable, CEPAD and a growing number of Nicaraguan Christians had begun struggling with how to resist the human rights abuses of the Somoza dictatorship and how to confront root causes of poverty such as landlessness. Development projects among Nicaraguan peasants had awakened them to the need for justice and structural change. "Why didn't you talk to us about nonviolence then?"

Aguirre was not simply dodging the violence-nonviolence question. In one of our afternoon meetings he elaborated: "I have a lot of respect for the peace churches. Your history and your Christian ethics can teach us so much. I plead for you to play a role throughout Latin

America. Please, help our brothers and sisters in places like Chile, Brazil, and Guatemala prepare for what we were not prepared for."

A person no less prominent than Nicaragua's foreign minister, Father Miguel D'Escoto, has bemoaned the fact that when resistance to Somoza was heating up, no one within Nicaragua's society and its churches had consciously promoted nonviolence.[4] But to accept such an invitation to teach nonviolence is no light matter. In 1972, amid the trauma of the Vietnam War, James E. Bristol wrote an essay warning North American pacifists that "Nonviolence [is] not First for Export." He observed that "pacifist advice will carry very little weight when given from several thousand miles away, especially if it has been devised . . . in the pleasant, aloof atmosphere of an affluent society starkly in contrast with the misery and repression in which the revolutionary movement is forced to operate."[5]

Actually, nonviolence is never first for export. A person cannot really practice it without real integrity and without seeking truth with a commitment so deep that it demands one's own conversion. That may be why only a few persons seem able to follow Bristol's further counsel:

> Go live for some years under the point of the plow in a country where over the years you can identify with the oppressed peoples and become fully conversant with all that operates there. Become aware of how vicious and total the tyranny is in the perception of those who actually suffer it day by day. Then, out of your experience of identification with the oppressed, you might in time be able to develop nonviolent methods and even a nonviolent strategy that could be viable in that situation, if not to the extent of making the revolution a gandhian one, at least to the extent of introducing a number of nonviolent qualities and emphases into the pattern of the struggle. Only in this way can your advocacy of nonviolence speak with sufficient authority to lend credence to your words.[6]

Yet the preceding chapters have made it clear that there are many more situations than we thought in which nonviolence does not need to be imported, much less imposed—because it is already there! It is there in Latin American culture, but ignored, unnamed, and neglected. The task of the social change promoter, whether the promoter be Latin or North American, is not first of all to introduce anything. Rather it is to witness and legitimate the people's rediscovery of their own cultural values. As they express their values through barrio assemblies, land recoveries, Christian base communities, Indian cultural resistance, defense of human rights, farming cooperatives, and the process of *conscientización,* it may often be appropriate to name those values authentic Latin American nonviolence.

Lessons to learn

Far from having proven irrelevant in Latin America, nonviolence there has much to teach those of us North Americans who are committed to peace, justice, social change, and nonviolence. Latin American nonviolence suggests nothing less than that we redesign the framework of our own nonviolent action. In North America we like the word "action" and call ourselves "activists." But Latin American nonviolence would teach us to dwell first not so much on strategies and tactics as on going back to our own people. By going back we may rescue the best of our cultural values and rebuild community. Wider use of the word "solidarity" in the last fifteen years could be a sign that some of this community-building is already happening. But the image that "solidarity work" and "activism" still evokes is one of frenzy. If we are not jumping from issue to issue, then we are constantly hurrying to keep abreast of the latest developments on a given issue, to find new strategies, to plan new campaigns, and above all to react to whatever is issuing forth from Washington or Ottawa.

As we editors approached writers who might contribute to this book we sought as many engaging stories of nonviolent campaigns and actions in Latin America as possible. At times this became a point of discussion. A couple of the writers warned us against casting the people's own stories in a way not authentically Latin American. My own chapter on the Honduran peasant movement took on a life of its own when one co-op leader repeatedly turned our conversation away from the twenty-four times his community had to occupy the land before it was theirs. He preferred to tell me about their everyday achievements in learning to conduct meetings, bookkeeping, and pest control.[7]

To be sure, Latin Americans have developed very creative tactics in situations of crisis. Among groups committed to nonviolence there is also an appreciation of the value of preparation and training. But our contacts over the years confirm that many nonviolent Latin American activists are surprisingly unselfconscious about the "how" of nonviolent action. They simply have faith that when the time comes the people will find the appropriate actions. At least they will if they are first conscious of their own identity, roots, and collective power. Before all else the role of the activist in Latin America is to be in touch with those roots. That is what the unwieldy-yet-essential term "preferential option for the poor" is all about. The nonviolence that Latin America urges upon us is not just a strategy, much less a philosophy or a dogma.

Nonviolence fundamentally involves the building or rescuing of community.

For all our questioning "the system" and talk of "changing structures," we are often blind to the ways that destructive tendencies within North American culture permeate our work. More than anything else, individualism permeates that culture. Activists for peace and social change often take the culture of individualism for granted—or even reinforce it. The pluralism we value is too often a pluralism of atomized "lifestyles" rather than a thriving multiplicity of ethnic or religious communities and regional subcultures. We claim to put a premium on "tolerance," yet in practice our movements regularly splinter into factions and in-fighting.

Without some melding of wills in search of the common good, no community can endure. And to be more than a tactical interest group within society, more than a momentary encounter group, more than a shifting coalition, we must offer communities with an abiding quality. That quality is what will prove our stated alternatives are socially viable and worth taking seriously.

A strong strain of individualism runs also through Latin American culture. Peasants can be fiercely independent, labor leaders may compete for the symbols of status, machismo is an unruly demon, and bruised honor can forever destroy a friendship. But it is precisely where the poor overcome this individualism and learn to work together through grassroots democracy and Christian base community, that bottom-up change has broken out in unexpected ways throughout Latin America.

Likewise, nationally and continent-wide, the challenge in Latin America is to build or rescue community. The struggle for human rights there is much more than a tactical Trojan horse to draw the attention of the international community toward Third World injustice. It is the wrenching cry of those whom the elites have excluded from all national dialogue, whether as "subversive" individuals, exploited classes or embarrassingly "backward" ethnic groups. Human rights is the cry of the marginalized, the cry to be let in, the demand to be accepted as part of national communities that ancient Conquest and modern repression alike have shattered, or which never existed at all. What makes the National Security Doctrine so dangerous is not that it posits a higher common good for national communities but that it proclaims a false national community, one that brutally excludes rather than justly includes the impoverished majorities.

Though the Latin American conception of active nonviolence as building and rescuing community is usually only implicit, Fernando Aliaga of SERPAJ/Chile has outlined its basis and its implications. In 1983 he elaborated a "Proposal for 'Active Nonviolence'." It was aimed

Epilogue 259

at overthrowing the military dictatorship of General Augusto Pinochet not from the top but through "constructing a [new] society from the bases, through recomposition of the social fabric." The patient work of organizing and consolidating the experiences of *la base* [the base level of society] might not have the same luster as "exhibitionist actions," even nonviolent ones, but Aliaga insisted that it was surer. The SERPAJ leader observed that armed revolutionary vanguards repeat the "historical sin" of right-wing generals in "postponing the people's role as social actor." But he also warned leaders of nonviolent movements to beware of any methodology that would alienate them from their roots. "The proposal of active nonviolence . . . cannot be reduced to a methodology of protests," he said, "but must be the alternative of a new democratic society." The "permanent" task of nonviolent groups like SERPAJ is to "engender communitarian expressions that endeavor to make solidarity and justice a reality at the local, national, and international level."[8]

How then are we learning, or might we learn, from Latin American nonviolence?

First, we too must stay attuned to the deepest aspirations of our peoples. While Latin American activists have desperately tried to insert their voices within national communities and recover the legitimacy that the National Security State has denied them, First World peace activists have sometimes played an inverse role: We have disdained and questioned the legitimacy of our national community entirely, rather than valuing it to transform it. A fresh model for this task comes from Frances Moore Lappé's *Rediscovering America's Values*. In arguing for a more economic and truly participatory democracy Lappé even finds common cause in overlooked passages of Adam Smith who, unlike fellow bulwarks of capitalist thought Thomas Hobbes and John Locke, emphasized a common social good over and above the competition of individual self-interests.[9] Even more to the point why *should* the average citizen listen to our critique if our behavior suggests that we are unable or unwilling to listen to his or her experience? In identifying with a counterculture many activists put the accent on differing from social institutions that dominate others, and less on how those institutions depart from—in fact betray—our common political and religious heritage.

Second, Latin American nonviolence reminds us that no direct action, however dramatic and media-grabbing, can take the place of patient, persistent, and empathetic grassroots political education and community organization. Fernando Aliaga's nonviolent strategy for Chile involved five points, with nonviolent direct action as only the last one. First came personal self-examination, support for grassroots expressions of community among the poor, socio-political formation as an expression of faith, and a pedagogy of peace. Only then would "training in how to plan and carry out nonviolent actions" be in order.[10] Too much emphasis on the "direct action" part of "nonviolent direct action" may actually alienate peace and social activists from our own peoples.[11]

Third, the faith of Latin Americans struggling for change has already done much for North American activists. It has reinvigorated our spiritual vitality and restored a concern to give religion and reflection on sacred texts their rightful place in our efforts. Yet even many of us who claim a faith still participate in grassroots faith communities only vicariously. Should we not see the task of *evangelización* as a more integral, fundamental part of our nonviolent action? Should we not place greater emphasis on building grassroots faith communities ourselves? Since the 1960s, the black civil rights movement has been the model in the United States for all sorts of social change. But whites, including white liberals, have tended to overlook a key fact: The civil rights movement would have been almost unimaginable without the network of black churches that was invisible to most whites and without Dr. King's articulation of the gospel. Fortunately, in the 1980s U.S. churches have been much more visible, indeed the main structure, in resistance to President Ronald Reagan's Central American policy. North American and Latin American churches have rediscovered a common biblical language capable of transcending national and cultural borders. With a new ability to communicate they have gathered and provided alternative information when the U.S. administration dominated the media agenda. Those of us with religious orientation ought to be even more intentional about these links. Nor should any of us let the New Right monopolize the language of recovering fundamental values. Here too the civil rights movement was exemplary as it called U.S. society back to its better values.

Finally, both Latin Americans and we in North America must build beyond local communities, faith communities, and just and inclusive national communities; we must go on to build community internationally. Local, faith, and justice communities built from the bottom-up are absolutely fundamental, but the nonviolence of small groups cannot take on international systems of hegemony alone. Where the powers that be are international in structure, nonviolent action and networks of solidarity must also be international. Otherwise, nonviolence will appear to fail. Chapter One explains why. In 1944 Guatemalans launched a decade of reform through a nonviolent uprising; it helped that the United States, being preoccupied with defeating fascism in Europe, barely noticed events in Central America. Ten years later when the U.S. government was intent on renewing its imperial dominance of Central America, Guatemalans had a very hard time informing the U.S. public in the face of CIA disinformation about their revolution. The U.S. government went on to destroy the revolution-born-in-nonviolence there.

Recently a new page has been turned. One of the many stories that did not fit in this book is that of the *Grupo de Apoyo Mutuo* (Mutual Support Group or GAM) in Guatemala. GAM is one of Latin America's many organizations of relatives of the "disappeared." In 1984, while the government's state terrorism raged, women whose loved ones had disappeared banded together to denounce the violence and demand an accounting from the government. Their stunning courage was clearly the key factor in the group's emergence and survival. But help from Peace Brigades International (PBI), an organization committed to Gandhian nonviolence, was probably also essential. A small PBI team largely made up of North Americans and Europeans provided a safe place for GAM to hold meetings, offered other organizational support, and played a very key role by accompanying GAM members. PBI's support did not prevent the kidnapping and murder of two GAM members in 1985; however since PBI initiated round-the-clock accompaniment of GAM leaders immediately thereafter, none of those being accompanied has been harmed.

More than one task

The relationship between GAM and PBI is only one in the widening community of inter-American solidarity that can make nonviolent struggle for liberation ever more viable. Yet all too often liberation movements and popular organizations in Latin America attract attention and spawn international "solidarity groups" only when they turn or seem about to turn violent. By then about the only contribution North Americans can make is to minimize a tragedy, rather than to open space for Latin American creativity.

If even the most just of armed revolutions involves tragedy, a further tragedy is that doubts about the viability of nonviolence in Latin America become self-fulfilling prophecies. A nonviolent action that no one knows about is like a tree falling in the forest that no one hears. The tree has made no sound; in the worlds of politics and the media the action has not even happened. So the event can scarcely influence public opinion, much less move the usually inactive mass of observers to action. Information does not flow of its own will. Where nonviolence in Latin America "doesn't work" at least part of the reason it doesn't is likely to be that potential allies neglect it. In other words, so long as the desperate poor of the Third World can get the attention of First World opinion leaders only when they take up guns, of course nonviolence "doesn't work." And we potential allies share the blame.

Even where a historical process is in a late polarized phase, with the openings for nonviolent initiatives almost all closed off, the values of nonviolence remain. And those values—generosity, reconciliation, and respect for human rights—can temper and humanize the perceived tragic necessity of violence.[12] In cases where armed insurrection has triumphed there are usually lonely individuals and groups seeking to play prophetic roles of constructive rather than counter-revolutionary criticism. Norman Bent, the Nicaraguan Moravian Church pastor who speaks in Chapter Twelve, is one such. In 1983 he told *Sojourners* magazine: "I have a personal problem. The revolutionary leadership does not trust me because I am a church leader of the Indian people. Neither am I trusted by my own people, because of my revolutionary approach to interpreting the Scripture. So you see where I am: I am the meat of the sandwich."[13] Yet that meat may be exactly what gives strength to keep the revolution headed toward its own best ideals. To ignore such an opportunity does a disservice to the revolution, and shows lack of imagination.

Only a few North American pacifists—those with proven skills of listening, crossing cultures, and suppressing any deeply-embedded "Yankee imperialism"—will actually have the opportunity to help Latin Americans discover nonviolence within their own historical situations. Such people deserve commendation rather than suspicion. But more important, many others can help create networks of solidarity with nonviolent movements in Latin America and elsewhere in the Third World.

There are enough tasks for all. No task requires us North Americans either arrogantly to impose programs of nonviolence on the desperate or to abandon hope in nonviolence as a way to support their just aims. Those are not the choices, even if some calculate the ethics or efficacy of nonviolence and violence differently than do we.

It is true that North Americans and Latin Americans generally come from different angles as they commit themselves to nonviolence. It is dangerous to generalize, but the broad strokes are clear. Both are discovering that peace and justice need each other, yet the original preoccupation of North American pacifists tends to be *peace;* that of Latin Americans, *justice.* If North American nonviolence has roots in the teaching of Gandhi or of King or of historic peace churches, the Latin American varieties almost always have roots in Catholic social teaching. And even as Catholic teaching since Vatican II has increasingly encouraged nonviolent alternatives, it nevertheless has not renounced the legitimacy of "just war" or "just revolution" against extreme tyrants. And finally, we have seen in this book that many Latin Americans are practicing something akin to active nonviolence quite spontaneously, scarcely realizing how historic is their strategy.

They do so simply because numbers, persistence, and organization are the poor's most accessible weapons.

Given the variety of priorities, moods, and roots, nonviolent activists in Latin America tell their North American colleagues that where there is grinding injustice and cruel repression, no one should expect to get anywhere without cooperative alliances with all people who work in good faith for just social change—even those who resort to violent means. To maintain a smug isolation from others who struggle for liberation is a luxury they do not have. This may be one more manifestation of the deep Latin American longing for the sense of community and solidarity of which their societies have been deprived. In any case it is something else from which we as North Americans must learn. We must seek more and earlier solidarity with nonviolent movements in Latin America, but without a judgmental spirit toward those who in tragic circumstances turn finally to armed resistance.

Does this mean those of us committed to nonviolence should hold that commitment lightly or even discard it? Hardly. If we are listening aright the call is to expand and link our communities, not exchange one for another; we must deepen our roots in the communities, the spiritualities, and the nonviolence that have nurtured us, while spreading our branches toward others.

There need be no contradiction between hearing the cry of the poor, whatever their means of struggling for social change, and reaffirming our own confidence in the power of thoroughgoing nonviolence. Gandhi's conviction that there is "that of God" in every person, even the oppressor, is the abiding root of many people's nonviolence. Jesus' urging of love for the enemy is the abiding root of many others'. However both roots generate not only strength of conviction but also vulnerability toward others' claims to truth. For instance as I worked in the mid-1980s in Nicaragua, my pacifist convictions urged me to support the rights of true conscientious objectors who could not kill "enemies" by participating in the Nicaraguan military. Yet these same convictions also urged me to explain to fellow North Americans why many other Nicaraguans—supposed "enemies" of the United States— felt they had no choice but to mount the strongest possible armed defense against possible U.S. intervention. "Love of enemy" demanded both.

It can be excruciating both to nurture the nonviolence of my own community and to build links of solidarity with those who believe they must defend their communities with force of arms. While there may not be a logical contradiction, there is an existential one. Listening to the armed revolutionaries forces me to examine and re-examine my own pacifism, my peace church's tradition, even the words of Jesus.

Fortunately that existential tension is our best hope. If we welcome that tension instead of prematurely seeking to alleviate it, the tension can be a creative dialectic. According to dialectical thought, history moves forward when apparent contradiction gives birth—with all the labor and pain the word implies—to a new synthesis. A sure way to abort the dialectic is to settle quickly for either an easy and pedantic pacifism or a reactive and equally doctrinaire advocacy of violence in the name of justice.

After all, the new synthesis we seek is not so much an idea, nor even a strategy, as it is living, involved people. We seek people who are as committed to peaceful, nonviolent means as they are to just ends, and as committed to building just societies as they are to living peacefully and nonviolently. Such folks will be willing to live out the dialectic, maintain the existential tension, and accept even the risk of their own lives. They will be people of both passion for their conviction and compassion for those who suffer injustice.

In a way, we are back to the first task: to hear the cry of the poor and deepen our practice of nonviolence at home. If the process of structural change stands any chance of creating fewer victims than it delivers, it will not so much be because concerned people have proposed alternative solutions or imposed some alternative means, so much as because they have taken the struggle for both within themselves, and have been ready to sweat and strain until new kinds of lives emerge. Along with those new lives and new experiences there will also come new strategies and nonviolent defenses and equitable social patterns. They will be strategies that make active nonviolence a genuine option for revolutionary skeptics. They will be defenses that seem real to the insecure. They will be social patterns that challenge even the managers of the status quo. Yet neither the strategies nor the defenses nor the social patterns will come to be if we turn a deaf ear to one or the other, nonviolence or concern for justice, and thereby abort the dialectic.

To maintain this creative tension between hope and tragedy we need sustenance. We all need it, whether we are Latin or North Americans. We need both to nurture one another and, as liberation theologian Gustavo Gutiérrez has written, to "drink from our own wells." For us North American pacifists our own wells are the teachings, communities, and traditions that have nurtured us and set us on journeys toward the poor. Encountering the oppression of the poor may have made us realize that for too long our pacifism has been passive. Yet we dare not cut ourselves off from our fonts. Even the freshest of wells can grow stagnant. But it is disuse, not age, that turns the water into mire; it is generous sharing with neighbors that keeps the well fresh.

Notes

1. From the conclusion of a preparatory document for the watershed conference of bishops in which the bishops sought to apply Vatican II specifically to their continent. Quoted in Esther and Mortimer Arias, *The Cry of My People: Out of Captivity in Latin America* (New York: Friendship Press, 1980), p. 109.

2. Earl and Pat Hostetter Martin, "Tell It to the Marines," *Sojourners*, April 1983, pp. 18-20. Additional details come from personal conversations.

3. See page 169 and following.

4. Miguel D'Escoto, "An Unfinished Canvas: Building a new Nicaragua," *Sojourners*, March 1983, p. 17.

5. James E. Bristol, "Nonviolence Not First for Export," reprinted from *Gandhi Marg*, October 1972, by National Peace Literature Service, American Friends Service Committee, Philadelphia, p. 9.

6. Ibid., p. 8.

7. See pp. 72-75.

8. Fernando Aliaga, "A Proposal of 'Active Nonviolence'," SERPAJ/Chile document, December 1983.

9. Frances Moore Lappé, *Rediscovering America's Values* (New York: Ballantine Books, 1989), pp. 12-14 and passim.

10. Aliaga, "A Proposal."

11. See Maurice Isserman, "The Irony of American Pacifism," *Peace and Change* 11, 1986, pp. 47-66.

12. See Chapter 9, "Nicaragua: Planting Seeds of Nonviolence in the Midst of War."

13. "Bordering on Reconciliation: A Miskito pastor reflects on the tension between his people and the Nicaraguan government," *Sojourners*, March 1983, p. 27.

For further reading

Berryman, Phillip. "Ethics of the Revolutionary *Proyecto*." In *The Religious Roots of Rebellion: Christians in Central American Revolutions*, Maryknoll, NY: Orbis Books, 1984, pp. 281-330.

Bristol, James E. "Nonviolence not first for export." Reprinted from *Gandhi Marg*, October 1972. Philadelphia: National Peace Literature Service, American Friends Service Committee.

D'Escoto, Miguel. "An Unfinished Canvas: Building a new Nicaragua." *Sojourners* (March 1983), pp. 14-18.

Isserman, Maurice. "The Irony of American Pacifism." *Peace and Change* 11 (1986): pp. 47-65.

Martin, Earl and Pat Hostetter. "Tell It to the Marines." *Sojourners* (April 1983), pp. 18-20.

Schlabach, Gerald. *Identification with the People in a Revolutionary Situation*. MCC Occasional Paper, no. 2. Akron, Pa.: Mennonite Central Committee, 1988.

Seeger, Daniel. "Pacifists and Third World Liberation Movements." *Friends Journal* 25, no. 9, 1979.

Swomley, John M., Jr. *Liberation Ethics*. New York: The Macmillan Company, 1972.

Wink, Walter. *Violence and Nonviolence in South Africa: Jesus' Third Way*. Philadelphia, PA, Santa Cruz, CA: New Society Publishers in cooperation with the Fellowship of Reconciliation, 1987.

APPENDIX A

A Spirituality of Nonviolence

Introduction

In 1982 Father Domingos Barbé spoke at the continental meeting of Servicio Paz y Justicia (SERPAJ). Until his death in 1988 Barbé worked with the poor and the labor movement in São Paulo, Brazil. He was also a leading member of Serviço Nacional Justiça e Não-Violência, the Brazilian branch of the SERPAJ network. A priest from a wealthy family in France, he had come to Brazil twenty years earlier and, in the words of Creuza Maciel, former General Coordinator of SERPAJ in Latin America, "pitched his tent among the poor, to whom he dedicated his life. He was a principal theologian and systematizer of nonviolence in Brazil." The following article is drawn from Father Barbé's talk.

Barbé takes his listeners along the inward journey of many who struggle for liberation in Latin America. Much of what he says may at first seem familiar—the concept of love, the basic principles of nonviolence. Yet his words are rooted in a mindset radically different from that of many North Americans in the nonviolent movement for social change. Compared to his, North American versions of nonviolence are often embarrassing in their rationalism, secularity, and materialism. It seems difficult for North American activists to grasp how Christian is the Latin American struggle. And yet if we do not grasp that fact we remain outsiders, unable to contact the living pulse of a powerful movement that is shaking the hemisphere and the world.

In North American movements for social change there is little to compare to the concepts of Grace and Cross as Father Barbé presents them. According to him, those who do not recognize and work within the phenomenon of Grace aim to take over secular power as the ultimate tool of the revolution. This is a sobering thought. Where do North American activists place their hopes for radically transforming not only society's structures but its spirit? Barbé speaks of difficulties in even the simplest small-scale collective life, pointing to the way the individual ego resists any yielding of its autonomy to the demands of socialization. While acknowledging the contributions of Marxist thought and depth psychology he maintains that there are depths of the human psyche and sources of its complex forces that are beyond the reach of such materialistic systems of thought. He opens a door into mystical dimensions that North Americans seldom associate with political struggle.

Barbé focuses especially on the meaning of the central symbol of Christianity—the Cross—and confronts his listeners with the outrageous, scandalous demands that this central fact of Christianity makes on us. He insists on the two sides of the Cross, sacrifice and resurrection, and on the triumph of life over death. Again and again he warns that there are no cheap ways to transform the world.

Barbé speaks much of *partilha* and *socialização*—concepts that the English translations "sharing" and "socialization" scarcely capture. His point that these are the very essence of true revolution flies in the face of North America's persistent individualism.

Read seriously, this is a deeply challenging and even shocking article. It leaves no room for escape. As Barbé points out, the number of actual casualties in nonviolent combat is relatively small. But the willingness to give up our lives, the insistence that it is for us and not our enemies to die in the struggle, is at the heart of the strategy of nonviolent liberation. At a time when many U.S. citizens find that the crisis in Central America has intensified the need for nonviolent direct action and increased its risks, this message is particularly timely.

Introduction by Judith Hurley

The Spiritual Basis of Nonviolence
Domingos Barbé

Something new: a revolutionary discourse that is religious

Creative people, those who make really new and original contributions, often are hardly conscious of their own accomplishments. Here, in today's Latin America,[1] a momentous new social phenomenon is emerging. Throughout this continent workers, peasants, blacks, indigenous peoples are all actively in search of radical social change. From all this an ideology of revolution is coming. Yet in essence its theoretical base and its practical strategy are not political but spiritual—and specifically, Christian. It has been centuries since such an important phenomenon has taken hold of so large a part of the Christian world.

Father Domingos Barbé, São Paulo, Brazil, 1987. Photo by Mev Puleo.

Religion has hardly been a part of the revolutions sweeping Europe and Asia since the eighteenth century. Revolution has come instead from dramatic leaps in political consciousness and analysis. The realm of the mystical and the realm of the political remained completely separated. However in present-day Latin America the very opposite is happening: religion is bringing new energy and insight to politics, and politics new energy and insight to religion!

We have not been quick enough to notice these developments and their importance. The theology of liberation is native to our own Latin

American experience. It may well be that, in coming centuries, historians of the Catholic Church will remember only two or three events of importance during this period: the phenomenon of the French worker-priests, Vatican II, and the theology of liberation. No doubt these events will continue to shake the very ground of the Church, provoking a crisis and setting off attempts to snuff them out.

When we speak of a spiritual or Christian basis for revolution, we are stating a simple and self-evident truth—that the gospel, correctly read, puts its followers on a path of radical social and cultural change. As we shall see, the Bible may serve as a handbook for revolution. We must become sensitive to the revolutionary thrust of Jesus' teachings. While he does not go into details about the organization of a new society, he does indicate a revolutionary stance.

Here in Latin America, to their surprise and enthusiasm, Christians have rediscovered that they need not embrace Marxism to live the revolutionary life. This is not to deny the political and analytical tools that Marxism and other purely rationalistic disciplines can provide. But in our struggles we no longer turn to such sources for our inspiration or ethics, or for how to live them out.

Christian combat and the three dimensions of liberation theology

Nonviolent combat? Why is a Christian life necessarily one of combat?

We usually understand evangelization, the spreading of the gospel, as the spreading of doctrine. And indeed, that is an important part. Yet to evangelize is essentially to transform the world into a place where all the children of the one Parent can live together in peace and security. In essence to evangelize is to transform society so that it may reveal the Kingdom of God. In all the vocabulary of Christianity there are three words by which we may accurately sum up the theology of liberation. They are Love, the Cross, and Grace.

Love

Love is the dimension of our faith that sets the ultimate goals of the Christian path, and the axis around which all else revolves. The Christian faith is not dogma, cult, or sacramentalism. To awaken the gospel's energies and give us strength we need reflection and celebration, in prayer and liturgy. But to achieve the final goal—love across the face of the earth—we must go beyond words. Among other things the commandment of Love must lead us into politics. In a society of bitter inequality, Love can never be fully realized: how can one speak of Love in a freezing cold *favela*[2] surrounded by the houses of the wealthy who shut their eyes and offer no help? Love requires radical social transformation.

This transformation must take root and grow in the hearts and consciousness of individuals. But it is necessary that these individual conversions show themselves in the creation of new social structures. This is the Christian basis for involvement in politics. For politics is the art of reorganizing society for the greater happiness of all people.

Pope Pius XI used to say that political work is the greatest expression of Love. Pope Paul VI dedicated his great encyclicals to the construction of a civilization based on Love, or in other words a social order marked by justice and a cultural order marked by the affirmation of Love as its highest value. Pope John Paul II specifically speaks about the social dimensions of Love. We cannot achieve the objectives that such teachings imply without serious political involvement, a kind of involvement both deeply human and profoundly intelligent.

But while the Christian understanding of liberation definitely includes the political dimension, it also goes further. After all, the Christian understanding is that the root of evil runs deeper than politics. It lies in the human soul. We believe that there can be elimination of evil, or sin, only through a living contact with the Divine Source of our being. Our ultimate struggle and goal is not only a more just social order but to create the conditions for God's presence among us. The Spirit of God fills all that it touches with joy. We do not live by bread alone! To be happy we need bread and Love.

So our vision goes beyond just social structures. We look for an order characterized by *participação* and *partilha*.[3] This is Love—and it is only in Love that God is revealed. In an unloving, nonsharing society, God cannot be revealed. The early Church had a beautiful saying: "Fishes swim, birds fly, and God moves in Love." An unloving, nonsharing society such as ours is structurally atheistic, for it prevents expression of the Divine Being. To live we need God, as we need air to breathe.

Most of today's Christians still see God almost like ancient Romans did. Consciously or unconsciously, they believe in a Jupiter-like God— one who needs only to send out a ray of power to solve the problems of humanity. But with such a God, the existence of injustice and suffering is incomprehensible. If God is all-powerful, why does God not intervene in the war in El Salvador? Why does God permit children to die of hunger? But Love limits God's power. True Love does not impose itself. Thus, in a certain way, Love is weak. God can accomplish anything, even overcome death, if I open the door to God. What limits the power of God is my human will. As the Book of the Apocalypse says, "If anyone hears my voice and opens the door, I will come and sit down and have supper with him" (Revelation 3:20). Jesus could work no miracles in Nazareth because the crowd lacked faith (Mark 6:5-6). In a sense God was expelled from God's own creation. Grace fled the earth not because God willed it but because human selfishness left it no room. By itself no political action, no human force, can compel the return of Grace. Only acts of Love can call it back.

Grace can return as we remove obstacles to it—fill in the ravines, level the mountains, smooth the ways (Luke 3:4-6). We do that by overcoming the gross injustice that concentrates enormous wealth in the hands of a few while the many suffer from hunger and misery. Injustice not only kills the body; it leads to mistrust and hatred and thereby to separation from God.

Every good and honest person is potentially an opening through whom God may enter into our human community. But the poor in particular represent the strategic point through which God may enter and return to humanity. "Blessed are the poor, for theirs is the Kingdom of God" (Matthew 5:3). The poor are blessed not because poverty is a good in itself but because, in their poverty, they naturally seek to move the world toward *partilha*, sharing. The *favela*-dweller cannot fail to see the misery of her neighbor. The thin-walled shanties do not permit people to hide their misery. Under these circumstances hypocrisy is impossible. So is private property, since by force of circumstance the land, water, and electricity belong to all. The rich on the other hand, being satisfied with things the way they are, are not motivated toward social change. Like a bunch of rats, each with his own fat cheese, they live isolated from each other. Here Love is impossible, and despair very great.

The Cross

Christian hope seeks the transformation of this earth, the launching of the Kingdom of God in the here and now. But over the earth looms the image of the Cross. Like Christ our teacher, whoever embraces the problems of the people inevitably embraces the Cross. Inspired by the spiritual gifts that graced them, some early Christians felt that the transformation of the world had already occurred, and in their elation they were tempted to ignore the sacrifices that lie in the path. Paul's response was to preach the Cross and bring them back to a wholesome realism. "We proclaim Christ—yes, Christ nailed to the Cross; though this is a stumbling block to Jews and folly to Greeks" (I Corinthians 1:23). The Cross was the very opposite of what the Jews and Greeks had been hoping for. The former looked for the Messiah to appear in glory, not defeat, and the Cross seemed like defeat. The latter looked for a higher Wisdom, not absurdity; and the Cross, which brought not the slightest increase in human happiness but only the contrary, seemed like nothing but folly. We too must get beyond a superficial understanding of what it means to be a Christian.

Grace

Just as one should not think that the spiritual gifts will suffice without the sacrifice of the Cross, it is also a misunderstanding to suppose that by our human strength alone—by such human instruments as parties, unions, class organizations, and economic power—we will overcome the crushing forces of oppression. As spiritual beings we have to have the flow of Divine Life from the Creator, just as material bodies have to be nourished by the circulation of blood. Ultimately, the sickness of our world is a spiritual illness that comes from a lack of a living relationship with God. This living relationship with God does not depend wholly on us. What we mean by Grace is the act of Love whereby God takes the first steps in our direction, in response to our call, however weakly we call out, however little we open our lives to God. *Without the workings of Grace, no power can succeed in bringing about deep and lasting social change.*

Where can we look for the strength to lift up the masses of Latin America, to transform them into truly socialized[4] beings committed to communal sharing of material and human resources? We do not believe that any external power can bring this about, not even the revolutionary power of the proletariat. Bureaucratic, totalitarian, and dictatorial societies have made many efforts to force the individual ego to submit to the process of socialization. In each case the true meaning of socialization has been lost. The will to personal autonomy is so great that it will never truly surrender to external force. Which reader who has been part of a socialistic experiment such as living in a communal household or sharing ownership of a car would not agree? How difficult it is to accept the discipline of collectivity! The car breaks down and no one fixes it. The bathroom is filthy, the phone bill astronomical, the garbage never taken out. The group reacts by making rules, with notices on every wall. Law conquers Grace, external authority overwhelms the law of the heart. But they do not work. People ignore the notices. And if the situation improves, it does so only because of the friendship of the members and their strong sense of common purpose.

Before the experience of socialization, people do not naturally have the will to yield to the demands of community life. Some say that such egoism comes from the bourgeois mentality of the dominant class, which the working class internalizes. But we think that the roots of egoism run deeper, in human nature, and represent a mysterious aberration of the human race. So far no approach to political re-education has taken sufficient account of this fact. Perhaps that is why re-education efforts of various socialist countries—such as the psychiatric wards of the Soviet Union—become so monstrous. To refashion the souls of individuals and overcome the structures of oppression within the psyche requires tools beyond the political, even beyond those of depth psychology. What is needed is what we call "Grace." Grace is the gift that leads people to trust. From trust comes unity, which in turn allows organization. Grace is the opposite of power; it works not by mandate but by inspiration.

Nonetheless, Grace, like power, has a political function. The source of sharing (*partilha*), the quality of fellowship (*convívio*) that is the very heart of communal life, derives not from power but from Grace. Power is at best an organizing tool to serve the heart that Grace awakens.

We must rediscover the political function of Grace. Those groups that do not acknowledge Grace as a revolutionary tool are reduced to taking political and economic power, as the ultimate tool of revolution. We do not deny the importance of such power, in the hands of the people, to create the structures they need to realize the revolution. But Grace goes deeper.

Active nonviolence as a strategy for radical Christian action in Latin America

How can active nonviolence contribute to the Church and to related land, labor, and indigenous movements as they work out their strategy of radical ministry? It can contribute at both levels, theology and practice. Consciously or unconsciously, whoever helps create Christian base communities and form popular cadres inevitably helps to bring on social warfare. And every war needs weapons. Here active nonviolence contributes, by training popular cadres in the weapons of Gandhi, King, and others. Active nonviolence contributes to a theology and a ministry of conflict.

In the second half of the twentieth century the Church has already taken several important steps in this direction:

1. The Church has affirmed its presence in the world to serve the world, not itself. Further, it has recognized that within itself there is concentrated a certain people, with its own culture—the people of God. Within this community each person has both the right and the responsibility to raise a voice in the Church, and to enter the struggle of Christ in this world.

2. Through the sufferings of millions of poor, the people of Latin America discovered that the Church must go beyond speaking, and take a second step: action. As Christians became active in social struggle, the theology of liberation was born.

3. Active nonviolence still wrestles with a serious question: Now that we have entered the struggle, what is distinctly Christian about our actions? We sense deeply that for the Christian, Life and Resurrection are the central reality. So we affirm that Life is at the heart of the Christian struggle, and that any struggle that brings Death rather than Life is not Christian. If individuals die in the struggle against injustice, it should be the death of the just, who have been led by Life to pay the price, the price of confronting and destroying the evil that is in both structures and mentalities.

The communal character of Christian combat

Nonviolence is not the only essential characteristic in Christian modes of struggle. Another distinctive feature is that it is communal and not individualistic. When two or more are gathered in Christ's name, the Christ-energy is present. This divine energy is never present when the individual seeks to solve problems alone. Individual power may not be wrong, but only in a climate of fraternal Love can the Grace of God approach. This Christ-energy gives us the strength to sacrifice our lives to bring about *partilha*, voluntary sharing.

The congregation is where we celebrate our faith and remember Jesus as he called us to do. Through the Eucharist we receive the strength that carried him to sacrifice his own self; through the Scriptures we understand his words and ideas. In the congregation we also experience the bread of Love, the strength of our sister- and brotherhood. But the bond of Love must not only be inside it. Love must spill out into the struggle on the streets so that the civilization of Love of which Pope Paul VI spoke might come into being. Faith lives not in the Church but in the street, the factory, the union. There it fights for electricity, for water, for child care, or for a political party. By such means we try to transform history. Without separating the living of faith from the celebrating of faith it is useful to distinguish between them. What we practice in daily life we celebrate in the Church. By celebrating what we are trying to practice we constantly reanimate the energies that Christ awakens in us through baptism. This is essential. Those who cease to pray, to nourish themselves on the Word of God, and to take of the Lord's Supper and its mystery of his body and blood—those people run the risk of becoming weak in the energies of the risen Christ who confronts and transcends Death. Without that energy our struggle for the Kingdom is like raising a new Tower of Babel.

Theological foundations of active nonviolence

To interpret the Word of God correctly it is not enough just to take the text of the Bible in hand. How one reads a biblical text depends a great deal on the community to which one belongs and the place that community occupies in the structure of society. The reading of the Bible is never a neutral act; it is always engaged, and we may read the same text in a variety of ways. For example, over the centuries the Church has sometimes understood Jesus' famous teaching, "Blessed are the poor," as inviting the poor to accept their misery in this world in anticipation of the happiness that awaits them in the world beyond. We can read the miracle of the loaves as an alienating text or, alternatively, as a liberating one. The alienating reading is: people are hungry, but since I am not the Son of God and do not have supernatural powers there is nothing I can do; so I keep my arms folded. The liberating alternative is: the people are hungry, and Jesus does not ask if we have any money but rather how many loaves, what resources, we do have. In sharing—*partilha*—all of the little that each has, the amount will be just enough for all. With this sharing comes Love, and Love attracts the Grace and the multiplying power of God. We must roll up our sleeves and work for *partilha*; history is in our own hands.

Violence and the Bible

People often quote from the Bible to justify their use of violence, and indeed there are many passages they can cite. We think the crucial point is that Jesus himself was always both vigorous and gentle, at the same time. Severe, unceasing conflict dogged his whole life, and became all the more acute as his hour approached. Yet never did he kill anyone physically, or express rejection in words. To address someone with scorn is to kill that person morally—to say in effect, "to me you are already dead." From this attitude it is only a small step to physical violence. Jesus kept even his enemies within the circle of his caring.

Another argument Christians frequently use to legitimize violence is the thesis that Jesus was a Zealot. Jesus surely had close contacts with the Zealots of his time, that is, with the anti-Roman guerrillas who attempted to liberate Palestine from the Roman oppressors. The contact was natural, since his preaching and activities had many points in common with theirs. Jesus invited the people to freedom, sharing, and justice. He defended the poor and fearlessly attacked the rich, the high priests, the scribes, and the Pharisees. That is, he attacked the wealthy, the powerful, and the teachers of the prevailing ideology. The multitudes accorded him enormous prestige, and on several occasions the Zealots tried to take advantage of his extra-ordinary influence over the masses. They tried to turn him into a national revolutionary leader. After the miracle of the loaves, the enthusiastic crowd, perhaps at the Zealots' behest, wanted to make Jesus king!

Jesus' own apostles sensed his enormous political prestige. Apparently a number were from Zealot backgrounds. In those days as in ours, the guerrillas went about armed. Most guerrillas were poor peasants who had left the large landholdings where the aristocracy had exploited them. They were ultra-nationalist, anti-Roman and anti-high priest; and they were ready to sacrifice themselves for the liberation of their country. From desert hideouts they emerged like wolves to attack government convoys and travelers. Like the Master from Nazareth they had not a stone on which to lay their heads. Judas may have betrayed Jesus out of bitterness that Jesus refused to transform his extraordinary influence into political power. Quite often the multitude showed clearly that it wanted to take up armed, nationalist revolution—that it wanted to expel the Romans and proclaim that its leader was King of the Jews. This intention was so clear that it appeared on the Cross as the principal reason for the Romans' sentence of death: "Jesus of Nazareth, King of the Jews."

But Jesus consistently refused. He did not want to be king. Pilate, the Roman who passed the sentence, understood this well and said, "I find no crime in him at all." But the crowd preferred to save Barabbas, who was probably a guerrilla taken prisoner after an attack. At the end the liberation movement's ultra-nationalists joined forces with the conservatives and reactionaries of the dominant class to eliminate Jesus. He was dangerous to the former and threatened the class interests of the latter because he had his own objectives and drew people away from armed struggle.

His course makes us ask, Why did Jesus refuse armed struggle? We believe he had three principal reasons:

1. As a penetrating observer of his day's political reality, Jesus clearly perceived that the balance of power did not favor armed revolt. Roman power was at its height. Barely forty years later when the Zealots finally created a popular uprising they were drowned in blood. Jesus' analysis proved correct: In a situation of weakness, vigorous nonviolent resistance accomplishes more than armed revolt.

2. But Jesus' refusal to take up arms was not only tactical. He was opposing an attitude of intense nationalism. That attitude, present not only among the Zealots but in the very soul of the Jewish people, utterly contradicted the universality of Jesus' message. Had he affiliated with the Zealots his message would have amounted to nothing more than a call for internal reform of the religion of Israel. Instead he preached a religious revolution that transcended national boundaries.

3. Moreover every partisan revolution recreates the structures of oppression. It does so by its need to eliminate one nation or class in

order to put another in its place. At the heart of Christian nonviolence lies this basic challenge: how do we engage in the struggle without using the weapons of the enemy? How do we arrive at a social situation that is genuinely new?

Jesus taught, "Whoever uses the sword will perish by the sword." Those who use the violent tactics of the dominant classes, even to overthrow oppression, will find their new order contaminated with new forms of oppression and elitism.

The resurrection of Jesus as foundation for a theology of nonviolence

Our faith in Jesus Christ must guide our rereading of the Bible. There are many phenomena in Christianity that are merely peripheral, not lying on the central axis of Christian truth. Of the guiding principles at the axis the most central is love of the enemy. Jesus' teaching us to love our enemy implies that we do have enemies—including class enemies. While acknowledging this fact Jesus also taught that our enemies are all children of the same Parent, of the God "who makes the sun shine on good and bad alike" (Matthew 5:45). To love our enemy and fulfill the spirit of Jesus' teaching we must act so that our enemy can actually sense our love. So the problem is how to translate this commandment of Love into political action, how to engage in the struggle for justice in a way that is both politically effective and faithful to the spirit of Love. The Bible enjoins us to engage in class struggle on the side of the poor—but in the spirit of Jesus.

The most important and original point of our faith is the resurrection of our Lord. In our daily lives the resurrection signifies that life is stronger than death, good is stronger than evil, grace is stronger than alienation. Death does not have the last word. Therefore, every struggle that afflicts death upon another as a principle of combat departs entirely from the Kingdom axis. How, then, could I use killing to bring about justice?

The struggle for the Kingdom is the struggle of the Suffering Servant (Isaiah 42 and 53). It is the struggle of the Lamb of God who sacrifices itself to take away the sins of the world. For many years Miguel D'Escoto—priest, revolutionary, and foreign minister of the Nicaraguan government—has urged the Church to adopt nonviolent means of social struggle. In an interview in December 1978 before the Nicaraguan uprising, he spoke powerfully on the subject of Christian methods of struggle. The title of the interview became "The Power of the Cross." Said he:

> Traditionally, in Latin America, we are inclined to look upon the
> Cross as a lamentable thing over which we weep, at least in Lent and

Holy Week, something we wish didn't happen, instead of looking upon the Cross as the most magnificent act of life. . . . Nonviolence must be looked upon as a constitutive element of preaching the gospel, which means I do not think we are preaching the gospel adequately if we are not instilling the spirituality and the idea of nonviolence as a means of liberation from oppression. It is essential to the gospel. . . . The Cross is not optional, it is the central thing. We must preach the Cross, and to preach the Cross is to preach nonviolence. Not the nonviolence of acquiescence, but the nonviolence of risking our life for the sake of preaching the demands of [fraternity]. When we do that, we suffer the retaliation of those who oppress others, and that is the Cross. When we suffer the Cross, we participate in the birth pangs of Christ for the new humanity. [5]

Nonviolence cannot be improvised

Nonviolence as a method of struggle requires different preparation than armed struggle. This is true for both leaders and masses. It achieves its victory at the conclusion of a long historical process, after being explicitly chosen and worked out, step by step, over a long period of time. It does not fall from the sky, but requires arduous efforts. When an entire historical process follows the path of violence there is no way to suddenly improvise a nonviolent outcome at the last moment. The incarnation of Jesus required centuries of preparation; the coming of Grace presupposes extraordinary conditions. If sacrifice and intense effort are not a part of the process, we will achieve only superficial solutions, devoid of Grace.

Gandhi used to say, "The work of personal transformation, of self-purification, is a hundred times closer to my heart than so-called 'political action'." In the end what unifies a people is the pure-heartedness of our struggle and of the methods we choose, and the goals we set. This purity of heart, combined with courage, moves the indifferent, unites the humble, and isolates the perverse. The secret of nonviolence is the spread of compassion in the hearts of the masses.

To say that violence is antithetical to the gospel is not to say that we can always avoid it. Unfortunately we cannot. But if my brother feels forced to take up arms, it may be because I have stood by with my arms folded. "It is better to be violent than passive," said Gandhi. The worst attitude, when evil confronts us, is to not face up to it. What is crucial is an unshakeable faith in the liberating power of nonviolence and an inexhaustible energy for systematically realizing it.

The key elements of active nonviolent struggle are strength and gentleness. With these psychological mechanisms, it is possible to develop a complete strategy and tactics of combat.

An illustration comes from the struggle at Alagamar, in Paraíba, Brazil. A small group of thugs, armed to the teeth, attempted to force two hundred *posseiros*[6] off the land. The *posseiros* were unarmed but at least superficially trained in nonviolent struggle. The thugs approached with threats. Without uttering a single word the *posseiros* encircled them and took the weapons out of their hands. The psychological effect of dozens of men silently approaching and forming a circle was overwhelming.

Let us imagine an alternative scenario: The thugs confront an equal number of *posseiros*—but some of them are armed. With their lives threatened, the thugs are quick to shoot. Or another alternative: There are only fifty unarmed *posseiros* against five armed thugs. Once again, altered circumstances affect the combat. Five armed thugs are in a position to defeat fifty unarmed men, while they would not have time to shoot two hundred men down before being overcome themselves.

Each situation supplies its own appropriate nonviolent response. What was a valid response at one moment in the struggle may not be a valid response a year later. Social and political conditions and the climate of repression vary constantly. Active nonviolence carefully guards against idealism or sentimentality. An effective popular force depends upon a high degree of militancy. Exact information is an essential element of this strength.

The engine of nonviolent combat is the inward disposition not to kill or humiliate. Such combat presupposes a high level of moral integrity and strategic unity. One individual assailing the adversary with insulting or humiliating remarks, or one person purchasing a revolver, can be enough to lower the ethical level of the struggle and destroy the critical mechanisms of nonviolence.

At every instant we must be like good generals and study the terrain for the best position for counterattack. Yet we must never discard the possibility of sacrifice. It is better to die than to kill! Nonviolence does not mean suicide—the militant does everything in his power to preserve life, his own and others'—but he or she is ready to die if necessary. Scripture tells us that there is no salvation without the shedding of blood. The question is: Whose blood? The answer holds the key to what is truly revolutionary about nonviolence. The nonviolent response is that the blood spilled must be the blood of those who fight against injustice. This is the logic of the Cross, the heritage of Jesus, who died to remove sin from the world. However, the sacrifice of the just is so effective that far fewer die in nonviolent combat than in conventional warfare.

The elements of nonviolent strategy

We can now summarize these elements of a nonviolent strategy:

1. The power of the poor lies in their greater number, a number constantly increasing.

2. The power of the poor derives from the place they occupy in the economy. The poor have their hands on the means of production. If they put down their spades or stop the machines the entire country comes to a halt, no matter how great the armies of the rich.

3. The weakness of the poor lies in their lack of unity and organization. This is where active nonviolence comes in. How do we unify the poor and make inroads among the rich? The answer: by the purity of our combat. I emphasize this purity because many of those who struggle for justice undervalue it. It is a fact that people come together more firmly, with more strength of purpose, in support of one of their number who is persecuted while unarmed than in support of a military leader, however good and just the military person might be. But it is essential that the struggle be visible, public and organized. A struggle that is not made public, fully and courageously, accomplishes nothing. Truth hidden cannot do its work. It is as Jesus taught us, "Don't hide your light under a basket" (Matthew 5:15).

Principles of active nonviolence

Active nonviolence presupposes the following:

1. Ongoing political training; constant analysis of the political and economic situation and the climate of oppression in order to find the most appropriate response.

2. The organization of a powerful popular force, based on the most noble sentiments.

3. Ongoing psychological training:

  i. Never to kill.
  ii. Never to injure.
  iii. Always to remain united.
  iv. Always to remain alert.
  v. Never to run away (unless by previous decision, for tactical reasons).
  vi. Never to become discouraged; to act with relentless persistence.
  vii. To know how to risk one's life; to overcome the fear of death.
  viii. Not to hide: nonviolence can never be clandestine. To hide is to negate its essence which comes from the force of truth.
  ix. To keep oneself from hatred, to pray for one's enemies, to love them: constant self-purification.
  x. To disobey those laws that would destroy the people and its organizations.

4. Finally, when all other resources are exhausted, all these efforts must follow the way of massive and organized civil disobedience.

translated from Portuguese by Judith Hurley

Notes

1. The term "Latin America" is unfortunate. The presence on the continent of blacks and indigenous peoples requires of us that we come up with a more appropriate designation.

2. *Favela:* shantytown; squatter settlement found on the peripheries of most Latin American cities.—Trans.

3. *"Participação"* looks like our "participation" but has a depth of meaning derived from the Christian experience of the sacraments, through which the faithful enter a new reality. The same quality of depth applies to *"partilha,"* which we may translate literally as "sharing." Throughout this article Barbé uses both words, along with *"socialização,"* to indicate the quality of a transformed world.—Trans.

4. *"Socialização"* implies an inner conversion that goes far beyond the external changes normally contained in words such as "socialist." Like *"participação"* and *"partilha,"* *"socialização"* is a key word for grasping the vision of the transformed world.—Trans.

5. Miguel D'Escoto, M.M., "The Power of the Cross," *The Catholic Worker,* February 1979, pp. 1, 6.

6. Untitled small landholders.—Trans.

For further reading

Barbé, Dominique. *Grace and Power: Base Communities and Nonviolence in Brazil.* Maryknoll, N.Y. Orbis Books, 1987.

Barbé, Dominique. *A Theology of Conflict and Other Writings on Nonviolence.* Foreword by James W. Douglas. Maryknoll, N.Y.: Orbis, 1989.

APPENDIX B

Preparing for Nonviolence

The following document from the Brazilian branch of the international Servicio Paz y Justicia (SERPAJ) network explores the principles of active nonviolence from the perspective of the popular movements and discusses the need for and the content of training for nonviolent action. It is only one example of nonviolence training materials. It reflects the horizons of struggle of the group that produced it. As such it is limited by the time (the mid-1970s) and the setting (Brazil) in which it was written. Nonetheless it is a useful illustration of how nonviolence training is approached in at least some Latin American settings.

Excerpted from Antônio Fragoso, et al., *A Firmeza Permanente—A Força da Não-violência* [Relentless Persistence: The Power of Nonviolence], (São Paulo: Loyola-Vega, 1977), pp. 29-32; 119-127.

Convictions and Consequences of Active Nonviolence

Active nonviolence offers to both the oppressed and the oppressor the possibility of safeguarding their honor and their person. In the unjust, it attempts to nurture understanding, transformation, and even collaboration toward the good of all. It does not seek the humiliation of the enemy, nor his or her destruction, and it is careful not to be unnecessarily provocative.

This struggle enriches the adversaries—both aggressor and victim. Even if in the first stage of the struggle the victims are not able to achieve their objectives or to emerge victorious, they should not allow apparent failure to discourage them or diminish their struggle. Even without immediate positive or visible results, our conviction—and the guarantee of nonviolent action—is that truthful and loving action has within it an all-encompassing, redeeming, and life-giving value: "To wish to save all humankind, including the oppressor."

This "universality" of the act of liberating nonviolence has infinite repercussions in the lives of men and women. Active nonviolence seeks to be the expression of authentic love at the core of political combat.

Some principles of nonviolence

1. In order to attain a just society, we need means that are better than intrigue, plotting, coups d'etat, torture, murder, and terrorism. To achieve justice and peace it is necessary to find just and peaceful means. Since such means are consistent with the ends we desire in the long run, they will be simpler and more effective.

2. *Firmeza permanente* [or relentless persistence, a term sometimes used in place of active nonviolence] is in no way cowardly submission to the oppressors. To the contrary, it opposes the tyrants and the violent ones with all its strength. The *queixada*[1] continually attempts to overcome bad with good, lies with truth, hatred with love.

3. The struggle of *firmeza permanente* draws all of its strength from truth. To withdraw from truth is to withdraw from the source of our strength. Therefore the struggle cannot be clandestine. If you act in secret, you end up lying in order to disguise your efforts.

4. Violence may be impressive at first sight if it is part of a courageous search for justice. With time however, we find that the way of violence does not deliver the hoped for result.

5. Courage in isolation is not enough. The struggle must be collective and organized. The struggle brings persecutions, but persecution and the action of the group nurture a class consciousness.

6. If the people do not want to use the very weapons that dehumanize

the oppressor, the only solution is to accept, without retreating, the blows and the brutality of the adversary. There is no such thing as a human being who wishes to be inhuman until the end. Such is our hope.

7. Those who use violence attempt to provoke the *queixadas* in order to get them to abandon their principal weapon: the use of *firmeza permanente*.

8. In a situation of weakness, *firmeza permanente* is more effective than violence.

9. By overcoming the oppressor through violence, one achieves only a partial victory. The roots of injustice remain within the oppressor who was defeated and within the victor who is liberated from the oppressor, since both used violence and so kept within themselves the evil that they fought.

10. We cannot offer any guarantees to anybody that they will not be imprisoned. We can only guarantee that we will go together and nobody will skip out on the others.

11. Since its first commitment is to truth and justice, *firmeza permanente* is not limited to strictly legal actions.

12. Violence comes from aggressive impulses that are not channeled constructively. Since it is irrational it leads to hatred. The *queixada,* fed by the conviction that we are all brothers and sisters, aspires to act for justice through the control of reason over instinct.

13. Violence is often impatient. *Firmeza permanente* endeavors to wait and to respect the necessary stages, recognizing that the conservatives know how to compromise or to change when they need to.

14. In the face of the *queixada,* the anger and the might of the oppressor are useless. He loses his sense of self-assurance because of the attitude of the victim and the appeals to reason that the victim makes. The transformation and the defeat that he suffers then are moral. Instead of humiliating him, they enrich him.

15. The important thing is not to be brave once in a while, but rather persistent all of the time. "We may die, but we are not going to run," pledged the workers of PERUS in the strike of 1967.

16. If you cannot commit yourself to be nonviolent, be violent. What you cannot be is submissive.

17. When somebody attacks another in an act of physical violence and the victim replies in kind or flees, the response of the victim gives the aggressor a great security and moral support, since it shows that the moral values of the victim are the same as those of the attacker. Any attitude of fight or flight on the part of the victim reinforces the morale of the aggressor. But if the attitude of the victim is calm and firm, the fruit of self-discipline and self-control, the aggressor is disarmed by the show of love and the respect for him or her as a person. This only happens because the victim does not respond to the violence

of the aggressor either with cowardice or with counter-violence. Instead the victim attacks the aggressor at the level of thought, of intelligence, of reason, using the weapons of truth, justice, and love.

Training for nonviolent action

Firmeza permanente is not improvised. We must take *training* for nonviolent action seriously. *Firmeza permanente* requires training that is as much spiritual as practical, as much in the inspiration as in the tactics of nonviolence.

Practical training

The reality of current events is right in front of us and it presents us with an increasingly urgent challenge.

Facts:

* In Arenópolis, Mato Grosso, 200 families, close to one thousand poor people, are in a legal struggle against Mr. Satoshi, who lives in Cuiabá, and who claims to be the owner of the Fazenda União. Recently, the situation has resulted in armed confrontations, with some people being killed and others imprisoned.

* In Sítio do Mato, Bahia, the *grileiros* (literally "landgrabbers"), with the help of hired gunmen, are threatening more than forty families to get them to leave their fields. They want to kill the Rev. José Moreira Cardoso for defending the workers. A place that four years ago was peaceful is now a setting of fear, terror, and tension.

* In Paraíba, 120 *posseiros*[2] of the Fazenda Mucatú have confronted some of the people of wealth of Recife who are trying to buy the *fazenda*[3] from Mr. Herculano Lundgreen with the intention of replacing the crops with pasture land and cattle ranching, which will generate more profit. The government intervened in a timely manner and seized the land in support of the *posseiros'* claims.

* The massacre in Merurí, Mato Grosso, resulted in three killed and many Indians wounded. Among the dead were the Indian Simão and Father Rudolf Lunbenkein who paid with his life for his peaceful struggle in defense of the Indians.

* In São Felix do Araguaia, in Acre—in fact in that whole region—the bursting of the boils of a sick body are evident. Who can forget the death of Father João Penido Burnier and the kidnapping of Dom Adriano, Bishop of Nova Iguaçú?

Analysis and method

We do not propose to elaborate an overall strategy to resolve the land tenure problem nor to offer complete solutions to the cases listed above. This is necessary, but we must be more modest. What we want to do is simply to offer some ideas that perhaps will help us to *resist and attack* in the way of active nonviolence when violent conflicts like these emerge. Let us consider two specific examples:

a) A big landholder, in order to expel the *posseiros* from the land he claims to own, uses the following method: Since he is not able to intimidate the *posseiros* through the use of a great variety of threats, he decides to rent the area in dispute to a contractor to plant and thus pull the rug out from under the *posseiros*. The *posseiros* feel that they have a legitimate case so they make the rounds of the quarters of all of the peasants hired by the contractor and ask them to leave. When they arrive at the cabin of the contractor, he greets them with a gunshot. *How should they confront this contractor?*

b) In a factory, three workers file a complaint against the company. In accordance with the law, they are seeking salaries equal to those of other workers who are doing the same work. After various unsuccessful attempts to reach an agreement, they ask for a meeting with the manager. *How should they prepare for this conversation/conflict, knowing that the company has a number of lawyers backing it up, while they only have the assistance of the one union lawyer who has to handle many other cases besides?*

Socio-drama[4]

Socio-drama is one of the best known and undoubtedly one of the most emotionally engaging training methods. It is a preview, in the form of theater, of a conflict that the participants are actually going to encounter. For example:

The case of the workers: Role play the conversation between the workers and the manager. Each one should give careful attention to preparing his or her role. Who will play the part of the manager and how? Of the workers? Of the lawyer from the union who accompanies them? Of the boss's secretary? Imagine the content of the conversation, the ambiance, the arguments each side will use. Anticipate the emotional reactions of the manager, the feelings of the workers. Divide up the tasks: During the conversation, who is going to speak? When? What tactic will you use?

The *companheiro* who will train the others in this socio-drama should define with great care the *theme* (the principal problem which will be confronted), the *setting* (what will the environment be like?) and the *place* (where?) of the action. The roles of the other persons who are present should also be explained in detail. The actors assume their roles while the other members of the group constitute the public. Each person takes a few moments to get into his or her role and then the simulation begins. When the coordinator gives a signal, the simulation is stopped and the group critiques the actors. Did they represent, or better said, *really express* the feelings of the boss? Of the workers? Of the union representative? Was it realistic? Were there mistakes? Insights? Would the tactic they used work? Did the arguments carry weight? Are there other approaches?

The case of the posseiros: Since this case is more complicated, violent, and dramatic, and the actors more numerous, the simulation is also more complicated.

The actors: The peasants hired by the contractor, including the women and children; the *posseiros,* the group of men who are going to protest (imagine what their wives will say to them before they leave); a leader, since any effective action depends on having someone to make decisions during the action; the contractor.

The theme: In the first stage, convince the hired peasants and the contractor to leave the area occupied by the *posseiros*; try to win their solidarity in this nonviolent action for justice.

The setting: Very tense; the men are tired, nervous, fearful. The number of militants experienced in *firmeza permanente* is ten. The other fifty *posseiros* have little training in nonviolence.

The place: Open air, a jungle area, dirt roads, the cabins grouped together. The contractor's cabin is near the edge of town.

Preliminary meeting: Get the *posseiros* together and sketch the situation on the blackboard. Then each group (the hired peasants, the *posseiros,* and the contractor) should think about the best way to assume its role. Do not forget the role of the women and the children. (What will they say to their husbands and fathers? What is their role in the action?)

Simulation: Act out the scenario. In this socio-drama, undoubtedly the most dramatic moment will be when the group of *posseiros* arrives in front of the cabin of the contractor (imagine the conversation, the action . . .) The socio-drama obliges the actors to seek solutions and to assume attitudes they may not be anticipating. After all, they may only have planned their action theoretically, or not planned it at all. For example:

A big group always causes fear and mistrust. If the objective of an action is to establish contact with a less numerous adversary, the most effective approach is to just send a few representatives so as not to frighten the adversary. In the case we are studying, it is good to stage both possibilities.

* If the contractor does not shoot (this is the first objective, before anything else), what should participants say? What should they do to convince him to leave?

* If the contractor starts shooting in the air, what attitude should participants take? Should they risk trying to talk with him? How? Is there a volunteer? How can they disarm his violence without unduly risking their lives?

Anticipate the most likely attitude of the contractor and act out the scenario accordingly.

Anticipate the need for quick decision-making. Plan that the *companheiros* of *firmeza permanente* are going to confront a lone, armed adversary. Then suddenly, a jeep shows up loaded with armed goons who shout out, "You have thirty seconds to get out of here." What should be done? This could happen in the midst of the socio-drama, without telling the actors about it beforehand. This permits the actors to see their own reactions and spirit of decision in a critical moment.

Evaluation of the socio-drama

The goal of *firmeza permanente* is the efficacy of nonviolence. We want to achieve the objective without anyone dying, either morally or physically. A socio-drama permits us to evaluate realistically the resources that we actually have to carry an action through to the end. In the case above, if the actor who plays the part of the contractor decides to respond by shooting, it is important to ask, before actually undertaking such an action, if the means in fact exist to turn around the situation without retreating and without using violence. If neither local action, much less the authorities, were sufficient to resolve the case, are we ready to organize a public pressure campaign in the press and to call on the International Red Cross? (This actually happened, but, unhappily, only after the death of one of the *posseiros*.)

Among the innumerable advantages that the socio-drama offers, we would single out the following:

* It situates the action in its actual setting: the place (where will it be?); the time (exactly when? for how long?).
* It familiarizes the *companheiros* with the situations in which they are engaged. Through the physical and emotional reactions that surface in the training, they are able to develop more appropriate responses to various situations, such as contact with the adversary, prison, shooting, negotiations with the authorities, surprise developments. This practical preparation for nonviolent action is very important because the diverse exercises enable one to take into account the psychological factors (critical to the course of an action), the rational factors (cool analysis of what should in fact

be done), and the practical factors (which a simple theoretical study of the situation would not allow one to foresee). As such, the goal of a socio-drama goes far beyond traditional, superficial preparation, sitting around a table.

* It attempts to comprehend the position of the adversary. This is an important step in nonviolence. It is necessary to put oneself in the place of the adversary in order to know why s/he acts in that manner. In this way, it is possible to prevent irresponsible actions in which the only result is to uselessly provoke the adversary and reinforce his or her error. There is no point in humiliating one's opponent. Rather, through truth and justice, we must find an honorable way out for everyone. Experiencing the difficulties that the adversary must overcome enables us to discover the adversary's strong points and, as a result, makes our action more effective, because we will know when and where to act to maximize the chances of success.

* It reinforces and nurtures the unity of the group. How? It develops the confidence of each individual in the group, stretches the bonds of friendship, and familiarizes the group with tense situations. Often the training enables the discharge of internal tensions, allowing each individual to regain a sense of calm at the time of the action.

* It reinforces and nurtures self-confidence in each individual. This is a crucial aspect. This trust in oneself develops if the person comprehends that s/he has the power to react in certain situations, that s/he is a member of a group that offers support, and finally, that s/he can take part in the unfolding of a situation in which the phases are known and understood. S/he is no longer a pawn.

* It teaches the group to do self-evaluation. Evaluation is the essential phase of the training. It gives an opportunity to judge the success or failure of the exercise and, above all, to see whether or not adequate resources actually exist to undertake an action. New and original ideas come up to overcome obstacles. There is no training without evaluation.

Additional preparation

Let's suppose that our activists are prepared thanks to the techniques that we have just presented. They have a variety of methods of action at their disposal; they know how to select among them, how to control their nerves, how to seize the initiative; they are capable of working as a group. Yet if they go into an action, they run the risk of being disillusioned because they are lacking other sorts of preparation. "Direct action is not all direct action."

1. Technical information

Medical: Just as the women of a village often learn first aid in order to be ready when the need arises, it also makes sense for nonviolent activists to do the same in anticipation of confrontations and repression. Especially in the case of a mass action, having somebody trained in first aid is very useful.

Legal: Activists who understand that their attitude may lead them to face the police or even end up in jail have every reason to be familiar with their legal rights. The use of a primer on human rights and the laws that guarantee the security of the citizen can accomplish this.

Security: Often nonviolent activists are characterized by a certain inconsistency when it comes to security. It is better not to say everything over the telephone, not to let just anyone participate in any meeting, not to pass out address lists as though they were leaflets, etc.

Techniques: Many groups depend on a "specialist" who knows how to use a mimeograph machine, design a poster, type. The editing of a pamphlet or of a press release (content and form), the production of a poster, the use of a mimeograph machine are all skills to acquire.

2. Reconnoitering the terrain

Information of this type is very useful for an analysis of the situation. Here we refer not just to geographical information (the nerve centers of a city, how many doors a building has . . .) but also familiarizing oneself with the customs of the place and the people who frequent it. For example, note the time that the factory manager arrives in order to arrange a direct contact with him.

Spiritual training

Finally, we cannot forget this fundamental aspect of training. The apostle Paul reminds us that even in the most dramatic situations, "the fruit of the Spirit is love, joy, peace, patience, kindness, goodness, trustfulness, gentleness, and self-control." (Galatians 5:22).

Fasting and prayer are powerful weapons of nonviolence. Before any action that is likely to awaken the strongest passions, everyone should do such things as increase their vigils of prayer, ask the pardon of their brothers and sisters, purify themselves of evil, do justice in their own life, and fast.

Why all of this? Because we believe in the power of truth. It is truth that is going to triumph in the social, political, and other realms of human endeavor. Gandhi wrote: "By its very nature, truth gives evidence of itself. From the moment we leave behind all the stubborn webs of ignorance, the truth shines in splendor. . . . The way of truth is full of unimaginable obstacles. But in the faithful lover of truth there is neither deception nor defeat. For the truth is all-powerful, and the disciple of truth can never be overcome."

Translated from Portuguese by Philip McManus

Notes

1. *Queixada* is the name given to the workers of the PERUS cement factory in São Paulo during their struggle against the powerful Grupo Abdalla. *Queixadas* are wild boars who, when in danger, gather together in groups and, snarling and grinding their teeth, turn to face the hunter. See Chapter 2.—Trans.
2. Untitled small landholders.—Trans.
3. A large private landholding.—Trans.
4. This section is indebted to an article by J. Fabre and P. Jacquenet, published in the magazine of the International Fellowship of Reconciliation.

RESOURCES

The following list, while very incomplete, includes some organizations working with nonviolent popular movements in Latin America.

American Friends Service Committee
1501 Cherry St.   Philadelphia, PA 19102   (215) 241-7159
• Since 1961 the American Friends Service Committee has been working in Latin America, focusing on human need, development, and the democratic empowerment of people in the region.

Fellowship of Reconciliation Task Force on Latin America and the Caribbean
515 Broadway   Santa Cruz, CA 95060   (408) 423-1626
• The work of FOR's Task Force on Latin America and the Caribbean includes delegations to Latin America, an Exchange Residency Program through which Latin American activists visit the U.S., Americas Connections through which U.S. activists visit Latin America, an urgent action network and other programs aimed at strengthening North/South communication and collaboration.

Mennonite Central Committee
21 S. 12th St.   Akron, PA 17501   (717) 859-1151
• The Mennonite Central Committee is the arm of the Mennonite churches of North America for relief, development and peacemaking projects. MCC maintains a staff of some 150 working throughout Latin America and the Caribbean in cooperation with Latin American church groups and local organizations.

Peace Brigades International Central America Project
193 Yonge St. Suite 502   Toronto, Ontario   Canada M5B1M8
(416) 594-0429
• Inspired by Gandhi, Peace Brigades International fosters nonviolent action and reconciliation. PBI provides unarmed, non-sectarian peace teams in areas of violent repression and conflict. Teams in Guatemala and El Salvador provide protective accompaniment for those whose lives may be in danger. The teams also offer education and training in nonviolence and human rights.

Resource Center for Nonviolence Latin America Program
515 Broadway   Santa Cruz, CA 95060   (408) 423-1626

• The Resource Center for Nonviolence works to raise public awareness in the U.S. about Latin American issues and to build ties with Latin American nonviolent popular movements. Projects include Project Abraço: In Solidarity with the People of Brazil, an urgent action network, a U.S.-Latin America exchange program, and extensive networking both within the U.S. and abroad.

Witness for Peace
2201 P Street NW, Room 109   Washington, DC 20037   (202) 797-1160
• Since 1983 Witness for Peace has maintained a continuous presence first in Nicaragua and more recently in Guatemala at the invitation of Central American churches in order "to develop an ever-broadening, prayerful, biblically-based community of U.S. citizens who stand with the Nicaraguan and other Central American people by acting in continuous nonviolent resistance to U.S. covert or overt intervention in their countries and to mobilize public opinion and help change U.S. policy to one which fosters justice, peace and friendship."

Some other groups working on Latin America issues

Center for Global Education
Augsburg College   731 21st Ave. S.   Minneapolis, MN 55454
(612) 330-1159
• tours to Central America

Committee in Solidarity with the People of El Salvador (CISPES)
P.O. Box 50139   F St. Station   Washington, DC 20004   (202) 887-5019
• solidarity work

The Environmental Project on Central America (EPOCA)
300 Broadway, Suite 28   San Francisco, CA 94133   (415) 788-3666
• provides resources to promote sound environmental practices with peace and justice in Central America

Global Exchange
2940 16th St. No. 307   San Francisco, CA 94103   (415) 255-7296
• reality tours, speaking tours of Latin American activists, educational resources

Institute for Food and Development Policy/Food First
145 9th St.   San Francisco, CA 94103   (415) 864-8555
• educational resources on food and development issues

MADRE
121 West 27th Street, Room 301   New York, NY 10001   (212) 627-0444
• national friendship and humanitarian-aid association; through its health and childcare programs, MADRE connects women and children in Central America and the Caribbean with women and children in the U.S.

National Central America Health Rights Network (NCAHRN)
853 Broadway, Suite 416   New York, NY 10003   (212) 420-9635
• promotes health in Central America and education in the U.S. about the impact of poverty and U.S. intervention on health, and creation of a more humane U.S. foreign policy

Neighbor to Neighbor
2940 16th St. Suite 200-2   San Francisco, CA 94103   (415) 621-3711
• grassroots lobbying work around Central America issues

Network in Solidarity with the People of Guatemala (NISGUA)
1314 14th St. NW Suite 17   Washington, DC 20005   (202) 483-0050
• solidarity work

294 *Relentless Persistence*

Nicaragua Network
2025 I St. NW Suite 212   Washington, DC 20006   (202) 223-2328
• solidarity work

Pledge of Resistance
4228 Telegraph Ave. Suite 100   Oakland, CA 94609   (415) 655-1181
• direct action protest of U.S. intervention in Central America

Quest for Peace
Quixote Center   P.O. Box 5206   Hyattsville, MD 20782
• material aid for Nicaragua

Religious Task Force on Central America
1747 Connecticut Ave. NW   Washington, DC 20009   (202) 387-7652
• resources for the faith-based Central America network in the U.S.

The Resource Center
P.O. Box 4506   Albuquerque, NM 87196   (505) 266-5009
• educational resources on Latin America

War Resisters League
339 Lafayette St.   New York, NY 10012   (212) 228-0450
• solidarity work from a pacifist perspective; connection with SERPAJ through War Resisters International

Sources for human rights documentation on Latin America

Americas Watch
1522 K St. NW   Washington, DC 20005   (202) 371-6592

Amnesty International
322 8th Ave.   New York, NY 10001   (212) 807-8400

Washington Office on Latin America (WOLA)
110 Maryland Ave. NE   Washington, DC 20002   (202) 544-8045

Organizations in Latin America

Popular movements in Latin America are made up of many thousands of different groups. One network which works with a broad spectrum of popular organizations is Servicio Paz y Justicia (the Service for Peace and Justice). Founded in 1974 under the leadership of Nobel Peace Laureate Adolfo Pérez Esquivel, SERPAJ has chapters in eleven Latin American countries and one in Europe. SERPAJ participates in the movement of oppressed peoples in search of their own liberation and facilitates intercommunication among groups struggling for justice through nonviolence. It is an international service of support, guidance, networking, training, formation and education for peace with justice in Latin America.

SERPAJ-AL (international office)
Casilla 8667   Guayaquil, Ecuador   (593 4) 20-3600

SERPAJ Argentina
Mexico 479   1097 Buenos Aires, Argentina   (541) 334-7036

SERPAJ Brasil
SDS—Ed. Venâncio V—Bloco R S/313   Brasilia, DF 70.302   Brasil
(55 61) 225-8738

SERPAJ Bolivia
Casilla 5807   La Paz, Bolivia   (591 2) 35-1179

SERPAJ Ecuador
Casilla 3280   Guayaquil, Ecuador   (593 4) 20-1536

SERPAJ Chile
Casilla 139   Santiago 3, Chile   (56 2) 22-56872

SERPAJ México
Apartado 70-575   México, DF 04511   México   (52 5) 871-6725

SERPAJ Nicaragua
Apdo. 5602   Managua, Nicaragua   (505 2) 7-3388

SERPAJ Panamá
Apartado 861   Panamá 1, Panamá   (507) 62-2472

SERPAJ Perú
Apartado 5602   Lima 100, Perú   (51 14) 27-7303

SERPAJ Paraguay
Casilla de Correo 1072   Asunción, Paraguay   (595 21) 3-3962

SERPAJ Uruguay
Joaquín Requena 1642   Montevideo, Uruguay   (598 2) 48-5301

SERPAJ Europa
Palaststrasse 3   5500 Trier—BRG   (49 651) 4-3572

Some periodicals which cover Latin America

Most of the SERPAJ chapters publish their own newsletters. So does the international office in Ecuador.

Andean Focus
198 Broadway, Rm 302   New York, NY 10038   (212) 964-6730
• Published by the Ecumenical Committee on the Andes (ECO-Andes); focuses on the Andean region; quarterly.

Central America Report:
The Weekly Review of Economics and Politics
Inforpress Centroamericana
9a Calle "A" 3-56   Zona 1, Guatemala City   Guatemala

Latin America Press
Apartado 5594   Lima, Perú
• Published weekly; covers all of Latin America including frequent reports on church issues; *Noticias Aliadas* is a sister publication in Spanish.

NACLA Report on the Americas
151 W. 19 St.   New York, NY 10011   (202) 989-8890
• Published by the North American Congress on Latin America; in-depth analysis of political and economic trends throughout Latin America; bi-monthly.

Solidarity
24 E. Wall St.   Bethlehem PA 18018
• Published by the Committee in Solidarity with Latin American Nonviolent Movements and the Fellowship of Reconciliation Task Force on Latin America and the Caribbean; promotes exchange between North American and Latin American activists; published in English and Spanish.

ABOUT
THE RESOURCE CENTER
FOR NONVIOLENCE

Founded in 1976, the Resource Center for Nonviolence in Santa Cruz, CA offers a wide-ranging public education program in the history, theory, methodology and current practice of nonviolence as a force for personal and social change. Resource Center activities include lectures and workshops, nonviolence training and leadership development programs, speaking tours, delegations abroad, urgent action appeals, exchange programs with Third World activists, internships, local organizing around racial and economic justice issues, and extensive networking with peace and justice groups in the U.S. and abroad, with special foci on Latin America and the Middle East.

The Resource Center for Nonviolence offers books, pamphlets and literature for sale in its New Society Bookstore and publishes a periodic "Center Update." In addition RCNV has published a number of other resources, including this book and *Neither Victims Nor Executioners*, by Albert Camus, both of which are co-published with New Society Publishers. For more information contact RCNV at 515 Broadway, Santa Cruz, CA 95060, (408) 423-1626.

ABOUT THE EDITORS

PHILIP MCMANUS is the Latin America staff person at the Resource Center for Nonviolence in Santa Cruz, CA and the Chair of the U.S. Fellowship of Reconciliation Task Force on Latin America and the Caribbean. He has traveled extensively in Latin America and he has lived in Mexico. He has also worked for several months as a team member of Witness for Peace (WFP) in Nicaragua and he continues to serve on the WFP Philosophy and Strategy Committee.

As part of his Latin America-related work he has taken several delegations to Central America, established the U.S./Latin America Exchange Program (in conjunction with Servicio Paz y Justicia), and organized an urgent action network to support Latin American popular nonviolent movements. McManus' articles on the process of social change in Latin America have been published by *Fellowship*, the *National Catholic Reporter*, and *Commonweal*, among others.

He and his wife, Betsy Fairbanks, have two children, Timothy and Kevin.

GERALD SCHLABACH has lived in Central America during various periods since 1970. As a writer and program administrator with Mennonite Central Committee (MCC), the relief and development arm of North American Mennonite churches, he has worked for peace and justice in that region since 1980.

From 1983 through 1985 Gerald Schlabach and his wife Joetta Handrich, served as MCC country representatives in Nicaragua. During that time Schlabach served as a consultant to CEPAD, the Council of Evangelical Churches of Nicaragua, in its efforts to propose and negotiate an alternative service for conscientious objectors to military conscription that would be appropriate and constructive within the context of the Nicaraguan revolution. He and his wife assisted the first Witness for Peace volunteers as they set up a long-term program, and also participated in the formation of a Nicaraguan chapter of Servicio Paz y Justicia (SERPAJ).

While in Nicaragua, Schlabach worked to develop a region-wide "Peace Portfolio" for MCC in Central America. That portfolio became his full-time assignment in Honduras, beginning in January 1986. While promoting theological education and practical training related to peace and justice issues together with Central American Mennonite leaders, he has also written various articles on the challenges Central America presents to the historic peace churches in North America.

Schlabach graduated from Goshen (Ind.) College in 1979 with a degree in history and journalism, and from the Associated Mennonite Biblical Seminaries in Elkhart, Ind., with an M.A. in Theological Studies in 1990. He is the author of *And Who is My Neighbor?: Poverty, Privilege and the Gospel of Christ* (Scottdale, Pa. and Kitchener, Ont.: Herald Press, 1990). He is a graduate student in theology and ethics at the University of Notre Dame. He and his wife have two sons, Gabriel and Jacob.

CONTRIBUTORS' BIOGRAPHIES

OSCAR ALIAGA-ABANTO works as a lawyer with Servicios Educativos Rurales (SER) in Lima, Peru. SER is an organization dedicated to training, advising and advocating on behalf of Peruvian peasants. From 1980 to 1987 he worked in the legal department of the Comisión Episcopal de Acción Social (CEAS) of the Peruvian conference of Catholic bishops. He has published a number of articles on human rights and popular struggles in Peru.

DOMINGOS BARBÉ was a French Catholic priest who lived the last twenty years of his life among the poor and oppressed in the *favelas* of São Paulo, Brazil. He was a tireless advocate on behalf of the poor and he also worked with the Ministry to Workers of the São Paulo Archdiocese. He was a founding member of the Secretariado Justiça e Não-Violência, the Brazilian branch of the Latin American network Servicio Paz y Justicia and, until his death in 1988, he was a principal theologian and systemizer of nonviolence in Brazil. His works in French and English are published under his French name, Dominique Barbé.

LEONARDO BOFF is a Franciscan priest and professor of systematic theology at the Petrópolis Institute for Philosophy and Theology near Rio de Janeiro, Brazil. He has been a leader in the development of liberation theology and he is one of its best known exponents. In part this is because of his well-publicized conflicts with the Vatican during which he has been backed by powerful progressive elements of the Brazilian Church, including bishops and cardinals. He has written many books, a number of which have been published in English.

WILSON T. BOOTS is Council Director for the Council on Ministries of the New York Conference of the United Methodist Church. He is a member of the Governing Board of the National Council of Churches of Christ in America and he is a past Director of the General Board of Global Ministries. He has served as a missionary in Bolivia and Argentina. His articles have appeared in *Christianity and Crisis*, the *Christian Century*, *New World Outlook*, and elsewhere.

MÁRIO CARVALHO DE JESUS is a labor lawyer in São Paulo, Brazil. He was instrumental in the founding of the Frente Nacional do Trabalho in 1960 and in 1978 of the Secretariado Justiça e Não-Violência (the Brazilian branch of the Latin American network Servicio Paz y Justicia). He was jailed four times by the Brazilian military dictatorship for his labor advocacy work.

JUDITH HURLEY is Coordinator of Project Abraço: In Solidarity with the People of Brazil at the Resource Center for Nonviolence in Santa Cruz, CA. As a child she was powerless to help her European Jewish family members who were killed in the

298

concentration camps. This experience left an indelible imprint, leading her to pursue understanding of how to break the chain of violence and how to empower the disempowered. Her 1982 travels in Brazil revolutionized her thinking as she saw both the devastation wrought by U.S.-led "development" and the dynamism of the popular resistance, especially in Christian base communities.

PAUL JEFFREY is a United Methodist missionary in Nicaragua. Since 1984 he has traveled throughout the country as part of his work with CEPAD, the Council of Evangelical Churches of Nicaragua. He produces a monthly newsletter for CEPAD and he writes about the Nicaraguan church scene for *Latin America Press, Religious News Service, Christian Century, Christianity and Crisis* and other journals. He and his wife, the Reverend Lyda Pierce, have two children.

EDMUNDO LEÓN Y LEÓN has been in charge of rural programs for the Comisión Episcopal de Acción Social (CEAS) of the Peruvian Catholic bishops conference since 1977. During that time he has played a key role in the development of the rural ministry of the Catholic Church and in promoting the Church's preferential option for the poor. He is the founder and current President of Servicios Educativos Rurales (SER), an organization dedicated to training, advising and advocating on behalf of Peruvian peasants. He is the author of numerous articles on agrarian, labor and church issues.

KATHERINE ROBERTS is a graduate student in international affairs at Columbia University. During 1987 she was supported by a university fellowship to do human rights work and research in Montevideo, Uruguay.

SECRETARIADO JUSTIÇA E NÃO-VIOLÊNCIA is the original name of the Brazilian branch of the Latin American network Servicio Paz y Justicia. Founded in 1978, it is now known as Serviço Nacional Justiça e Não-Violência. Its headquarters are in the Brazilian capital, Brasilia.

PABLO STANFIELD has lived in Spain, Ecuador, Mexico and Central America as well as the USA. A former linguist and teacher of languages, he now holds a master's degree in Whole Systems Design focused on Latin American studies, especially Latin/Anglo-American intercultural conflict resolution. He made five trips to Central America to work with Peace Brigades International teams in the region. He is a member of University Friends Meeting (a Quaker) in Seattle, WA, a calligrapher, and a chef.

OMAR WILLIAMS LÓPEZ, is National Coordinator of Servicio Paz y Justicia (SERPAJ) in Chile. A sociologist by training, he has served two terms as Regional Coordinator of SERPAJ in Antofagasta, Chile. He is also the Director of the Centro de Estudios para el Desararollo Humano "AINE."

BLANCA YÁÑEZ BERRÍOS is a sociologist who has worked with Servicio Paz y Justicia (SERPAJ) in Antofagasta, Chile, since 1979. She is Coordinator of the national women's program and she has served on the national coordinating committee of SERPAJ/Chile. She and her husband, Omar Williams López, have two children.

GLOSSARY

active nonviolence—A means of struggle for social change based on an unswerving commitment to speak the truth and a willingness to put oneself at risk in the process while refusing to harm others. Major components of nonviolent action include reflection, dialogue, education, challenging existing power relations, and building alternative structures to create a just and compassionate world.

animator—A person who contributes leadership to a group by stimulating the full participation of others; one who asks the right questions rather than gives all the answers; hence one who empowers others, a change agent.

barrio—Literally neighborhood; in Latin America the term typically refers to poorer neighborhoods.

base-level—Referring to the sector at the base of societies characterized by a social pyramid: a small elite, a somewhat larger middle class, and a vast majority of poor.

caceroleada—Spanish; banging of pots and pans as a form of protest.

Christian base community (comunidad eclesial de base)—A small group typically from among the poor, which gathers together to study the scriptures in the light of their own experience. While they are sometimes joined by a priest or other religious, their great significance lies in the fact that the poor themselves interpret and then apply the gospel message. They often undertake social action, and in some cases they have been the catalyst for the creation of popular movements. They emerged in Latin America in the mid-60s, in part as a result of the changes in the Roman Catholic Church after the Second Vatican Council.

compañero, compañera (Spanish) companheiro, companheira (Portuguese)—Literally "companion"; frequently used to denote those involved in a shared struggle.

comunidad eclesial de base (CEB)—Spanish; see "Christian base community."

conscientización (Spanish) conscientzação (Portuguese)—The process whereby the poor acquire critical consciousness of their role as actors in the world, the creators of their own history.

contras—Short for the Spanish "contrarevolucionarios." Refers to the irregular armed force of Nicaraguans, created by and wholly dependent on the U.S. government, which fought throughout the 1980s to overthrow the Nicaraguan revolutionary government, led by the Frente Sandinista de Liberación Nacional (FSLN).

disappeared—Refers to a person who has been kidnapped, usually by government forces, against whom no charges are filed, and who is held incomunicado in unacknowledged detention, usually until s/he is murdered. At that point the body is usually disposed of secretly so as to leave no trace. As a result of the widespread use of the practice in parts of Latin America from the 1960s on, the term has also come to be used as a transitive verb, i.e., "to disappear" someone is to take him or her without warning, without trial, and without leaving behind any sign. The term "disappearance" has come to be used to refer to that particular crime against humanity of which the "disappeared" are the victims.

evangelical—In the broad sense, anything related to the Christian gospel. In Latin America the term is also widely used to refer to the Protestant—as opposed to Catholic or orthodox—churches and to their members.

evangelization—Literally the task of preaching the Christian gospel. In Latin America the term is often understood to refer to Christian ministry and the responsibility of Christians in a much broader sense, as in this quote from Domingos Barbé: ". . . to evangelize is to transform the world into a place where all the children of one Parent can live together in peace and security. In essence to evangelize is to transform society so that it may reveal the Kingdom of God."

fast—Abstaining from some or all foods with the aim of self-purification and/or seeking change in the understanding and behavior of oneself or others. A fast (as opposed to a hunger strike) is not tied to and contingent upon specific demands.

favela—Portuguese; a shantytown in or near a city. Inhabitants are among the most marginalized people of Brazil; living conditions are desperate.

fazenda—Portuguese; a large private landholding.

firmeza permanente—Portuguese and Spanish; relentless persistence; a term used in parts of Latin America to refer to what in English would be called active nonviolence.

formation—The process of personal development; includes intellectual development and acquiring specific skills as well as the less quantifiable but even more important process of empowerment, the development of the awareness and the confidence essential to full participation and the realization of one's potential.

gringo—Spanish; usually refers to someone from the U.S.; can also refer to non-Latin foreigners in general.

Gross Domestic Product (GDP)—The total value of the annual output of goods and services within a given nation.

hunger strike—Abstaining from some or all foods with the aim of pressuring others to meet specific demands.

ladino—Spanish; in Latin America refers to a person of European rather than Indian descent.

liberation—The achievement of social, economic, political, and spiritual self-determination wherein human needs are met, human rights are protected and human relations are based on respect and solidarity.

liberation theology—An approach to Christian thought and action based on commitment to liberation. Liberation theology is the product of lived struggles rather than intellectualized theology. It emerged in the 1960s in Latin America. More a way of doing theology than a distinct body of thought, it finds expression in the interpretation of the Bible from the perspective of the poor and oppressed, rooted in the recognition that liberation is a fundamental biblical concept.

lightning action (mitín relámpago)—In situations where public protests are prohibited, a well-organized demonstration that lasts long enough to make a clear public statement but usually ends quickly enough to avoid arrest. Common in Chile under the Pinochet dictatorship.

macho—Spanish; strong, tough, displaying male qualities; often carries a pejorative connotation; "machismo" refers to the qualities that make one macho.

marginalized—Refers to the condition of being excluded, by virtue of poverty and lack of political power, from full participation as a member in society; also used to refer to those in that condition, as in "the socially marginalized."

Medellín—Refers to the meeting of Latin American Roman Catholic bishops which took place in 1968 in Medellín, Colombia. It was especially noteworthy for its bold denunciation of the injustice of the status quo and for its unprecedented proclamation of the church's "preferential option for the poor."

mística—Spanish; refers to a shared vision or inspiration capable of motivating, guiding, and giving cohesion to a group, institution or movement. By implication, participation is a privilege that is its own reward.

mitín relámpago—Spanish; see "lightning action."

National Security Doctrine—An ideological teaching based on the division of the world into "Western, Christian civilization" and its "enemies" in the form of communism and subversion. Its proponents, chiefly the United States government and some Latin American militaries, assert that a permanent state of war exists between the two and that all means, including murder, torture and disappearance, may be necessary and therefore acceptable. They see communist subversion everywhere, and hence they tend to brand all efforts for basic change as communist.

nonviolence—See "active nonviolence."

peasant—An agricultural worker, usually poor, who may or may not own the land s/he works.

pedagogy—The art or science of teaching. In Latin America the revolutionary pedagogy promoted by the Brazilian educator Paulo Friere and others, with its focus on the learning process as an empowering and liberating experience, has had far-reaching effects on movements for social change.

popular—Of or by the poor majority in societies characterized by a social pyramid; as in "popular movements." "Lower income" captures part of the meaning of the term but in Latin America the term "popular" also incorporates the idea of caste in that economic and social mobility is limited.

popular education—Education with adults from among the poor majority. In the experiences described in this book it refers more specifically to a dynamic education/action process aimed at addressing the basic needs of participants while developing a critical consciousness of one's social, political and cultural reality.

las posadas—Spanish; a Christmas festivity usually lasting nine days in which barrio residents accompany a couple playing Joseph and Mary going door to door seeking hospitality.

posseiro—Portuguese; a small landholder, often a landowner—by virtue of actually working a piece of land for a minimum period—who is nonetheless untitled and therefore more vulnerable to the strongarm tactics of the wealthy.

praxis—In contemporary philosophical and ideological discussion, a dynamic interaction between theory and practice, between action and reflection. Theory tested by practice, and practice corrected by theory.

preferential option for the poor—A position articulated by the Latin American Catholic Church, influenced by the Second Vatican Council, which identifies the needs of the poor as the Church's highest priority since, all people being equal in God's eyes, it is the poor whose humanity is most clearly denied by grinding poverty and injustice. Seeking to follow the example of Jesus, the preferential option for the poor has meant getting physically and culturally close to the problems of the poor majority, sharing their pain and their joy.

Puebla—Refers to the meeting of Latin American Roman Catholic bishops which took place in 1979 in the Mexican city of Puebla. It was noteworthy for its reaffirmation, despite conservative church pressures, of the "preferential option for the poor" proclaimed at the Medellín meeting and for its affirmation that the poor themselves must be the primary agents of change.

queixada—Portuguese; a term used to refer to the striking workers at the PERUS cement factory. (See Chapter 2.) Queixadas are wild boars who, when in danger, will pull together in a group, snarling and grinding their teeth, and directly confront the hunter.

recoveries (recuperaciones)—Nonviolent land takeovers which through direct action seek to put into practice land reform laws which are unenforced because of the pressure of wealthy landowners. Peasants use the term "recoveries" both because such actions are based on legal rights under existing law and because they often entail the recovery of land which was taken either from them or from their forebears.

recuperaciones—Spanish; see "recoveries."

romaria—Portuguese; a religious pilgrimage or march.

rondas campesinas—Spanish; peasant, volunteer patrols which serve primarily to prevent crime, especially cattle rustling, in rural communities in Peru. They may also take on a variety of other roles. In some communities they have come to be the primary source of authority.

Second Vatican Council (1962-65)—A major gathering of Roman Catholic bishops. It became a watershed experience that redefined the role of the Catholic Church in the modern world, placing greater emphasis on the Church's role in the world rather than apart from it and on the Church as a community of equals, whether laity, priest or bishop, each with some gift to contribute and responsibility to share.

theology of liberation—See "liberation theology."

Third World— The less-developed countries of the world, especially in Latin America, Africa and Asia. In this case, "development" refers to a process that has been dominated—through colonization, military action, and political and economic coercion—by the industrial powers of the North in order to serve their needs, often at the cost of the increased impoverishment of the Third World poor.

Vatican II—See "Second Vatican Council."

INDEX

304

national security state, 34, 259
National Security Doctrine, 5, 88-90, 100,
103-105, 108, 114, 250, 258
U.S. promotion of, 5, 29, 30, 89-90, 103,
106-107
early test of, 29
as hemispheric system, 29
National Union of Peasants [Honduras], UNC, 66,
70, 72
nationalism, 28, 276
Nazism, 22, 89
neighborhood groups, 117, 125-128, 131-132,
134, 199, 206ff, 240, 245, 256
New Deal, 22, 30
New People's Army [the Philippines], 254
Nicaragua, 25, 153ff, 174, 211ff, 231, 246-247,
249, 255-256, 263
Niño, Gustavo, see Astiz, Alfredo
Nixon, Richard
administration
human rights policy, 98
nonviolence
armed struggle and, 9, 16, 20, 119-120, 136,
153, 155ff, 181, 187, 191, 231, 246, 275ff,
252ff
as community-building, 257-259, 263
and ecology, x, 7, 247-248
and economics, 3, 35, 67-68, 72, 74, 106-108,
115, 127-128, 132, 138, 142, 188, 199, 206,
247-248, 270
"Five Commandments of . . . ," 193, 280
in Europe, 91, 163, 170, 193ff, 238, 243, 249-251
distinctively Latin American, 8-9, 16, 21, 29,
63-64, 67, 76, 77, 102, 109, 111-112,
121-122, 136-137, 141-143, 149, 157, 171-
172, 187, 189, 240, 242-244, 246-247,
256-263, 266ff
liberation theologies and, ix, x
nature of, viii, ix-x, 6-10, 16, 20, 34, 37, 39, 40,
49, 61, 64, 76, 94-95, 111, 114-115, 120,
130-131, 137, 185, 188, 191-193, 223, 234,
238, 241, 246-247, 257ff, 278-279
in North America, 6, 9-10, 30, 91, 154-155,
160, 163, 170ff, 181, 193ff, 226, 238, 240ff,
243, 249-251, 252ff, 266-267
power of, ix, 6, 21, 37, 50, 52, 60, 64, 67-68, 70,
72, 76-77, 95, 110-111, 123, 130, 131-132,
142-143, 162-163, 185, 193, 191ff, 226,
233, 239, 246-249, 255, 257, 279-280
principles of, 7-8, 39-41, 46-47, 67, 93, 96-97,
119, 123, 132-133, 137-138, 163, 171, 193,
239, 241, 243, 247-248, 256, 261-262, 274,
280ff, 282ff
spirituality of, spiritual basis, viii, ix-x, 3, 9,
39-43, 47, 60-61, 64, 76-77, 82, 101, 107,
133, 137-138, 142-143, 149-150, 162-164,
171, 185-189, 192-194, 211ff, 231, 234,
239-242, 244-245, 250, 260, 263-264,
266ff, 283, 290
strategy of, 7-8, 29, 75-76, 108-111, 119,
130-132, 155, 162, 194, 214ff, 233,
247-249, 255-260, 264, 277-279, 279ff
tactics and actions, 257, 259
advertisements, 86, 91
caceroleadas, 102, 111-112
cultural symbols, use of, 16, 109, 157ff

demonstrations, 16, 18-19, 35, 55, 81-82,
88, 91-92, 112, 121-122, 132, 135, 181,
189, 209, 248
denunciations, 110, 234, 250
excommunication, interdict, 59
fasts, 41, 48ff, 91, 102, 110ff, 158, 166ff,
181, 227, 290
leafletting, 19, 34, 121, 123
legal system, use of, 34, 37, 39, 40-45, 138,
181
letters, telegrams, etc., 58
lightning actions, 121-122, 124, 134-135
marches, 1, 10, 18-19, 65, 68, 70-71, 82, 88,
91-93, 109, 112, 132, 134, 157, 164, 181,
184, 187, 226-227, 247-248
mediation, conflict resolution, 56, 59-61,
143, 169, 211ff
observer groups, accompaniment, 52, 56, 61,
168, 170-172, 191
occupations and recoveries, land, 64, 148,
181ff, 231, 236, 246, 256
petitions, 18, 41, 45, 86, 88, 91, 104, 113
prayer, 91, 102, 166
protests, 7, 16, 19, 86, 110, 112, 121,
131-132, 135, 164, 248, 259
publishing human rights reports, 86, 114
religious processions, 19, 157ff, 181, 184,
187, 209-210
silent reflection, 102
strikes, 34, 41ff, 164
strikes, general, 16-20, 69-70, 93, 112
strikes, hunger, 48ff, 131
strikes, sit-down, 138
vigils, 85-86, 88, 91, 102, 166, 171, 181
other, 1, 7, 10, 138, 170-171, 190-191
training and preparation for, 7, 9, 34, 67, 75, 85,
96, 100, 115, 119, 124, 126-128, 131-133,
135-136, 147ff, 164, 180, 187-189, 192,
207, 209ff, 214, 230-232, 247-248, 257,
259-260, 273, 278, 280, 282ff
See also pacifism
Nonviolence Schools [Chile], 131, 133
Nova Ronda Alta, Brazil, 181, 183, 188-189
Nutritional Institute for Central America and
Panamá, INCAP, 77

Obando y Bravo, Miguel, 162
occupations, land, see nonviolence—tactics and
actions, occupations and recoveries, land
Olancho, Honduras, 71
Olivera, Ademar, 111
ollas comunes, see soup kitchens
Operation Success, 25
La Opinión [Argentina], 84
option for the poor, see preferential option for the
poor
Ordóñez, David, 19
Organization of American States, OAS, 25
Commission on Human Rights, 91-92
Ortega, Daniel, 155
os Sem Terra, see Movement of Landless Rural Workers
Osorio, Jorge, 111

Pachamama, 148
pacifism, 7-8, 12, 64, 67, 76-77, 137, 155,
165-166, 169, 187, 254-256, 262-264